DATE DUE

APR 2 0 1996	NOV 2 6 2003
OCT 2 1996	
MAR - 6 1997	
APR 3 1997	
APR 1 9 1997	
OCT 3 1 1997	
Nov 12	
Nov 21	
APR 1 4 1998	
JUN 1 8 1998	
FEB 2 4 2000	
FEB 2 4 2000	
APR 3 2000	
DEC 5 2000	
DEC - 3 2001	
JAN 09 2002	
MAR 2 4 2003	
04.02.03	

BRODART, INC.   Cat. No. 23-221

Beyond Trauma

Cultural and Societal Dynamics

The Plenum Series on Stress and Coping

Series Editor:
Donald Meichenbaum, *University of Waterloo, Waterloo, Ontario, Canada*

Current Volumes in the Series:

BEYOND TRAUMA
Cultural and Societal Dynamics
Edited by Rolf J. Kleber, Charles R. Figley, and Berthold P. R. Gersons

COMBAT STRESS REACTION
The Enduring Toll of War
Zahava Solomon

COMMUTING STRESS
Causes, Effects, and Methods of Coping
Meni Koslowsky, Avraham N. Kluger, and Mordechai Reich

COPING WITH WAR-INDUCED STRESS
The Gulf War and the Israeli Response
Zahava Solomon

INTERNATIONAL HANDBOOK OF TRAUMATIC STRESS SYNDROMES
Edited by John P. Wilson and Beverley Raphael

PSYCHOTRAUMATOLOGY
Key Papers and Core Concepts in Post-Traumatic Stress
Edited by George S. Everly, Jr. and Jeffrey M. Lating

STRESS AND MENTAL HEALTH
Contemporary Issues and Prospects for the Future
Edited by William R. Avison and Ian H. Gotlib

TRAUMATIC STRESS
From Theory to Practice
Edited by John R. Freedy and Stevan E. Hobfoll

THE UNNOTICED MAJORITY IN PSYCHIATRIC INPATIENT CARE
Charles A. Kiesler and Celeste G. Simpkins

Ludmilla I. Meijler-Iljina, Department of Psychiatry, Utrecht University, 3584 CS Utrecht, The Netherlands

Diana E. H. Russell, Emerita Professor of Sociology, Mills College, and Russell Research on Sexual Assault, 2432 Grant Street, Berkeley, California 94703

Victor W. Sidel, Montefiore Medical Center, Albert Einstein College of Medicine, Bronx, New York 10467-2490

Michael A. Simpson, Centre for Traumatic Stress, P.O. Box 51, Pretoria 0001, South Africa

Derek Summerfield, Medical Foundation for the Care of Victims of Torture, 96–98 Grafton Road, London NW5 3EJ; and Department of Community Psychiatry, St. George's Hospital Medical School, London SW17 ORE, United Kingdom

Jan van den Bout, Department of Clinical and Health Psychology, Utrecht University, 3584 CS Utrecht, The Netherlands

Guus van der Veer, Pharos Foundation, Health Service for Refugees, Department of Mental Health, Prins Hendrikkade 120, 1011 AM Amsterdam, The Netherlands

Jos M. P. Weerts, BNMO-Centre (Veterans Center), 3940 AG Doorn, The Netherlands

Eliezer Witztum, Jerusalem Community Health Center, Ezrath Nashim, Jerusalem 91001, Israel

Contributors

David Becker, Latin American Institute of Mental Health and Human Rights, Providencia Santiago, Chile

Aor. Konrad Brendler, Department of Educational Sciences, University of Wuppertal, 42097 Wuppertal, Germany

Daniel Brom, Latner Institute for the Study of Social Psychiatry and Psychotherapy, Herzog Hospital, Jerusalem 91351, Israel

Mark Creamer, Department of Psychology, University of Melbourne, Parkville, Victoria 3052, Australia

Charles R. Figley, Psychosocial Stress Research Program, Florida State University, Tallahassee, Florida 32306-4097

Berthold P. R. Gersons, Department of Psychiatry, Academic Medical Center, University of Amsterdam, 1105 BC Amsterdam, The Netherlands

Isabelita Z. Guiao, University of Texas, Health Science Center at San Antonio, San Antonio, Texas 78284-7948

Johan M. Havenaar, Department of Psychiatry, Utrecht University, 3584 CS Utrecht, The Netherlands

Rolf J. Kleber, Department of Clinical and Health Psychology, Utrecht University, and Institute for Psychotrauma, 3584 CS Utrecht, The Netherlands

Elizabeth Lira Kornfeld, Latin American Institute of Mental Health and Human Rights, Providencia Santiago, Chile

Alexander C. McFarlane, Glenside Hospital, Eastwood, South Australia 5063, Australia

Library of Congress Cataloging-in-Publication Data

Beyond trauma : cultural and societal dynamics / edited by Rolf J.
  Kleber, Charles R. Figley, and Berthold P.R. Gersons.
       p.   cm. -- (The Plenum series on stress and coping)
    Includes bibliographical references and index.
    ISBN 0-306-45058-5
    1. Post-traumatic stress disorder--Social aspects. 2. Psychic
  trauma--Social aspects.   I. Kleber, R. J. (Rolf Jan) II. Figley,
  Charles R., 1944-   . III. Gersons, Berthold P. R., 1945-   .
  IV. Series.
  RC552.P67B49 1995
  616.85'21--dc20   95-40998
                                                                  CIP

ISBN 0-306-45058-5

© 1995 Plenum Press, New York
A Division of Plenum Publishing Corporation
233 Spring Street, New York, N. Y. 10013

Beyond Trauma
Cultural and Societal Dynamics

Edited by

Rolf J. Kleber

*Utrecht University
and Institute for Psychotrauma
Utrecht, The Netherlands*

Charles R. Figley

*Florida State University
Tallahassee, Florida*

and

Berthold P. R. Gersons

*Academic Medical Center
and University of Amsterdam
Amsterdam, The Netherlands*

Published in cooperation with

THE INTERNATIONAL SOCIETY FOR
TRAUMATIC**stress**
STUDIES

PLENUM PRESS • NEW YORK AND LONDON

Foreword

The editors of *Beyond Trauma: Cultural and Societal Dynamics* have created a volume that goes beyond the individual's psychological dynamics of trauma, exploring its social, cultural, political, and ethical dimensions from an international as well as a global perspective.

In the opening address as International Chair of the First World Conference of the International Society for Traumatic Stress Studies on Trauma and Tragedy: The Origins, Management, and Prevention of Traumatic Stress in Today's World, June 22–26, 1992, Amsterdam, The Netherlands, the conference that formed the foundation for the collected chapters in this volume, I commented:

> This meeting is a landmark in accomplishing the Society's universal mission. Our distinguished International Scientific Advisory Committee and Honorary Committee, whose membership was drawn from over 60 countries, the cooperation of six United Nations bodies, and the participation and endorsement of numerous nongovernmental organizations and institutions attest to the Society's emerging presence as a major international forum for professionals of all disciplines working with victims and trauma survivors.
>
> On a personal note, it was also in June, 1986, that I last shared a podium at the RAI International Congress Centre as a member of a panel on War Trauma and Adult Development with, among others, Dr. Robert Laufer, who was later elected president of the Society. Another close Dutch friend, colleague, and pioneer in our field, Dr. Edie de Wind, was present as well. Like so many other Holocaust survivors, both died prematurely. These were friends of mine and of the Society. But June is also an anniversary of the birth of a young Amsterdam girl who has become a friend and symbol to millions. Earlier this month, on June 12, Anne Frank would have been 63.
>
> Being here today has an additional historic poignancy. For it was 50 years ago to this day, on June 22, 1942, that Adolf Eichmann, head of the Jewish department of the Gestapo in the Reich Central Security Office, informed Karl Rademacher, the Jewish affairs expert in the Foreign Office, that arrangements had been concluded with the railways for the deportation of Jews from the Netherlands, Belgium, and Occupied France to Auschwitz.

From July 1942 until September 1944, 93 transports left Westerbork—Holland's gateway to hell. Following centuries when they found a safe haven in the Netherlands, of the 140,000 Jews living there at the time of the German invasion, 110,000 were murdered; only 3,000 people returned of the 103,000 who were deported; 15,000 Jews were saved in hiding. Despite initial courageous protest, undaunted, unforgotten rescuers, and heroic resistance fighters, as in the rest of Europe, some were collaborators and many more were bystanders in a silently acquiescing world. In the end, 79% of the Dutch Jews were murdered, the highest percentage in Western Europe.

Living as we do in an era of astonishingly rapid and sometimes cataclysmic global changes, which have *again* upended the dynamic of the international community and transformed world realities, makes acute the need and affords us with the opportunity to reexamine the ways we live together on our planet earth.

As Elie Wiesel (1972) reflects, "After the reckoning, one feels discouragement and shame. The balance sheet is disheartening. . . . Society has changed so little [that] only one conclusion is possible: namely, that the failure of the black years has begotten yet another failure. Nothing has been learned: Auschwitz has not even served as warning" (p. 15).

Indeed, until recently, most of the very issues we will be discussing here over the next five days were shrouded in silence. This conference is a milestone in paving the way to adjust the balance sheet: to share what we *have* learned and what we *can* apply to help all victims and trauma survivors of past and the traumata of *today's* world, and to prevent new ones from looming in the future. Time constraints allow for but a mere mention of some of the sources of the immense suffering demanding our attention around the world today: the abandoned and abused children in the streets of the big cities, at home, and in institutions; violated women; victims of torture and other crimes; indigenous peoples; the plight of refugees and displaced people; ethnic strife and deprivation; political instability and other upheavals; poverty and starvation; oppression; and natural and technological disasters and their aftermath. June 4 marked the anniversary of Tiananmen Square. . . .

Just 20 days before the betrayal that led to her deportation to Westerbork, Auschwitz, and Bergen Belsen, Anne Frank wrote in her legendary diary of living in hiding, "[I]n spite of everything I still believe that people are really good at heart." I am heartened to say that this World Conference, in her city, and in yours, Your Majesty, Mr. Mayor, is abundant with people who will act on her words. For we are here not only to learn from victims/survivors of past and present generations but also to do our best to make the world a better place for them, and for us, and for generations to come.

The meeting fulfilled much of its promise. The editors of *Beyond Trauma: Cultural and Societal Dynamics* selected some of the distinguished, path-breaking presentations at the conference to explore trauma beyond its individual dynamics and to view it in a *multidimensional, interdisciplinary, integrative framework.*

Considered within such a framework (Danieli, 1985), an individual's identity involves a complex interplay of multiple spheres or systems. Among these are the physical and intrapsychic; the interpersonal–

familial, social, communal; the educational–professional–occupational; and the material–economic, political, national, and international. These systems coexist dynamically along the time dimension to create a continuous conception of life from past through present to the future. Ideally, the individual should simultaneously have free psychological access to and movement within all these identity dimensions.

Victimization causes a rupture, a possible regression, and a state of being "stuck" in this free flow (which I have termed *fixity*) that may render the individual vulnerable, particularly to further traumatic events and ruptures throughout the life cycle. The time, duration, extent, and meaning of the trauma for its victims and survivors; the heterogeneous survival mechanisms and strategies they have used to adapt to it; and postvictimization traumata such as the conspiracy of silence (Danieli, 1988) and second wound (Symonds, 1980)—all will determine the elements and degree of the rupture, the disorganization and disorientation, and the severity of the fixity. This multidimensional, interdisciplinary, integrative framework allows the evaluation of whether and how much of each system was ruptured or proved resilient and may thus inform the choice of optimal systemic interventions.

Systems can change and recover independently of other systems. For example, there may be progress in the social system but not in the religious system. While there can be isolated, independent recovery in various systems, they may also be related and interdependent. Also, with a multidimensional framework for the multiple levels of posttraumatic adaptation, the finding that survivors have areas of vulnerability and resilience is not a paradoxical one. In addition, tracing one's history of multiple traumata along the time dimension at different stages of development reveals that, while for many people time heals ills, in traumatized persons time may not heal but rather magnify the response to further trauma. To be healing and even potentially self-actualizing, the integration of traumatic experiences must indeed be examined from the perspective of the totality of the survivors' and their family members' lives. The book does so with authority, excellence, and great care.

The editors of the present collection selected authors representing different parts of the world, reflecting cultural richness and intricacies and moral and political nuances that shape individuals' responses to their particular trauma. The chapters demonstrate a wide range of methodologies and theoretical formulations. As a founder and past president of the International Society for Traumatic Stress Studies, I am delighted that this important book brings us a step closer to appreciating the complexities of our field, and to fulfilling the society's mission "to provide a forum for developing and disseminating research, clinical strategies, public policy concerns, and theoretical formulations around the world."

YAEL DANIELI, PH.D., Director
Group Project for Holocaust Survivors
and Their Children
New York, New York

REFERENCES

Danieli, Y. (1985). The treatment and prevention of long-term effects and intergenerational transmission of victimization: A lesson from Holocaust survivors and their children. In C. R. Figley (Ed.), *Trauma and its wake* (Vol. 1, pp. 295–313). New York: Brunner/Mazel.

Danieli, Y. (1988). On not confronting the Holocaust: Psychological reactions to victim/survivors and their children. In *Remembering for the Future: The Impact of the Holocaust on the Contemporary World*, Theme II (pp. 1257–1271). Oxford: Pergamon Press.

Symonds, M. (1980). The "second injury" to victims. *Evaluation and Change* (special issue), pp. 36–38.

Wiesel, E. (1972). *One generation after*. New York: Avon.

Acknowledgments

Writing is a solitary activity and frequently even a lonely endeavor. When different authors from all over the world are working together on the same book, the combination of all their single activities becomes a rather complicated and often perplexing challenge. Letters are mailed over the oceans, faxes are sent, and many conversations are held on the telephone.

Many things can go wrong on the lengthy road to completion. Faxes may never arrive, editorial instructions may not be understood, letters may get lost, and computer problems may obstruct the understanding of messages and manuscripts. But in the end, all obstacles and barriers have been overcome.

The joining of ideas and thoughts by authors and experts from all over the world and from various backgrounds has been a gratifying and fascinating enterprise. The editors are grateful to the contributing authors for their cooperation and their ability to cope with the perplexities of international traffic. Their belief in a successful outcome has also been most stimulating and rewarding. To them we owe an international perspective on traumatic stress that embraces many viewpoints.

The contributions to this volume have been reviewed by experts who were members of the editorial review committee. Their careful and skillful comments and criticisms concerning scientific criteria have been most helpful. We are very thankful to the following colleagues: Dora Black, M.B., F.R.C. Psych., D.P.M. (Royal Free Hospital, London, England); Danny Brom, Ph.D. (Latner Institute for Research, Jerusalem, Israel); Dr. Ate Dyregrov (Center for Crisis Psychology, Norway); Dr. J. Mia Groenenberg (Social Psychiatric Service for Refugees, Amsterdam, The Netherlands); Dr. Jean Harris Hendriks (Royal Free Hospital, London); Dr. Wolter S. de Loos (Utrecht, The Netherlands); Henry Krystal, M.D. (Southfield, Michigan, USA); Dr. Henk A. W. Schut (Utrecht, The

Netherlands); Dr. Michael A. Simpson (Pretoria, South Africa); James Thompson, Ph.D., Dip. Clin. Psychol., C. Psychol., F.B.Ps.S. (London, England); Dr. Paul Valent (Melbourne, Australia); Dr. M. A. A. (Guus) van der Veer (Social Psychiatric Service for Refugees, Amsterdam, The Netherlands); and Dr. Victor M. Vládar Rivero (The Hague, The Netherlands).

The editors are indebted to the organizing committee of the First World Conference on Traumatic Stress in Amsterdam. It supported this volume financially and psychologically. In particular, we appreciate the efforts of Jos Weerts, formerly director of the National Institute for War Victims in The Netherlands.

Finally, the energetic contribution of Trudy Mooren, who carefully went through all the chapters, and the sustaining support of Ellen Muller throughout the long and often dragging process of creating this book are acknowledged with gratitude.

Editing is an endeavor in communicating, writing, traveling, and becoming friends. Places to remember are Alligator Point in Florida, where the idea of this book was conceptualized; the riverside walk in San Antonio, where we discussed the progress of the volume; and Berthold's Oosterpark house in Amsterdam.

Contents

Chapter 1. Introduction   1

Rolf J. Kleber, Charles R. Figley, and Berthold P. R. Gersons

Trauma, Society, and Culture   2
The First World Conference on Traumatic Stress   4
Outline of the Book   5
Part I: Conceptual Issues   5
Part II: Societal and Political Issues   6
Part III: Ethical Considerations   8
References   9

PART I. CONCEPTUAL ISSUES

**Chapter 2. Addressing Human Response to War and Atrocity:
    Major Challenges in Research and Practices and the
    Limitations of Western Psychiatric Models** 17

Derek Summerfield

Introduction 17
The Medical Model of Trauma 18
Trauma as Collective Experience 19
Beyond Victimology: Challenges in Research and Practice 22
Treatment 24
Advocacy 25
Conclusions 27
References 28

**Chapter 3. The Severity of the Trauma: Issues about Its Role
in Posttraumatic Stress Disorder** 31

Alexander C. McFarlane

Introduction 31
The Political and Social Context of Trauma 32
Issues in the Relationship between Stressor and Disorder 34
Measurement of Exposure 38
Statistical Modeling and Analysis 44
Conclusion 50
References 52

**Chapter 4. A Cognitive Processing Formulation
of Posttrauma Reactions** 55

Mark Creamer

Introduction 55
The Proposed Model 57
The Study 62
Results 66
Discussion 69
References 73

**Chapter 5. Beyond the "Victim": Secondary
Traumatic Stress** 75

Charles R. Figley and Rolf J. Kleber

State of the Field 76
The Neglect of the Surrounding Others 76
Definition of Secondary Traumatic Stress 77
Who Are the Significant Others? 79
The Impact of Traumatic Stress on Family Members 80
Worker-Related Secondary Traumatic Stress 87
Theoretical Perspectives on Secondary Traumatic Stress 92
Conclusion 95
References 95

Chapter 6. The Deficiency of the Concept of Posttraumatic
Stress Disorder When Dealing with Victims of Human
Rights Violations 99

David Becker

Introduction 99
The Delusion of the Term *Post* 100
The Inadequacy of the Term *Disorder* 103
Conceptualizing Trauma 104
Conclusions 107
References 109

PART II. SOCIETAL AND POLITICAL ISSUES

Chapter 7. The Development of Treatment Approaches
for Victims of Human Rights Violations in Chile 115

Elizabeth Lira Kornfeld

Introduction 115
The Social "Imaginary" of Human Rights Issues 118
Therapy under the Dictatorship 122
Conceptualizing a Psychotherapeutic Approach 124
Developing Resources to Support Therapists in Their
Therapeutic Work 125
The Conflicts and Anxieties of the Therapist 126
Social and Political Signals in the Field of Human Rights after
the Dictatorship 128
Final Comments 130
References 130

Chapter 8. Cultural Analysis of Research Findings
on the Political Instability in the Philippines 133

Isabelita Z. Guiao

Introduction 133
Political Instability in the Philippines 134
The Study in Brief 135
Main Statistical Findings 137
An Interpretation from the Perspective of Filipino Culture 139

General Discussion and Conclusion 144
Recommendations for Future Study 145
References 147

Chapter 9. Psychotherapeutic Work with Refugees 151

Guus Van der Veer

Introduction 151
Traumatization as a Cumulative Ongoing Process 152
Uprooting 154
Phases in the Experiences of Refugees 154
Overcoming Cultural Differences 155
Adjusting Therapeutic Techniques 160
Developing Cultural Empathy 160
Language Problems 161
Cultural Bias and Diagnosis 161
Using Interpreters 162
The Attitude of the Psychotherapist 165
Final Remarks 168
References 168

**Chapter 10. The Prevalence, Trauma, and Sociocultural Causes
    of Incestuous Abuse of Females: A Human Rights Issue** ... 171

Diana E. H. Russell

Introduction 171
Definitions and Terminology 172
The Prevalence of Incestuous Abuse 173
The Trauma of Incestuous Abuse 176
Some Sociocultural Causes of Incestuous Abuse 178
Conclusion 184
References 186

**Chapter 11. What Went Wrong?: Diagnostic and Ethical
    Problems in Dealing with the Effects of Torture
    and Repression in South Africa** 187

Michael A. Simpson

The Nature of Apartheid and Its Related Trauma 188
The Effects of Belief Systems on Trauma and Responses to It ... 189

Problems of Psychiatric Diagnosis in Torture Victims 192
Ethical Aspects of Torture, Human Rights Abuses, and the
    Participation of Health Professionals 200
Conclusion 209
Postscript 210
References 210

**Chapter 12. Health Problems in Areas Contaminated
    by the Chernobyl Disaster: Radiation, Traumatic Stress,
    or Chronic Stress?** 213

Jan van den Bout, Johan M. Havenaar, and Ludmilla I. Meijler-Iljina

Introduction 213
The Disaster and Its Aftermath: Social, Cultural and
    Socioeconomic Aspects 216
Psychosocial Stressors after the Chernobyl Accident 219
Characteristic Reactions of the Inhabitants 222
Health Attributions: Some Illustrative Data 225
Radiation, Traumatic Stress, and Chronic Stress in Relation
    to Health Problems 227
A Psychosocial Stress Model for the Development of Health
    Problems and Illness Behavior 228
Concluding Remarks 230
References 232

PART III. ETHICAL CONSIDERATIONS

**Chapter 13. When Political Reality Enters Therapy:
    Ethical Considerations in the Treatment
    of Posttraumatic Stress Disorder** 237

Daniel Brom and Eliezer Witztum

Introduction 237
Israel and Intifada 238
Theoretical Conceptions of PTSD and the Place of the Therapist 238
The Concept of Disorder 242
Treatment Approach 245
Discussion 246
References 248

Chapter 14. Working through the Holocaust: Still a Task for Germany's Youth? 249

Aor. Konrad Brendler

Approach and Aim 249
Methodology 251
The Sample 253
Results 254
Explaining the Different Levels of Coping with Nazi History 264
Discussion of Results 270
Epilogue 273
References 274

Chapter 15. Primary Prevention of Traumatic Stress Caused by War 277

Victor W. Sidel, Berthold P. R. Gersons, and Jos M. P. Weerts

Introduction 278
The Role of Health Professionals in Prevention of Health Problems 279
The Health Consequences of Modern Warfare 280
Causes of Violence and War 284
From the Individual's Perspective to the Collective 286
Collective Security 288
The Role of Health Professionals in the Prevention of War 289
Conclusion 294
References 295

Chapter 16. Epilogue 299

Rolf J. Kleber

The Hidden Majority 300
Posttraumatic Stress Disorder and Complex Trauma 301
The Illusion of *Post* 302
Coping as a Collective Process 303
References 305

About the Editors 307

Index 309

1

Introduction

ROLF J. KLEBER, CHARLES R. FIGLEY,
and BERTHOLD P. R. GERSONS

Trauma goes beyond the individual. It has a far wider context. We interpret war, loss, violence, and disasters in ways shaped by our culture, by our society, and by its values and norms. We cope with serious life events in ways provided and approved by our surroundings.

Traumatic stress does not occur in a vacuum. Victims of traumatic stress live in specific situations in specific societies. The characteristics of these circumstances determine the intensity and severity of the consequences of extreme life events, such as combat, disaster, sudden bereavement, and violence. They even determine the occurrence of the events themselves: Such diverse situations as political repression and technological disasters are human-made and create intense feelings of helplessness, disruption, and despair.

This book is devoted to the societal and cultural dimensions of traumatic stress. Researchers and clinicians can understand the aftereffects of war, violence, disaster, and loss only by taking these dimensions into account. It is essential to pay attention to these dimensions explicitly and in depth. The authors of this book deal with conceptual issues con-

ROLF J. KLEBER • Department of Clinical and Health Psychology, Utrecht University, and Institute for Psychotrauma, 3584 CS Utrecht, The Netherlands.   CHARLES R. FIGLEY • Psychosocial Stress Research Program, Florida State University, Tallahassee, Florida 32306-4097. BERTHOLD P. R. GERSONS • Division of Psychiatry, Academic Medical Hospital, 1105 BC Amsterdam, The Netherlands.
Beyond Trauma: Cultural and Societal Dynamics, edited by Rolf J. Kleber, Charles R. Figley, and Berthold P. R. Gersons. New York, Plenum Press, 1995.

cerning trauma and its societal context. They analyze controversies and shortcomings in the well-known diagnosis of posttraumatic stress disorder and point to necessary developments in concepts. They discuss political issues that have to be examined if we are to understand the problems of victims of violence, disaster, and war, and they place the aftermaths of traumatic events in a societal perspective. Finally, they focus on the ethical and moral implications of traumatic stress research and the treatment of victims, and they make clear that the psychotherapeutic treatment of victims and survivors is affected by these implications.

TRAUMA, SOCIETY, AND CULTURE

In 1980, the third edition of the *Diagnostic and Statistical Manual of Mental Disorders* (DSM-III; American Psychiatric Association, 1980) was published. It included a separate category to denote the psychological disturbances resulting from extreme life events. Since then, the concept of posttraumatic stress disorder has been increasingly applied in clinical practice and scientific research. There is now a wealth of research and clinical writings on posttraumatic stress disorder. It is clear that this category, redefined in the revised third and fourth editions of the DSM (DSM-III-R, and DSM-IV; APA, 1987, 1994) and in the ninth and tenth editions of the International Classification of Diseases (ICD-9 and ICD-10; World Health Organization, 1991, 1992), fulfills a strongly felt need.

Posttraumatic stress disorder is a syndrome that occurs following all types of extreme stressors. However, it is not only the event itself that causes the characteristic symptoms. The psychological atmosphere in a society is clearly a factor that facilitates or hinders the process of coping with stressful life events. It may be precisely this climate that will enlarge or even cause the problems of victims and survivors. The following examples have made this point clear.

It is now well known that victims of World War II had to endure lack of recognition by their surroundings in the first decades after 1945. For many survivors, the return to society after the war proved to be a new traumatic experience. Relatives had been murdered, possessions were missing, and houses had been devastated or occupied by others. The survivors were frequently treated with indifference and lack of interest. Most inhabitants of European countries suffered under German occupation. Material losses were tremendous, and society had to be rebuilt. As a result, the recognition of the hardships and losses of the individual survivors was rather minimal.

Many authors (e.g. Keilson, 1979) described the sequential traumatization of Jewish concentration camp survivors. Postwar society was not what the war victims had imagined it would be. In the camps, the hope had been cherished that the world after the liberation would be a different world, in which oppression and injustice no longer existed. The confrontation with the hassles of daily life and the return of many prewar irritations, however, resulted in a general atmosphere of disillusionment. A feeling of emotional isolation was often present, aggravated by the fact that the painful and long-term effects of concentration camps and other war-related stressors were underestimated and even ignored. It took a long time before it was generally accepted—even in mental health care—that traumatic situations may produce long-enduring changes in adjustment and personality.

The same lack of recognition seriously intensified the problems for Vietnam veterans. A relevant explanation of the many problems of Vietnam veterans is the social reception given to these soldiers in the United States. At the end of the 1960s and the beginning of the 1970s, the United States was vehemently debating the sense of fighting the Vietnam war. Subsequently and with increasing frequency, public opinion turned against the American intervention. Many veterans felt estranged from the society to which they had returned. They were considered to be representatives of this abominable war. It was difficult to share their often horrible experiences.

Consequently, many Vietnam veterans secluded themselves from others. They developed bitterness and resentment toward official authorities. Feelings of detachment and isolation as well as significant problems in the areas of intimacy and sociability have been reported among combat veterans. As for the veterans themselves, the war and their involvement in it received a negative connotation, which resulted in low self-esteem.

In his analysis of a devastating flood, the Buffalo Creek disaster, Erikson (1976) spoke of two traumas: first, the occurrence of the traumatic event itself and, second, the destruction of community life and loss of social contacts. He emphasized the relevance of the sociocultural nature of the area and its population in understanding the long-term effects. The survivors remained in the area, where they were confronted by memories of the disaster every day. Many continued to be employed at the mining company, the same company that had built the dam that collapsed and caused the flood. They had few opportunities for other work or social activities. The inhabitants were put up in emergency accommodations, without consideration of existing relationships between neighbors and relatives, so that the community ties, which were essential to them, were severely disrupted. In short, reorientation and reconstruction were extremely difficult in this small, isolated community.

These examples point to the importance of the social and cultural climate in determining the intensity of psychological disturbances after extreme stress. The disturbances of victims and survivors are determined at least as much by this sociocultural trauma as by the trauma of the event itself.

Nietzsche described the human being as a *nicht festgestelltes Tier,* an animal determined only partly by heredity. Culture supplies people with behavioral patterns, ways of thinking, and feelings. It is an acquired "lens" through which individuals perceive and understand the world that they inhabit, and through which they learn how to live within it (Jahoda, 1982). Such cultural elements form an intrinsic part of an individual's personality and behavior, although we are usually not aware of most of them. A person is raised in a culture that has taught him or her to perceive, think, and evaluate in a certain way. These cultural influences have become internalized by the person in the course of this socialization process and shape his or her responses to extreme and unpredictable events. They determine how a traumatic experience may challenge an individual sense of identity, as well as the violation and disruption associated with the experience. Culture has a distinct impact on the appraisal of events and on the process of coping with extreme stress.

The concept *posttraumatic stress disorder* has become so fashionable that it is dominating the debate worldwide about human responses to catastrophic events. Western conceptual frameworks dominate the field. Nevertheless, the concept has inherent limitations in capturing the complex ways in which individuals, communities, and indeed whole societies register tragedy.

THE FIRST WORLD CONFERENCE ON TRAUMATIC STRESS

The First World Conference on Traumatic Stress, held in Amsterdam in 1992, fulfilled the distinct need of communication between researchers, clinicians, and other delegates from all continents of the world. It paid attention to human rights violations, to the aftermath of human-made and natural disasters, to the traumatic experiences of people living in war-stricken countries, to the late sequelae of World War II, and to the violence in modern society.

The many contributions to the conference made clear that the experience of traumatic stress is shaped by the specific cultural and societal context, in the sense that:

- The problems and issues that confront the individual after serious life events are to a large extent defined by the society or culture in which he or she lives.
- This context provides ways of interpreting the traumatic events and the ways of coping with it.
- This context provides facilities for helping victims of traumatic events or blocks possible ways of supporting and treating victims and survivors.

OUTLINE OF THE BOOK

This book is a contribution to the understanding of the societal and cultural dimensions of traumatic stress. The editors have brought together a diverse array of contributors from all over the world since they realize that no single perspective can illuminate the many contours of the complex phenomena that are the subject of the book. They have integrated the contributions by this opening chapter and by introductions to each part of the book.

The book is divided into three sections. Part I examines conceptual issues. Its chapters explore the possibilities and the limitations of the concepts of posttraumatic stress disorder and consider alternatives. Part II focuses on societal issues, such as the sequelae of political repression and understanding the plight of those victimized by events and circumstances around them. Part III considers the ethical issues related to traumatic stress. It deals with moral implications and with the need for individuals as well as society at large to work through fundamental issues concerning traumatic stress.

PART I: CONCEPTUAL ISSUES

Part I of the book deals with conceptual issues. Although the field of traumatic stress has realized significant achievements, serious doubts exist about the concepts and theoretical notions underlying these concepts. Are they adequate enough to describe the various consequences of traumatic events? Are they applicable to differing situations? Are they not formulated too strictly and too rigidly, so that differences in the consequences in complex circumstances or in other societies are overlooked?

The first chapter, by Summerfield, makes clear the shortcomings of Western models of understanding human reactions to war and atrocity. He underlines that it is in a social setting that traumatized individuals reveal themselves. The concept of posttraumatic stress disorder has limitations in grasping the complex ways in which individuals perceive and comprehend loss and violence. It cannot capture by which mechanisms people search for a meaning.

The next chapter goes into the role of the stressor as the central factor in determining the typical symptoms of posttraumatic stress disorder. McFarlane raises a series of central issues about causation, treatment, and prevention. He analyzes assumptions concerning the relationship between the traumatic event and subsequent psychopathology, and presents solutions to the many inconsistencies and contradictions. His chapter makes it clear that defining a traumatic event on the surface seems a simple and straightforward process, yet on detailed examination it is quite a complex problem.

Cognitive processing is central to the consequences of traumatic stress. One could argue that a cognitive approach unites the analysis of the individual with an analysis of the context. The third chapter, by Creamer, integrates existing conceptualizations of reactions to traumatic events into a longitudinal model. The implications of this formulation of treatment lend support to interventions in which exposure to the traumatic event is essential. Recovery from trauma may be facilitated in societies that encourage discussion of the traumatic experiences and that provide strong social support.

The next contribution considers the concept of secondary traumatic stress. It is striking that most publications on posttraumatic stress disorder ignore those who are traumatized indirectly or secondarily: spouses, children, other family members, friends, colleagues, and helping professionals. Figley and Kleber deal with the responses of those people who have been traumatized by the knowledge of a traumatic stress event experienced by a significant other. In addition, the authors present explanations of the transmission of trauma.

Finally, Becker describes the limitations of the concept of posttraumatic stress disorder based on his experience with victims of human rights violations and other forms of organized violence. Latin American regimes created political repression in the 1970s. Many people still suffer the aftereffects today. Becker analyzes and specifies the consequences of extreme traumatization.

PART II: SOCIETAL AND POLITICAL ISSUES

Part II focuses on situations of abuse that have their roots in societal and political conditions, varying from massive human rights violations in countries where injustice rules to the abuse of women and to neglect and technological mishaps. All chapters deal with specific themes concerning the impact of a political system on human experience and reactions to trauma. They underscore the importance of the political context of trauma—*political* in the sense of power relationships and social governance. All trauma is to some extent determined by political forces, effects, and motives. These political forces are clear in the case of crimes against humanity, but they are also relevant in the circumstances of natural disasters. The unemployed and the homeless are always more affected. The chapters all consider significant issues of mental health care resulting from the situations of abuse, inhumanity, and human rights violations.

In the first chapter, Lira Kornfeld describes the development of a clinical approach to survivors of human rights violations in Chile. The chapter emphasizes the repercussions on therapists and their strategies of coping with the extreme traumas of victims of political violence. The author stresses that, by working through these painful experiences, the Chilean people can find the basis and roots to build social peace.

Guiao examines the impact of political conflict and instability on various indicators of mental distress in Filipino women. She integrates empirical findings from a study using a general stress and coping perspective with an analysis of specific attributes of Filipino culture. Her work lays a bridge between psychological research and cultural anthropological analysis. She also emphasizes adequate coping strategies of people in prolonged and severe circumstances. Resilience is a concept that is, unfortunately, neglected in traumatic stress research.

For refugees, traumatization is not a relatively isolated incident or set of events, but a cumulative, ongoing process. In his chapter, Van der Veer illustrates this enduring process that continues during exile. The process is a chain of traumatic and stressful experiences. Van der Veer focuses on the necessity of overcoming cultural differences as an important ingredient in working with traumatized refugees. Various manifestations of these differences create serious communication problems. In order to overcome these problems, the therapist must become informed about the cultural differences. The chapter ends with concrete implications for therapy with traumatized refugees.

When violence takes the form of incestuous abuse, victims do not often receive the necessary attention by policymakers or public opinion leaders with regard to rescue, treatment, and prevention. Russell describes the sociocultural causes of sexual assault and considers it a massive, gender-related human rights issue. After showing the ubiquitous prevalence of rape, sexual abuse, and incestuous abuse in the Western world, she develops a distinct theory in which society's conception of masculinity is a key to understanding the sexual assault of females.

In the next chapter, Simpson emphasizes that the political context of trauma has been comprehensively neglected, although it is essential for a sufficient understanding of trauma and its effects. In particular, he focuses on the experiences under the apartheid regime in South Africa. Presenting many illustrative examples from the situation in the 1980s and 1990s, he criticizes in a constructive way the diagnostic concept of posttraumatic stress disorder and reviews important forensic problems. Finally, the author examines the ethnical issues of how health professionals become involved in facilitating torture and political trauma.

The last chapter of Part II deals with the type of disaster that has emerged in the last decades: the technological catastrophe, defined as the breakdown of human-made technical systems. The authors, Van den Bout, Havenaar, and Meijler-Iljina, visited areas in the former Soviet Union that were contaminated by the massive explosion of the Chernobyl nuclear power plant. They show that the inhabitants of these areas are suffering from a pervasive distrust. Because the authorities withheld a great deal of information about the accident during the first three years after the disaster, people became suspicious: They have turned cynical and do not trust anyone or anything. The authors propose a psychosocial hypothesis for the occurrence of the many health problems in the contaminated areas.

PART III: ETHICAL CONSIDERATIONS

Part III considers the ethical issues related to traumatic stress, which are often overlooked. Their neglect is rather remarkable. Trauma implies a breach between the individual and the context, between a human being and his or her close environment. The individual has lost the sense of control, the sense of certainty, and the sense of connectedness with other people. Trauma is a shattering of a person's fundamental assumptions and rules and therefore implies a breach between the life before the events and the life after them. It is therefore an existential experience with moral and ethical implications.

Brom and Witztum present the ethical and professional dilemmas in the treatment of posttraumatic stress disorder. They analyze one case example with regard to the Intifada in Israel. It is their opinion that therapists cannot pretend not to be involved in conflicts with moral and political implications: To a certain extent, their choice in these conflicts determines their treatment strategies.

Brendler focuses on the problems of coming to terms with Nazi history. How do the generations of those who were on the wrong side in World War II cope with the terror and the evil of war? In an analysis of interviews with German youth, he shows the traumatic as well as the educational effects of the legacy of silence within the family and the confrontation with the facts of the Holocaust. There is no enclave in the world where a later generation can flee from the shadows cast by the memory of the Nazi crimes against humanity. Working through the Holocaust is an unavoidable task.

The last chapter, by Sidel, Gersons, and Weerts, pays attention to the role of mental health professionals in the prevention of war. After illustrating the successful attempts by physicians to apply primary prevention to the health consequences of war, the authors suggest avenues for the involvement of mental health specialists in the primary prevention of traumatic stress: by providing advice on methods for prevention, informing people of the traumatic sequelae of war, education, the advocacy of measures that promote collective security, and collective actions. The responsibility to prevent the wounds is at least as important as the responsibility to bind the wounds after they have occurred.

The epilogue examines some common themes in the numerous issues that the authors of *Beyond Trauma* have raised. The trauma field has grown immensely since the concept of posttraumatic stress disorder was introduced. Significant contributions to theory, research, intervention, and psychotherapy have been made. Victims of violence, war, abuse and disaster are being recognized by society, and receive more and more recognition. Knowledge of trauma has reached a large audience and many ideas that were novel in the 1970s and 1980s have become well-known and well-accepted in the 1990s. Nonetheless, the expression *beyond trauma* also refers to the conviction that the scientific study of traumatic experiences has to evolve beyond the current state of insights and concepts. New perspectives on coping with trauma have to be developed, and new strategies on helping people have to be conceived. There are definite challenges for the near future.

REFERENCES

American Psychiatric Association (1980). *Diagnostic and statistical manual of mental disorders* (3rd ed.). Washington, DC: Author.
American Psychiatric Association (1987). *Diagnostic and statistical manual of mental disorders* (3rd ed., rev.). Washington, DC: Author.
American Psychiatric Association (1994). *Diagnostic and statistical manual mental disorders* (4th ed.). Washington, DC: Author.

Erikson, K. T. (1976). *Everything in its path: Destruction of community in the Buffalo Creek flood.* New York: Simon and Schuster.

Jahoda, G. (1982). *Psychology and anthropology: A psychological perspective.* New York: Academic Press.

Keilson, H. (1979). Sequentielle Traumatisierung bei Kindern. Stuttgart: Ferdinand Enke Verlag.

World Health Organization (1991). *International classification of diseases* (9th ed.). Geneva: Author.

World Health Organization (1992). *International classification of diseases* (draft for the 10th ed.). Geneva: Author.

I

Conceptual Issues

Trauma has become a very popular concept in psychology, psychiatry, and the social sciences, and its popularity is still growing rapidly. The starting point of this exceptional development was the introduction of the diagnostic concept of *posttraumatic stress disorder* in 1980. The sudden and broad acceptance of trauma is remarkable. As early as the end of the 19th century, scientists were studying the consequences of shocking events on their patients. Hermann Oppenheim introduced the concept of traumatic neurosis. Pierre Janet, Josef Breuer, and Sigmund Freud examined the traumatic nature of the disturbance of hysteria. The term *trauma* became established in the scientific vocabulary, but gradually, the interest in phenomena related to the impact of violence, abuse, and other extreme events moved to the background. Nevertheless, it returned cyclically, after World War I, after World War II, and after other dramatic catastrophes and calamities. The current concern developed as a result of the aftermath of the interference of the United States in Vietnam, the increasing attention to victims of urban violence, and the need to help abused women and children. This interest appears to be rather permanent, but it remains an intriguing and fascinating question whether it will be cyclical once again or whether trauma has decisively acquired an inherent position in modern science of human beings.

Essential to the scientific study of trauma is that attention be focused on events, situations, and circumstances. Starting points are serious life conditions that confront an individual with powerlessness, disruption, and death, as in acts of violence, human-made and natural disasters, combat, human rights violations, and the sudden loss of loved ones. The origin of the individual's problems is found in an external factor, something outside the person. The scientific study of trauma uncovers the effects of atrocities, war, and losses on individuals and explains how and why their adjustment may be disturbed. In a sense, one could speak of a paradigmatic break in psychology and psychiatry. While, in the traditional approach, clinicians and researchers concentrated on personality and other intrapersonal factors, now they start their investigation with something outside the person.

It appears to be a rather simple point of departure: a distinct event that can be determined by everybody and that can be defined as very painful and obnoxious by everybody. For instance, the *Diagnostic and Statistical Manual of Mental Disorders* of the American Psychiatric Association starts its description of the concept of posttraumatic stress disorder with the assumption that the individual has experienced an event that is outside the range of usual human experience and that would be markedly distressing to almost anyone. It seems clear, then, that people suffer because of these experiences and that they develop well-defined types of disorders that can be examined in research and health care.

Unfortunately, it is not that easy. There are several conceptual confusions, in particular in relation to the apparently uncomplicated concept of *posttraumatic stress disorder*. What do we mean by the seemingly innocent expression "beyond usual human experience"? How do we assess the severity of an event? What is the subjective meaning of trauma? There is considerable puzzlement about the following significant issues:

1. To which events do the concepts of *trauma* and *posttraumatic stress disorder* apply? What are the characteristics of the specific stressor?
2. What is the precise relation between the event and its consequences?
3. Is disorder the necessary result of an extreme event? Is anyone who has been confronted with the particular event by definition a patient?
4. To which persons does the term apply—victims in the literal sense, bystanders, rescue workers and other professionals, or family members?
5. Are *trauma* and *posttraumatic stress disorder* universal concepts in the sense that they allow us to understand the behavior of people of other cultures?

These issues are addressed in the chapters of the first part of *Beyond Trauma*. These chapters all deal with conceptual matters and dilemmas in the field of traumatic stress; they all attempt to provide answers and solutions; and they all make clear from different perspectives that many recent publications on traumatic stress lack conceptual clarity. Common to all these chapters is the statement that contextual and circumstantial factors in the traumatizing experience and in their aftermath have to be taken into serious consideration.

This statement is central to the first chapter. Summerfield argues that behavior is as much socially constructed as it is a function of the psychological attributes of an individual. Most models in medicine and psychology are limited because they do not embody a socialized view of mental health. However, exposure to trauma and its aftermath is not generally a private experience. It is in a social setting that the traumatized who need help reveal themselves and that the processes that determine how victims cope with the events are played out over time. Summerfield states that traumatic experiences need to be conceptualized in terms of dynamic interactions between the victimized individual and the surrounding society, evolving over time, and not only as a relatively static, confined entity to be located within the individual. The role of social forces in transforming individual traumatic experiences is a theme of this chapter, as well as the search of victims for social justice. The narrow application of the traditional scientific method frequently leads to a separation of illness from its social roots and, therefore, from issues of human rights. Posttraumatic symptoms are not just a private and individual problem but also an indictment of the social contexts that produced them. The author illustrates this fact with examples from his own research on war-displaced peasants in Nicaragua.

As mentioned above, the trauma literature has grown significantly since the advent of the concept of posttraumatic stress disorder. The inclusion of this diagnostic concept in psychiatric and psychological nomenclature has played a central role in focusing society's concern on the impact of trauma. Previously, there was a tendency to underestimate the role of trauma and to use individual vulnerability as the reason for people's suffering. This meant that the victim's suffering was dismissed and stigmatized. However, careful examination of the literature suggests that traumatic events do not have a uniquely powerful relationship to the onset of subsequent symptomatology.

Against this background, McFarlane addresses a series of fundamental issues. He suggests that contradictions and problems arising out of the complex relationship between the stressor and posttraumatic stress disorder are often ignored for a variety of political, social, and cultural reasons. The traumatic stress literature has not systematically grappled with questions concerning the role of the stressor in causing the typical symptoms of disorder, although there is a clear need to examine the reasons why such variability exists between different traumatic events.

There is a series of problems of definition and measurement of traumatic events that need to be refined in future research. In his chapter, McFarlane examines these problems in depth and suggests significant solutions. First, the reliability and validity of measures of the intensity of an individual's exposure have not been systematically examined. The assumptions inherent in the construction of exposure scales require discussion. Second, there are a number of problems in the statistical models used to analyze the data. The current statistical models of the effects of trauma and the methods of statistical analysis contain a series of built-in assumptions that are seldom questioned. For instance, current methods of statistical analysis have tended to assume simple causal relationships rather than to examine the possibility that triggering and vulnerability factors may have different acute and longitudinal effects. Again, McFarlane ends with the conclusion that central to understanding the impact of trauma is the fact that the context plays a critical role in influencing the interpretation of the event and the method used to cope with it.

The purpose of the next chapter, by Creamer, is to develop a cognitive processing model of the reactions after traumatic stress and to evaluate that model empirically. Cognitive processing models are particularly attractive from a cultural and social perspective on trauma. They explain the interrelationships between cultural and societal variables, on the one hand, and individual behavior and experience, on the other. How a potentially traumatic event is interpreted may be influenced largely by cultural expectations and social norms; what is traumatic in one culture or one society may not be so in another. During the recovery phase, rituals, attitudes, and expectations may facilitate or impair the survivor's ability to come to terms with the experience.

Cognitive processing models have been central to the understanding of posttrauma reactions. They focus on schemata containing information about the individual's past experience, as well as assumptions and expectations regarding future events. A traumatic event shatters these preexisting views. For recovery to occur, the new information from the traumatic experience must be processed until it can be made congruent with these inner models, and preexisting schemata must be modified to accommodate the new information. These attempts to integrate threat-related information result in considerable distress and a desire to avoid, or escape, thoughts and reminders of the trauma.

The chapter by Creamer integrates existing conceptualizations into a longitudinal model that is empirically evaluated. Data were obtained following a multiple shooting in a city office block in Melbourne, Australia, in which people died and were injured. In its implications for treatment, this model highlights the importance of confronting the traumatic memories. Since such activation is likely to be accompanied by high levels of distress, however, it is important to provide strategies and interventions for managing or reducing these aversive responses. It can be speculated also that recovery from trauma may be facilitated in those cultures that encourage activation of the traumatic memory networks.

Mere knowledge of the exposure of a loved one to a traumatic event may be traumatizing as well. Nevertheless, most publications that focus on people confronted with traumatic events exclude those who experienced the events indirectly. The chapter by Figley and Kleber focuses on these secondary victims: the victim's spouse and/or children, friends and neighbors, colleagues at work, and helping professionals such as rescue workers, emergency personnel and psychotherapists. These people are in some way close to the victim or survivor. Secondary traumatic stress refers to the stress symptoms resulting from hearing about an extreme event experienced by a friend or loved one or from attempting to help the traumatized or suffering person. This exposure may be a confrontation with powerlessness and disruption as well.

The authors review the scientific literature associated with secondary effects of traumatic stress and describe the various groups of people indirectly influenced and touched by trauma. Conceptual issues and theoretical explanations are examined as well. What is the distinction between primary traumatic stress and secondary traumatic stress? Where is the demarcation line between direct effects and indirect effects of combat, disaster, war and violence? Which psychological problems can be still regarded as consequences of traumatic stress? Which causes of secondary traumatic stress can be distinguished?

The last chapter of Part I is again a critical discussion of well-known concepts in the modern scientific literature. Human rights violations and the suffering of the victims have often been the starting point in trauma research for critical reflections on well-known concepts. Many clinical experiences and research findings have been accumulated concerning the physical and mental care of victims of human rights violations in Chile since 1973, during the dictatorship as well as in the slow transition to democracy. The Chilean scientist Becker examines the concept of *posttraumatic stress disorder* on the basis of this expertise. The successive process of traumatization is, in his view, highly important. Traumatic experiences are often continuous, and a definite termination cannot be distinguished. Introducing the idea of sequence to trauma theory makes it possible to understand the chronic problems of victims. Becker also emphasizes that the proposed changes in scientific concepts make generalizations in future research more difficult, as we have to analyze trauma in reference to specific social and cultural contexts. Any comprehensive analysis must be built on the differences much more than on the similarities. Trauma is indeed context-bound. That fact creates an enormous task of carefully constructing context-bound definitions of illness, trauma, and expectable symptomatology.

2

Addressing Human Response to War and Atrocity
Major Challenges in Research and Practices and the Limitations of Western Psychiatric Models

DEREK SUMMERFIELD

INTRODUCTION

According to studies undertaken for the International Symposium of Children and War in 1983, 5% of all casualties in World War I were civilians, 50% in World War II, and over 80% in the Vietnam war (UNICEF, 1986). In current armed conflicts, over 90% of all casualties are civilians, typically from the poorest sectors of society. What predominates is the use of terror to exert social control, if necessary by disrupting the fabric of grassroots social, economic, and cultural relations. The target is often population rather than territory, and psychological warfare is a central element. Atrocity, including public execution, disappearances, torture and sexual violation, is the norm, and those whose work symbolizes shared values are also targeted: community leaders, priests, health workers, and teachers. These strategies, frequently played out on the terrain of subsistence economies, can be devastatingly effec-

DEREK SUMMERFIELD • Medical Foundation for the Care of Victims of Torture, 96–98 Grafton Road, London NW5 3EJ; and Department of Community Psychiatry, St. George's Hospital Medical School, London, SW17 ORE, United Kingdom.
Beyond Trauma: Cultural and Societal Dynamics, edited by Rolf J. Kleber, Charles R. Figley, and Berthold P. R. Gersons. New York, Plenum Press, 1995.

17

tive. Mozambique, Angola, Sudan, Somalia, El Salvador, Guatemala, Nicaragua, Peru, Afghanistan, Iraq, Iran, Indonesia, the Philippines, Sri Lanka, the Israeli occupied territories, and the former Yugoslavia have all provided examples of this pattern of war or civil conflict in the past decade. At present, the United Nations High Commission for Refugees counts about 18 million refugees who have fled across an international frontier, though there are at least as many again, no less destitute, who are internally displaced. There have been an estimated 150 wars in the Third World since 1945, which have left 22 million people dead. So far, we have learned little of the health and social costs for the millions left behind, let alone the patterns of their distress and adaptation over time.

THE MEDICAL MODEL OF TRAUMA

The successor to formulations like *concentration camp syndrome, survivor syndrome,* and *war neurosis,* the *posttraumatic stress disorder* (PTSD) first introduced in the *Diagnostic and Statistical Manual of Mental Disorders,* Third Edition (DSM-III; American Psychiatric Association, 1980) has become so fashionable that it is dominating the debate worldwide about human response to catastrophic events. Most publications in the medical or psychological literature have used PTSD to measure traumatization in the subject sample. PTSD embodies a core set of ongoing disturbances of physiological and psychological arousal and drive—disturbed sleep with recurrent nightmares, variability of mood, poor concentration and memorizing, sensitivity to environmental stimuli, liability to reexperience aspects of the original trauma—that are assumed to be universal human reactions. Underlying the concept of PTSD is the assumption that the essence of human experience of war and atrocity can be captured by negative psychological effects as they are understood and categorized in the West, to be elicited in the mental life of each individual victim. This view of trauma as an individual-centered event bound to soma or psyche is in line with the tradition in this century in both Western biomedicine and Western psychoanalysis of regarding the single human being as the basic unit of study.

It is simplistic to regard victimhood as a "pure" state, and to view victims as mere passive receptacles of psychopathological phenomena that can be adjusted "present" or "absent." Whether in clinic or population studies, a checklist of mental state features cannot provide a rigorous distinction between subjective distress and objective disorder. Much of the distress experienced and communicated by victims of extreme trauma is normal, even adaptive, and is colored by their own active interpretations and choices. The features of PTSD are reportedly prevalent worldwide, but it is a mistake to assume that, because signs and symptoms may be regularly identified in different social settings, they mean the same thing in those settings. This is what Kleinman (1987) calls a *category fallacy*. For one person, recurrent violent nightmares may be an irrelevance, revealed only under direct questioning; to a second person, they may indicate a need to visit a mental health professional for treatment; to a third, they may represent a helpful message from his or her ancestors.

It follows that PTSD, like other psychiatric models of mental disorder, does not easily encompass the complex and shifting relationship between subjective mental life and observable behavior. Behavior is as much socially constructed as it is a function of the supposedly unique psychological endowments of any individual. It is thus predictable that a diagnosis of PTSD will correlate poorly with the ability to function socially, and to keep going despite hardships, nor does it necessarily imply a need for psychological treatment. PTSD was first highlighted in U.S. Vietnam war veterans, shown to have a lifetime rate of 15% after 10–15 years in one of the more comprehensive studies (Centers for Disease Control Vietnam Experience Study, 1988). By comparison, a recent study of British service personnel who saw intense, although shortlived, fighting in the Falklands showed an even higher prevalence of PTSD 5 years later (nearly one in four), but all subjects had unremarkable work and social lives (O'Brien & Hughes, 1991).

In my own studies of war-displaced peasants in Nicaragua, all survivors of atrocities, I found PTSD features to be very common, but they were not what the subjects themselves were attending to. Where they did have concerns about their health, these generally took the form of psychosomatic ailments that were not part of PTSD. These people were anything but psychiatric casualties; they were active and effective in maintaining their social world as best they could in the face of the continuing threat of further attacks (Summerfield & Toser, 1991). Indeed, this thereat rendered a PTSD "symptom" like hypervigilance lifesaving. In a subsequent study of war-injured ex-soldiers in the same country, I found that three-quarters of those with diagnosable PTSD were basically well adjusted and functioning unremarkably (Summerfield & Hume, 1993). Comparable findings have been made, for example, in Cambodian war refugees in both clinic and population studies (Mollica, Wyshak, & Lavelle, 1987; Kinzie & Sack, 1991).

TRAUMA AS COLLECTIVE EXPERIENCE

Medical models are limited because they do not embody a socialized view of mental health. Exposure to a massive trauma, and its aftermath, is not generally a private experience. It is in a social setting that the traumatized who need help reveal themselves and that the processes that determine how victims become survivors (as the majority do) are played out over time. The case of the U.S. Vietnam war veterans is instructive. These men and women returned to find that their nation, and even their families, had disowned their own guilt for the war and were blaming them instead. Attended by feelings of shame, guilt, and betrayal and a sense of wasted sacrifice, the trauma of the war continued for them back home. In stark contrast, the British Falklands war veterans came home to national acclaim for an honorable job well done.

   Victims react to extreme trauma in accordance with what it means to them. Generating these meanings is an activity that is socially, culturally, and often politically framed. Enduring, evolving over time, meanings are what count rather than diagnoses. Since all experience is relative, there will be no easy prediction of how victims prioritize their personal traumas. For instance, the debate about torture in Western countries has been concerned with the long-term effects of what is seen as an extreme violation of individual integrity and identity. But what of non-Western peoples who have a different notion of self in its relation to others and the supernatural? What if the maintenance of harmonious relations within a family and community is given more significance than an individual's own thoughts, fantasies, and aspirations? Here, the cultural emphasis will be on dependency and interdependency rather than on the autonomy and individuation on which many Western ideas about mental injury have been predicated. Most torture worldwide does not take place as an isolated act but in the context of the destruction and terrorization of whole communities, as noted before. The meaning of torture to many victims may primarily relate to the familial and social rupture accompanying it. In the Philippines, women raped by soldiers during "low-intensity" warfare offensives end up as prostitutes in Manila. The definitive injury that rape has inflicted on them, a catastrophic one, is social, because there is now no place for them in their rural communities. Some torture survivors say that this was not the worst thing that has happened to them. They cite other experiences, like the ominous disappearance of a younger brother, the witnessing of the gruesome death of a close friend, or the destruction of their community, as having affected them more. There are proposals for rape counseling projects for Bosnian refugees arriving in European countries. These women have all experienced multiple traumas, and we cannot necessarily assume that it is "rape victim" that primarily defines them in their own eyes, or that the rape victim can be meaningfully separated from the "bereaved mother," "widow," or "refugee." Nor can we predict which of these experiences may be the hardest to survive in each woman's case.

Fifty years ago, Bettelheim (1960) noted at Auschwitz that those incarcerated as communists rather than as Jews could draw on their political ideals to better withstand what was happening to them. My clinical practice in London with survivors of torture bears this observation out on a regular basis. In Gaza, strong identification with the aspirations of Palestinian nationhood seems to offer psychological protection to children facing high levels of violence from the Israeli army (Abu Hein, Quota, Thabet, & El Sarraj, 1993). Similar observations have been made in South Africa about young activists (Swartz & Levett, 1989). In Nicaragua, war-maimed young men have been fortified by the belief that they made a worthwhile sacrifice for the war effort and the social values it was defending (Summerfield & Hume, 1993). But such beliefs, and the strength people draw from them in adversity, may change with circumstances. Some of these same men had been sufficiently disappointed by postwar politics and economic crises to abandon this sense of having suffered in a good cause. They now feared it had all been in vain and for the second time were having to come to terms, different terms, with their physical disability and other losses. On the other hand, the grief of a mother for a 10-year-old son shot dead on the streets of Soweto by the South African police may be eased since the cause for which he died has had a positive outcome in a more egalitarian society. This outcome provides the validation that the U.S. Vietnam veterans were denied. We should note that the distinction between the trauma and the posttrauma phase is often unclear or artificial. For some, notably those with lives mired in regions with endemic conflicts (perhaps the majority), it is nonexistent.

War and organized violence in the Third World damage social and cultural institutions, and this damage is usually no accident. As the psychologist Martin-Baro (1990) wrote of its impact in his own country, what was left traumatized were not just El Salvadoran individuals but El Salvadoran society. Elsewhere, what has been termed *cultural bereavement* may turn out to be a key determinant of longer-term psychosocial outcomes for whole societies. In Africa, there are subsistence peoples who may not be able to imagine personal survival if their way of life does not survive. In Mozambique, fleeing survivors are haunted by the spirits of their dead relatives, for whom the traditionally prescribed burial rituals have not been enacted (Harrell-Bond & Wilson, 1990). One study of teenagers displaced by the Sudan civil war revealed that none could write a history of their clan and many did not even know the names of their grandparents or the village their clan came from. Not one could name any traditional social ceremonies (Panos, 1988). Eisenbruch (1991) described culturally bereaved Cambodians in the United States, who continue to feel guilty about abandoning their homeland and their un-fulfilled obligations to the dead, and who are haunted by painful memo-ries and unable to concentrate on the tasks facing them in an alien society. He pointed out that Cambodian adolescents in Australia, where there was less pressure to conform and where they were able to practice some traditional ceremonies, did better than those in the United States.

In summary, traumatic experience needs to be conceptualized in terms of a dynamic, two-way interaction between the victimized individ-ual and the surrounding society, evolving over time, and not only as a relatively static, circumscribable entity to be located and addressed with-in the individual psychology of those affected. The role of social forces in transforming individual traumatic experience, for good or ill, is a theme of this chapter. The reparative power of social justice will be further discussed later.

BEYOND VICTIMOLOGY: CHALLENGES IN RESEARCH AND PRACTICE

Even the "new" cross-cultural psychiatry, which recognizes the eth-nocentricity of Western categories of mental disorder and seeks to un-derstand people from non-Western cultures in their own terms, runs up against the core conundrums of the relativism–universalism discourse. Are there shared features which unite all humankind? How can one culture be made truly intelligible to another?

The survivors of war and atrocity worldwide are effectively separ-able into two groups. The first is of those refugees able to reach Western countries. It is these peoples, particularly from Latin America and Indo-china, who have featured to date in most published research papers. On top of their history of persecution and atrocity are added the disorient-ing experiences of refugeedom, and it is not easy to delineate the rela-tive contributions of pre- and postflight traumas to the overall burdens they carry, and to outcomes. It has been argued both that their specific traumatic experiences are too little addressed and, the opposite empha-sis, that the undermining effects of insecurity over deportation, money, poor housing, and racism are underestimated and should be distin-guished from what is generally meant by the stresses of acculturation. The research literature to date has tended to regard specific contact with extreme violence as the central and defining trauma and has neglected other dimensions, including refugeedom itself. One of the pressures of refugeedom is fear of deportation, often all too realistic. Some of the Guatemalan and El Salvadoran refugees forcibly returned by the United

States in recent years have been subsequently documented as victims of the army or death squads. The literature of both the anthropological and the mental health fields (in the latter case, starting with the classic study of Freud and Burlingham, 1943) gives a convincing demonstration of the positive effects of family attachment and of wider social supports in combating the influence of trauma and disruption.

The second group represents the millions who remain in or near the war-devastated areas of the Third World, the overwhelming majority. We need to know more about traditional coping patterns mobilized in time of crisis in a particular society and whether these have been disrupted by conflicts destroying not only peoples but also ways of life. Where these patterns still exist, helping agencies can seek to facilitate or at least not retard their function. A body of indigenous writings about these questions does exist but is rarely translated into Western languages and published in major journals (Baker, 1992). Arguably, the central question is not so much how or why individuals become psychosocial casualties, but how or why the vast majority do not. This is what might be called a "survivorological" inquiry, in contrast to the "victimological" framework which tends to be deployed by health professionals. This means more of a focus on social, cultural, and situational variables than on individual psychology. Closer working alliances between the mental health field and other disciplines—anthropologists, sociologists, historians, and political economists—would afford the best chance of a more richly textured understanding of human responses to extreme violence and its determinants.

Perhaps the most resonant question of all is whether the exposure of whole generations to mass atrocity and the destruction of their social and cultural worlds will have long-term, traceable consequences. So far, this question has centered on whether persisting effects were identifiable in the children and grandchildren of Jewish Holocaust survivors. In a review of the post-Holocaust literature, Solkoff (1992) noted that psychoanalytically oriented studies tended to support this conclusion but that community-based research did not bear it out. The variables to which researchers must attend do not lie just with the subjects themselves. Those who emerged alive in 1945 mostly sought to rebuild their social and work lives and put their traumas behind them. Most did not seek, nor were they offered, psychological help, and postwar societies did not see them as carrying a permanent psychological wound.

In contrast, today's victims of torture and also, for example, of rape or childhood sexual abuse are commonly held to have a kind of life sentence and to be in need of psychological treatment, a "working through," to at least moderate the damage. Through the popular media, the general public has become familiar with these concepts, and terms like *emotional scarring* are in commonplace usage. As discussed before, socially held beliefs about trauma outcomes influence individual victims, shaping what they feel has been done to them, whether or how they seek help, and their expectations of recovery. In the clinic setting, mental health workers also have the power to influence this process, including the very words victims come to use to describe themselves and the legacy of their histories. Researchers into long-term effects must take account of the way these social constructions of trauma change over time, and from one culture to another. The reference some make to the "natural history of PTSD" will not suffice, nor will conclusions based primarily on clinic populations. It may be that a sociological framework will yield more generalizable insights than that of individual psychology, with its victimological focus. The effects of holocaustic experience may be usefully traced through in shifts of the collective worldview and group identity of survivors and their children, and in the social and political institutions which represent these. Oral histories and other ethnographic material would also assist. From the human rights point of view, the moral outrage which legitimately attaches to such events pushes us, rightly, to recognize victims. However, it would be an affront to the uncounted millions who do reassemble their lives afterward to assume that they are intrinsically damaged human beings who cannot but hand this damage on to their children. Human suffering, even after catastrophe, cannot lightly be labeled psychological "damage." The question of long-term and transgenerational effects is one that still awaits conclusive answers.

TREATMENT

Most studies have so far been based on clinic populations in specialist centers in the United States and Europe. The use of Western psychotherapeutic techniques with predominantly non-Western refugees obviously raises cross-cultural questions. White and Marsella (1982) noted that the use of "talk therapy" aimed at change through gaining insights into one's psychological life is firmly rooted in a Western conception of a person as a distinct and independent individual capable of self-transformation in relative isolation from social context. It is also worth remembering that the notion that traumatic experience is better dealt with if thoughts and feelings associated with it are ventilated, often in a professional setting, has only recently become familiar to the general public in Western countries. Many non-Western cultures have little place for the revelation of intimate and personal material outside the close family circle. Many survivors see clinics as the place to present their general health concerns, mostly couched in a somatic idiom, as well as to seek practical help with their social predicament. However, it may be that, despite the cultural gulf, these people can draw from therapeutic encounters the nonspecific elements which amount to a validation of what they have endured: the chance to be heard and believed in a place safe and sympathetic enough to permit the expression of emotion and the regeneration of hope. To date, the specific efficacy of pharmacotherapy or Western psychotherapies has not yet been conclusively established through well-designed trials.

The World Health Organization (WHO) stresses that, in the Third World, mental health must be viewed as an integral part of public health and social welfare programs, not merely addressed via a specialized set of skills and knowledge. Moreover, many conflict situations are still changing or fraught with danger (scarcely the completed trauma envisaged by PTSD). Individual approaches can have only a small part to play, even if educating primary health workers, often the only network available, allows for greater recognition and sympathetic handling of the more traumatized cases. The emphasis must be on capacity to function, not on subjective mental state features or symptoms, to distinguish between those who are coping and those who are not. But interventions do not necessarily have to be "psychological." Collective recovery over time is intrinsically linked to reconstruction of social and economic networks and of cultural identity. Thus, tracing schemes that reunite war orphans with members of their extended family, work with teachers that helps them to manage war-affected children in the classroom, and the provision of material for shrouds to allow for traditional burial rites are examples of useful projects. Traditional healers are beginning to have their capacities recognized, even by the WHO. Anything which improves the economic state of families will ameliorate the psychological effects of war on their children. We should give material support to indigenous organizations operating at the grass roots to enable victims to rebuild their lives and networks. Moreover, there are possibilities for collaboration with international aid and development organizations, like Oxfam or Save the Children Fund, that have witnessed what the upheavals of war have done to their development programs and are responsive to contributions from the mental health field (Summerfield, 1991).

ADVOCACY

Some torture victims seek psychological help, but all of them want social justice. It is an ethical imperative that a human rights framework

informs the way those in the trauma field address their patients, colleagues, and the wider public. It may be no coincidence that the most
trenchant criticism of medical models like PTSD has come from professionals in oppressive societies, notably in Latin America, where work
with traumatized victims is unavoidably also human rights work. They
charge that the narrow application of the scientific method can amount
to reductionist medicalizing, with health and illness being separated
from their social roots. Posttraumatic symptoms are not just a private
and individual problem but also an indictment of the social contexts
which produced them.

There are too few studies which "bridge" individual psychological
responses and the sociopolitical dynamics of marginalization and persecution which are the traditional lot of so many. In El Salvador, which
has long had one of the most atrocious human rights records in the
Western Hemisphere, Martin-Baro (1990) saw psychosocial trauma as
the normal consequence of social systems based on exploitation and
dehumanizing oppression. He described how destructively polarized
choices imposed themselves on the developmental processes of El Salvadoran children who had to grow up with this social "normal abnor-
mality," a climate of unremitting state terror, militarization of social life,
and institutionalized lying. If prevention is to be as important as cure,
there must be as much rigor in the analysis of the causes of mass trauma
as of its effects. Some issues will be global ones, notably the tacit insis-
tence of Western governments and businesspeople (particularly arms
manufacturers) that human rights considerations should not significantly influence the alliances they choose in the Third World (Siward,
1989). Relatively empowered and unpersecuted Western professionals
are in a position to publicize the human costs of these decisions.

Local human rights organizations in the Third World need to be
helped to publicize their findings in the West. Such solidarity would also
make it harder for authoritarian regimes to silence courageous activists
and their work. The testimonies they collect can provide for a more
complete counting of the human costs of exposure to extreme violence.
It is significant that, in El Salvador, people are worried that they have
begun to forget all the names of those murdered by the military in the
1980s. The collated testimonies of survivors could be part of a kind of
grassroots history, a counter to the official accounts generated by those
with power to abuse and thus a public validation of their suffering. As
Primo Levi, a survivor of the Jewish Holocaust, wrote of what he had
witnessed, "If understanding is impossible, knowing is imperative".

An allied vital question is that of official reparation for human
rights crimes. Victims may better become survivors if some part of the

legacy of the past can be addressed: This may be something approaching a universal value, even though we must also acknowledge the pessimistic lessons of history, that there has always been little redemption for those massively wronged and that historical accounts are seldom settled. (Indeed, what has been called the first genocide of the 20th century, of up to 1.5 million Armenians by Turkey in 1915, is still officially denied in toto.) In recent years, ostensibly democratizing civilian governments have replaced brutal military regimes in, for example, Uruguay, Chile, Argentina, and, most recently, El Salvador and yet have been reluctant to allow full investigation into past human right offenses or have given retrospective amnesty to the perpetrators. A government which refuses to own up to atrocious acts committed by agents in its name seems still to insist that the extrajudicially executed, tortured, and "disappeared" are the guilty ones and denies their relatives the recognition and validation they need to make sense of their losses. These decisions need to be highlighted and resisted. Justice, even if long delayed, is reparative. We should also note that some participants in torture have been doctors and other health professionals. This facet of medical ethics has been most publicized and condemned in relation to the former Soviet Union, Latin American countries, and South Africa. Most recently, publicity about the role of Israeli army doctors in routinely colluding with what Amnesty International has called the institutionalized torture of Palestinian detainees during interrogation has finally forced the Israeli Medical Association to take a stand on this issue (Fine, 1993). It has been noted that medical bodies in countries which routinely torture their citizens are often remarkably passive about this issue (British Medical Association, 1992).

CONCLUSIONS

The patterns of war and conflict worldwide show little distinction between combatants and bystanders; terrorization of whole populations is used as a means of social control. The context of atrocity is frequently the intended destruction of the economic, social, and cultural worlds of the victims. Western mental health professionals and their conceptual frameworks have been prominent in the contemporary debate about human responses to such events. Psychiatric models like PTSD, even if the DSM-IV version brings improvements, have inherent limitations in capturing the complex ways in which individuals, communities, and, indeed, whole societies register massive trauma, socialize their grief, and reconstitute meaningful existence. Traumatic experience, and the search for meaning which it triggers, must be understood in terms of the relationship between the individual and his or her society, with outcomes influenced by cultural, social, and political forces (which themselves evolve over time). In order to better understand the suffering of victims and the ways they cope and transcend, as well as how and why a minority cannot, the mental health field must make common cause with other disciplines and with the testimonies of the survivor populations themselves. As far as therapeutic practice is concerned, there will be some victims whose psychological difficulties, particularly when they are socially dysfunctional, will merit individual treatment. However, the majority will cope with recovery as a collective activity, seeking assistance directed primarily at their social rather than their mental lives. Part of what mental health professionals can do to assist both distressed individuals and distressed societies is to endorse the link between psychological recovery and societal reparation and justice. Thus, it is important that the trauma debate be conducted within a human rights framework and not as if it is just a new specialism.

REFERENCES

Abu Hein, F., Quota, S., Thabet A., & El Sarraj, E. (1993). Trauma and mental health of children in Gaza. *British Medical Journal, 306,* 1130–1131.

American Psychiatric Association (1980). *Diagnostic and statistical manual of mental disorders.* (3rd ed.). Washington, DC: Author.

Baker, R. (1992). Psychosocial consequences for tortured refugees seeking asylum and refugee status in Europe. In M. Basoglu (Ed.), *Torture and its consequences* (pp. 83–106). Cambridge: Cambridge University Press.

Bettelheim, B. (1960). *The informed heart.* New York: Free Press.

British Medical Association. (1992). *Medicine betrayed—The participation of doctors in human rights abuses.* London: Zed Books.

Centers for Disease Control Vietnam Experience Study. (1988). Health status of Vietnam veterans: 1. Psychosocial characteristics. *Journal of the American Medical Association, 259,* 2701–2707.

Eisenbruch, M. (1991). From post-traumatic stress disorder to cultural bereavement: Diagnosis of Southeast Asian refugees. *Social Science and medicine, 33*(6), 673–680.

Fine, J. (1993). Torture in Israel and the occupied territories. *Lancet, 342,* 169.

Freud, A., & Burlingham, D. (1943). *War and children.* New York: Ernst Willard.

Harrell-Bond, B., & Wilson, K. (1990). Dealing with dying: Some anthropological reflections on the need for assistance by refugee relief programmes for bereavement and burial. *Journal of Refugee Studies, 3*(3), 228–243.

Kinzie, J., & Sack, W. (1991). Severely traumatized Cambodian children: Research findings and clinical implications. In F. Ahearn & J. Athey (Eds.), *Refugee children: Theory, research and services* (pp. 92–105). Baltimore, MD: Johns Hopkins University Press.

Kleinman, A. (1987). Anthropology and psychiatry: The role of culture in cross-cultural research on illness. *British Journal of Psychiatry, 151,* 447–454.

Martin-Baro, I. (1990). *War and the psychosocial trauma of Salvadoran children.* Posthumous presentation to the Annual Meeting of the American Psychological Association, Boston.

Mollica, R., Wyshak, G., & Lavelle, J. (1987). The psychosocial impact of war trauma and torture on Southeast Asian refugees. *American Journal of Psychiatry, 144,* 1567–1572.

O'Brien, L., & Hughes, S. (1991). Symptoms of post-traumatic stress disorder in Falklands veterans 5 years after the conflict. *British Journal of Psychiatry, 159,* 135–141.

Panos Institute. (1988). *War wounds: Development costs of conflict in southern Sudan.* London: Panos.

Siward, R. (1989). *World military and social expenditures.* Washington, DC: World Priorities.

Solkoff, N. (1992). The Holocaust: Survivors and their children. In M. Basoglu (Ed.), *Torture and its consequences* (pp. 136–148). Cambridge: Cambridge University Press.

Summerfield, D. (1991). The psychosocial effects of conflict in the Third World, *Development in Practice, 1*(3), 159–173.

Summerfield, D., & Hume, F. (1993). War and posttraumatic stress disorder: The question of social context. *Journal of Nervous and Mental Disease, 181,* 522.

Summerfield, D., & Toser, L. (1991). "Low intensity" war and mental trauma in Nicaragua: A study in a rural community. *Medicine and War, 7,* 84–99.

Swartz, L., & Levett, A. (1989). Political repression and children in South Africa. *Social Science and Medicine, 28,* 741–750.

UNICEF. (1986). *Children in situations of armed conflict.* New York: Author, E/ICEF.CRP.2.

White, G., & Marsella, A. (1982). Introduction. In A. Marsella & G. White (Eds.), *Cultural conceptions of mental health and therapy* (p. 9). Dordrecht: Reidel.

3

The Severity of the Trauma
Issues about Its Role in Posttraumatic Stress Disorder

ALEXANDER C. McFARLANE

INTRODUCTION

History is always an ambiguous affair. Facts are hard to establish, and capable of being given many meanings. Reality is built on our own prejudices, gullibility, and ignorance, as well as on knowledge and analysis.

Salman Rushdie
"*'Errata': Unreliable Narration*
Midnight's Children"

Constructing an objective picture of the impact of a traumatic event and its effects is a complex task. It is a central issue in traumatic stress studies because the cornerstone of posttraumatic stress disorder is the accepted role of the stressor as the primary etiological factor determining the typical pattern of symptoms. Posttraumatic stress disorder (PTSD) is unusual in psychiatric classification because it is one of the few disorders where a clearly defined cause is stated in the diagnostic criteria (DSM-III, American Psychiatric Association, 1987).

Against this background, this chapter examines three issues. First, it is suggested that contradictions and issues arising out of the relationship

ALEXANDER C. McFARLANE • Glenside Hospital, Eastwood, South Australia 5063, Australia.

Beyond Trauma: Cultural and Societal Dynamics, edited by Rolf J. Kleber, Charles R. Figley, and Berthold P. R. Gersons. New York, Plenum Press, 1995.

between the stressor and posttraumatic stress disorder are often ignored for a variety of political, social, and cultural reasons. Second, there are a series of problems of definition and measurement of traumatic events which need to be refined in future research. Finally, the current statistical models of the effects of trauma and the methods of statistical analysis contain a series of built-in assumptions which are seldom questioned.

THE POLITICAL AND SOCIAL CONTEXT OF TRAUMA

The role of the stressor in PTSD embodies a series of issues about causation, treatment, and prevention. Currently, some of these relationships are oversimplified, and the doubts and questions are avoided for a number of reasons.

Implicit in the stressor criterion is a series of assumptions about the etiology of posttraumatic symptoms. Given the current state of knowledge, it is perhaps somewhat surprising the extent to which the role of trauma has been minimized in the past. Within certain circles of the psychiatric profession, continuing skepticism remains about the importance of posttraumatic stress disorder and dissociative processes (Ellard, 1992). This attitude needs to be recognized in the context of the series of powerful social, cultural, and political forces that have molded society's acceptance of victims and conceptualization of the role of trauma which have influenced the development of the concept of PTSD.

Acceptance of the importance of trauma has not come easily to psychiatry, and its role has long been a matter of controversy. Herman (1992) highlighted how political forces have been very influential in society's accepting the prevalence of sexual abuse and acknowledging the horrors of war and the prevalence of torture as tool of repression in many states. The acceptance of the role of the stressor in PTSD has been shaped by a range of forces and has not been just a matter of science. As a consequence of this political backdrop, many of the uncertainties have not been openly discussed despite their importance in developing a better understanding of the effects of trauma. The political atmosphere in the traumatic stress discipline can leave one vulnerable to suspicion if one is not clearly a true believer.

The most important issue has arguably been the conceptualization of the effects of trauma in the military. Military discipline demands that soldiers obey commands, and the failure of a soldier to act in battle evokes the specter of cowardice. Thus, there is an uneasy interface between the articles of war which define cowardice and the protocols for treating the effects of acute battle trauma. In addition, the military psychiatrist's role is one that raises a series of ethical issues about whether the primary allegiance is to the soldier or to the military objectives of a fighting unit. Cusack (1993) argued that the psychiatrist or psychologist is placed in an impossible dilemma in this role and is unable to acknowledge the suffering of the individual soldier. This legacy of the two world wars has profoundly influenced psychiatry's neglect of the long-term effects of trauma. It was only in the context of the politically unpopular Vietnam war that the these issues came to be debated with due political recognition. A profound change in attitude occurred when the plight of the individual soldier could no longer be dismissed as necessarily subservient to the social good. The trauma of war was not the consequence of the individual soldier's lack of courage and premorbid vulnerability.

Sigmund Freud initially proposed that trauma was the major cause of hysteria, yet he subsequently rejected his earlier views because he could not accept the prevalence of childhood sexual abuse which he apparently observed. This is the most striking example of psychiatry's ambivalence about the role of trauma (Van der Kolk & Van der Hart, 1991) and probably occurred because the social and political environment was not ready to accept such confronting observations (Herman, 1992). The feminist movement has played an essential role in advocating the extent of sexual abuse and domestic violence. The relationship between trauma and psychiatric symptoms is a confronting and socially charged issue and can dominate the scientific issues in question.

Thus, posttraumatic stress disorder embodies in part the age-old arguments about the relative importance of nature and nurture. At one level, it challenges society on whether it is responsible for the individual's suffering or whether it is due to their moral degeneracy and inferiority, as was considered the case at the end of World War I. The development of the welfare state and the increasing embodiment of human rights in legislation and social values are a context which has allowed a greater focusing on the role of trauma. However, it is easy to see how there would be a less ready acceptance of these views in a more totalitarian society and particularly in underdeveloped countries.

Central characteristics of traumatic stress are the experiences of helplessness, powerlessness, and the threat to one's life and sense of control. Trauma attacks the individual's sense of self and the predictability of the world. Surprisingly, there has been little discussion of the determinants of these dimensions of trauma and whether they had such importance at other times in history. Western society, in its current historical context, places far greater emphasis on the rights of the individual than on the value of obedience to the broader dicta of one's culture.

The relevance of this question is apparent when Eastern cultures are examined such as Chinese and Indian (Prakash, 1992), where the concept of the individual and the accepted determinants of affect states are somewhat different. Cultural values may influence how an unpredictable event will challenge an individual's sense of identity as well as determine the quality of the sense of violation associated with traumas such as rape.

There is no doubt that the definition of PTSD in the DSM-III was a major breakthrough as it created an objective definition which has formed the basis for more valid and reliable studies. However, many issues remain unresolved, despite the systematic methodology involved in constructing the DSM-IV (American Psychiatric Association, 1994). For example, although the role of the stressor was further examined in the field trials for the DSM-IV (Kilpatrick & Resnick, 1993), this revision has not confronted a number of core issues—perhaps understandably, given their controversial nature. The authority that the DSM-III has come to acquire means that the conclusions of any revision are perhaps not scrutinized as thoroughly as necessary for the health of the traumatic stress discipline. For example, these field trials examined the role of the stressor within specific populations that had experienced a limited range of traumatic experiences. In addition, the trials were confined to the cultural environment of the United States. The importance of property loss as a determinant of PTSD in disaster populations is not reflected in the new criteria because the field trial largely addressed the consequences of violence against the individual. This issue about the definition of a traumatic event is likely to become more contentious with the publication of a competing definition in the 10th edition of the *International Classification of Disease* (World Health Organization, 1992). The incorporation of a category of personality disorder attributable to the effects of trauma in the ICD-10 also means there will be increased debate as to what are the symptoms and behaviors that are particularly causally related to traumatic events.

ISSUES IN THE RELATIONSHIP BETWEEN STRESSOR AND DISORDER

The stressor criterion implies a different relationship between environmental factors and patterns of disordered arousal and affect in contrast to other psychiatric disorders. It suggests that individual variability plays a less important role in the determination of these abnormalities than in other psychiatric disorders. Yet, the findings such as the prevalence of comorbidity provides a series of conceptual challenges to this association which require a more adequate discussion (McFarlane & Papay, 1992). In particular, most systematic studies have found that the majority of victims of trauma develop a range of other disorders (e.g., major depressive disorder, panic disorder, and generalized anxiety disorder) as well as PTSD. Thus, trauma does not have a unique association with the constellation of symptoms in PTSD and may have an equal ability to precipitate a range of other symptomatic outcomes. This is an issue which needs to be considered by any biological or psychological etiological model of the effects of trauma and argues against the specificity of the effects of traumatic stress.

Apart from its importance in etiology, the stressor is also central to the issues of treatment. The accepted psychotherapies for PTSD all propose focusing on and working through the triggering trauma. Particularly cognitive, behavioral, and psychodynamic forms of treatment place an unusual importance on dealing with the reality of external threat. These techniques attend to the individual's conceptualization of his or her experience and associated disruptions of the self-concept and worldview. Thus, in contrast to most other psychiatric disorders, there is an unusual focus on external reality, and by implication, this is specific to the type of events defined by the stressor criterion. It has also been argued that events defined by the stressor criterion cause a unique pattern of biological response leading to the development of specific biological models that have implications for treatment (Van der Kolk & Saporta, 1991).

Equally, the stressor implicit in the definition of posttraumatic stress disorder also implies that unusual opportunities exist for prevention because the occurrence of such an event is predictably followed by significant morbidity. The growth of services for a variety of groups such as the survivors of disasters and the victims of crime, as well as special debriefing services for emergency service personnel, embodies the optimism that it is possible to mitigate the effects of trauma. However, in contrast to the resources committed to prevention, very few systematic data exist which demonstrate the effectiveness of these interventions.

Assumptions about Etiology: The Contradictions

There remains a variety of evidence that tends to be avoided by the community interested in traumatic stress which does not confirm the powerful relationship between the stressor and subsequent symptoms. Quarantelli (1985) stated, "In our judgement, the individual trauma approach is still at the mythological stage that most social and behav-

ioural disasters were at about two decades ago" (p. 204). It is surprising
(or perhaps not) how such challenges are largely sidestepped in the
traumatic stress literature. Systematic reviews of the literature about
disasters come to similar conclusions.

For example, Breslau and Davis (1987a), after reviewing the available published evidence, concluded that "literature on disasters, civilian
and wartime, . . . does not support the view that extreme stressors form
a discrete class of events in terms of the probability of psychiatric sequelae or the distinctive nature of subsequent psychopathology"
(p. 255). The traumatic stress literature similarly tends to dodge the
issues. Often authors selectively review the literature, presenting only
those articles that support their own contentions and hypotheses.

Table 1 provides some examples of how contradictory opinions can
exist within the literature about similar stressors. The table gives examples of studies which demonstrate more complex relationships between
the stressor and the symptomatology as well as of those that demonstrate
a direct exposure effect. Those studies that have found a powerful and
distinct relationship between the stressor and the symptoms require no
discussion. The divergence of opinion can be striking where some studies find that more than 50% of the causal variance in a population of
victims is accounted for by the disaster experience, whereas other stud-

**Table 1. Summary of Contradictory Reports
in the Literature**

Proportional relationship with severity of stressor	
Buydens-Branchey et al., 1990	War
Nader et al., 1990	Sniper attack
Green et al., 1989	War
Shore et al., 1986	Volcanic eruption
Card, 1987	War
Green et al., 1986	Supper club fire
More complex relationship or no difference from other life events	
Breslau & Davis, 1987a	
Solomon & Canino, 1990	Disasters
Phifer & Norris, 1990	Flood
Palinkas & Coben, 1987	Timing of injury in combat
McFarlane, 1988a	Fire
Helzer et al., 1979	War
Yager et al., 1984	War
Bromet et al., 1982	Nuclear incident
Feinstein & Dolman, 1991	Accident victims
Norman et al., 1991	Accident victims
Carr et al., 1991	Earthquake

ies have found that the size of the causal effect of the trauma, despite its magnitude, is no greater than the 10% associated with less extreme adversity. The reasons for this divergence are numerous and arise in part from the sample selection and the method of data analysis. Some of the most challenging studies have gone virtually unnoticed despite their implications.

One example of the more complex relationships comes from the study of Palinkas and Coben (1987), which examined psychiatric casualties in Vietnam. Rather than supporting the conventional view that increased rates of physical casualties are followed by increased rates of psychiatric casualties, they found the reverse relationship, where psychiatric casualties preceded an increased rate of combat casualties. Such data provide major challenges to conceptualizations of conventional measures of combat severity. These challenges raise a series of important methodological issues about how best to measure the severity of combat, as there is the obvious potential for these measures to be confounded measures of disorder. The lack of predictive power of objective measures of exposure was shown by Feinstein and Dolman (1991), who found little relationship between the actual severity of injury in traumatic accident and the onset of posttraumatic stress disorder. Rather, they found that the issues of perception and meaning were more important.

Resolution of These Issues

It would seem important to the further development of the traumatic stress area that these contradictions and inconsistencies be given systematic analysis and discussion. Apart from the obvious scientific importance of this process, to fail to do so leaves the traumatic stress area open to being discredited by those whose political and social views are still very threatened by the concepts embodied in posttraumatic stress disorder.

Such a process requires a series of steps. First, reviewers' articles need to ensure that authors will not selectively review the literature but convey the complexity of the argument. This is particularly important if authors are examining populations that have been involved in a single type of event. It is essential that the range of findings within that event be acknowledged. This is probably most apparent in the disaster literature, where there is a very considerable divergence of opinion about the role of the stressor.

Second, studies are required which examine the different effects of chronic and pervasive traumatic events such as wars involving multiple dimensions of threat and loss, in contrast to dramatic and short-lived events such as disasters. In addition, the impact of these events need to be viewed in a cultural, social, and political context.

Third, although there has now been a series of papers which suggest that there is not a qualitatively different relationship between traumatic stressors and life events, again this issue has been substantially avoided (Breslau & Davis, 1987b; McFarlane, 1987; Solomon & Canino, 1990). Solomon and Canino (1990) found that, in two populations that had been subjected to disasters, day-to-day stressors were equally important determinants of psychiatric morbidity.

Fourth, inherent in these contradictions is the apparent different impact of stresses which emerge from community samples in contrast to patient populations. The majority of studies which have tended to suggest the primacy of the stressor have examined patient populations. This examination introduces a series of potential biases and sources of error, such as the role that the stressor may play in predicting the seeking of treatment as against the onset of symptoms, as well as statistical relationships that have been examined between the severity of symptoms and the stressor in ill populations, rather than examining these questions in more representative groups.

Thus, the relationship between PTSD and the traumatic event is not as clear-cut as the literature tends to convey. Another central issue is the measurement of the severity of the stressor.

MEASUREMENT OF EXPOSURE

The measurement of the severity of life events and the associated distress has proved a vexing issue (Paykel, 1978). The many problems associated with measurement have been responsible in part for the decrease in research activity in this area since the mid-1970s. Against this background, it is perhaps surprising that few of the lessons from the life-events literature have been considered in the traumatic stress area.

Issues in Constructing Measures of a Stressor

First, scales that quantify the severity of stress associated with a range of experiences had to be developed in different populations from those being tested. The reason was to overcome the problem of "effort after meaning" (Andrews & Tennant, 1978). In other words, people who had experienced particular types of adversity which had led to the onset of symptoms were likely to rank such adversity as being more distressing and demanding greater degrees of change than people who had not become ill but had experienced these events. This tendency to exaggerate the importance of an event arose from people's attempt to search their environment for cause that would explain their distress. In addition, with scales such as the schedule for life events, an important stage in development was to compare a variety of different populations and the extent to which there were similarities and differences in their ranking of life events (Finlay-Jones, 1981). In the traumatic stress area, there has been little attempt to develop scaled measures of traumatic stress and to use them to compare different groups unexposed to the trauma. No attempt has been made to look at social and cultural influences affecting the perception of trauma. For example, trained personnel may perceive certain traumatic experiences as being much less distressing than those without training. In addition, certain cultural and religious expectations about fate may similarly modify the perception of individual traumatic events.

Other assumptions about the construction of trauma scales have largely gone unexamined. Life event scales have also assumed that individual events have an additive effect (Brown & Harris, 1978). The logic and rationale for using additive scales in the disaster area have not been established. Another major problem demonstrated in the life events literature is the low test–retest reliability of most scales (Paykel, 1983). Even over relatively short periods of time, a great deal of variability of recall exists.

There is some suggestion that the retrospective assessment of the severity of traumatic events inevitably biases the finding to demonstrate the role of the stressor. Even though part of the phenomenology of posttraumatic stress disorder is the powerful imprinting of memories, the normal process of adaptation involves forgetting. It is easy to see how unaffected groups will tend to forget or minimize the severity of the traumatic stress if assessed some time after the event (McFarlane, 1989).

The issue of test–retest reliability in traumatic settings is particularly important in the area of disasters because of the natural process of forgetting involved in adaptation. Thus, the very process of remembering is likely to be different in those who have PTSD and those who do not, and thus, retrospective recall of the traumatic event may naturally bias the data toward the finding of high levels of exposure in the PTSD group. The importance of avoidance as a mechanism of adaptation is also an important issue. A number of studies (Kinzie, Boehnlein et al., 1990; Kolb, 1989) have demonstrated how avoidance may lead to a complete denial of the trauma. Clinical practice would also suggest that the trauma history depends on the method of examination.

The impact of extremely traumatic events on the victims' behavior and mental state during the event may also be an important issue affecting the validity of measures of exposure. Dissociation is a common response during extremely traumatic events that could lead to the underreporting and the misperception of various aspects of the trauma. It is important that objective measures of the event be used to validate individuals' recall if at all possible.

While major traumatic events are clearly independent events in the sense that they cannot possibly have been caused by the individual, individuals' mental state may have important effects on their behavior and consequent danger. People who panic or who respond in other maladaptive ways may effectively increase their apparent exposure. Thus, exposure can be a confounded measure of the individual's mental state at the time and the severity of the trauma.

In contrast to the effort put into the development of valid and reliable measures of adverse life events, surprisingly little attention has been given to the issue in the area of traumatic stress. Furthermore, the impact of social and cultural issues on people's recall has not been explored; for example, the relative importance of property loss or personal loss in different cultural settings needs to be examined. One of the only populations to rate the stressfulness of the items in the Holmes and Rahe scale in a significantly different way was a group of earthquake victims. Surprisingly, they rated the severity of the impact of major losses as less than populations unaffected by disaster (Janney, Masuda, & Holmes, 1977). This finding suggests that traumatized groups may have a different perspective on their experience from populations that have not confronted that particular event. This possibility has the potential to create significant errors when one is trying to judge the severity of traumatic stressors and to identify the events that are markedly distressing to most people.

Finally, there has been little systematic examination of the different dimensions of a traumatic experience and their interrelationship. In attempts to grade exposure, the relative importance of a range of variables has not been considered. Figure 1 lists a series of components of a traumatic experience which include the actual impingement of the event on the individual, such as injury, as well as the events the person saw. These issues will be influenced by the person's mental state (for example, whether he or she panicked or dissociated) and the person's perception of the risks and capacity to act adaptively. On one hand, there will be objective measures of exposure such as seeing death and injury or actually being injured. Similarly, a duration of exposure and awareness of destruction and loss are objective issues. In contrast, matters that might be equally important in determining an individual's traumatization in-

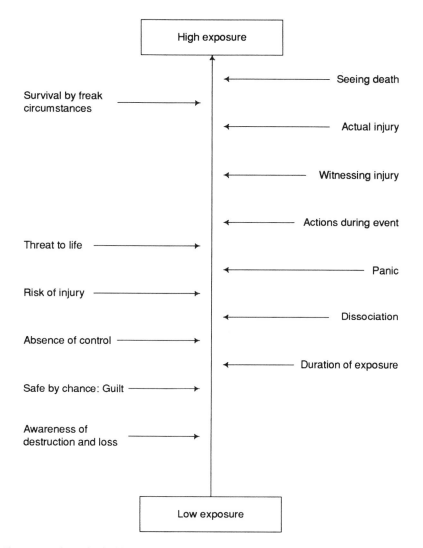

Figure 1. A hypothetical hierarchy of elements of a traumatic experience.

clude survival by freak circumstances, being safe by chance, and having no control of the circumstances or one's behavior. The relative importance of these subjective components has been increasingly demonstrated to be the important issues in determining subsequent symptomatology (Feinstein & Dolman, 1991).

How to measure and combine these variables requires examination.

Figure 1 implies a gradation of experience with increasing distress and threat occurring with increasing intensity of exposure. There has been little systematic validation of the interrelationship of these phenomena or of whether it is appropriate to construct composite scales. The extent to which such a scale can be legitimately transferred from one population to another has not been examined, an issue because subjective experiences may also be quite variable within different cultural and social groups. Therefore, the development of scales to quantify the severity of an individual's traumatic exposure is a complex and difficult issue (see Figure 1). Whether meaningful scales can be developed that combine a range of very different experiences needs careful theoretical and methodological examination. For example, in a disaster situation, how does one compare the different effects of coming close to being killed oneself and losing one's house? If an individual were further to have lost a relative, does this loss make her or his exposure and the impact twice or three times as bad? There has been little systematic examination of the assumptions and issues involved in constructing a valid quantitative representation of the experience of trauma. Figure 1 lists a possible hierarchy of traumatic components of a disaster.

Representations of the Trauma

The cognitive reprocessing model of traumatic stress implies that the representations or meanings developed for the traumatic experience play a central role in the incompatibility of the traumatic experience with the individual's existing schemata and beliefs (Horowitz, 1986). To date, there has been relatively little investigation of the process and the temporal sequence involved in the formation of these representations. Figure 2 presents these issues schematically, emphasizing that the meaning of a traumatic event is derived not just during the duration of the experience but b, a number of factors which precede and follow the trauma. This was particularly demonstrated by Shalev's study (1992) of the survivors of a terrorist bombing, where their acute traumatic responses were poor predictors of their longer-term adjustment. There may have been a number of reasons.

First, the extent of individuals' training and prior anticipation of a traumatic event may play an important role by modifying their behavior during the event. Weisaeth (1989) found that workers who had had previous experience in emergency situations were less likely to develop posttraumatic stress disorders following an industrial accident. Similarly, people who anticipate and heed possible risks in a disaster situation may be able to institute adaptive behaviors that will minimize the impact of

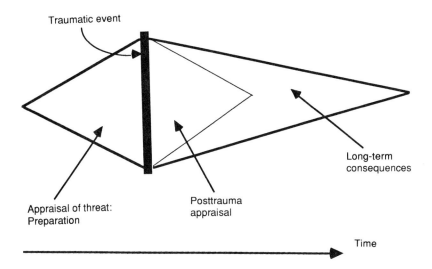

Figure 2. Time periods during which the meaning of a traumatic stressor is determined.

the event. Equally, their anticipation and acceptance of the risks made the consequence of trauma more compatible with preexisting schemata.

Second, the duration of a traumatic event may be extremely brief. For example, a terrorist bombing or a severe motor vehicle accident may last for seconds. Figure 2 demonstrates schematically how the temporal duration of the trauma may be insignificant in contrast to the preparatory and postdisaster periods. The individual may have relatively little information about the significance or consequence of the trauma during the emergency. The impact and the likely disability for many victims will become an objective fact only once their injuries have been assessed and treated. Similarly, they may be unaware of the death or injury of close relatives during the incident. The actual memory of the event may be a cameo which is subsequently imbued with major meaning according to a variety of information that is acquired or provided in the posttrauma period. One example is of a man involved in a holdup who was unaware of the fact that he had nearly been hit by a bullet until he viewed a videotape of the scene, only to see a bullet strike a partition several inches from his head. In contrast to the actual experience, the traumatic image from the video was the major content of his preoccupations.

The impact of losses and changes in an individual's life in the posttrauma period is also likely to be a factor leading to a constant reinterpretation of the traumatic experience. The process of rehabilitation after injuries and assistance in reconstruction after natural disasters may be critical in influencing people's perception of the consequence of their losses. It is similarly understandable how adversarial compensation schemes can have a very detrimental impact and substantially exacerbate individuals' sense of traumatization. Examining a range of traumatic events in different social and cultural contexts is likely to elucidate the role of this constant reinterpretation of the trauma.

Hence, defining where a traumatic event begins and ends on he surface seems a simple and straightforward process yet, on detailed examination, is a far more complex problem (see Figure 2).

STATISTICAL MODELING AND ANALYSIS

The methods of data analysis used to explore the relationship between the stressor and the consequent symptoms embody many assumptions that are seldom discussed. These issues account for a number of the apparent contradictions in the PTSD literature.

The Shape of Relationships: Threshold Effects

While statistics have become the descriptive language of psychosocial research, and the trauma area is no exception, the appropriateness of the inherent assumptions is seldom discussed. Figure 3 indicates sche-

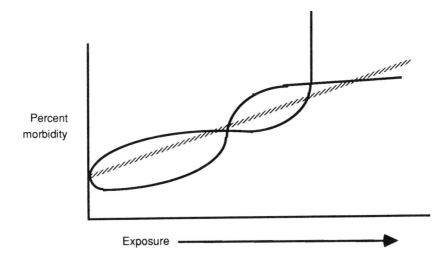

Figure 3. Different possible relationships between the severity of exposure and the recruitment of morbidity.

matically a series of possible patterns of recruitment of the prevalence of disorder with the increasing severity of a trauma. The implications of these different possible threshold effects are highlighted because they are important to developing an understanding of the role of the stressor in PTSD (McFarlane, 1988a). For example, PTSD may emerge at lower levels of exposure in people who are vulnerable for a variety of reasons, whereas PTSD which emerges at very high levels of threat may involve a more central role for the stressor. The commonly used statistical methods mean that these issues do not get investigated. Similarly, most methods of analysis fail to take account of the preexisting disorder that is known to be present in most communities on the basis of epidemiological studies. These are important issues in the light of the divergent findings about the role of the trauma in PTSD.

The first assumption arises from the use of correlational analysis in most studies, which implies linearity of relationships (see the straight line in Figure 3). When these assumptions are examined, some data (McFarlane, 1988b) suggest that embedded data may be a variety of threshold effects. For example, it is possible that a relatively low threshold of exposure to a traumatic stressor may be necessary to recruit a significant number of symptoms of trauma response, and then only at a very high exposure do another set of symptoms become recruited. Conversely, it may be at levels of only moderate exposure that there is a major categorical shift in people's psychological response, and that further increases in the intensity of exposure lead to little or no change in the type of symptoms or their severity (see Figure 3). The consistency of these threshold effects needs to be considered across a variety of cultural groups and traumas.

These effects have been examined in collaboration with Cao in her study of a major earthquake in Yunnan Province which killed 748 people in 1988 (McFarlane & Cao, 1993). In this study, three villages were examined 20 kilometers, 37 kilometers, and 60 kilometers from the epicenter. There was a significant increase in the General Health Questionnaire (GHQ) score between the control village and the two villages with lesser degrees of exposure (see Figure 4). However, there was no difference in the total GHQ score between these two villages, a finding suggesting an initial threshold effect. A second threshold appeared, as the most intensely exposed village again had a significant increase in symptoms. Thus, there was an apparent two-step recruitment effect within this sample of 1,294 victims.

Within the region of this earthquake, a group of indigenous people living close to the epicenter of the earthquake who were illiterate and had very different cultural and ethnic origins from the other disaster

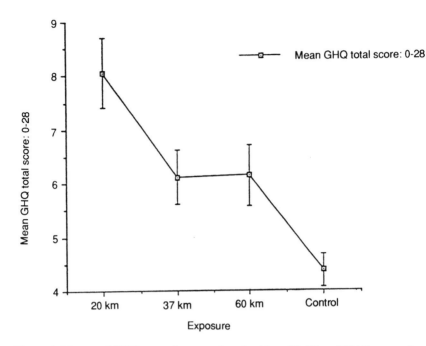

Figure 4. Mean total GHQ scores for controls and subjects 20, 37, and 60 kilometers from the epicenter of earthquake.

victims were studied. While problems may exist in the data collection from this group because they was collected through an interpreter, these people had significantly fewer symptoms than the Chinese villagers, even though a much higher proportion of this group was killed. Given these findings, the impact of a variety of social and cultural factors on the existence of such threshold effects needs to be examined.

Differential Effects of Triggers and Vulnerability Factors

Most etiological studies of posttraumatic stress disorder simultaneously place measures of exposure and a variety of other predictive or vulnerability variables and postdisaster variables in multivariate analyses. This approach fails to consider the process of symptom recruitment and how exposure to a trauma will have a very different etiological impact from an individual characteristic such as neuroticism. Similarly, etiological models have seldom considered the different role that the traumatic experience may have in the different subsets of symptoms in posttraumatic stress disorder. An investigation of the statistical paths between the traumatic event and the disorder arousal (see Figure 5) suggested that the traumatic event had a direct causal link with the disorder arousal only via the intensity of the intrusive phenomena (McFarlane, 1992). The avoidance and estrangement phenomena were associated directly only with intrusion (Figure 5). This finding suggests that avoidance and intrusive phenomena occur in some of the victims of traumatic experiences in the absence of disordered arousal. The avoidance phenomena represent the individual's attempts to modulate the distressing memories and recollections and do not have a direct relationship to the severity of the person's arousal. This implies that there is a multidimensional set of relationships within the phenomena of PTSD. These findings are similar to those of others (Creamer, Burgess, & Pattison, 1990).

Building on this model, it was found that some subjects had high levels of intrusion following traumatic events but did not go on to develop the other symptoms. It was found that the path from intrusion to disordered arousal was predicted by high levels of neuroticism and a family history of psychiatric disorder (McFarlane, 1988b). This finding implies that the traumatic event may account for the intensity of an individual's distress, but that the recruitment of symptoms leading to the disordered arousal of PTSD requires an interaction with a set of vulnerability factors (Figure 6). Figure 6 also indicates how the intensity of an individual's intrusive thoughts or distress is a consequence not only of the intensity of exposure to the trauma but also of a series of other variables, such as past traumatic experiences, the availability of social support, and personality traits. Once the individual's intrusions have emerged, it becomes critical how these are modulated and worked through. Figure 6 represents how a second series of protective and

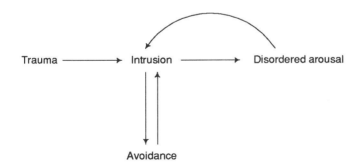

Figure 5. Path demonstrating the link between arousal and exposure is by intrusion (McFarlane, 1992).

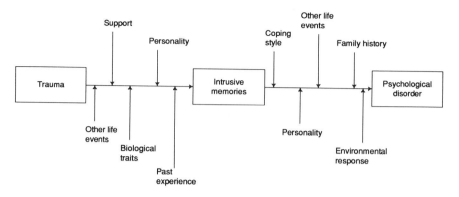

Figure 6. Etiological factors influencing the transition from distress to disorder following trauma.

vulnerability factors come into play at this point, including coping style, other life events, and a past personal or family psychiatric history. This figure provides a conceptual model for examining the cumulative etiological path involved in the onset of PTSD and the errors which may arise in using simple regression models.

These findings are supported by Goldberg, True, Eisen, and Henderson's examination (1990) of over 2,000 monozygotic twin pairs from the U.S. military, some of whom were discordant for Vietnam service. Combat exposure of one twin was associated with an odds ratio of 9.2 for the onset of posttraumatic stress disorder, a finding demonstrating a clear association between combat exposure and PTSD. An odds ratio greater than 1 conveys the increased risk of developing PTSD or the component symptoms if an individual who has experienced the trauma is compared with the cotwin who did not experience the trauma. The greater the odds ratio, the greater the size of the effect. Thus, Goldberg et al.'s study is important because it demonstrates the apparently significant contribution of the experience of the trauma (war) when the genetic and shared early environmental experiences of twins are controlled for.

However, careful examination of Goldberg et al.'s data suggested that there were very different effects of combat on the subsets of PTSD symptoms. In particular, the odds ratio for avoidance and the intrusive items of PTSD were generally greater than 7.2, a finding arguing for the primary role of the combat in the development of these symptoms. In contrast, the estrangement and disturbed arousal had odds ratios as low as 1.8, a finding suggesting that genetic factors play a much greater role in these symptoms of PTSD. The low odds ratio (approaching 1) suggests that the effect of the variable being examined (war experience) is not substantial. As indicated in Figure 6, models are required that examine the interactions of vulnerability or protective factors at two points along an etiological path. Goldberg et al.'s data highlight the determinants of the second step, where factors facilitate an individual's progress from being highly distressed to the onset of disordered arousal. These data demonstrate that the war experience is important in determining the intrusive memories, but that the shared genes and early environment of the twins are the major contributor to the development of the anxiety symptoms of PTSD.

Examining these etiological paths in different cultural and social groups will be important to teasing apart the different roles of social, environmental, and cultural factors in the onset of PTSD. The study of the Yunnan earthquake suggests that the same etiological paths exist and that the role of various factors is currently being analyzed.

Different Effects of the Passage of Time

There has been very little examination of the longitudinal course of posttraumatic stress disorder and the way in which the traumatic experience contributes to symptomatology. Very few studies have used the time between the trauma and the point of measurement as a covariate in analyses. The quality of the postdisaster environment, particularly in disaster-affected communities where an individual's physical living circumstances may have been severely changed as a consequence of the event, may have important interactive effects with the traumatic exposure. These effects may contrast with the effects of a combat experience, where the individual then returns to a civilian lifestyle. Thus, current models do not take account of the environmental, social, or cultural context within which individuals attempt to adapt to their acute posttraumatic reactions.

Table 2 summarizes three studies conducted after the 1983 Ash Wednesday bushfires and the relative contribution of a range of variables to the etiology of symptoms in three groups after the disaster, demonstrating the changing effects with the passage of time. These findings are then compared with the data from the study of a second disaster (McFarlane & Cao, 1993). The first study, examining a group of firefighters, demonstrates how the causal variances accounted for by the fire decreased to 0 across the 29 months (McFarlane, 1989). In contrast, other environmental events which were often related to the disaster came to play an increasingly important role in predicting the presence

Table 2. Nature of Relationship between Disaster Experience and Symptoms

Group	N	Time (months)	Other events (%)	Fire (%)
Firefighters	469	4 mo	4	8
		11 mo	4	4
		29 mo	12	0
Registered victims	1,421	12 mo	13	5
Children	808	2 mo	—	5
		8 mo	—	0
		29 mo	2	NS

of symptomatology. Similarly, in a group of 808 primary-school children studied after this disaster, the causal variance explained by the fire was again no longer significant at 29 months. In contrast, other environmental events played a significant role. In these children, the major contributing factor, however, was the presence of posttraumatic symptomatology among their parents.

A study of 1,421 victims of this disaster (Table 2) also indicated that the consequences of the disaster in terms of financial difficulties and difficulties of rebuilding contributed more to their symptomatology than did the impact of the fire (Clayer, Bookless-Pratz, & McFarlane, 1985). Thus, these data imply that the postdisaster environment is as important in the maintenance of posttraumatic symptoms as the enduring memories of the trauma. Currently, these different effects are not accounted for in most correlational models. An examination of this issue in the Yunnan earthquake demonstrated a similar relationship, where the postdisaster environment appeared to be making a substantial contribution to the victims' symptoms. Eight months after that disaster, the events which followed the earthquake accounted for double the causal variance (8%) compared with the threat, losses, and injury caused by the earthquake (4%).

As well as being an important theoretical issue, examining the relative impact of the trauma and the posttrauma environment following a range of events will assist in understanding the persistence of posttraumatic stress disorder symptoms and how the environmental context may assist in their amelioration.

CONCLUSION

While the role of the stressor is a primary characteristic of posttraumatic stress disorder and central to its definition, a series of questions remain about its role in causing the typical symptoms of this disorder. The discussion of these issues is inhibited by the often polarized political and social issues which have influenced a recognition of the effects of trauma. It can be difficult to examine the objective evidence in an area where advocacy for victims plays an important part in the work of clinicians and researchers alike. In particular, in some circles, there is a desire to minimize the importance of trauma, such as by defendants' expert witnesses in personal injury cases and by pension and compensation authorities that have an interest in limiting their liability. Despite these influences, it is important that the contradictions in this area be debated in a reasoned discourse if the knowledge base in traumatic stress is to increase.

The complexity of the relationship between the stressor and subsequent morbidity is often ignored. There are now many papers in the literature which suggest quite different relationships in different populations. There is a need to develop more complex models of etiology in posttraumatic stress disorder which take account of this variability of outcome. While these models are likely to emerge in research settings, they have important implications for planning prevention strategies and treatment. For example, the process by which the meaning of a traumatic experience is accumulated across time has implications for how to prevent victims from developing distorted perceptions (Figure 2). Similarly, recognition that there is a stepwise development of symptoms (Figures 5 and 6) implies that there are various points in this process where clinical interventions can be planned, and that there is a need to differentiate the different groups of symptoms in PTSD.

Scrutiny of much of the available research also suggests that more development needs to occur in the measurement of traumatic stressors. The first step will involve defining more carefully the components of the traumatic experience (Figure 2). To date, few measures of exposure have taken account of the methodological problems which are known to be important in the life events area. Recognition of these issues is also important in the clinical assessment of patients. Second, current methods of statistical analysis have tended to assume simple causal relationships rather than to examine the possibility that triggering and vulnerability factors may have different acute and longitudinal effects. Central to understanding the impact of trauma is the fact that the context plays a critical role in influencing the interpretation of the event and the method used to cope with it.

Finally, the trauma response is made up of a range of symptom groups which may have different etiologies. To date, most studies have tended to treat PTSD as though there is a similar etiology for each of the groups of diagnostic criteria. However quite different mechanisms and variables may contribute to the onset and severity of intrusions, disordered arousal, and avoidance and estrangement. This possibility has important implications not only for researchers, but also for clinicians, because different treatment strategies may be required for the subgroups of symptoms.

While important gains have been made since the mid-1970s in understanding the effects of traumatic stress, the uncertainties are not insubstantial. Freud's comment in 1917 that this is "a disorder which we are far from understanding" (Freud, 1973, p. 314) remains pertinent. Equally, his statement in 1933 that "traumatic neuroses are not in their essence the same thing as the spontaneous neuroses" (Freud, 1973, p. 428) emphasizes the unique impact of trauma and the dependence of the symptoms of PTSD a series of specific psychopathological processes which require further elucidation. This elucidation will depend on the development of improved measures of the effects of trauma as well as on more sophisticated etiological models.

REFERENCES

American Psychiatric Association (1987). *Diagnostic and statistical manual of mental disorders* (3rd ed., rev.; DSM-III-R). Washington, DC: Author.

American Psychiatric Association. (1994). *Diagnostic and statistical manual of mental disorders* (4th ed.; DSM-IV). Washington, DC: Author.

Andrews, G., & Tennant, C. (1978). Being upset and becoming ill: An appraisal of the relationship between life events and physical illness. *Medical Journal of Australia, 1,* 324–327.

Breslau, N., & Davis, G. C. (1987a). Posttraumatic stress disorder: The stressor criterion. *Journal of Nervous and Mental Disease, 175*(5), 255–264.

Breslau, N., & Davis, G. C. (1987b). Posttraumatic stress disorder: The etiologic specificity of wartime stressors. 139th Annual Meeting of the American Psychiatric Association (1986, Washington, DC). *American Journal of Psychiatry, 144*(5), 578–583.

Bromet, E. J., Schulberg, H. C., & Dunn, L. O. (1982). Reactions of psychiatric patients to the Three Mile Island nuclear accident. *Archives of General Psychiatry, 39*(6), 725–730.

Brown, G. W., & Harris, T. (1978). *The social origins of depression: A study of psychiatric disorder in women.* London: Tavistock.

Buydens-Branchey, L., Noumair, D., & Branchey, M. (1990). Duration and intensity of combat exposure and posttraumatic stress disorder in Vietnam veterans. *Journal of Nervous and Mental Disease, 178*(9), 582–587.

Card, J. J. (1987). Epidemiology of PTSD in a national cohort of Vietnam veterans. *Journal of Clinical Psychology, 43*(1), 6–16.

Carr, V. J., Lewin, T. J., Carter, G. L., & Webster, R. A. (1992). Patterns of service utilisation following the 1989 Newcastle earthquake: findings from Phase 1 of the Quake Impact Study. *Australian Journal of Public Health, 16*(4), 360–369.

Clayer, J. R., Bookless-Pratz, C., & McFarlane, A. C. (1985). *The health and social impact of the*

Ash Wednesday Bushfires: A survey of the twelve months following the bushfires of February 1983. Mental Health Research and Evaluation Centre, South Australian Health Commission.

Creamer, M., Burgess, P., & Pattison, P. (1990). Cognitive processing in posttrauma reactions: Some preliminary findings. *Psychological Medicine, 20*(3), 597–604.

Cusack, J. R. (1993). The wounds of war. *American Journal of Psychiatry, 150*(7), 997–999.

Ellard, J. (1992). New white elephants for old sacred cows: Some notes on diagnosis. *Australian and New Zealand Journal of Psychiatry, 26*(4), 546–549.

Feinstein, A., & Dolman, R. (1991). Predictors of posttraumatic stress disorder following physical trauma: An examination of the stressor criterion. *Psychological Medicine, 21*(1), 85–91.

Finlay-Jones, R. (1981). Showing that life events are a cause of depression—A review. *Australian and New Zealand Journal of Psychiatry, 15*, 229–238.

Freud, S. (1973). *The New Introductory Lectures in Psychoanalysis.* New York: Penguin.

Goldberg, J., True, W. R., Eisen, S. A., & Henderson, W. G. (1990). A twin study of the effects of the Vietnam war on posttraumatic stress disorder. *Journal of the American Medical Association, 263*(9), 1227–1232.

Green, B. L., Grace, M. C., & Gleser, G. C. (1986). Identifying survivors at risk: long term impairment following the Beverly Hills Supper Club fire. *Journal of Consulting Clinical Psychology, 53*, 672–678.

Green, B. L., Lindy, J. D., Grace, M. C., & Gleser, G. C. (1989). Multiple diagnosis in posttraumatic stress disorder: The role of war stressors. *Journal of Nervous and Mental Disease, 177*(6), 329–335.

Helzer, J. E., et al. (1979). Depression in Vietnam veterans and civilian controls. *American Journal of Psychiatry, 136*, 526–529.

Herman, J. (1992). *Trauma and recovery.* New York: Basic Books.

Horowitz, M. J. (1986). *Stress response syndromes.* New York: Jason Aronson.

Janney, J. G., Masuda, M., & Holmes, T. H. (1977). Impact of a natural catastrophe on life events. *Journal of Human Stress, 3*, 22–35.

Kilpatrick, D. G., & Resnick, H. S. (1993). A description of posttraumatic disorder field trial. In J. R. T. Davidson & F. B. Foa (Eds.), *Posttraumatic stress disorder DSM-IV and beyond.* Washington, DC: American Psychiatric Association Press.

Kinzie, D. J., Boehnlein, J. K., et al. (1990). The prevalence of posttraumatic stress disorder and its clinical significance among Southeast Asian refugees. *American Journal of Psychiatry, 147*(7), 913–917.

Kolb, L. C. (1989). Chronic post-traumatic stress disorder: Implications of recent epidemiological and neuropsychological studies. *Psychological Medicine, 19*(4), 821–824.

McFarlane, A. C. (1987). Life events and psychiatric disorder: The role of a natural disaster. *British Journal of Psychiatry, 151*, 362–367.

McFarlane, A. C. (1988a). Relationship between psychiatric impairment and a natural disaster: The role of distress. *Psychological Medicine, 18*, 129–139.

McFarlane, A. C. (1988b). The longitudinal course of posttraumatic morbidity: The range of outcomes and their predictors. *Journal of Nervous and Mental Disease, 176*(1), 30–39.

McFarlane, A. C. (1989). The treatment of post-traumatic stress disorder. *British Journal of Medical Psychology, 62*(1), 81–90.

McFarlane, A. C. (1992). Avoidance and intrusion in posttraumatic stress disorder. *Journal of Nervous and Mental Disease, 180*(7), 439–445.

McFarlane, A. C., & Cao, H. (1993). Study of a major disaster in the People's Republic of China: The Yunnan earthquake. In B. Raphael & J. Wilson (Eds.), *The international handbook of traumatic stress syndromes* (pp. 493–498). New York: Plenum Press.

McFarlane, A. C., & Papay, P. (1992). Multiple diagnoses in posttraumatic stress disorder in the victims of a natural disaster. *Journal of Nervous and Mental Disease, 180*(8), 498–504.

Nader, K., Pynoos, R., Fairbanks, L., & Frederick, C. (1990). Children's PTSD reactions one year after a sniper attack at their school. Annual Meeting of the American Academy of Child and Adolescent Psychiatry (1988, Seattle, Washington). *American Journal of Psychiatry, 147*(11), 1526–1530.

Norman, E. M., Getek, D. M., & Griffin, C. C. (1991). Post-traumatic stress disorder in an urban trauma population. *Applied Nursing Research, 4*(4), 171–176.

Palinkas, L. A., & Coben, P. (1987). Psychiatric disorders among United States Marines wounded in action in Vietnam. *Journal of Nervous and Mental Disease, 175*(5), 291–300.

Paykel, E. S. (1978). Contribution of life events to causation of psychiatric illness. *Psychological Medicine, 8*, 245–253.

Paykel, E. S. (1983). Methodological aspects of life events research. *Journal of Psychosomatic Research, 27*, 341–352.

Phifer, J. F., & Norris, F. H. (1990). Psychological symptoms in older adults following natural disaster: Nature, timing, duration, and course. *Journal of Gerontology, 44*, 207–217.

Prakash, S. (1992). *"God, money and success."* Ph.D. thesis, Flinders University of South Australia.

Quarantelli, E. L. (1985). An assessment of conflicting view on mental health: the consequences of traumatic events. In Ch. R. Figley (Ed.), *Trauma and its wake* (pp. 173–215). New York: Brunner/Mazel.

Shalev, A. (1992). Posttraumatic stress disorder among injured survivors of a terrorist attack: Predictive value of early intrusion and avoidance symptoms. *Journal of Nervous and Mental Disease, 180*, 505–509.

Shore, J. H., Tatum, E. L., & Vollmer, W. M. (1986). Psychiatric reactions to disaster: The Mount Saint Helens experience. *American Journal of Psychiatry, 143*(5), 590–595.

Solomon, S. D., & Canino, G. J. (1990). Appropriateness of DSM-III-R criteria for posttraumatic stress disorder. Fifth Annual Meeting of the Society for Traumatic Stress Studies (1989, San Francisco, California). *Comprehensive Psychiatry, 31*(3), 227–237.

Van der Kolk, B. A., & Saporta, J. (1991). The biological response to psychic trauma: mechanisms and treatment of intrusion and numbing. *Anxiety Research, 4*, 199–212.

Van der Kolk, B. A., & Van der Hart, O. (1991). The intrusive past: The flexibility of memory and the engraving of trauma. *American Imago, 48*(4), 425–454.

Weisaeth, L. (1989). The stressors and the post-traumatic stress syndrome after an industrial disaster. Special Issue: Traumatic stress: Empirical studies from Norway. *Acta Psychiatrica Scandinavica, 80*, 25–37.

World Health Organization. (1992). *Mental disorders: Glossary and guide to their classification in accordance with the tenth revision of the International Classification of Disease.* Geneva: World Health Organization.

Yager, T., Laufer, R., & Gallops, M. (1984). Some problems associated with war experience in men of the Vietnam generation. *Archives of General Psychiatry, 41*, 327–333.

4

A Cognitive Processing Formulation of Posttrauma Reactions

MARK CREAMER

INTRODUCTION

In recent years, considerable interest has been directed toward cognitive processing theories of posttrauma reactions. Such conceptualizations are attractive, since they attempt to explain the underlying mechanisms rather than to replace existing models. From a cultural perspective of trauma, cognitive processing models are perhaps especially appealing. Such an approach may help to explain the interrelationships between cultural and social variables, on the one hand, and individual behavior and experience, on the other. The way in which a potentially traumatic event is appraised and interpreted may be largely influenced by cultural expectations and norms; what is traumatic for one culture may not be so for another. During the recovery phase, cultural rituals, attitudes, and expectations may facilitate or impair the survivor's ability to process, or come to terms with, the experience.

The purpose of this chapter is to develop a cognitive processing model based on a synthesis and reformulation of some existing theories

MARK CREAMER • Department of Psychology, University of Melbourne, Parkville, Victoria 3052, Australia.
Beyond Trauma: Cultural and Societal Dynamics, edited by Rolf J. Kleber, Charles R. Figley, and Berthold P. R. Gersons. New York, Plenum Press, 1995.

(e.g., Foa, Steketee, & Rothbaum, 1989; Horowitz, 1986) and to evaluate that model empirically. Therefore, the chapter provides additional data in support of the model originally proposed by Creamer, Burgess, and Pattison (1992). It would be assumed that the model is not culture-bound, being applicable to survivors from a range of traumatic experiences and from a variety of cultural backgrounds. Equally, as noted below, societal norms and expectations may play a prominent role in influencing particular stages. Further research is required, however, to replicate the current findings with alternative cultural groups.

A comprehensive review of earlier cognitive processing models is beyond the scope of this chapter; discussion will be limited to a brief summary of the major approaches. Cognitive processing theories propose that individuals enter novel situations with preexisting mental schemata, or memory networks. These schemata contain detailed information about the individual's past experience, as well as assumptions and expectations regarding future events (Hollon & Kriss, 1984). Therefore, these expectations, or "models of the world," are likely to be influenced by cultural norms and belief systems. The experience of a trauma confronts the survivor with information that is likely to be inconsistent with these preexisting views of the world. For recovery to occur, this new information from the traumatic experience must be processed until it can be made congruent with these inner models (Horowitz, 1986). In addition, preexisting schemata may be modified to accommodate the new information. These attempts to integrate threat-related information require the individual to confront the traumatic memories. This confrontation is likely to result in considerable distress and a desire to avoid, or escape, thoughts and reminders of the trauma. Horowitz (1986) argued that, until the traumatic experience can be assimilated and integrated into existing views of the world, it is stored in "active" memory and will continue to produce intrusive and emotionally upsetting recollections. The numbing (both psychological and physiological) that occurs in posttraumatic stress disorder (PTSD: American Psychiatric Association, 1987) is seen as an attempt to block out these intrusive images.

Building on the earlier work of Lang (1977, 1985), Foa et al. (1989) proposed a similar theory, suggesting that the experience of a traumatic event results in the formation of a trauma-related memory network. This network contains not only stimulus information about the traumatic event, but also response information (in cognitive, affective, physiological, and behavioral domains), as well as interpretive information about the meaning of the stimulus and response elements of the network. Foa et al. argued that two conditions are required for recovery from trauma. First, reminders of the experience must be made available in a manner that will activate the traumatic memory network: If the network remains dormant and out of consciousness, it will not be available for modification. Second, information that is inconsistent with that contained in the network must be made available, so that modification can occur. Effective processing of this new information results in a weakening of stimulus–response elements in the network and allows the meaning placed on the experience to be modified.

Many other authors (e.g., Chemtob, Roitblat, Hamada, Carlson, & Twentyman, 1988; Janoff-Bulman, 1985; Wilson, 1989) have argued from similar perspectives. In each case, the central theme is successfully processing or integrating the trauma into a view of the world that restores feelings of security and invulnerability.

The above theories have made significant contributions to our understanding of posttrauma reactions, and some empirical support has been provided for discrete elements of such formulations (Litz & Keane, 1989). Some modifications are required, however, if empirical support for such models is to be generated by means of a longitudinal study. The following section provides an outline of such a formulation.

THE PROPOSED MODEL

The proposed longitudinal model, originally presented by Creamer et al. (1992), represents a synthesis and conceptualization of existing models. This formulation clearly does not include all elements influencing posttrauma adjustment; factors such as pretrauma personality (Wilson, 1989), the recovery environment (Green, Wilson, & Lindy, 1985), and the biological sequelae of trauma (Kolb, 1987; Schwartz, 1990) are all likely to contribute to subsequent pathology. Rather, the model aims to provide an explanation of the cognitive processing mechanisms of recovery. Figure 1 (as originally proposed by Creamer et al., 1992) shows the model as applied to a posttrauma reaction sampled at three points in time, consistent with the data reported in this chapter.

Stage 1: Objective Exposure

It is widely accepted that the severity of the trauma is a critical factor in the development of subsequent pathology (e.g., Foy, Carroll, & Donahoe, 1987; Green, 1982; Kilpatrick, Saunders, Amick-McMullan, Best, Veronen, & Resnick, 1989). Clearly, however, trauma severity is not the only determinant of adjustment; individuals exposed to the same inci-

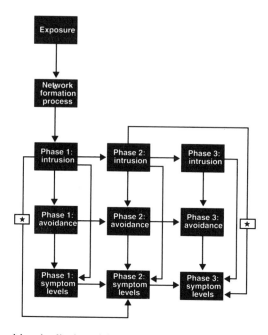

Figure 1. Proposed longitudinal model of cognitive processing in posttrauma reactions. (*indicates a negative association.)

dent respond with different levels of subsequent pathology. It is proposed, therefore, that severity of exposure to trauma does not impact directly on subsequent adjustment; rather, its influence is mediated by the processing variables discussed below.

Stage 2: Network Formation

It has been argued that the individual's subjective perception and appraisal of the event influence both initial and long-term adjustment to trauma (Foa et al., 1989; Green et al., 1985; Horowitz, 1986). This proposition has long been accepted in the stress literature and is central to cognitive theories of human psychopathology (e.g., Beck & Emery, 1985). This stage of appraisal is essential in the development of PTSD; if the incident is not perceived as frightening or threatening, activation of the traumatic memories will not be distressing. For example, in a study of rape victims, Kilpatrick et al. (1989) found that those victims who perceived the assault to be life-threatening were more likely to develop PTSD than those who did not have this perception.

The nature and content of the traumatic memory network is determined largely by characteristics of the trauma: what happened, how the threat was appraised, how the individual responded, the meaning attached to the experience, and so on. In addition, however, formation of the network may be affected by other factors not shown in Figure 1, such as pretrauma personality, prior life experiences, and cultural expectations. Such factors may affect the way in which elements of the trauma are processed. Detailed discussion of these factors, however, is beyond the scope of this chapter.

Thus, the processing of the traumatic event and the interpretation or meaning attached to the experience result in the formation of the traumatic memory network. Such interpretations and meanings are based not only on the individual's own prior experience, but presumably also on culturally determined expectations and norms. Creamer et al. (1992) termed this stage "network formation." It is proposed that this stage is influenced by the level of exposure to trauma and will itself predict the level of intrusive thoughts.

Stage 3: Intrusion

In order for recovery to take place, the memory network must be activated and modified. Creamer et al. (1992) referred to this stage as "network resolution processing." The network is activated, according to Lang (1977), when the individual is presented with information that matches material contained in the memory network. Since the network contains both stimulus and response information, activation results not only in intrusive memories of the experience, but also in aversive response elements (i.e., distressing symptoms). However, the proposed model suggests that, while intrusive memories are associated with distress at the time, they can also be conceptualized as a form of "processing" the trauma. The reexperiencing phenomena indicate that the network has been activated and that the individual is being exposed to trauma-related memories. This exposure allows associations between stimulus and response components to be weakened and prompts modification of the meaning associated with the incident (e.g., the individual learns that he or she is not always vulnerable to a recurrence). As Horowitz (1986) argued, intrusive thoughts may be adaptive and may lead to "revising the automatic processing of such information, to revising the relevant schemas, . . . and to completing the processing of the stressful information" (p. 99).

It is argued here that some intrusive experiences may be functional, that is, associated with reduced symptom levels in the long run as the traumatic memory network is gradually modified. Other intrusive experiences may be dysfunctional, since they result in very high arousal and prompt the individual to "escape" or block out the traumatic memories. This apparent contradiction is highlighted by the fact that some people with PTSD continue to experience intrusive memories for many years without recovery. Creamer et al. (1992) suggested that a possible explanation lies in the length of exposure to the traumatic memories. Research on other anxiety disorders has shown that brief exposures do not allow for extinction to occur (Chaplin & Levine, 1980; Rabavilas, Boulougouris, & Stefanis, 1976; Stern & Marks, 1973). The reason may be that they are associated with states of very high arousal under which processing of the new ("corrective") information does not occur effectively. On the other hand, it is possible that some survivors, particularly in the early stages posttrauma, do not attempt to block out the intrusive memories as soon as they occur; instead, they allow themselves to think about their experiences for prolonged periods, even if such thoughts are distressing. Current measures of "intrusive distressing recollections" (DSM-III-R; American Psychiatric Association, 1987, p. 250) do not allow for such distinctions, and it is therefore difficult to control for the duration of individual episodes of intrusion. Future research on cognitive processing models may attempt to address this issue.

Escape and avoidance may be best conceptualized as coping strategies, although often maladaptive, in response to discomfort resulting from intrusive memories. This conceptualization differs from the model proposed by Horowitz (1986), in which avoidance precedes intrusion. In that model, it is the "outcry" stage (equivalent to the network formation stage in the current model) that prompts avoidance, with intrusion occurring as the powerful memories break through this defensive mechanism. It is argued here, however, that intrusion of cognitive, affective, physiological, and behavioral elements of the trauma occurs once the traumatic memory network is formed, since the network is easily activated by a wide range of stimuli. The current model proposes, therefore, that high levels of intrusion are associated with high symptom levels at the time, but with reduced symptom levels in the future. According to the model, exposure to severe trauma and negative interpretations of the incident results in a powerful memory network and thus high levels of intrusion. It is also reasonable to assume that levels of intrusion at later points in time will be predicted by earlier levels.

It must be emphasized that intrusion is only one form of network resolution and that effective recovery is characterized by more adaptive examples of voluntary activation of the memory network. These may include talking about the trauma and personal reactions with friends and family, therapeutic exposure to trauma-related stimuli, and deliberate attempts to get new information about the incident. In such instances, the memories are not considered intrusive, since the individual is making a conscious effort to recall the trauma. Presumably, they are of longer duration, thereby facilitating extinction. These other forms of cognitive processing have been omitted from Figure 1, since they were not assessed in the current research; nevertheless, they would occur at the same stage as intrusion. These more adaptive forms of processing, however, are less likely to result in avoidance, since activation of the fear network is more controlled. It is likely that factors such as social support, the recovery environment, cultural attitudes towards the survivor, and personal expectations are of importance at this stage. Activation of the network is inevitably distressing, and cultural and subcultural influences may facilitate or impede such confrontation of the traumatic memories.

Stage 4: Avoidance

The current model proposes that escape and avoidance are coping strategies in response to the discomfort caused by the intrusion stage. As noted above, the experience of intrusive thoughts indicates that the memory network has been activated, and this activation is likely to be accompanied by considerable distress. Active attempts to block out the traumatic memories, and to avoid reminders of the trauma, may assist in reducing this distress. The degree of avoidance may, to a certain extent, be culturally determined; such behaviour may be reinforced by familial or societal expectations not to discuss the trauma. An example of this process was apparent following the Vietnam war; veterans returned to an unsupportive environment in which discussion of their combat experiences was actively discouraged.

Escape and avoidance, while reducing immediate distress, may be maladaptive in the long run. The model proposes that effective recovery depends on the network's being activated for long enough to allow for modification, and this tends not to occur while escape and avoidance levels are high. Thus, it is suggested that high levels of avoidance are associated with the continued presence of psychological symptoms. It is also to be expected that later avoidance will be predicted by earlier levels of avoidance.

Avoidance levels are presumably determined not only by the degree of intrusion, but also by preexisting styles of coping. Those individuals who habitually use denial and avoidance as strategies to cope with stressful situations will presumably continue to do so following a traumatic incident. It may be speculated that cultural expectations regarding acceptable behavior are important in the development of these strategies.

Some societies clearly reinforce stoicism and discourage the outward expression of emotions, particularly by males. Unfortunately, it is difficult to control for this variable in posttrauma research, since attempts to measure pretrauma personality style following the incident are inevitably contaminated by experience of the trauma.

Stage 5: Outcome

The model proposes that activation of the memories, and the incorporation of new information, allows network resolution processing to take place. Thus, although activation of the network results in current high symptom levels, it will result in reduced symptom levels in the future as the memories are modified. Since posttrauma reactions tend toward chronicity, later symptom levels are also influenced by earlier levels.

THE STUDY

Full details of the research project have been provided elsewhere (Creamer, Burgess, Buckingham, & Pattison, 1989; Creamer et al., 1992), and only details relevant to the present study are provided here.

The Incident

The study investigated reactions to a multiple shooting that occurred in an 18-story office building located in the center of Melbourne, Australia. A gunman entered the building at 4.20 p.m. on December 8, 1987, and proceeded through three floors, killing eight people and severely injuring four others. Following a brief struggle, during which the gun was taken from him, he jumped through a window and fell to his death on the pavement below. The police, fearing that the incident was a hostage situation, took some time to get to two of the affected floors. Further time elapsed before the building was declared safe and ambulance officers were allowed in to attend to the injured. The people in the building experienced a range of exposure to trauma, and many were in fear for their lives.

It should be noted that this incident was the second random multiple shooting to occur in Melbourne within four months. The population of the city, and indeed the state, was deeply affected by these incidents, which were seen as "something that happens in America, but not in Australia." These two acts of unprovoked violence were seen by many as symbolizing the end of Australia's innocence. For those directly involved, there was a powerful need to answer the questions: Why? Why did he do it? Why choose our building? Why those particular floors? The fact that the perpetrator died during the incident perhaps made answers to those questions more difficult to find. Nevertheless, the coroner's inquest into the nine deaths brought to light some information regarding the gunman and was probably an important, although painful, therapeutic process.

A comprehensive mental-health-recovery operation was conducted in the building for 12 months following the shooting. Described in detail elsewhere (Creamer, Buckingham, & Burgess, 1991), the program was designed to develop a subculture which maximized the recovery potential of the posttrauma environment. A strong emphasis was placed on the dissemination of accurate information about the incident and related issues. Staff in the building were educated about common responses to trauma and were reassured that these were normal responses to an abnormal situation. Attempts were made to facilitate exposure to trauma-related stimuli and to encourage individuals to confront, rather than avoid, the traumatic memories. The program encouraged active involvement in the recovery process by staff at all levels and promoted the development and utilization of social support networks. In terms of the proposed model, such a recovery program may be seen as facilitating the activation and modification of the traumatic memory network. Although not always successful, attempts were made to develop a subculture within the building that would promote recovery. The results of the current research need to be seen in this context.

The Sample

All people employed in the building were surveyed initially ($N = 838$); it is estimated that approximately 540 of these were actually in the building at the time of the shootings. For the purposes of these analyses, however, only those people who were present in the building at the time of the shootings and who responded in full to all phases of the research were examined ($N = 108$). Predictably, response rates decreased over the three phases of the research (4 months: $N = 291$; 14 months: $N = 164$; 27 months: $N = 108$). This, of course, raises questions regarding the extent to which the final group is representative of the total possible sample. Nevertheless, it has been noted elsewhere that, as far as it was possible to ascertain, there were no differences between completers and noncompleters on any of the major variables, including level of exposure to trauma and symptom levels (Creamer et al., 1989). This issue of subject selection is a problem common to most posttrauma research (Green, 1982). Such research is routinely oriented toward volunteer populations and is frequently restricted to those who have presented for treatment.

The subject group was predominantly male (54%), and the average age of the sample was 34.9 years ($SD = 9.3$). The majority of respondents were married (63%), and most people (94%) had received at least four years of high school education. In terms of ethnicity, the sample was largely homogeneous, 77% having been born in Australia and less than 10% having been born in non-English-speaking countries. It is not possible, therefore, to comment in detail on ethnic differences in either initial levels of distress or patterns of subsequent recovery. The sample size was not sufficiently large to test the model separately for different ethnic groups.

Methodology

The research utilized a repeated-measures survey design, with data collection at 4, 14, and 27 months posttrauma. Questions relating to exposure and network formation (Stages 1 and 2 of the model) were asked only at 4 months posttrauma; intrusion, avoidance, and symptom development measures were employed in all three phases of the research. The timing of the data collection was dictated by the practicalities of the research; the data in this chapter provide an improvement on those reported by Creamer et al. (1992), since the measurement intervals are more equal. The self-report method was chosen for practical reasons, given the large subject groups.

Measurement Strategies

Stage 1: Exposure to Trauma. It was considered essential that measurement at this stage rely on the objective elements of the trauma and not on individual interpretations of the event or personal reactions. Thus, a dichotomous measure of objective exposure to trauma was used (Exposure). Subjects scored 1 if they were in the building at the time of the shootings and 2 if they were on one of the floors on which the shootings occurred.

Stage 2: Network Formation. The individual's interpretation of the threatening elements of the trauma was the most difficult stage of the model to assess empirically. It is recognized that a retrospective judgment was required and that a memory bias may have been operating.

That is, those people with severe posttrauma reactions may be more likely to remember the event as being threatening than those who have recovered well. It is acknowledged, therefore, that there are methodological difficulties with the measurement of this stage and that it is important that future research in the area be designed to more fully access information regarding this stage in the model. Nevertheless, subjects were asked, "During the incident, did you fear for your safety?" and responded on a 9-point scale ranging from "not at all" (0) to "extremely" (9). (This question is referred to as Fear below). It is argued that such a question provides on indication of the formation of a fear network.

Stages 3 and 4: Intrusion and Avoidance. The Impact of Events Scale (IES; Horowitz, Wilner, & Alvarez, 1979) is a widely used 15-item scale with good psychometric properties (Zilberg, Weiss & Horowitz, 1982). It comprises the two subscales of Intrusion and Avoidance. The Intrusion subscale, which contains questions such as "I think about it when I don't mean to," is appropriate for measuring the Intrusion stage of the model (although, as noted above, it does not allow for differentiation between intrusive experiences of long and short duration). Similarly, the Avoidance subscale is an appropriate instrument for assessment of the Avoidance stage of the model. The questions tap both escape components (e.g., "I avoid letting myself get upset when I think about it or am reminded of it") and avoidance components (e.g., "I stay away from reminders of it"). Indeed, although originally developed as a measure of current distress related to a specific event (Horowitz et al., 1979), it has been suggested (Creamer, Burgess, & Pattison, 1990) that scores on the IES are better interpreted as indications of cognitive processing.

Stage 5: Outcome. Posttrauma reactions are typically pervasive and are not necessarily confined to those symptoms required for a formal diagnosis of PTSD. Anxiety and depression are common, as well as associated problems such as guilt, hostility, and substance abuse (DSM-III-R; APA, 1987). In evaluating the proposed model, the interest is not in a formal diagnosis of PTSD, but in relative levels of posttrauma adjustment. Therefore, a broad psychological symptom measure was required, and the Symptom Check List 90 Revised (SCL-90-R) (Derogatis, 1977) was chosen. The Global Severity Index (GSI), an overall measure of the number and severity of problems, represents the "best single indicator of the current level or depth of the disorder" (Derogatis, 1977, p. 11) and is used for the analyses reported in this chapter.

RESULTS

Descriptive Data

Table 1 shows the mean scores on the Intrusion and Avoidance subscales of the IES and the GSI in all three phases of the research. In order to illustrate the role of Exposure, the group has been divided in this table into high-exposure and low-exposure groups. Although not reported in detail here, data were collected also on a comparison group in the first two phases of this research. This group comprised workers from a similarly sized office building in the central business district of Melbourne, and further details on this sample have been provided elsewhere (Creamer et al., 1989). Differences between the groups were significant on all scales at the .0001 level, with the "trauma" group reporting greater distress. It is therefore reasonable to assume that the high symptom levels reported by the subject group were a function of exposure to the traumatic incident.

Sample scores on the Intrusion and Avoidance scales showed appropriate distribution characteristics. Scores on the GSI were skewed, however, which was expected because of the large proportion of subjects with relatively low exposure to trauma. The GSI data were therefore transformed to enable the use of multivariate analyses. The negative

Table 1. Mean and Standard Deviations for High- and Low-Exposure Subgroups on Intrusion, Avoidance, and the Global Severity Index (GSI) at 4, 14, and 27 Months Posttrauma

	High exposure (N = 24)	Low exposure (N = 84)	Total group (N = 108)
Phase 1 (4 months)			
Intrusion	18.17 (8.87)	11.21 (8.15)	12.76 (8.76)
Avoidance	15.67 (8.11)	10.35 (8.31)	11.53 (8.52)
GSI	.72 (.74)	.50 (.49)	.55 (.56)
Phase 2 (14 months)			
Intrusion	15.83 (8.76)	8.96 (7.13)	10.49 (8.01)
Avoidance	15.92 (9.58)	8.54 (8.22)	10.18 (9.03)
GSI	.64 (.80)	.56 (.58)	.58 (.63)
Phase 3 (27 months)			
Intrusion	13.08 (7.96)	8.04 (7.37)	9.16 (7.76)
Avoidance	13.50 (9.70)	8.49 (8.13)	9.60 (8.72)
GSI	.61 (.73)	.51 (.53)	.54 (.58)

Table 2. Correlation Matrix among Variables in the Model ($N = 108$)[a]

	Fear	P1Int	P1Avd	P1GSI	P2Int	P2Avd	P2GSI	P3Int	P3Avd	P3GSI
Fear										
P1Int	.44									
P1Avd	.36	.69								
P1GSI	.14	.59	.52							
P2Int	.35	.77	.57	.58						
P2Avd	.28	.64	.71	.52	.65					
P2GSI	.13	.54	.49	.79	.62	.59				
P3Int	.31	.62	.50	.42	.62	.43	.39			
P3Avd	.22	.61	.67	.52	.58	.71	.51	.63		
P3GSI	.14	.47	.41	.62	.52	.50	.76	.52	.55	
Exposure	.39	.33	.28	.16	.35	.35	.04	.26	.24	.06

[a] P1 = Phase 1; P2 = Phase 2; P3 = Phase 3; Int = Intrusion; Avd = Avoidance; GSI = Global Severity Index

reciprocal transformation yielded a near-normal distribution, and all analyses reported below utilize transformed scores for the GSI.

As noted in Table 1, the range of scores on the Exposure index was also skewed, with high numbers of respondents scoring 1 (i.e., "low" exposure) on the scale. This is to be expected because people in the building were distributed throughout all 18 floors, while the shootings actually occurred only on the 5th, 11th, and 12th floors. It should be emphasized, however, that people throughout the building were aware that a shooting was taking place and barricaded themselves into their work areas. They could hear the gunshots and feel the reverberations through the building. Thus, even those scoring 1 on Exposure experienced a considerable degree of trauma. Scores on the Fear question were normally distributed (mean = 4.3; SD = 2.5).

Empirical Validation of the Model

In order to validate the proposed model empirically, the LISREL program (Jöreskog & Sorbom, 1986) was used to undertake a path analysis. In addition to path coefficients and indices of variance accounted for by the regression (i.e., R^2), LISREL also provides indices and statistical tests for overall goodness of fit for the model (Jöreskog, 1978; Long, 1983). The first model tested was that shown in Figure 1, based on the correlation matrix shown in Table 2.

The maximum likelihood method was used to estimate the parameters of the model. Since a more robust model generally results when fewer paths are estimated, those links hypothesized to be equivalent in

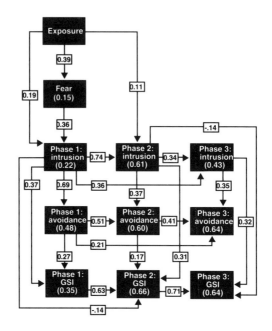

Figure 2. Regression coefficients of observed model. Figures in parentheses indicate the amount of variance (R^2) on each variable accounted for by the model, as calculated by the LISREL program.

each phase of the research were constrained to be equal. Although such a model provided a reasonable account of the data, a number of modifications were required to achieve acceptable levels for goodness of fit. These improvements in the basic model were made on the basis of modification indices provided by the LISREL program, examination of the residual covariance, and the deletion of nonsignificant paths. The model accepted on that basis is presented in Figure 2, with the regression coefficient for each link. The amount of variance accounted for by the model on each variable is also shown in Figure 2. This path model is almost identical to that reported by Creamer et al. (1992).

It can be seen that this revised model required the addition of a number of extra paths, notably (1) paths from Phase 1 to Phase 3 on Intrusion, Avoidance, and GSI; (2) a path from Exposure to Intrusion in Phase 2; and (3) a path from Exposure to Intrusion in Phase 1. In addition, one hypothesized path was removed (i.e., between Avoidance and GSI scores in Phase 3). Two sets of paths were found not to be equal in each phase of the research (i.e., between Intrusion and Avoidance, and between Avoidance and GSI). The revised model provides a good account of the data, with acceptable levels for both chi squared ($\chi^2(36)$ = 39.08; p = .33) and goodness of fit (.94).

A number of variations of this model were tested according to alternative conceptualizations. In particular, the GSI was placed before the IES subscales in the model to determine whether the IES was a mediating variable between exposure to trauma and symptom development, rather than an alternative outcome measure. Also, Avoidance was placed before Intrusion, in order to determine whether avoidance was a reaction to the threatening elements of the trauma itself (as proposed by Horowitz, 1986), rather than a reaction to the intrusion occurring as a result of activation of the fear network. Neither of these two alternatives provided an adequate account of the data; in both cases, a significant chi-squared value and poor goodness of fit indices were obtained, and modification indices suggested a return to the model shown in Figure 2.

DISCUSSION

The empirical data provide additional support for the model proposed above, using an alternative data set to that described by Creamer et al. (1992). All those links that were hypothesized to be present were significant, with the exception of the link between Avoidance and symptom levels in Phase 3. Further, the data provide support for the temporal sequencing of the various stages. While some of the path coefficients were relatively small, a number of specific points are worthy of note. First, there was no direct relationship between either the objective index of exposure to trauma, or the immediate subjective appraisals of the event, and subsequent symptom levels. That link was mediated by the two subscales of the IES, which, as discussed earlier, may be interpreted as an indication of the individual's cognitive processing of the traumatic memories. This finding is in line with previous conceptualizations of cognitive processing in posttrauma reactions (e.g., Foa et al., 1989; Horowitz, 1986).

Similarly, neither subjective or objective exposure to trauma was directly associated with Avoidance; the relationship between these variables is mediated by Intrusion. This finding suggests that cognitive and behavioral avoidance may be a coping strategy in response to the discomfort caused by the intrusive memories of the trauma, rather than a direct response to the threatening elements of the trauma itself. At first sight, this finding appears to contradict Horowitz's model (1986). However, it is perhaps more useful to conceptualize his outcry and avoidance stages as characterizing the shock and numbness occurring in the period immediately following the trauma. The current research, with initial data collection at four months posttrauma, may have occurred too late to elucidate those mechanisms.

The relationship between the network formation stage (Fear) and Intrusion appeared to be stronger than that between the objective index of exposure and Intrusion. The individual's appraisal of the threatening elements of the trauma, therefore, seems to be a more important predictor of intrusive thoughts and images than the actual objective experience of the trauma. This finding is in line with previous research findings regarding the importance of appraisal and interpretation of the trauma in subsequent symptom development. Equally, objective severity of the trauma is clearly also important. Although the path coefficient is low, Exposure predicted Intrusion scores not only at 4 months but also at 14 months posttrauma, a finding suggesting that Intrusion scores at 14 months were not simply a function of Intrusion scores at 4 months. Rather, they were, in part, independently predicted by the objective elements of the trauma. Similarly, levels of Intrusion, Avoidance and GSI in Phase 3 were predicted both by Phase 1 levels and by Phase 2 levels on the respective measure.

Intrusion consistently predicted more global psychopathology (GSI) in all three phases of the research, providing additional support for a cognitive processing model of posttrauma reactions. As noted in the introduction, the network contains not only the memories of what happened, but also response information, notably in affective and physiological domains. The occurrence of intrusive thoughts indicates that the memory network has been activated, and as predicted, this activation is associated with the experience of more global psychophysiological response elements. Importantly, however, the characteristics of the model were not acceptable when symptom levels (GSI) were placed before Intrusion in the model, a finding suggesting that intrusive thoughts result in more global pathology rather than vice versa.

The relationship between Avoidance and GSI was not found to be constant; rather, it reduced over time. While at 4 months posttrauma, avoidance was a reasonably good predictor of symptom levels, at 14 months it was less so, and at 27 months avoidance did not predict symptom levels at all. A possible explanation is that, while avoidance impairs processing and therefore results in higher symptom levels in the short run, in the long run it may be an adequate coping strategy for some people who are presumably utilizing this strategy effectively. This finding may have implications for therapy; clearly, not all avoidance is maladaptive.

Interestingly, the ability of Intrusion to predict Avoidance also reduced over time. It may be that cognitive and behavioral avoidance is initially a direct result of intrusive, distressing memories. Over time, however, the avoidance behavior may become entrenched as a coping strategy in its own right and may be less dependent on high levels of intrusion. As this occurs, it appears that avoidance becomes a less detrimental strategy and is less likely to result in high symptom levels. It may be that some survivors of trauma are able to adjust to their experiences, and to function quite adequately, by adopting such strategies.

The negative association between Intrusion in one phase and symptom levels (GSI) in the subsequent phase is most interesting. That is, while high levels of intrusion are associated with high symptom levels at the time, they appear to predict a reduction in symptom levels some months later. This finding adds support to Horowitz's suggestion (1986) that intrusion is a means by which individuals process the trauma. The strength of the path coefficient, however, suggests that this mechanism was not operating for the whole sample. It was noted that Intrusion (at least, as measured by the IES) may be both functional and dysfunctional. It is possible that this negative link was operating for those subjects who were able to expose themselves to the traumatic memories often enough, and for long enough periods, to facilitate processing and recovery. In other cases, however, the intrusive memories may have occurred in a more pathological sense (less under voluntary control and for briefer periods), the result being extreme arousal and avoidance behavior. Unfortunately, a more detailed analysis of the mechanisms involved was beyond the scope of this study, and such propositions must remain largely speculative at this stage. Nevertheless, it is reasonable to assume that activation of the traumatic memory network may be, at least in part, culturally determined. That is, cultural expectations and societal norms may influence the degree to which individuals feel comfortable talking about their experiences and expressing openly the accompanying emotions. Widely held beliefs about the way people "should" cope with such events may promote or inhibit this process of modifying the memory network and may influence how survivors interpret their own reactions.

Finally, it appears that the proposed model is able to account for a considerable amount of variance. Over 20% of the variance on Intrusion at four months posttrauma, for example, is accounted for solely by objective and subjective indices of exposure to trauma. Similarly, the model is able to account for 35% of the variance on the GSI at four months. While other factors not incorporated into the proposed model (such as pretrauma personality and social support) are presumably required to explain the remaining variance, the model highlights the important role that objective and subjective experience of the trauma, intrusive thoughts, and avoidance behavior play in the development of subsequent psychopathology. The amount of variance accounted for by the model at subsequent phases of the research is considerably higher, of course, since earlier scores on the same measure are strong predictors. This finding reflects the tendency toward chronicity in posttrauma reactions.

Clearly, there were limitations in the measurement strategies adopted in the current study. While measurement of the degree of exposure to trauma was purely objective, it provided a very limited range of scores. The network formation stage of the model was limited to a retrospective assessment of the immediate processing of the threatening elements of the trauma. The individual's processing of the traumatic memories was measured solely by intrusion and avoidance and did not take into account other more adaptive forms of processing, such as education about the event and personal reactions, talking through the trauma, or other self-directed exposure. Finally, the model does not include other factors that may influence processing, such as personal characteristics or the recovery environment. Refinements in measurement strategies, especially regarding the network formation stage, will better illuminate the role of cognitive processing in posttrauma reactions. Further replications of this model on new data sets are clearly required before firm conclusions may be drawn. In particular, it would seem important to replicate this model with different cultural and ethnic groups.

Notwithstanding those methodological issues, the current data set is important in providing preliminary evidence for a longitudinal cognitive processing model of posttrauma reactions. In terms of implications for treatment, the model highlights the importance of confronting the traumatic memories. The network needs to be activated frequently enough, and for long enough periods, for modification to occur. Since such activation is likely to be accompanied by high levels of distress, however (as evidenced by the links of intrusion to symptom levels at the same point in time), it is also important to provide strategies to manage or reduce these aversive responses. Such interventions may include some kind of anxiety management, as well as encouraging the use of social support networks. Indeed, these approaches to treatment (exposure combined with anxiety management) have received support in recent empirical trials (Foa, Rothbaum, Riggs, & Murdock, 1991). It can be speculated also that recovery from trauma may be facilitated in those cultures which encourage activation of the traumatic memory networks. This may take the form of open discussion of the traumatic experiences and the provision of strong social support under such circumstances. This is in contrast to many Western cultures which, at least until recently, have tended to discourage survivors from talking about their experiences and, in more severe cases, have actively alienated the trauma victim.

ACKNOWLEDGMENT. This research was funded in part by the Victorian Health Promotion Foundation and was supported by the Office of Psychiatric Services, Health Department Victoria.

REFERENCES

American Psychiatric Association (1987). *Diagnostic and statistical manual of mental disorders* (3rd ed., rev.; DSM-III-R). Washington, DC: Author.

Beck, A. T., & Emery, G. (1985). *Anxiety disorders and phobias: A cognitive perspective.* New York: Basic Books.

Chaplin, E. W. & Levine, B. A. (1980). The effects of total exposure duration and interrupted versus continuous exposure of flooding. *Behavior Therapy, 12,* 360–368.

Chemtob, C., Roitblat, H. L., Hamada, R. S., Carlson, J. G., & Twentyman, C. T. (1988). A cognitive action theory of posttraumatic stress disorder. *Journal of Anxiety Disorders, 2,* 253–275.

Creamer, M., Burgess, P., Buckingham, W. J., & Pattison, P. (1989). *The psychological aftermath of the Queen Street shootings.* Department of Psychology, University of Melbourne, Australia.

Creamer, M., Burgess, P., & Pattison, P. (1990). Cognitive processing in post-trauma reactions: Some preliminary findings. *Psychological Medicine, 20,* 597–604.

Creamer, M. Buckingham, W. J., & Burgess, P. (1991). A community based mental health response to a multiple shooting. *Australian Psychologist, 26,* 2.

Creamer, M., Burgess, P., & Pattison, P. (1992). Reaction to trauma: A cognitive processing model. *Journal of Abnormal Psychology, 101,* 452–459.

Derogatis, L. (1977). *SCL-90-R Version: Manual-I.* Baltimore, MD: Johns Hopkins University Press.

Foa, E. B., Steketee, G., & Rothbaum, B. O. (1989). Behavioral-cognitive conceptualizations of posttraumatic stress disorder. *Behavior Therapy, 20,* 155–176.

Foa, E. B., Rothbaum, B. O., Riggs, D. S., & Murdock, T. B. (1991). Treatment of post-traumatic stress disorder in rape victims: A comparison between cognitive-behavioral treatments and counselling. *Journal of Consulting and Clinical Psychology, 59,* 715–723.

Foy, D. W., Carroll, E. M., & Donahue, C. P. (1987). Etiological factors in the development of PTSD in clinical samples of Vietnam combat veterans. *Journal of Clinical Psychology, 43,* 17–27.

Green, B. L. (1982). Assessing levels of psychological impairment following disaster: Consideration of actual and methodological dimensions. *Journal of Nervous and Mental Disease, 170,* 544–552.

Green, B. L., Wilson, J. P., & Lindy, J. D. (1985). Conceptualizing posttraumatic stress disorder: A psychosocial framework. In C. Figley (Ed.), *Trauma and its wake* (Vol. 1). New York: Brunner/Mazel.

Hollon, S. D., & Kriss, M. R. (1984). Cognitive factors in clinical research and practice. *Clinical Psychology Review, 4,* 35–76.

Horowitz, M. J. (1973). Phase orientated treatment of stress response syndromes. *American Journal of Psychotherapy, 27,* 506–515.

Horowitz, M. J. (1986). *Stress response syndromes* (2nd ed.). New York: Jason Aronson.

Horowitz, M. J., Wilner, N., & Alvarez, W. (1979). The Impact of Events Scale: A measure of subjective stress. *Psychosomatic Medicine, 41*, 209–218.

Janoff-Bulman, R. (1985). The aftermath of victimization: Rebuilding shattered assumptions. In C. Figley (Ed.), *Trauma and its wake* (Vol. 1). New York: Brunner/Mazel.

Jöreskog, K. G. (1978). Structural analysis of covariance and correlation and matrices. *Psychometrika, 43*, 443–477.

Jöreskog, K. G., & Sorbom, D. (1986). *Analysis of linear structural relationships by the method of maximum likelihood.* University of Uppsala, Sweden.

Kilpatrick, D. G., Saunders, B., Amick-McMullan, A. E., Best, C. L., Veronen, L. J., & Resnick, H. (1989). Victim and crime factors associated with the development of posttraumatic stress disorder. *Behavior Therapy, 20*, 199–214.

Kolb, L. C. (1987). A neuropsychological hypothesis explaining posttraumatic stress disorders. *American Journal of Psychiatry, 144*, 989–995.

Lang, P. J. (1977). Imagery in therapy: An information processing analysis of fear. *Behavior Therapy, 8*, 862–886.

Lang, P. J. (1985). The cognitive psychophysiology of emotion: Fear and anxiety. In A. H. Tuma & J. D. Maser (Eds.), *Anxiety and the anxiety disorder.* Hillsdale, NJ: Erlbaum.

Litz, B. T., & Keane, T. M. (1989). Information processing in anxiety disorders: Application to the understanding of posttraumatic stress disorder. *Clinical Psychology Review, 9*, 243–257.

Long, J. S. (1983). *Covariance structure models: An introduction to LISREL.* Beverly Hills and London: Sage.

Rabavilas, A. D., Boulougouris, J. C., & Stefanis, C. (1976). Duration of flooding sessions in the treatment of obsessive-compulsive patients. *Behavior Research and Therapy, 14*, 349–355.

Schwartz, L. S. (1990). A biopsychosocial treatment approach to posttraumatic stress disorder. *Journal of Traumatic Stress, 3*, 221–238.

Stern, R. S., & Marks, I. M. (1973). Brief and prolonged flooding: A comparison in agoraphobic patients. *Archives of General Psychiatry, 28*, 270–276.

Wilson, J. P. (1989). *Trauma, transformation and healing.* New York: Brunner/Mazel.

Zilberg, N. J., Weiss, D. S., & Horowitz, M. J. (1982). The Impact of Events Scale: A cross validation study and some empirical evidence supporting a conceptual model of stress response syndromes. *Journal of Consulting and Clinical Psychology, 50*, 407–414.

5

Beyond the "Victim"
Secondary Traumatic Stress

CHARLES R. FIGLEY and ROLF J. KLEBER

A local elementary-school janitor walked into a cafeteria in Florida in the United States, filled with chattering schoolchildren, and shot his supervisor in the chest with a shotgun. As a children and teachers watched in horror, the murderer left the room, fired the remaining shot over the playground, and left the campus. The county sheriff's office caught the man within an hour. The elementary school implemented its "code blue" system, which kept all children safely in their classrooms, while school counselors from throughout the county converged to provide crisis counseling. School officials informed parents of the events and provided suggestions for helping their children overcome the extreme event. Indeed, the plans for protecting children and promoting their emotional recovery were state-of-the-art, and the school system carried them out effectively. All the "victims" were cared for. All, except the parents of the children. However, they, too, were confronted with the frightening experience. They listened to the stories of the children and the officials. They identified with the reactions of their children. And they felt angry and frightened.

This chapter focuses on these secondary victims. What follows is an

CHARLES R. FIGLEY • Psychosocial Stress Research Program, Florida State University, Tallahassee, Florida 32306-4097.   ROLF J. KLEBER • Department of Clinical and Health Psychology, Utrecht University, and Institute for Psychotherapy, 3584 CS Utrecht, The Netherlands.
Beyond Trauma: Cultural and Societal Dynamics, edited by Rolf J. Kleber, Charles R. Figley, and Berthold P. R. Gersons. New York, Plenum Press, 1995.

explication of secondary traumatic stress, since the indirect and peripheral responses to trauma have received the least attention by scholars and practitioners in the field of traumatic stress. This discussion is followed by a review of the theoretical and research literature that supports the existence of secondary traumatic stress.

STATE OF THE FIELD

The diagnosis of posttraumatic stress disorder (PTSD) is widely utilized in mental health research and practice. Its application has influenced case law and mental health compensation. In a review of trauma-related articles cited in *Psychological Abstracts* (Blake, Albano, & Keane, 1992), 1,596 citations were identified between 1970 and 1990. This finding supports the fact that the trauma literature has been growing significantly since the advent of the concept of posttraumatic stress disorder.

Psychotraumatology, or the field of traumatic stress studies, appears to have been literally invented in the last decades. Even though the origin of the study of human reactions to traumatic events can be traced to the earliest medical writings in *Kunyus Pyprus* published in 1900 B.C. in Egypt (Trimble, 1981), the justification for a distinct field of study and treatment emerged only recently (Figley, 1988; Kleber & Brom, 1992). A field devoted exclusively to the study and treatment of traumatized people is a culmination of many factors. One factor is a much greater awareness of the number and extraordinary impact of various traumatic events on people.

Many identify the introduction of posttraumatic stress disorder in the third edition of the *Diagnostic and Statistical Manual of Mental Disorders* (DSM-III) by the American Psychiatric Association in 1980 (APA, 1980), as a major milestone. The common symptoms experienced by a wide variety of traumatized persons were now viewed as a psychiatric disorder, one that could be accurately diagnosed and treated. Since this introduction and the subsequent editions of the DSM-III-R and the DSM-IV, the popularity with professionals working with traumatized people (including lawyers, therapists, emergency professionals, and researchers) has been growing, and empirical studies have been accumulating.

THE NEGLECT OF THE SURROUNDING OTHERS

After 15 years of use, the diagnosis of posttraumatic stress disorder is commonly applied to people traumatized by one of many types of traumatic events. Yet, an examination of the scientific literature yields the following proposition: Nearly all publications focusing on people confronted with extreme stress events exclude those who have experienced the event indirectly or secondarily and concentrate on those who were directly traumatized (i.e., the "victims" or "survivors"). Yet, diagnostic descriptions of what constitutes a traumatic event (i.e., Category A in the DSM descriptions of post-traumatic stress disorder) clearly suggest that mere knowledge of the exposure of a loved one to a traumatic event can be traumatizing as well.

The quotation below is taken from the posttraumatic stress disorder description (DSM-IV) of what constitutes a sufficiently traumatic experience. The italicized sections emphasize that people can be traumatized without actually being physically harmed or threatened with harm (i.e., a secondary traumatic stressor):

> The essential feature of Post-traumatic Stress Disorder is the development of characteristic symptoms following exposure to an extreme traumatic stressor involving direct personal experience of an event that involves actual or threatened death or serious injury, or other threat to one's physical integrity or *witnessing an event that involves death, injury, or a threat to the physical integrity of another person* or *learning about unexpected or violent death, serious harm, or threat of death or injury experienced by a family member or other close associate.* (APA, 1994, p. 424; italics added)

This definition has led to a conceptual conundrum in the field, although few have noted it: Why are there so few reports of these secondarily traumatized people? One explanation is that they are not perceived as being traumatized; and that supporters (family, friends, colleagues, acquaintances, and professionals, including therapists) themselves regard their reactions as simply signs of "caring." Yet, little is written about the "cost of caring": How and why can these same supporters become upset, too.

DEFINITION OF SECONDARY TRAUMATIC STRESS

Human beings do not live in a vacuum. They are surrounded by others. And those others will be confronted with the traumatic event, too, in particular, the implications. These people hear about the event, they perceive the suffering of the victims, and they have to cope with the changes caused by the event and the suffering.

Bolin (1985) made a distinction between primary and secondary victims: The former experience physical damage; the latter witness the event but are not damaged by it. This is a rather unsatisfactory differentiation. Physical damage is, of course, important, but those who are very close to the victim are left out of this categorization. Being directly exposed to the event itself or not is the separating criterion.

An extreme or traumatic situation is psychologically defined by the following two elements (Kleber & Brom, 1992), namely:

1. *Powerlessness.* An individual barely has any influence on the occurrence and development of the event. In "Jenseits des Lustprinzips" (1920, 1955), Freud already proposed that "the essence of a traumatic situation is an experience of helplessness that is brought about either externally or internally."

2. *Disruption.* The situation crudely disrupts the course of daily existence. One is cut off from the previously secure environment. The existing certainties of life have disappeared. The world does not make sense anymore. The images one holds of oneself and the environment no longer adequately fit the new situation. In the words of Janoff-Bulman (1992), basic assumptions have been shattered.

Being a victim of a traumatizing event means being the target of an overwhelming event. The direct confrontation with such an extreme event could be defined as a primary stressor.

We would like to define a secondary traumatic stressor as the knowledge of a traumatizing event experienced by a significant other. For people who are in some way close to a victim, the exposure to this knowledge may also be a confrontation with powerlessness and disruption. *Secondary traumatic stress* refers to the behaviors and emotions resulting from this knowledge. It is the stress resulting from hearing about the event and/or from helping or attempting to help a traumatized or suffering person. This conceptualization of primary and secondary traumatic stress describes the distinction between those "in harm's way" and those who care for them and become impaired in the process.

The phenomenon of the transmission of trauma has been examined in a few dozen publications in the general area of traumatic stress studies. The concepts vary greatly. Miller, Stiff, and Ellis (1988) wrote about "emotional contagion," defined as an affective process in which "an individual observing another person suffering experiences emotional responses parallel to that person's actual or anticipated emotions" (p. 254). Dixon (1991) identified as "peripheral victims" those who were not present at the location of the disaster but who easily could have been. Others mention "proximity" effects on female partners of war veterans (Verbosky & Ryan, 1988) or the need for family "detoxification" from war-related traumatic stress (Rosenbeck & Thomson, 1986). Figley (1991) coined the term "secondary traumatic stress disorder (STSD)", a disorder produced by exposure to and out of concern for a person experiencing primary traumatic stress. Other concepts are *vicarious traumatization* (McCann & Pearlman, 1990), *secondary survivor* (Remer & Elliott, 1988a,b), *the ripple effect,* and *trauma infection.* Also related is the notion of transgenerational effects of trauma (Danieli, 1982).

We prefer the term *secondary traumatic stress* (Figley, 1983, 1985) because it combines and integrates the many aspects mentioned in the other concepts. It is the exposure to knowledge of a traumatizing event experienced by a significant other that is associated with posttraumatic stress symptoms.

WHO ARE THE SIGNIFICANT OTHERS?

Which people are we referring to? A model of the circles surrounding the victim makes this clear.

First of all, there is the spouse of the victim and his or her children. Research findings on war veterans clearly show the long-term impact of combat stress on the family. Individuals very close to a person with a posttraumatic disorder may suffer most. Difficulties with family cohesion and intimacy arise. Spouses feel helpless and lonely, while children may experience developmental difficulties and impaired social relationships.

Also, friends and neighbors of a victim of violence or of another serious life event will be confronted with the suffering of that person. They perceive the pains of the person and have to cope with their own reactions in some way.

Next, the colleagues at work are influenced by the repercussions of the traumatic event. Unfortunately, the dimension of work is often neglected in psychotherapy and mental health care. Employees of banks, police officers, and workers in department stores may become victimized by violence or calamities. Their resulting reactions, such as irritation and feelings of uncertainty, have a clear influence on the behavior of their fellow workers. These identify with the victim and become afraid that they themselves will be the target of extreme events. They, too, may suffer from absenteeism and poorer performance.

Finally, there are the helping professionals, such as rescue workers, emergency personnel, social workers, nurses, physicians, and psychologists, who are particularly vulnerable to developing stress reactions because of the high emotional burden of working with clients distressed by their exposure to horrifying events.

The point of departure of this chapter is that traumatic events affect a much wider range of people than is often assumed. We will demonstrate this by a review of the psychotraumatology literature associated with the secondary effects of traumatic stress. The analysis is based on a general distinction of groups of people indirectly influenced and touched by trauma: family members (respectively, the family as a system, spouses, and children) and people who are exposed to victims in the work setting (colleagues, rescue workers, and mental health professionals).

A crucial dilemma in this review is the issue of dividing lines. What is the distinction between primary traumatic stress and secondary traumatic stress? Where is the demarcation line between direct effects and indirect effects of war, combat, and violence? This issue is also apparent in the question of the extent of secondary traumatic stress. Which psychological problems of people can still be regarded as consequences of traumatic stress? For instance, should we consider the difficulties of adult children of World War II survivors as the result—direct or indirect—of their parents' traumatic experiences?

THE IMPACT OF TRAUMATIC STRESS ON FAMILY MEMBERS

When viewed as a system, the family in its responses to stress, including traumatic stress, provides considerable insight into how individuals cope with stress and why. Among the first efforts to recognize the role of these social relationships was the classic study of World War II war veteran families by Hill (1949). Most observers viewed Hill as having originated the concept of family stress. He was the first to suggest that the system of the family is greatly affected by crisis events such as war and postwar reunion. This sociological orientation emerged into what was later to be called the *ABCX model of family crisis* and has evolved into various subsequent models.

In the next sections, we describe the various forms of secondary stress experienced within the family context that result from a traumatic event. A distinction is made among the whole family, the spouse, and, finally, the children.

Israeli War Veteran Families

Findings with regard to the impact of war on family members are not limited to the United States. Cohen and Dotan (1976) investigated the role of communication in the family as a function of war-related stress. During the 1973 Middle East war and the eight months following this war, Israeli families were studied through interviews with women residing in Jerusalem who had at least one child between the ages of 6 and 18. The results showed that, during the war, there was more stress in the family and more interpersonal communication and consumption of mass media compared with peacetime.

Significant are the studies of Zahava Solomon and her colleagues on family characteristics and posttraumatic stress disorder in Israeli combat-stress-reaction casualties. In one study (Solomon, Mikulincer, Freid, & Wosner, 1987), they investigated the role of family status and family relationships in the course of combat-related posttraumatic stress disorder. The data source was medical records and questionnaires on a sample of 382 Israeli soldiers who had suffered combat stress reactions during the 1982 Lebanon war. In contrast to theories and studies that suggest that intimate relationships help in the recovery from traumatic experiences, their results did not show this. One year after the war, married soldiers had higher rates of posttraumatic stress disorder than did unmarried soldiers. It is revealing that Solomon et al. also found higher rates of posttraumatic stress disorder to be associated with low expressiveness, low cohesiveness, and high conflict in the families. This finding lends support to the notion of the deleterious impact of war-related posttraumatic stress disorder on families and challenges the simplistic notion that the availability of a family of procreation automatically ameliorates the symptoms of posttraumatic stress disorder. Without information about family life before the war, however, we are unable to conclude that posttraumatic stress disorder caused the dysfunction among these families.

Acknowledging that the literature on the detrimental effects of combat-related posttraumatic stress disorder indicates guilt feelings, emotional withdrawal, and elevated levels of aggression in the returning veteran, a next study (Solomon, 1988) hypothesized that those with posttraumatic stress disorder would have a greater negative effect on family life than those without PTSD. Thus, the former group's experiences would make it difficult, perhaps even impossible, to fully resume the formal roles of father, husband, and breadwinner. Wives and children of veterans would begin to show psychiatric symptoms themselves. Despite these hardships, the families would generally be reluctant to seek professional help.

Subsequent research by Solomon and her associates has confirmed these hypotheses. For example, Solomon, Waysman, Avitzur, and Enoch (1991) found that the wives of soldiers with posttraumatic stress disorder are much more likely to suffer from levels of psychopathology and social dysfunction than those married to soldiers without posttraumatic stress disorder. Also, a next study (Solomon, Waysman, Belkin, Levy, Mikulincer, & Enoch, 1992) found that, over time, the marital relations of Israeli combat veterans who had sustained combat stress reactions were more conflictual, less intimate, less consensual, and less cohesive; reported less marital satisfaction; and were less expressive than couples without combat stress reactions. Solomon, Waysman, Levy, Fried, Mikulincer, Benbenishty, Florian, and Bleich (1992) found that wives of veterans with posttraumatic stress disorder, in contrast to wives of veterans without this disorder, had impaired social relations in a broad range of contexts, from inner feelings of loneliness, through impaired marital and family relations, and extending to the wider social network.

Spouses of Vietnam War Veterans

Secondary traumatic stress of spouses can be seen as "the stress of caring too much." Spouses may be at particular risk because of the especially close, often emotionally intense nature of the spousal relationship. According to Gilbert (1995), the stress may be the result of direct (proximal) or indirect (distal) exposure to the primary victimization of one's spouse. Spouses also may experience a type of resonating secondary traumatic stress reaction, in which one partner's response acts as a trigger for the other's response.

The development of secondary traumatic stress responses in spouses results from their need to make sense of their partner's traumatic experience and its aftermath. It is complicated by their efforts to maintain a stable and workable dyadic relationship. These reactions may cause the secondarily affected spouse to become overly responsible for the primarily affected spouse. Efforts to protect may result in overprotection and isolation. Given the nature of the relationship, recovery requires that the victims learn new ways of thinking, new skills, new behaviors, and new interactional patterns.

Combat stress has a great impact on the spouses of veterans. In a study of U.S. veterans (Carroll, Rueger, Foy, & Donahoe, 1985), it was found that Vietnam combat veterans with posttraumatic stress disorder had more martial problems in terms of self-disclosure and expressiveness, hostility and aggression toward their partner, and global marital maladjustment. Similarly, another study (Rueger, 1983) showed that the wives of Vietnam veterans were less communicative, more angry, and more fearful of their partner than comparison groups of wives. These findings are consistent with the approach advocated by Levy and Neumann (1987), who found that the treatment of combat reactions was made more effective by involving families.

In a study of families of U.S. Navy prisoners of war, five years following reunion, researchers (Nice, McDonald, & McMillian, 1981) found that most were experiencing captivity-related stress. Marital stability and perceptions of marital adjustment and family environment were significantly lower among the group of prisoners of war repatriated from Vietnam than in a comparison group. Verbosky and Ryan (1988) studied the female partners of Vietnam veterans receiving treatment for posttraumatic stress disorder and suggested that these women were experiencing the stress of war by "proximity." The results of their study of 23 female partners showed a significant relationship between posttraumatic stress disorder symptoms of the veteran and the female partner's poor self-esteem, limited coping skills, and ineffective use of overcompensation to deal with problems. Verbosky and Ryan concluded, as have others (Figley, 1983; Figley & Sprenkle, 1978), that the perpetuation of the dysfunctional family system is enhanced both by the presence of posttraumatic stress disorder in one family member, such as the war veteran, and the existing (or resultant) characteristics of the partner.

Similarly, Maloney (1988) focused on posttraumatic stress disorder in the Vietnam veteran partner through interviews with a small sample of wives of Vietnam vets with posttraumatic stress disorder. The results indicated conflicted relationships between these women and their mothers, idealized relationships with their fathers, beliefs that their husbands had not grown past adolescence, and conflicted feelings about the military and a lifelong history of alcohol and physical abuse. Unfortunately, the author did not use a control group to contrast respondents with those in a different context. In spite of methodological flaws, this study makes a compelling argument that the families of war veterans absorb the aftermath of war.

This last conclusion is especially appropriate in more recent reports, such as the comprehensive investigation of the long-term psychosocial effects of war conducted by Kulka et al. (1991). Their study included a national, random household survey in which not only Vietnam veterans but also their families, were carefully interviewed. The results were startling but not entirely unexpected. First, the researchers found that family members tended to confirm the accounts of Vietnam veterans. This finding lent support and credibility to claims of the long-term, combat-related problems described by Vietnam veterans for years. Second, they found in general that there were more problems in the families of Vietnam veterans with posttraumatic stress disorder than in the families of Vietnam veterans without posttraumatic stress disorder. Third, they discovered that wives of veterans with posttraumatic stress disorder were significantly less happy and satisfied than wives of those without post-traumatic stress disorder. These women had more general distress, including feelings or thoughts that they might have a nervous breakdown. Fourth, they found that veteran families afflicted by posttraumatic stress disorder had more marital problems and family violence than veteran families that were not PTSD-afflicted. Fifth, they discovered that veterans with posttraumatic stress disorder were less effective as family members in fulfilling their role as father or husband. Sixth, they found that veterans with posttraumatic stress disorder tended to have been married to or living with their spouse or partner significantly less long than veterans without posttraumatic stress disorder (an average of 10 years versus 16 years, respectively).

Children

Directly or indirectly, children witness the effects of traumatic experiences on parents, siblings, or friends. However, much less literature has been published on the effects of trauma on children than on the adult victims. Not surprisingly therefore, research on secondary reactions of children is lacking. It is an area that has been neglected.

Witnessing may include observing the trauma of a loved one or merely having the knowledge that a loved one has experienced a trauma. Children of victims, exposed to their parents' symptomatology without themselves undergoing violence, persecution, or war, display the characteristic traumatic stress symptoms of intrusion, hyperarousal, and enactments similar to those of their parents (Steinberg, 1995). Parental reactions to the experience play a crucial role in the child's responses, at times determining the child's reaction to the traumatic event. Trauma clearly has a contagious effect. Nevertheless, Steinberg also observed that the child's resilience and available supports may modify the impact.

In the already-mentioned investigation of the long-term effects of the Vietnam war (Kulka et al., 1991), it was found that children with a veteran parent suffering from posttraumatic stress disorder had significantly more behavioral problems than did children of veteran parents without posttraumatic stress disorder. These findings highlight the interpersonal nature of trauma and may help explain the transmission of posttraumatic stress to offspring who were spared the actual traumatic experiences.

Evidence of the secondary impact of a single family member's traumatic stress is also shown in studies of the families of POWs. In a study of the children of U.S. prisoners of war held during the Vietnam war, McCubbin, Dahl, Lester, and Ross (1977) found indications of the transgenerational effects of captivity. The long-term strains of internment affected the parent–child relationships and child functioning generally, as was shown in, for example, school performance and dysfunctional symptoms of the child. A longitudinal analysis of the 42 families showed five major factors that could account for these effects, four of which were (1) the severity of the mental abuse suffered during internment; (2) the severity of physical abuse; (3) the wife's relationship with her parents; and (4) the wife's involvement in the activities of the former prisoner of war. The father's involvement in preparing the family for separation was found to be a positive factor in subsequent family relationships.

One of the most well-documented groups experiencing the indirect effects of trauma are the children of survivors of the Nazi Holocaust. In the 1960s, the first studies (Rakoff, Sigal, & Epstein, 1965) were conducted on the impact of the internment in the German concentration camps on the children of survivors. Children born after World War II to Holocaust survivors exhibited negative effects due to the traumatic experiences of their parents. However, the issue of the traumatization of these children—which is assumed in the concept of transgenerational traumatization—is not undisputed. The psychopathology of the offspring of survivors has sometimes been stressed to an extent unwarranted by empirical research (Solkoff, 1992).

In a number of clinical descriptions of children in families of Jewish World War II survivors (Freyberg, 1980; Sigal & Rakoff, 1971), it was found that separation from the parents and the development of individual autonomy were not facilitated. The parents had experienced so many losses and so many separations in the war that they felt threatened by the idea that their child was growing into an independent individual. They felt as if they were losing their child (Barocas & Barocas, 1980). Not being able to support a child to become independent may lead to an "anxious attachment" between parent and child (Bowlby, 1981), manifested in difficulties with separation and in overprotection (Russell, 1980). This is illustrated as follows. For a mother suffering from such traumatic war experiences, it is difficult to accept the child's wishes to become independent and to stimulate these wishes. When she is unable to encourage her child to explore the environment, the child becomes frustrated and angry. The frustration and anger cause panic, and the child feels abandoned because the mother's reactions give the impression that the child's desires and feelings are bad. As a result, feelings of guilt may arise. This "anxious" attachment may cause a stagnation in the child's identity development and in his or her social behavior.

Memories of war experiences may also disrupt family dynamics. The parents examined by Sigal, Silver, Rakoff, and Ellin (1973) and Russell (1980) were often not able to be intimate with their children. They were often so occupied with their war reminiscences that they could not pay enough attention to the emotional needs of their child. The intrusions of World War II made the parents psychologically vulnerable, and they turned to their children for support. As a result, children of Jewish war survivors may have felt responsible for the needs of their parents and for their parents' well-being. The instability in parent and child roles sometimes resulted in a reversal of roles in the family, as described in the phenomenon of parentification (Danieli, 1982; Sigal et al., 1973).

In the clinical literature, it has been reported that unfinished separation–individuation development and disrupted family dynamics continued to play a role in child–parent relationships when the children were adolescents and adults (Barocas & Barocas, 1980) and were manifested in anxiety, anger, and irritation. Excessive commitment and mistrust were also reported in relationships with friends or partners (Musaph, 1978). Furthermore, clinical investigations indicated reduced psychological well-being and more psychopathology in the later life of the second generation of war survivors (Russell, 1980), in particular feelings of depression and guilt (Rustin & Lipsig, 1972) and problems with the regulation of aggression.

Notwithstanding these clinical reports and impressions, many empirical studies of nonclinical groups of children of survivors did not support the findings of increased psychopathology among children of Jewish survivors of World War II (Leon, Butcher, Kleinman, Goldberg, & Almagor, 1981; Sigal & Weinfeld, 1985; Weiss, O'Connell, & Siter, 1986). Using standardized questionnaires and control groups, these studies did not confirm many of the earlier findings (Rose & Garske, 1987).

To deal with these contradictory findings Eland, Van der Velden, Kleber, and Steinmetz (1990) conducted a comparative investigation of the psychological problems of the Jewish second generation of World War II survivors in the Netherlands. Their findings supported some of the results of the qualitative studies of clinical groups, as noted above: (1) Children of Jewish war survivors viewed their childhood as characterized by more feelings of guilt and shame, and by more problems with separations from the family; (2) the reminiscences of the war were associated with difficulties in the child's development of separation and individuation; (3) parentification, problems with aggression, and overprotection by the parents were prevalent and were associated with disrupted family dynamics due to the strain of the war memories; (4) however, current social relationships of the Jewish second generation were hardly affected by the war experiences of the parents; (5) both the clinical observations and the self-report data showed some significant differences in psychological problems and contacts with mental health professionals; and (6) compared with the reference group, children of Jewish World War II survivors had had a more difficult youth that still bothered them but that was not generalized to all aspects of their current life. A controlled study using a similar research design was conducted in Israel (Brom, Kfir, & Dasberg, 1994) and showed that, even with more rigorous methods, modest differences between the offspring of Holocaust survivors and their matched peers could be demonstrated.

These and other empirical studies (Solkoff, 1992) made clear that there are some long-term aftereffects of war in the offspring of war survivors. Nevertheless, it appears that the concept of transgenerational traumatiziation is rather inappropriate. The children of concentration camp survivors have not themselves experienced traumatic events: They have not witnessed death, terror, and hunger. It is their upbringing that is hindered by war memories and their parents' feelings of guilt and loss. Danieli (1985) observed that the effects of the Holocaust on children are, in part, a function of the *postwar* adaptational styles of the survivor families. The war experiences of the survivors put a strain on their child-rearing capacities. The health symptoms and other psychological reactions of the adult children are related to these strains, and not so much to the war itself. Again, we encounter here the dilemma of definition that we mentioned earlier. Some reactions, such as parentification, can be considered the result of the knowledge of war. They are examples of "compassion fatigue." But other problems, such as the difficulties with separation and individuation, are mainly associated with developmental problems in a particular context. The disturbances of the offspring of war survivors are not as much an issue of transmission of trauma as an issue of a specific socialization.

WORKER-RELATED SECONDARY TRAUMATIC STRESS

Not only family members are exposed to the suffering of victims and survivors. In the work setting, too, people may be confronted with the traumatic stress reactions of other persons. Unfortunately, the relationship between work and trauma has been a rather ignored subject in scientific research, as well as in clinical practice and organizational matters, although there is growing interest in the theme. Here we review the phenomena of secondary traumatic stress in three categories: close colleagues in high-risk occupations, rescue workers and other helpers in crisis situations, and, finally, psychotherapists as helping professionals.

Colleagues in High-Risk Occupations

In several professions there is a serious risk of violence. Banks have always been the target of robberies, holdups, kidnappings, and blackmail. More and more organizations in the Western world, however, are being confronted with work-related violence and other calamities. Examples are employees of department stores and supermarkets confronted with holdups and hijackings, gas station personnel, workers in industrial plants, police officers involved in shooting incidents and accidents, personnel of security companies, prison guards, and penitentiary officers. By many estimations, posttraumatic stress disorder represents a most severe and disabling form of occupational stress. Recently, Mitchell and Everly (1995) observed that, among other things, work-related stress claims represent the fastest-growing and most costly, per incident, type of workers' compensation claim affecting commerce in the United States; those in high-risk occupations are most vulnerable to posttraumatic stress disorder.

The employees involved have to cope with the aftermath of the life-threatening events in their jobs (Kleber & Van der Velden, 1995), yet these events affect not only the individual directly involved, but also their colleagues who have not been confronted with the traumatic event itself. However, hardly any study pays attention to the negative impact on the surrounding colleagues.

A holdup of a bank is a good illustration of work-related stress. Two masked criminals carry out a surprise raid on a bank. Using automatic weapons, they yell for the money and force the manager and two of his employees to open up the vault. Within minutes after their disappearance, the police arrive. Afterward, the event itself, its course, and its aftermath are the topic of endless discussions among the employees of the bank. The details of the experience are transmitted to all members of the organization. They all look for explanations, and they all compare this experience with other accounts of robberies. Not only those who have actually experienced the holdup and those at the bank who witnessed the event, but also the co-workers who were not confronted with the event themselves go through many reactions in the days or weeks after the robbery.

The indirect effects are manifested in the following reactions;

1. *Increasing feelings of insecurity and uncertainty.* The employees are hypervigilant and are suspicious of any strange person who enters the bank.
2. *Increasing workload.* As the victims of the robbery often show absenteeism and/or impairment of their work performance, others are confronted with the bearing of extra work pressure.
3. *Increasing social tensions at the workplace.* The victimized workers are irritated and have outbursts of anger. They are constantly

watching the doors of the bank. These irritations and the discussions of why the event happened influence the other members of the organization as well and result in social strains.

4. *Increasing feelings of incompetence.* Experimental social psychological research has shown that stress reactions are stronger when one is in the presence of others and when one feels embarrassed about one's own behavior. One feels ashamed about one's functioning at the workplace, especially because being competent at work is so relevant.

Highly relevant in the aftermath of a traumatic event is the support and recognition by colleagues at work as well as by the management of the organization. The support that an individual receives in the form of close relationships with co-workers can mitigate the effects of occupational stressors on health outcomes. This support with regard to primary and secondary traumatic reactions is highly dependent on the organizational context. The idea that problems are only evoked by offers of assistance, and that it would be best to do as little as possible, is still rather persistent in many organizations: "As long as people do not talk about stress reactions, they will not experience them." Another prominent element of such an organizational culture is an emphasis on macho behavior, sometimes labeled as the *John Wayne culture.* The attitude of "keeping a stiff upper lip" or "being a tough guy" pervades many organizations in which workers are confronted with violence or accidents. Colleagues expressing emotional distress after acts of violence are sometimes publicly denounced as "soft." A change in the climate toward the acceptance of victim assistance within a company is an essential although a prolonged process. The organization must work to establish an atmosphere that acknowledges the normality of reactions to (secondary) traumatic stress (Brom & Kleber, 1989).

Crisis Workers and Other Helpers in Emergency Situations

Exposure to occupational trauma is frequent and repetitive for frontline first responders such as firefighters, law enforcement personnel, and rescue workers. The confrontation with the incident is often quite direct for these workers. But crisis workers also include persons who are perhaps physically removed from the trauma incident scene, such as emergency room nurses, but who are also exposed to trauma and "absorb" the resulting stress. Other categories of such nonimmediate crisis workers are unexpected responders (passersby and others in the event), body identification and burial personnel, crisis interveners (clergy, medical, and mental health professionals), voluntary personnel (Red Cross, Salvation Army, and caregivers), and remote responders (equipment maintenance personnel).

Crisis workers, by the nature of their duties and responsibilities, are at risk of experiencing primary traumatic stress (i.e., stress reactions that arise from exposure to a traumatizing event) and secondary traumatic stress (i.e., stress reactions that arise from assisting or wanting to assist a traumatized person). Unintended and deleterious effects may occur as a result of their providing help. These include negative health consequences, relationship problems, and substance abuse.

A fine example of secondary stress was presented by Dixon (1991). Among people referred to a mental health team in the three years following the ferryboat disaster near Zeebrugge, Belgium, a group of 17 workers was found who were afflicted in a similar way to victims of a disaster, although they had not been directly involved in a disaster or its aftermath. The group consisted of experienced personnel of the ferries that cross the English Channel. After the capsize of the *Herald of Free Enterprise,* they suffered from an increasing fear of the sea till they reached the point where they were unable to continue to function. It was as if they had experienced the disaster vicariously as if they had been there. These workers suffered from symptoms of posttraumatic stress disorder as well as dysfunctions in the areas of work, social activity, and relationships. With one exception, they were unable to return to work because of severe anxiety.

It is important to realize that these workers were repeatedly exposed to the same conditions as the victims of the disaster: the unpredictability of the weather of the English Channel, being at sea in the night, and staying on a ferryboat. Their stress symptoms were most pronounced at work, worsening in rough weather or when their boat made any unusual movement. It may be concluded that a large-scale disaster such as the Zeebrugge catastrophe broke through the defense of denial which helps people to cope with a job that exposes them to high risk. Here again, we see the shattering of basic assumptions (Janoff-Bulman, 1992) that make sense in daily life but that are destroyed by extreme life events.

In the last years, there has been a growing focus on the importance of promoting trauma resolution and healthy coping strategies in emergency workers. McCammon and Allison (1995) reviewed several debriefing models and noted that the common elements across the various models included (1) the structuring of opportunities to review the events of the traumatic situation and to ventilate feelings; (2) learning skills for integrating and mastering the event; and (3) obtaining assistance in identifying, enlisting, and accepting help from one's support system. Important, and often neglected, posttrauma activities include individual follow-up sessions and attention to anniversaries of traumatic events.

Helping Professionals: Psychotherapists

Therapists are not normally perceived as being in a high-risk occupation. However, they are especially vulnerable to secondary traumatic stress. Given the extraordinary experiences of traumatized people, it is not surprising to find that mental health professionals who work with these patients—psychotherapists and also researchers and other mental health workers—experience the influence of traumatic stress. For example, Berah, Jones, and Valent (1984) found that a majority of mental health workers experienced shock, confusion, and sadness, and that half became ill, experienced accidents, and noticed changes in eating, smoking, and drinking patterns and needed the support of other team members.

The concept of vicarious traumatization is relevant to describing traumatized therapists. McCann and Pearlman (1990) observed that therapists treating trauma victims find their inner experience of "self" and "other" transformed in ways that paralleled the experience of the trauma survivor. This transformation, which is called *vicarious traumatization,* includes changes in one's identity and worldview, in self-capacities, in ego resources, and in psychological needs and cognitive schematas. For instance, as a result of working with children abused by their parents, a therapist may become rather skeptical of other people's motives, more pessimistic, and more distrustful. A repeated exposure to stories of human cruelty inevitably challenges the therapist's faith and his or her sense of invulnerability. The therapist may lose confidence in his or her own skills and may start to feel as helpless and guilty as the patient. Herman (1992) portrayed the often bewildering imagery, bizarre dreams, and perceptual distortions of therapists working with survivors of childhood abuse.

McCann and Pearlman (1990) suggested that strategies to counteract the negative effects on the therapists who do trauma work should emphasize the need for balance, the use of external resources, self-acceptance, connection, and the need to foster one's sense of meaning, interdependence, and hope. Ultimately, working with victims may lead to an enhanced empathy for the suffering of people and a deeper sense of connection with others.

In a recent paper, Cerney (1995) focused on therapists who work with psychologically and physically traumatized patients, not just adult survivors. Cerney noted that these therapists are especially vulnerable to secondary stress reactions. The assault on these heroic treaters' sense of personal integrity and their belief in humanity can be so shattering that it places them within a special group of traumatized individuals similar in many ways to the individuals they treat, although each trauma victim, whether patient or therapist, is different.

Some view the problems faced by therapists whose own life experiences affect how they work with certain clients as a manifestation of countertransference. As concepts that emerged from psychoanalytic theory, transference is considered a distortion in the therapeutic relationship on the part of the client (e.g., unconsciously attributing to the therapist the attributes of a significant figure from the client's past), and countertransference is seen as a distortion on the part of therapist (i.e., the therapist's emotional reactions to the client's transference). In a more general sense (Lindy, 1993), countertransference includes all conscious and unconscious feelings or attitudes that a therapist has toward a client; these feelings and attitudes may be useful to successful treatment. Countertransference refers to the process of seeing oneself in the client, of overidentifying with the client, or of meeting needs through the client.

Secondary traumatic stress is not limited to what researchers and other professionals view as countertransference. First, countertransference happens only within the context of a specific psychotherapy, while "vicarious traumatization" is assumed to influence the general beliefs of a therapist. Second, countertransference is a reaction of the therapist to the transference actions of the client. Third, countertransference is often considered a negative consequence of therapy and should be prevented or eliminated. However, secondary traumatic stress is a rather natural consequence of caring between two people, one of whom has been initially traumatized and the other of whom is affected by the first's traumatic experiences. These affects are not necessarily a problem; they may be more a natural by-product of helping traumatized people.

THEORETICAL PERSPECTIVES ON SECONDARY TRAUMATIC STRESS

Why do bystanders, family members, and therapists suffer symptoms similar those of the directly afflicted victims and survivors? Which causes of secondary traumatic stress can be distinguished?

We would like to propose two general theoretical interpretations of the origins of traumatic stress. One is connected to the burnout literature and is discussed below. The other one has to do with the fact that an individual is very close to the victim or is in a similar situation, so that he or she will eventually experience the same psychological characteristics of the traumatic events as the victim. As was described in the beginning of this chapter (Kleber & Brom, 1992), he or she will also be confronted with the characteristic elements of a traumatic experience: the intense feelings of powerlessness and disruption. Individual assumptions of invulnerability and control will also be shattered. One could speak of a kind of contagion or, more positively formulated, of a form of empathy. Instead of *secondary traumatic stress*, the term *compassion fatigue* would be appropriate.

This empathy perspective suggests that members of systems, in an effort to generate an understanding of the victimized members, require identification with the victims and their suffering. They attempt to answer for themselves the five victim questions: What happened? Why did it happen? Why did I act as I did then? Why have I acted as I have since? If it happens again, will I be able to cope? (Figley, 1983). People surrounding the victim try to answer these questions for the victim in order to change her or his behavior accordingly. Yet, in the process of generating new information, the members of the social system experience emotions that are strikingly similar to those of the victim. These include visual images (e.g., flashbacks), sleeping problems, depression, and other symptoms that are a direct result of visualizing the victim's traumatic experiences, or of exposure to the symptoms of the victim, or both.

The second explanation has to do with the fact that a person provides so much support to a victim that he or she finally becomes exhausted. We would like to call this the *energy depletion perspective*. It suggests that members of a system are worn down, physically and emotionally, by exposure to a primary victim.

This perspective proposes that supporters become exhausted and overwhelmed in their effort to provide support. For example, this model would account, in part, for the phenomenon of the vicarious traumatization of therapists working with adult survivors of child victimization, noted by McCann and Pearlman (1990). It is a continuous assault on the therapist's schematas through working with many traumatized clients over the years and results in a gradual wearing down. This energy depletion accounts for the findings reported by Solomon and her colleagues, as noted earlier in this chapter. Living with a husband who is experiencing the stressful consequences of posttraumatic stress disorder, including nightmares, physical aggression, flashbacks, and other symptoms, makes a poor marital partner. And like those subjected to the strains of living with someone with a chronic, debilitating illness, few escape its effect. This explains how systems and their members appear to cope well initially but gradually develop traumatic stress symptoms and, eventually, disorders.

This perspective is remarkably similar to models of burnout. According to Pines and Aronson (1988), this concept refers to "a state of physical, emotional and mental exhaustion caused by long term involvement in emotionally demanding situations" (p. 9). Three aspects are particularly important in burnout (Maslach & Jackson, 1981): emotional exhaustion (e.g., "I feel emotionally drained from my work"), depersonalization (e.g., "I worry that the job is hardening me emotionally"), and reduced personal accomplishment (e.g., "I feel I am not able anymore to influence other people's lives positively through my work"). It is especially the emotional exhaustion that appears to be the key element.

Burnout is typically the result of the extended accumulation of intensive contact with clients. It is a process that begins gradually and becomes progressively worse. More and more, a person in a helping profession is exposed to job strain. Idealism is eroded away, and the person is confronted with the awareness of a void in his or her achievements. Burnout is manifested in a variety of symptoms, such as physical symptoms (e.g., fatigue and physical depletion or exhaustion, as well as sleep difficulties), emotional symptoms (e.g., irritability and depression), behavioral symptoms (e.g., aggression and substance abuse), work-related symptoms (e.g., poor work performance and absenteeism), and interpersonal symptoms (e.g., withdrawal from clients and co-workers).

Burnout has been associated with a reduced sense of personal accomplishment, and with discouragement as an employee (Maslach & Jackson, 1981). From a review of the research literature, it appears that the most salient factors of burnout are client problems that are perceived to be beyond the capacity of the service provider (Maslach & Schaufeli, 1993). Moreover, service providers are caught in a struggle between promoting the well-being of their clients and, at the same time, struggling with procedures and structures in the human-service delivery system that tend to stifle empowerment and well-being. A related, although somewhat different, explanation is learned helplessness (Seligman, 1975).

Burnout and secondary traumatization are highly related. Nevertheless, there are also differences. Secondary traumatization is more specific than burnout and sometimes more pervasive. It has to do with the impact of a horrifying, extreme experience itself on the surrounding people (e.g., the helpers). In contrast to burnout, secondary traumatic stress symptoms sometimes emerge suddenly without much warning. In addition, traumatic stress is especially manifested in feelings of helplessness, shock, and confusion, and there seems to be a faster rate of recovery from the symptoms.

The explanations of secondary traumatic stress in terms of empathy and energy depletion do not contradict each other. They are both valuable for the understanding of secondary reactions in family members, as well as in workers and professionals. As a matter of fact, both explanations are rather parallel. A traumatic event forces a person close to a victim to identify and to emphasize. In the long run, this compassion becomes a burden, and exhaustion develops. The energy depletion characteristic of secondary traumatic stress is, in part, due to one's loss of empathic ability, as well as the growing inability to find relief from one's reactions through a sense of satisfaction in helping to relieve suffering. There is a considerable overlap between the two explanations.

CONCLUSION

The concept of *traumatic stress* is mainly used with regard to a direct confrontation with disruption, abuse, and powerlessness. This chapter has shown that the experiences of a traumatized person affect those of other members of a social system in many ways. Not only are family and friends of people exposed to primary stressors (i.e., victims) vulnerable to secondary traumatic stress and disorders, but so are colleagues, mental health professionals, and other helpers. Human beings are social creatures; we seek the comfort of those we care about when we are exposed to traumatic events.

It is still rather unclear by which mechanisms primary traumatic stress influences other persons. What is the mode of transmission from the member of a social system with primary traumatic stress to members who, in the process of exposure to the traumatized member, develop secondary traumatic stress? Is it possible to predict who in the system will experience secondary stress in response to a member's stress reactions? If so, what are the conditions under which secondary traumatic stress reactions take place, for how long, and at what point in time? Given the substantial evidence of the existence of secondary traumatic stress, these questions pose a significant challenge for future investigations.

REFERENCES

American Psychiatric Association. (1980). *Diagnostic and statistical manual of mental disorders* (3rd ed.; DSM-III). Washington, DC: Author.
American Psychiatric Association. (1994). *Diagnostic and statistical manual of mental disorders* (4th ed.; DSM-IV). Washington, DC: Author.
Barocas, H., & Barocas, C. (1980). Separation-individuation conflicts in children of Holocaust survivors. *Journal of Contemporary Psychotherapy, 11,* 6–14.
Berah, E. F., Jones, H. J., & Valent, P. (1984). The experience of a mental health team involved in the early phase of a disaster. *Australian-New Zealand Journal of Psychiatry, 18,* pp. 354–358.
Blake, D. D., Albano, A. M., & Keane, T. M. (1992). Twenty years of trauma: Psychological abstracts 1970 through 1989. *Journal of Traumatic Stress, 5,* 477–485.

Bolin, R. (1985). Disaster characteristics and psychosocial impacts. In B. J. Sowder (Ed.), *Disaster and mental health: Selected contemporary perspectives* (pp. 3–28). Rockville, MD: U.S. Department of Health and Human Services.

Bowlby, J. (1981). *Attachment and loss* (3 vols.). London: Pelican Books.

Brom, D., & Kleber, R. J. (1989). prevention of posttraumatic stress disorders. *Journal of Traumatic Stress Studies, 2,* 335–351.

Brom, D., Kfir, R., & Dasberg, H. (1994). *A controlled double-blind study on the offspring of Holocaust survivors.* Poster presented at the Annual Conference of the Society of Traumatic Stress Studies, Chicago, November 1994.

Carroll, E. M., Rueger, D. B., Foy, D. W., & Donahoe, C. P. (1985). Vietnam combat veterans with PTSD: Analysis of marital and cohabiting. *Journal of Abnormal Psychology, 94,* 329–337.

Cerney, M. S. (1995). Treating the "heroic treaters." In C. R. Figley (Ed.), *Compassion fatigue: Coping with secondary traumatic stress disorder in those who treat the traumatized* (pp. 131–149). New York: Brunner/Mazel.

Cohen, A. A., & Dotan, J. (1976). Communication in the family as a function of stress during war and peace. *Journal of Marriage and the Family, 38,* 141–148.

Danieli, Y. (1982). Families of survivors of the Nazi Holocaust: Some short and long term effects. In C. D. Spielberger & I. G. Sarason (Eds.), *Stress and anxiety* (Vol. 8, pp. 405–421). New York: Hemisphere.

Danieli, Y. (1985). The treatment and prevention of long-term effects and intergenerational transmission of victimization: A lesson from Holocaust survivors and their children. In C. R. Figley (Ed.), *Trauma and its wake: The study and treatment of posttraumatic stress disorder* (pp. 295–313). New York: Brunner/Mazel.

Dixon, P. (1991). Vicarious victims of a maritime disaster. *British Journal of Guidance and Counselling, 19,* 8–12.

Eland, J., Van der Velden, P. G., Kleber, R. J., & Steinmetz, C. H. D. (1990). *Tweede generatie Joodse Nederlanders: Een onderzoek naar gezinsachtergronden en psychisch functioneren.* Deventer: Van Loghum Slaterus.

Figley, C. R. (1983). Catastrophes: An overview of family reactions. In C. R. Figley & H. I. McCubbin (Eds.), *Stress and the family: Vol. 2. Coping with catastrophe* (pp. 3–20). New York: Brunner/Mazel.

Figley, C. R. (1985). From victim to survivor: Social responsibility in the wake of catastrophe. In C. R. Figley (Ed.), *Trauma and its wake: The study and treatment of post-traumatic stress disorder* (pp. 398–415). New York: Brunner/Mazel.

Figley, C. R. (1988). Toward a field of traumatic stress. *Journal of Traumatic Stress, 1,* 3–6.

Figley, C. R. (1991). *Investigation of war-related stress among families of Gulf War military service personnel.* Unpublished research proposal, Florida State University Marriage and Family Therapy Center, Tallahassee, Florida.

Figley, C. R. (Ed.). (1995). *Compassion fatigue: Coping with secondary traumatic stress disorder in those who treat the traumatized.* New York: Brunner/Mazel.

Figley, C. R., & Sprenkle, D. H. (1978). Delayed stress response syndrome: Family therapy indications. *Journal of Marriage and Family Counseling, 4,* 53–60.

Freud, S. (1955). *Jenseits des Lustprinzips, Gesammelte Werke* (Vol. 13). London: Imago. (original work published 1920)

Freyberg, J. T. (1980). Difficulties in separation-individuation as experienced by offspring of Nazi Holocaust survivors. *American Journal of Orthopsychiatry, 50,* 87–95.

Gilbert, K. (1995). Couple coping: The loss of a child. In C. R. Figley, N. Mazze, & B. Bride (Eds.), *Death and trauma.* New York: Brunner/Mazel.

Herman, J. L. (1992). *Trauma and recovery: The aftermath of violence.* New York: Basic Books.

Hill, R. (1949). *Families under stress: Adjustment to the crisis of war separation and reunion.* New York: Harper.

Janoff-Bulman, R. (1992). *Shattered assumptions: Towards a new psychology of trauma*. New York: Free Press.

Kleber, R. J., & Brom, D., in collaboration with Defares, P. B. (1992). *Coping with trauma: Theory, prevention and treatment*. Amsterdam and Berwyn, Pennsylvania: Swets & Zeitlinger International.

Kleber, R. J., & Van der Velden, P. G. (1995). Acute stress at work. In M. J. Schabracq, J. A. M. Winnubst, & C. L. Cooper (Eds.), *Handbook of work and health psychology*. New York: Wiley.

Kulka, R. A., Schlenger, W. A., Fairbank, J. A., Hough, R. L., Jordan, B. K., Marmar, C. R., & Weiss, D. S. (1991). *Trauma and the Vietnam war veteran generation*. New York: Brunner/Mazel.

Leon, G. R., Butcher, J. N., Kleinman, M., Goldberg, A., & Almagor, M. (1981). Survivors of the Holocaust and their children: Current status and adjustment. *Journal of Personality and Social Psychology, 41*(3), 503–516.

Levy, A., & Neumann, M. (1987). Involving families in the treatment of combat reactions. *Journal of Family Therapy, 9,* 177–188.

Lindy, J. D. (1993). Focal psychoanalytic psychotherapy of posttraumatic stress disorder. In J. P. Wilson & B. Raphael (Eds.), *International handbook of traumatic stress syndromes* (pp. 803–809). New York: Plenum Press.

Maloney, L. J. (1988). Post traumatic stress on women partners in Vietnam veterans. *Smith College Studies in Social Work, 58,* 122–143.

Maslach, C., & Jackson, S. E. (1981). The measurement of experienced burnout. *Journal of Occupational Behaviour, 2,* 99–113.

Maslach, C., & Schaufeli, W. B. (1993). Historical and conceptual development of burnout. In W. B. Schaufeli, C. Maslach, & T. Marek (Eds.), *Professional burnout: Recent developments in therapy and research* (pp. 1–16). Washington, DC: Taylor & Francis.

McCammon, S. L., & Allison, E. J., Jr. (1995). Debriefing and treating emergency workers. In C. R. Figley (Ed.), *Compassion fatigue: Coping with secondary traumatic stress disorder in those who treat the traumatized* (pp. 115–130). New York: Brunner/Mazel.

McCann, I. L., & Pearlman, L. A. (1990). Vicarious traumatization: A contextual model for understanding the effects of trauma on helpers. *Journal of Traumatic Stress, 3,* 131–149.

McCubbin, H. I., Dahl, B. B., Lester, G., & Ross, B. (1977). The returned prisoner of war: Factors in family reintegration. *Journal of Marriage and the Family, 39,* 471–478.

Miller, K. I., Stiff, J. B., & Ellis, B. H. (1988). Communication and empathy as precursors to burnout among human services workers. *Communication Monographs, 55,* 277–301.

Mitchell, J. T., & Everly, G. S., Jr. (1995). Critical incident stress debriefing (CISD) and the prevention of work related traumatic stress among high risk occupational groups. In G. S. Everly, Jr., & J. M. Lating (Eds.), *Psychotraumatology: Key papers and core concepts in post-traumatic stress* (pp. 267–280). New York: Plenum Press.

Musaph, H. (1978). De tweede generatie oorlogsslachtoffers: Psychopathologische problemen. *Maandblad voor Geestelijke Volksgezondheid, 33*(12).

Nice, D. S., McDonald, B., & McMillian, T. (1981). The families of U.S. Navy prisoners of war from Vietnam five years after reunion. *Journal of Marriage and the Family, 43,* 431–437.

Pines, A., & Aronson, E. (1988). *Career burnout: Causes and cures*. New York: Free Press.

Rakoff, V., Sigal, J. J., & Epstein, N. (1965). Children and families of concentration camp survivors. *Canada's Mental Health, 14,* 24–26.

Remer, R., & Elliott, J. (1988a). Characteristics of secondary victims of sexual assault. *International Journal of Family Psychiatry, 9,* 373–387.

Remer, R., & Elliott, J. (1988b). Management of secondary victims of sexual assault. *International Journal of Family Psychiatry, 9,* 389–401.

Rose, S. L., & Garske, J. (1987). Family environment, adjustment and coping among children of Holocaust survivors: A comparative investigation. *American Journal of Orthopsychiatry, 57*(3).

Rosenbeck, R., & Thomson, J. (1986). "Detoxification" of Vietnam veterans' war trauma: A combined family-individual approach. *Family Process, 25,* 559–570.

Rueger, D. B. (1983). *PTSD: Analysis of female partners' relationship perception.* Paper presented at the annual meeting of the American Psychological Association, Anaheim, California.

Russell, A. (1980). Late effects—Influence on the children of the concentration camp survivor. In J. E. Dimsdale (Ed.), *Survivors, victims and perpetrators: Essays on the Nazi Holocaust* (pp. 175–204). Washington DC: Hemisphere.

Rustin, S., & Lipsig, F. (1972). Psychotherapy with adolescent children of concentration camp survivors. *Journal of Contemporary Psychotherapy, 4*(2), 87–94.

Seligman, M. E. P. (1975). *Helplessness: On depression, development and death.* San Francisco: Freeman.

Sigal, J. J., & Rakoff, V. (1971). Concentration camp survival: A pilot study of effects on the second generation. *Canadian Psychiatric Association Journal, 16,* 393–397.

Sigal, J. J., Silver, D., Rakoff, V., & Ellin, B. (1973). Some second generation effects of survival of the Nazi persecution. *American Journal of Orthopsychiatry, 43,* 320–327.

Sigal, J. J., & Weinfeld, M. (1985). Control of aggression in adult children of survivors of the Nazi persecution. *Journal of Abnormal Psychology, 94,* 556–564.

Solkoff, N. (1992). Children of survivors of the Nazi Holocaust: A critical review of the literature. *American Journal of Orthopsychiatry, 62,* 342–358.

Solomon, Z. (1988). Somatic complaints, stress reaction and posttraumatic stress disorder: A three year follow-up study. *Behavioral Medicine, 14,* 179–186.

Solomon, Z., Mikulincer, M., Fried, B., & Wosner, Y. (1987). Family characteristics of posttraumatic stress disorder: A follow-up of Israeli combat stress reaction casualties. *Family Process, 26,* 383–394.

Solomon, Z., Waysman, M., Avitzur, E., & Enoch, D. (1991). Psychiatric symptomatology among wives of soldiers following combat stress reaction: The role of the social network and marital relations. *Anxiety Research, 4,* 213–223.

Solomon, Z., Waysman, M., Belkin, R., Levy, G., Mikulincer, M., & Enoch, D. (1992). Martial relations and combat stress reaction: The wives' perspective. *Journal of Marriage and the Family, 54,* 316–326.

Solomon, Z., Waysman, M., Levy, G., Fried, B., Mikulincer, M., Benbenishty, R., Florian, V., & Bleich, A. (1992). From front line to home front: A study of secondary traumatization. *Family Process, 31,* 289–302.

Steinberg, I. (1995). Treating the loss of a child. In C. R. Figley, N. Mazze, & B. Bride (Eds.), *Death and trauma.* New York: Brunner/Mazel.

Trimble, M. R. (1981). *Post-traumatic neurosis: From railway spine to the whiplash.* Chichester: Wiley.

Verbosky, S. J., & Ryan, D. A. (1988). Female partners of Vietnam veterans: Stress by proximity. *Issues in Mental Health Nursing, 9,* 95–104.

Weiss, E., O'Connell, A. N., & Siter, R. (1986). Comparisons of second generation Holocaust survivors, immigrants and non-immigrants. *Journal of Personality and Social Psychology, 50*(4), 828–831.

6

The Deficiency of the Concept of Posttraumatic Stress Disorder When Dealing with Victims of Human Rights Violations

DAVID BECKER

INTRODUCTION

The classification and diagnosis of an illness is a noble task that, at first sight, seems to be a value-free activity, carried out in the best interest of scientific development and the health care necessities of a given patient. Unfortunately, science is never value free, and since Werner Heisenberg defined his principle of uncertainty, we definitely learned that, even in the so-called hard sciences, the way we look at things changes not only what we see but also what happens. Posttraumatic stress disorder (PTSD), as defined by the revised third edition of the *Diagnostic and Statistical Manual of Mental Disorders* (American Psychiatric Association, 1987), was probably never meant to be a concept, a theory of the aftereffects of traumatic

DAVID BECKER • Latin American Institute of Mental Health and Human Rights, Providencia Santiago, Chile. Revised version of a paper presented at the ISTSS Conference "Trauma and Tragedy," Amsterdam, The Netherlands, June 1992.
Beyond Trauma: Cultural and Societal Dynamics, edited by Rolf J. Kleber, Charles R. Figley, and Berthold P. R. Gersons. New York, Plenum Press, 1995.

experiences, but it ended up being just that. The PTSD concept defines the existence of the illness based on the appearance of certain symptoms within a certain time span. Without symptoms, there is no illness. PTSD is a form of diagnosis applicable to individuals. If the illness in question were to exist between individuals and not only in them, PTSD not only would be incapable of understanding the phenomenon but would also influence the appearance of the illness. In short, PTSD is, necessarily, a concept that shapes our way of understanding trauma, that determines treatment strategies, and, last not least, that possibly influences how persons suffering from trauma will deal with their problem.

In Chile, we have been giving physical and mental care to victims of human rights violations since 1977, that is, during dictatorship as well as within what we can now define as a slow transition to democracy. At the Latin American Institute for Mental Health and Human Rights (ILAS), since 1991, we have carried out a longitudinal study of the problems of more than 200 extremely traumatized families, afflicted by torture, death, or exile, and their evolution within the different kinds of treatment—that is, psychotherapeutical, medical and social—offered by our institution.

In this research, whose findings are currently being prepared for publication, we have registered and evaluated the life histories of 226 families affected by political repression in Chile. Of these families, 64 suffered the disappearance of one of more members; in 76 cases, at least one family member was detained and tortured; in 17 cases, one family member was killed; 60 families suffered exile as well as one of the other repressive situations mentioned; and 9 families suffered other repressive situations. A total of 147 of these families were treated in individual, family, and/or group therapy; 168 cases received medical treatment.

It is in this context that I would like to reflect on the limits of the concept of posttraumatic stress disorder. Basing my arguments on our clinical experience and our research (Becker, 1992; Becker & Lira, 1989; Lira & Castillo, 1991; Lira & Weinstein, 1984; Weinstein, Lira, & Rojas, 1987), I will try to show that PTSD, even in its own framework, is not an adequate diagnostic instrument and furthermore that it has ideological implications which are important to avoid when dealing with victims of human rights violations and other forms of organized violence.

THE DELUSION OF THE TERM *POST*

When evaluating the relationship between the life histories of our patients and PTSD diagnosis, a series of problems become immediately evident. First of all, the *P* of *PTSD* does not apply. The term *post* suggests that the traumatic event was limited to a certain moment in time, which lies in the past. But our patients experience cumulative and continuous trauma.

Juana and her two children, for example, came to ask for help in 1989, when she showed severe depressive symptomatology and her children showed aggressive behavior and problems in school. When did the traumatization of this family start? Doubtless in September 1973, after the military coup. But when did it stop? When she came out of prison? When her husband was killed? When her second husband was killed? When she reunited with her children, who had lived several years in exile, while she participated within the country in the struggle against dictatorship? When the democratic government was elected, not as product of a glorious victory over dictatorship, but as part of a political negotiation that opened a door to democracy but left Pinochet as commander in general? When?

Or take the case of the family of Diego and Cecilia and their sons, Roberto and Francisco. Diego and Cecilia first came to see me in 1983, right after the beginning of the mass protests. They described problems with their 5-year-old youngest son, Francisco, who expressed strong fears, never wanted to be left alone, and would get very angry if his parents did not react the way he wanted. In fact, they felt that he was controlling them and that they often had to invent complicated strategies to maintain some kind of liberty. When I asked the children to draw something, Francisco made a very detailed drawing of their apartment, putting both his parents in bed and himself and his brother playing on the floor; from behind closets and chairs, a couple of ghosts looked onto the scene. It soon became evident that he had made a drawing of something that had happened two years before he was born, when his father had been kidnapped by the secret police, severely tortured for weeks, and then brought back to the apartment accompanied by them. For 10 more days, the secret police had held the father, the mother, and the baby Roberto hostage and had tried to use the apartment as a trap for political friends of the father. When they finally left, they made the father sign a statement that he had never been imprisoned, and they also made it clear that, if he ever talked about his experience, it would be no problem to arrange a little accident. For the following two years, they reminded the family of this threat by regular telephone calls. Francisco officially knew nothing about all this. Both parents confirmed that not only had they never talked to the children about these events, but also they had not even talked between themselves. They had tried to forget and had stopped all political activity.

Within the ensuing family therapy the "family secret" was finally shared, and Francisco's symptoms soon disappeared. But Roberto developed relevant depressive symptomatology, the father confessed typical PTSD symptoms, and marital problems between the father and the mother became apparent. Although treatment with this family was quite successful, it continued with interruptions till 1990. In fact, every time the social situation in Chile began to change or turned somehow more threatening, the family came back to see me, presenting different kinds of symptomatology. The first treatment phase went from 1983 to 1985. When an attempt to assassinate the dictator Pinochet failed in 1986 and repression became very strong again for a couple of months, they returned. The same happened in 1988, just before the plebiscite, and in 1989, before the elections. Although they have not had any more problems since 1990, I am not sure if they will not need me again at some time.

The first case example makes it very obvious that Juana and her children were subjected to continuous traumatic experiences, that cannot be grasped by the term *post*. Symptomatology in this case occurred not in a measurable time span after trauma, but as part of a process that continued for 17 years. Some authors hold that the *post* in PTSD does not imply any reference to the duration of trauma but only marks the beginning. If so, then why use the term *post*? As the first case example showed, neither the beginning nor the end of a traumatic process can be clearly determined. The only recognizable "post" is the moment when we (the therapists) begin to know about the suffering of this family.

The second case example reveals a similar process and also highlights two other important issues:

1. The family as a totality forms part of the traumatic experience. The father seems to be eligible for the label of PTSD, but the symptomatic son, Francisco, how do we define him? Or how do we understand the fact that, only after the son's symptoms diminished did the father begin to show full-blown PTSD symptoms?
2. How do we account for the fact that, although severe traumatization occurred in 1976, continuing with threats till 1978, symptomatology occurred only in 1983? And how can we explain that, in direct dependency on the sociopolitical process, the family relapses into illness?

In short, *post* seems to have very little to do with the kind of traumatic experiences people undergo as a consequence of political repression. The Israeli psychotherapists Benyakar, Kutz, Dasberg, and Stern (1983) very impressively summed up the problem by citing a personal communication of Gabriel Dagan, a psychotherapist and Auschwitz survivor: "I think that in Auschwitz we have been hit in the core of the denial of death. Something has been damaged, smashed in this mechanism, and through this irreparable crack, Death keeps dripping into life. . . . I have survived hell but I have not been released from it. It is still inside me, day and night" (p. 443).

THE INADEQUACY OF THE TERM *DISORDER*

This leads us to a second crucial problem, which can be identified with the last letter of *PTSD*. When talking about genocide, torture, or political repression, it seems sort of strange to label the victims as *disordered*. Eissler (1963) titled an article of his with the following question: "The Assassination of How Many of His or Her Children Does a Human Being Have to Experience without Producing Symptoms, in Order to Show That He or She Has a Healthy Psychic Constitution?" In his article, Eissler discussed the rights of Shoah survivors to receive reparation, and the terrible postwar German psychiatrist, who often denied a connection between specific illnesses and the concentration camp experiences. The problem is evidently multiple.

First of all, it is important to notice that the justification given by those who exercise the terrors of human-made disasters is always that the victims are "disordered." Jews were considered a threat to humanity by the Nazis; Latin American dictatorships described their victims as a cancer to society, which therefore had to be eliminated. Victimizers in all parts of the world have used the supposed "disorder" of the victims to justify their acts of cruelty and destruction. The reality of political repression is masked by arguments that put the victims outside of the realm of social interaction. Pseudoscientific arguments about health, used for example in Latin America and in the Soviet Union, or about biology, as is the case in racism, try to block out all human characteristics of the victim and at the same time eliminate all possible evidence that the actions of the victimizers are crimes. If our clinical language voluntarily or accidentally mirrors this self-justifying attitude of the victimizers, we evidently run high risks of converting ourselves into traumatizing agents. The victims underwent an experience in which a sociopolitical act of power—torture, for example—was converted into an individual experience. If we call that experience a "disorder," we repeat the denial initiated by the victimizers, and we thereby deepen the trauma.

A second important point is made by Eissler: Is it a disorder if a person develops symptomatology after having witnessed the killing of his family, for example? Would it not be more correct to consider somebody disordered who does not become ill after such an experience? Is the above-cited Auschwitz survivor disordered, or are those people disordered who find it difficult to listen to him?

A third consideration comes from our patients. They not only react very sensibly to the word *disorder* but state very clearly that one of the important reasons they feel that they can ask for our help is that we are a human rights institution, not a hospital or an institution for the mentally ill. In fact, many of them are sick and show extreme symptomatology, and the help they ask for makes reference to these problems. The idea therefore cannot be to deny the high levels of individual destruction suffered by them. The point I am trying to make, though, is that, to these persons, it makes an enormous difference that we regard them less as individually disturbed and more as persons suffering the consequences of a disturbed society.

A fourth and very important issue in reference to the term *disorder* is that it suggests a set of clearly identifiable symptoms, a clear way in which the illness develops and the circumstances under which it can disappear. None of this is true of our patients. Although many present PTSD symptomatology, many also present other kinds of problems. Of 100 individually analyzed cases (within the research presented at the beginning of this paper), only 2 presented exclusively psychological symptoms. All others also presented varying kinds of somatic and psychosomatic illnesses. The timing of symptoms is uncertain, and they may appear a few days after the traumatic experience or many years afterwards. In many youths, we find less overt symptomatology, but relevant problems in social behavior, such as problems at work, dropping out of school, and premature marriages. Although we do believe that it is possible to identify a set of typical problems of survivor families, these do not fit into the PTSD diagnosis, and what is more complicated, they tend to appear and disappear following less an individually recognizable logic and much more a dependence on the social process.

CONCEPTUALIZING TRAUMA

We are thus left with the letters *T* and *S* of the concept *PTSD*. I strongly agree with Benyakar et al. (1989) that, within the conceptualization of PTSD, "trauma has become devoid of any of its original connotations of disruption and discontinuity and in fact has become meaningless, used in the vernacular to imply any terrible situation" (p. 432). They believe that trauma is an indispensable clinical concept because of the notion of injury and discontinuity it implies, which as a psychological concept makes reference to the perceived sense of irreparable tear of self and reality. In this context, the concept of *traumatic stress* appears to be basically self-contradictory. Trauma is qualitatively different from stress. As Benyakar et al. (1989) pointed out, the sequence of a stressogenic threat followed by a reorganizing response in which the structure of the person receiving the stress stays basically intact is quite different from what occurs in a traumatic experience, where the sequence could be described in terms of a catastrophic threat followed by a chaotic response, implying the occurrence of structural breakdown. In other words, if we want to learn about the meaning of "death dripping into life," the word *stress* will help us very little, and we will have to find out more about the trauma.

In 1943, Bruno Bettelheim wrote about his experience in a concentration camp and justified the need for a new term to describe the experiences he and his fellow prisoners had suffered: "What characterized it most was its inescapability, its uncertain duration, but potentially for life; the fact that nothing about it was predictable; that one's very life was in jeopardy at every moment and that one could do nothing about it" (p. 418). Bettelheim suggested the term *extreme situation*. He was the first to explain very clearly that traumatization as a product of human-made disaster, cannot be categorized in usual psychiatric or psychoanalytic language. This was something else, and the nature of the trauma required a new language. In the post-Shoah literature, the term *extreme traumatization* was developed. While this term emphasizes that trauma has occurred, the word *extreme* also conveys the special nature of the trauma, a trauma that, neither in its occurrence nor in its short- and long-term consequences nor in its symptomatology nor in its sociopolitical implications, can be compared to other traumatic events, like, for example, an accident, an earthquake, or a heart attack.

The idea already expressed by Freud that trauma may also be a product of several experiences was further developed by Khan (1977) and leads finally to his concept of "cumulative trauma," through which the dimensions of time and relationship are introduced to the discussion of trauma. Khan suggested speaking of cumulative trauma when a mother has not adequately fulfilled her role as a protective shield in the developmental process of the infant from early childhood to adolescence. The mother must have failed in all areas in which the child needed her to contain its developmental and structural insecurities. The important point that Khan made is that the ruptures of the stimulus barrier in the child are not traumatic each time they occur. They acquire traumatic qualities only a posteriori, because they accumulate. Following Khan, a trauma can be a product of a series of individually nontraumatic experiences which develop and accumulate within an interactional framework and finally lead to breakdown. These thoughts are highly important because, although initially limited to the mother–child relationship, they change the emphasis from trauma to the traumatic situation, converting the event into a process and, without denying the intrapsychic wound, focus on the importance of the interactional framework.

Both Bettelheim's and Khan's ideas were further developed by Hans Keilson (1992) in his concept of "sequential traumatization." In his very important follow-up study of Jewish war orphans in the Netherlands, he distinguished three traumatic sequences:

1. The occupation of the Netherlands by the enemy and the beginning of the terror against the Jewish minority. This implies attacks on the social and psychic integrity of the Jewish families.
2. The period of direct persecution, which included the deportation of parents and children, the separation of mother and child, the hiding of the children in foster families, and the experience of the concentration camps.
3. The postwar period, during which one of the main issues was appointing guardians for the parentless children. The alternatives were to let the children stay with their Dutch foster families or to return them to the original Jewish environment.

Keilson linked the concept of *cumulative trauma* with the concept of *extreme situation.* He not only emphasized the successive process of traumatization, showing how the different ages of the children influenced their pathology, but also convincingly pointed out that only the analysis of all three traumatic sequences permitted an adequate comprehension of the psychological problems of the children. Introducing the idea of sequence to trauma theory makes it possible to visualize chronic trauma, which otherwise implies an apparent contradiction. Trauma initially refers to an event. Chronic trauma can develop whenever the content of the traumatic situation is persecution and political repression. Keilson proved that a severe second traumatic sequence and a "good" third traumatic sequence imply a better long-term health perspective for the victim than a not-so-terrible second traumatic sequence and a "bad" third traumatic sequence. This point is highly important because it explains that traumatization can continue even when the actual persecution has already stopped. Also, we are thus able to understand why patients may present symptomatology immediately after the original traumatic event, and also why they may do so 20, 30, or 40 years later.

Not being able to use PTSD in reference to our own patients, and finding the thoughts of Bettelheim, Khan, and Keilson highly useful, we adopted the term *extreme traumatization* (Becker, 1990, 1992; Becker & Castillo, 1990), whose central characteristic in our definition is that of an individual and collective process that occurs in reference to and in dependence of a given social context: It is a process because of its intensity, its duration in time, and the interdependence of the social and the psychological processes. It exceeds the capacity of the psychic structure of the individuals and of society to answer adequately to this process. Its aim is the destruction of individuals, their sense of belonging to the society, and their social activities. Extreme traumatization is characterized by a structure of power within the society that is based on the elimination of some members of this society by others of the same society. The process of extreme traumatization is not limited in time and develops sequentially. In other words, in our own definition, we intend to transcend the individual level, without denying it, and to include the social reality. Or said in another way, extreme traumatization is never only individual destruction or only a sociopolitical process. It is always both.

CONCLUSIONS

The proposed change of concept has a series of implications. First of all, we have to realize that extreme traumatization cannot be integrated into a typical medical or psychological framework of diagnosis and treatment. Instead of diagnosing individual illnesses and specific symptoms, we will have to evaluate social processes that provoke trauma and convert a part of the population in a high-risk group, which may or may not need treatment. When symptoms occur, we will have to relate them to the traumatic process. In other words, we will not ask if cancer is a typical aftereffect of torture, but if we attend a patient with cancer and learn that he or she was tortured, we will imply that traumatization occurred and adapt our treatment strategy accordingly. Instead of symptoms, the traumatic experiences and sequences become our basic way of understanding patients. We will not be surprised by symptoms occurring many years after the persecution has stopped. We will also easily understand that whole family groups are primarily traumatized, and that their illness will always appear in relationship to a certain social context. We will understand that it makes an enormous difference if a torture victim is treated within his or her country, or if the treatment occurs in exile. Instead of dealing with persons who suffer from PTSD, we will be dealing with Shoah survivors, with torture victims, and with Vietnam veterans. The right to receive pensions and medical and therapeutical aid will not depend on showing PTSD symptomatology, but on the fact that somebody was a victim of political repression.

Health services that want to adapt to this kind of comprehension of trauma will have to focus on two issues:

1. They will have to teach health personnel in general that a traumatized person may appear with any kind of symptomatology in any kind of health service. Professionals will have to be able to question persons about whether traumatization occurred and will then have to adapt their treatment strategies accordingly.
2. During or after situations of social catastrophe, special health services will have to be established that offer medical, social, and psychotherapeutic help to victims. The basic criteria for receiving treatment would not be symptomatology but the simple fact that the victim asks for help.

Symptomatic diagnosis, like PTSD or certain psychoanalytic categories, evidently will help to define specific characteristics of the patients and their needs. Therefore, they will be used, but only in the limited sense of helping to *describe* specific difficulties of patients.

As researchers, we will have to accept the fact that the proposed change of concept makes generalizations more difficult, because we will be able to talk not about trauma as such, but only in reference to specific social contexts. Our comprehensive analysis will have to built on the differences much more than on the similarities. Or to state it in a different way, generalization in trauma theory cannot occur within positivistic thinking, but only within a framework that comprehends that the essential sameness of political trauma in different parts of the world is the fact that it is context-bound and that its characteristics therefore must be basically different. There remains an enormous task of carefully constructing context-bound definitions of illness, of trauma, of expectable symptomatology. Although we may have to face for sometime a certain amount of confusion and insecurity, we will also be able to understand certain phenomena which were out of reach up to now. We might begin to understand, for example, why the North American offer to teach the diagnosis and treatment of posttraumatic stress disorder in El Salvador (a country which suffered a 10-year civil war that was sponsored by the United States) produced a negative reaction not only by the guerrilla organizations, but also by the psychologists working with the military. The main problem of the soldiers from both sides in El Salvador today is not to be recognized as "sick," but the wish to be socially reintegrated and recognized as valuable members of society.

The concept of extreme traumatization helps us to understand that therapy is necessary and will help in many cases, but we will also know how much of the mental health of our patients depends on the willingness of society to deal with their issues. We will understand more easily why healing in these cases often has less to do with being symptom-free than with our disposition to sharing and understand destruction. Last but not least, we will understand that the treatment of extremely traumatized patients requires not only an interdisciplinary team and a disposition to work with a flexible setting, possibly for many years, but mainly what we have called a "bond of commitment," or what Kinston and Cohen (1986), in more careful psychoanalytic language, have called "primary relatedness." Without denying the reality of transference and countertransference, we have to work from a nonneutral standpoint, accepting a basic commitment to our patients, in which we help them to convert a sociopolitical crime, which has turned into an individual illness, once more into something that will facilitate social and thereby individual elaboration.

REFERENCES

American Psychiatric Association. (1987). *Diagnostic and statistical manual of mental disorders* (3rd ed.; DSM-III-R). Washington, DC: Author.

Becker, D. (1990). Ohne Hass keine Versöhnung: Aus der therapeutischen Arbeit mit Extremtraumatisierten in Chile. In E. Herdieckerhoff, D. von Ekesparre, R. Elgeti, & Marahrens-Schürg (Eds.), *Hassen und Versöhnen*. Göttingen: Verlag Vanderhoeck & Ruprecht.

Becker, D. (1992). *Ohne Hass keine Versöhnung: Das Trauma der Verfolgten*. Freiburg: Kore Verlag.

Becker, D., & Castillo, M. I. (1990). *Procesos de traumatización extrema y posibilidades de reparación*, unpublished paper, Instituto Latino Americano de Salud Mental y Derechos Humanos, Santiago, Chile.

Becker, D., & Lira, E. (Eds.). (1989). *Derechos Humanos: Todo es según el dolor con que se mira*. Santiago, Chile: Instituto Latino Americano de Salud Mental y Derechos Humanos.

Benyakar, M., Kutz, I., Dasberg, H., & Stern, M. J. (1989). The collapse of a structure: A structural approach to trauma. *Journal of Traumatic Stress, 2*, 431–450.

Bettelheim, B. (1943). Individual and mass behavior in extreme situations. *Journal of Abnormal and Social Psychology, 38*, 417–452.

Eissler, K. (1963). Die Ermordung von wie vielen seiner Kinder muss ein Mensch symptomfrei ertragen können, um eine normale Konstitution zu haben? *Psyche, 17*, 241–291.

Keilson, H. (1992). *Sequential traumatization in children*. Jerusalem: Magnes Press, Hebrew University. (Work first published 1979).

Khan, M. (1977). Das kumulative trauma. In M. Khan, *Selbsterfahrung in der Therapie*. München: Kindler Verlag.

Kinston, W., & Cohen, J. (1986). Primal repression: Clinical and theoretical aspects. *International Journal of Psychoanalysis, 67*, 337–355.

Lira, E., & Castillo, M. I. (1991). *Psicología de la amenaza política y del miedo*. Santiago, Chile: CESOC Ediciones/Instituto Latino Americano de Salud Mental y Derechos Humanos.

Lira, E., & Weinstein, E. (Eds.). (1984). *Psicoterapia y represión política*. Mexico City: Siglo XXI.

Weinstein, E., Lira, E., & Rojas, E. (Eds.). (1987). *Trauma, duelo y reparación*. Santiago, Chile: Eitorial Latinoamericana/FASIC.

II

Societal and Political Issues

This part of *Beyond Trauma* contains a group of chapters especially dedicated to the societal and political dimensions of traumatic stress. They all disclose the embeddedness of individual responses in the context of the larger society. A characteristic of all these chapters is that they deal with traumatic events that are caused by societal conditions: from situations of injustice and human rights violations to human-made catastrophes caused by prolonged neglect.

Abuse of human rights is a major issue in nearly all the chapters of Part II. The Chilean psychologist Kornfeld focuses on the conflicts and anxieties of therapists and mental health workers under the dictatorship in Chile and in the difficult period of transition to democracy. Victims of human rights violations have been diagnosed as extremely traumatized people. Their experiences range from the death and disappearance of loved ones to torture, exile, and general harassment. *Trauma* is a key concept, both at the individual level and at the social level. In therapy, it is important to uncover the meaning that the individual has given to these traumatic experiences. A fundamental dimension is the need to "historicize" these traumatic experiences. Patients and therapists are unable to give meaning to such experiences unless they link them to particular and concrete circumstances.

The repercussions on therapists are also examined by Kornfeld, who describes their coping strategies when working in the same social context as their patients and treating victims in a threatening social and political context, such as in Chile. She realized that the subjective impact of the violence, aggression, and anguish that the patients brought to the therapy was hardly reported. The demand for assistance was too immediate to allow a proper consideration of the effects on the therapists. The author shows how hard it is for professionals to express their aggressive feelings, to show their fears, and to discuss the differences between colleagues. The chapter analyzes the conceptualization of these psychotherapeutic experiences as a kind of coping strategy of the therapists. It describes this process through the experience of a Chilean team working for more than 10 years with victims of human rights violations under the dictatorship and afterward.

Guiao investigates the consequences of political conflict and instability with regard to mental health. In particular, she studies the impact on women of the prolonged and severe political turmoil in the Philippines. Her work is a synthesis of an analysis of characteristics of Filipino culture with a stress and coping research perspective. Thus, she integrates two distinct fields in the social sciences and combines quantitative findings and cultural analysis. Her chapter make clear that many people reach a certain level of resilience and stress tolerance. The author emphasizes the significance of culture as a buffer to the negative impact of political instability. Many women were able to cope rather adequately with the prolonged hardships of insecurity and unrest in the Philippines, a country plagued by many coups d'état, guerrilla warfare, assassinations, and terrorism in the last decades. At the end of her chapter, she poses a cluster of highly relevant questions for future research and interventions.

Many victims of human terror, human rights violations, and civil war have had to flee their homeland and migrate to foreign, often rather inhospitable, countries. The world is confronted more and more with the many difficulties of refugees. Van der Veer starts with the fact that, for refugees, traumatization is not a specific, isolated incident, but an enduring, cumulative process, a chain of experiences that confront the refugee with helplessness and that interfere with personal development over an extended period of time. The realization of cultural differences is significant in understanding the problems of the individual refugee as well as in the treatment of these disturbances. In his chapter, the author describes these differences and their implications for treatment, but he stresses at the same time that there is no reason to let oneself be intimidated by cultural differences. One has to be attentive and flexible. Genuine interest in, respect for, and tolerance of the anxiety of the client are basic conditions for counseling and therapy.

Van der Veer shows that psychotherapy with refugees is a matter not of inventing completely new techniques, but of creatively adjusting a variety of existing techniques. Psychotherapy with traumatized refugees is an ongoing effort to help or stimulate the client to regain her or his liberty, in the sense of acquiring control over posttraumatic symptoms that interfere with present psychological functioning and the opportunities for future psychological development. In that sense, it is very concrete. The author concludes with a rather positive message. Even with limited resources, it is possible to build up expertise with regard to psychotherapy with refugees. It is within the reach of the average professional in the mental health sector: assuming that he or she is ready to plunge into the backgrounds of the patients and to listen to the stories of refugees and is allowed to adapt procedures and organizational structures in a way that meets their specific needs.

The purpose of the chapter by Russell is to examine the trauma of incestuous abuse by summarizing some of the immediate and long-term effects and by analyzing some of the major causes. The chapter starts with the presentation of cross-national data on the prevalence of abuse. Two facts are articulated: the first is the high prevalence rates; the second is that the perpetrators are predominantly male. The author states that the severity of the trauma associated with incestuous abuse qualifies it in many instances as a form of torture, and she argues that it deserves to be taken at least as seriously as torture is, as a gender-related human rights issue. Again, we see here the dominant position of the human rights issue in trauma research. Russell raises the intriguing question of whether conceptualizing the more severe cases of incestuous abuse as torture would induce societies to take this ubiquitous crime more seriously instead of dismissing it as a private and nonpolitical matter. Finally, some of the major structural and cultural causes of incestuous abuse are discussed. The author concludes that incestuous abuse of females by males should be recognized as a political offense that both reflects and perpetuates the unequal power relations between males and females. Society's conception of masculinity is a key to understanding the incestuous abuse of females.

The next chapter also deals with abuses of human rights. Simpson examines the experiences in South Africa, a society that suffered the chronic trauma of apartheid and its system of repression and discrimination. His chapter forms a bridge between the conceptual matters of Part II and the ethical issues of Part III. The author shows how individual traumatic experiences were affected by the social and political context. Simpson eloquently argues that the political system has been comprehensively neglected, although it is essential to a full understanding of trauma and its aftereffects. He then reviews diagnostic and forensic problems arising from this neglect. He makes clear that there is no evidence of the existence of such a discrete syndrome as posttorture syndrome. At the same time, he explains the serious shortcomings of the concept of posttraumatic stress disorder when describing the disturbances of political detainees and victims of torture.

Finally, the author examines the ethical problem of how physicians, psychiatrists, and other health professionals become involved in facilitating torture and political trauma. The participation of these professionals in torture and human rights abuses is not merely an ethical problem;

it contributes greatly to the frequency with which such trauma is inflicted, and to the skill and efficacy with which its practitioners inflict traumatic stress disorders. Simpson presents a comprehensive model of the ways in which health professionals can be involved and of the conditions that facilitate this involvement, and he illustrates it with examples from South Africa. It his strong opinion that there was widespread political abuse of medicine and psychiatry. There was no lack, in South Africa, of professionals who were happy to assist by skillfully finding nothing wrong with political detainees, no matter how severe their symptoms, and by testifying that they were perfectly fit, no matter how damaged they might be.

One of the ironies of the human condition is the appearance of new scourges once old ones have been conquered. A new type of disaster has emerged in the last decades: the technological catastrophe, defined as the breakdown of human-made technical systems.

Catastrophes such as the nuclear plant disasters in Chernobyl (in the former Soviet Union) and Harrisburg (in the United States) have a large impact on mental and physical health. Symptoms are worries about one's own health, worries about the causal explanation with regard to any disease, worries about the future of one's children, plans to move, and distrust of authorities.

The radioactive threat is invisible; there is an expectation of future illness, so that the consequences are aggravated by the (initial) lack of information provided by the authorities and by the resulting ignorance of the population. The strong desire of the residents of the area for repeated measures of radioactivity and for physical examination of complaints of whatever nature shows that they are continuously striving to find out exactly what happened. Furthermore, the neglect of necessary safety procedures and technological mishaps result in a loss of confidence, not only in the future ability to control technology but also in the authorities.

As discussed by Van den Bout, Havenaar, and Meijler-Iljina, years after the Chernobyl disaster, the inhabitants of the contaminated areas are still very concerned about all kinds of health problems. These problems range from somatic complaints, such as headaches or gastrointestinal problems, to psychosomatic symptoms, such as sleeplessness and tiredness. These health problems generate many worries and are to a very large extent attributed to radiation by the people living in or near the contaminated areas. Radiation experts, however, generally hold the view that a direct link between radiation and most of the health problems of the population is highly improbable, with the exception of a rise in the incidence of thyroid cancer in children. A psychosocial stressor explanation of the occurrence of these health problems is proposed, stressing cognitive-emotional processes.

7

The Development of Treatment Approaches for Victims of Human Rights Violations in Chile

ELIZABETH LIRA KORNFELD

INTRODUCTION

The dictatorship of Augusto Pinochet, which ruled Chile from 1973 to 1990, was accused of human rights abuses throughout this period. Gross human rights violations have been described, including the systematic use of torture against political prisoners. The cases of detainees who disappeared, people who were executed, and attacks against people's lives committed by individuals justified by political pretext, were the basis for the creation of the National Commission of Truth and Reconciliation in 1990.[1]

---

[1]This commission was created at the beginning of the constitutionally elected government after dictatorship. Its aim was to establish the truth of human rights violations, restricted to cases that ended in death. The official figures confirmed that more than 4,000 people were assassinated for political reasons (National Commission of Truth and Reconciliation Report, 1991).

ELIZABETH LIRA KORNFELD • Latin American Institute of Mental Health and Human Rights, Providencia Santiago, Chile.
Beyond Trauma: Cultural and Societal Dynamics, edited by Rolf J. Kleber, Charles R. Figley, and Berthold P. R. Gersons. New York, Plenum Press, 1995.

More than one-half of the people whose deaths are classified as human rights violations in the commission's report were those killed by state agents or people in the state's service. Some of the victims were sentenced to death by wartime court martials (*consejos de guerra*). Other people were shot while supposedly trying to escape imprisonment (*ley de fuga*). Other situations that ended in death, justified under the "state of war," "state of siege" or "state of exception," were also included.

Many people were arrested in their homes, in front of their families, by large contingents of police who ransacked their houses. Sometimes, the arrests took place in the streets, either in the presence or in the absence of third parties. Commonly, there was a lack of information about the prisoner's whereabouts for periods of from 5 to 20 days. Authorities did not acknowledge that the arrest had occurred. The family, therefore, feared for the victim's life and worried constantly about the detained person's physical and psychological condition because they knew that he or she was in danger of being tortured or killed. More than 1,000 people were kidnapped and disappeared during this period.

Detention and confinement for several months or years without charges were a common situation for thousands of people between 1973 and 1975. Most of them were released without any judicial procedure. The authorities could also arrest, detain, or transfer any person to anywhere in the country, a practice that was institutionalized as "relegation," that is, internal exile. The attitude adopted by the judicial system caused an important aggravation of the process of systematic violations of human rights (Americas Watch Report, 1991).

Torture was very extensive under the dictatorship (National Commission Report, 1991). Methods of torture included the "grill," which consisted of electricity applied while the prisoner was tied to a metal bed. Another method was the prolonged suspension of the victim by wrists or knees. The "submarine" was the repeated submersion of the head in liquid, generally mixed with feces or urine, until the moment of near-suffocation. Other tortures included beatings and breaking bones or aggravating existing wounds by, for example, driving a vehicle over the victim's limbs. In some interrogation centers, rape was practiced regularly as well as other forms of sexual abuse (Americas Watch Report, 1991).

Torture consists of the deliberate and systematic application of excruciating pain to a person in an attempt to undermine the will, the affective links, and the loyalties, beliefs, and physical and psychic integrity of the individual. Life threats and physical pain are the essence of torture. At a broader level, the reason for torture is to intimidate third parties, thereby ensuring responses of fear, inhibition, paralysis, impotence, and conformity within society.

Violations of human rights cannot be viewed exclusively from the perspective of isolated individual abuses. Their implications are much more extensive, for they describe not only a system's response to conflict, but a general ambience of political threat, both of which lead to an atmosphere of chronic fear (Lira, 1988). Those violations have implied a strong threat affecting everyday life in Chilean society. Persecution of those identified as "enemies" of the ruling power in the country included not only political leaders, priests and religious women, trade union leaders, members of leftist parties, and human rights activists, but the general population as well. Insecurity, vulnerability, and fear were widespread feelings among people, whatever their actual political involvement. Fear, which is normally a reaction to a specific external or internal threat, became a permanent component of everyday personal and social life. This constant state of fear, while affecting more directly those people who identified themselves as possible targets of political repression, did not leave the uninvolved unscathed.

Fear, confusion, general distress, personal threat of death, and harrassment were some of the subjective consequences presented by the affected people. Feelings of helplessness, defenselessness, and impotence were engendered not only in those affected, but especially in those who were unable to discern what really might happen to them. For these people, the sense of constant threat became an unbearable feeling, an unending torture in itself, whether this threat materialized or not.

Torture, kidnappings, disappearances, and other forms of political repression can be understood as traumatic experiences for the victims. They may result in an individual trauma that implies the breakdown of the psychic structure. This occurred in a context where there was also a partial breakdown of social structures: the so-called regimes of exception. In many Latin American countries, the governments decreed partial or complete suspension of constitutional rights and liberties in the face of disorder and violence. Under a regime of exception, the constitutional presidents executed opponents, sent adversaries into exile, censored the press, jailed and abused authors and publishers, and confiscated property; in short, they ruled their nations with virtually absolute power. They usually did this in accord with the constitutions that purportedly guaranteed civil liberties, civil rights, and popular sovereignty (Loveman, 1993). In other words, legal and political structures that supposedly guaranteed human life and rights to all members of a given society became threatening and devastating for most of them during the "state of exception" period.

Ignacio Martin Baró (1984, 1990) developed the concept of *psychosocial trauma* with regard to traumatic experiences affecting a society:

This means looking at experiences that affect a whole population not only as individuals per se, but as social beings in a social context. Psychosocial trauma constitutes the concrete crystallization of aberrant and dehumanizing social relations in individuals, like those prevalent in a civil war. . . . This also means that the chain tends to break at its weakest link (the most unprotected social sectors) or the sectors most directly affected by the conflict and warfare. (1984, p. 504).

The purpose of this chapter is to describe both the therapeutic work of dealing with the consequences of human rights violation in victims and the therapist's anxieties about the oppressive background of political violence. These anxieties are acknowledged as a kind of countertransference due to the overwhelming nature of the violence suffered by the patients. The conceptualization of these psychotherapeutic experiences is considered a coping strategy of therapists in a threatening context. Therapists' anxieties also have been understood as an expression of the collective feelings existing in Chilean society.

This chapter describes this process through the experience of a Chilean team working for more than 10 years with victims of human rights violations both under the dictatorship and afterward. The therapist's challenge of dealing with the psychopathological consequences of political violence after the dictatorship formulates new theoretical and practical problems for psychotherapy as well as for the Chilean society because of the necessary healing processes related to human rights violations.

THE SOCIAL "IMAGINARY" OF HUMAN RIGHTS ISSUES

Chile was accused by the international community of violating human rights during the whole period of the dictatorship. This "issue" was not only political but also a social, ethical, psychosocial, and mental health problem for the Chilean society. It did not end with Pinochet's government. On the one hand, human rights issues were considered by the military regime a part of a conspiracy. Accordingly, it was said that, after their defeat, the leftists had organized an international campaign against the military regime and that Chile's enemies had invented the violations of human rights to damage the image of Chile and its government. Denial was the systematic official response to the condemnation of human rights abuses.

On the other hand, human rights violations brought responses from various sectors of Chilean society. Lawyers, social workers, physicians, psychotherapists, Catholic priests, and ministers of other churches turned the defense of human rights into a central issue in their lives.

Their efforts entailed a commitment to human life and human beings as well as to their values and beliefs. That commitment implied to many of them a way of rescuing their own life projects, disrupted by political conditions and political repression. Survivors and human rights workers projected their expectations, wishes, fears, frustrations, impotence, guilt, rage, aggression, sufferings, and losses onto the subject of "human rights." It implied also another way of participating in public affairs.

The victimizers had probably taken for granted that they would never be prosecuted. Belief in their impunity could be a key condition of their taking part in crimes and political repression. Condemnation and legal procedures such as habeas corpus, although useless for protecting human life for long, eventually allowed the start of legal proceedings against human rights violators, at the end of the dictatorship.

Silence was the predominant social reaction to fear and political threat, as it associated "human rights" with death and extreme danger. At the end of military rule (1990), all these perceptions and projections of the human rights issue generated a particular, subjective phenomenon, which encompassed the whole society. The victims and the human rights workers had known in excruciating concreteness what was meant by "human rights issues." They knew the "truth" through their own experiences. They had been witnesses to a social reality filled with arbitrariness, cruelty, and abuses.

Another part of society created a different social representation regarding the human rights issues: a "social imaginary," in the sense that Castoriadis (1975) gave to this concept. "Social imaginary" is our translation of the Spanish expression *imaginario social*. Castoriadis defined *imaginary* in terms of the capacity to have an image which represents a relationship with a symbolic object. The flag of the country is such an imaginary. He argued that, when the ordinary language defines *imaginary*, it takes for granted that it is unlike reality, whether it seeks to take its place (a lie) or if it does not (a novel). In this sense, human rights affairs have different and conflicting subjective meanings for the Chilean people, and for the people related to the international solidarity movement. Persecution, prison, torture, exile, anxiety and loss, hope and helplessness, and life and death became different realities and fantasies to different social groups. The meaning given depended on their experience and social interactions related to "human rights." Fantasies—a mixture of memories, real experiences, desires, nightmares, fear of threats, and danger—were elements of projection. These different images or "inventions" allowed people to fill the gap of former official censorship and denial.

As time passed, such meanings were transformed and apparently found a collective symbolization, in spite of all these contradictions. Most people agreed with the perception that something "terrible" had happened in Chile. Some people reacted as if human rights violations had essentially been a problem of believing or not believing that horrible things had really happened. They disregarded the consequences for the victims and for social relations as the true problem for society. These reactions in the postdictatorship period have allowed people to understand that these violations of human rights were an objective tragedy for Chilean society. However, they were interpreted, condemned, and justified from different, contradictory, ethical, and political standpoints.

This social imaginary has also determined the social, political, and subjective place assigned to the human rights issues since the end of military rule. The transition government of President Aylwin tried to make amends through different policies concerning the social, legal, and health consequences of former human rights violations leveled at the population. Nevertheless, the social and political contexts of this transition have implied severe limitations on justice and social reparation. They have implied that some aftereffects will probably remain irreparable. Paraphrasing Martin Baró, clearly nobody is going to return his youth to the imprisoned dissident, her innocence to the young woman who has been raped, his or her integrity to the person who has been tortured. Nobody is going to return those who disappeared to their families (Martin Baró, 1989).

THERAPY UNDER THE DICTATORSHIP

In the first years of the dictatorship, many people requested therapy immediately after they were released from prison or secret places of detention. Some of them came for consultation because they had been tortured or they had lost their jobs. Others emphasized their personal crises or the conflicting, destructive relationships in their families. The relatives of detained-disappeared[2] and assassinated people asked for help at various moments.

In all these cases, the memories of traumatic experiences related to political repression were extremely vivid. They were maintained as a terrible present that seemed to be impossible to close or forget. Many

---

[2]*Detained-disappeared* (*detenido desaparecido*) refers to people detained and unaccounted for up to the present. While many presume these people were murdered, their legal existence is still indeterminate.

people lived in fear because detention and torture or other repressive situations could recur in the following days, months, or years.

These patients' presentations were characterized at the time as "traumatic political experiences" (Cienfuegos & Monelli, 1983; Lira & Weinstein, 1984). The following is a first session's extract of an old man who consulted us in 1986:

> Therapist: Why have you come? . . . What has happened to you?
> Patient: Nothing. I had a little problem. I was arrested and detained for 12 or 13 days. When I was released, I got depressed. I resisted well there . . . but now every night I dream of the jail. I don't feel like doing anything. . . . I was also taken prisoner in 1974. Afterward things were catastrophic. Many searches. In my nightmares, I go back to the chains, to the tortures. . . . I want to get out of this jail . . . of this enormous loss of human dignity.

This fragment allows the recognition of several elements that characterized the reasons why people asked for assistance. Here, the subject directly associated his suffering and symptoms with the repressive experience, which was a threatening, repetitive and unending situation, in spite of his efforts to minimize it. His mood was depressive, and his final comment could be understood as a metaphor for either his personal situation or that of Chilean society.

From the end of the dictatorship to the present, it has been common for people not to relate their symptomatology to traumatic experiences. During the dictatorship, we observed the opposite. Patients attributed all their symptoms to the repressive experience. Their symptoms have not changed. They mainly manifest depressive or anxious reactions or a combination of both. Others show isolated symptoms, such as insomnia or irritability. Still others evidence psychosomatic illnesses and alcohol dependence. In a few cases, drug dependence has been uncovered. Some patients have presented physical sequelae of torture. Symptomatology has appeared to be almost chronic or acute, depending on the repressive situation and how much time has passed up to the moment of consultation.

In dealing with this type of case, most of the therapeutic processes were originally conceived of as brief therapy with a dynamic orientation. The first objective was catharsis through the reconstitution of the traumatic experience, its emotional elaboration, its connection to the existential and contextual meaning of the subject's life, and its relationship to his or her vital experience (Weinstein et al., 1987). It was thought that the process of healing required restoration of the individual's capacity to resume the course of his or her life. This involved making the patient's previous history—political commitment, personal relationships, work, and social connections—meaningful in the present and the future (Cienfuegos & Monelli, 1983).

Testimony was a method of the catharsis of recent traumatic experience. It was also useful to denounce human rights violations. Frequently, under torture, patients had to "betray" friends, allies, and eventually family members. Besides catharsis, testimony sometimes permitted a limited process of working through, relieving anxiety and guilt, and putting the painful experience in the context where it had happened. Sharing their own story of their trauma allowed patients to channel their anger constructively into the creation of a document that might be used as an indictment of the offenders. Testimony provided a link between the political and the psychological, between the public and the private, and because of its effectiveness, it may account for helping to restore affective ties and for integrating fragmented experiences (Mishler, 1992).

This therapeutic approach focused on understanding the traumas experienced by the patients and their consequences, related to the Chilean political situation. As Mishler (1992) underlined, for each individual the experience of violence and of the destructive effects of loss, anger, and the breakdown of one's expectations for the future is a personal one. The healing process required explicit attention to the collective nature of the victims' suffering.

CONCEPTUALIZING A PSYCHOTHERAPEUTIC APPROACH

The concept of *trauma* has been the basis for understanding the subjective impact and the consequences of human rights violations. *Extreme traumatization* as a specific concept denotes the specific political meaning of this type of trauma, which (Becker, Castillo, Gómez, Kovalskys, & Lira, 1989; Lira, Becker, & Castillo, 1990) is closely related to Bettelheim's theory (Bettelheim, 1981). This concept emphasizes the radical disruption in the goals and ideals that the individual had established during his or her life, along with its continuing destructive impact on his or her identity, and on his or her family and social relations.

The concept of extreme traumatization also implies a process. Persecution or torture can involve successive and cumulative traumatization, which can be repeatedly produced by political repression. It occurs when authorities have the power to violate human rights, in other words, to use suffering for regulating antiestablishment political behavior.

It is important to realize that, in Chile, political repression transformed the social context, making it threatening and traumatic, with
great destructive potential for many people. It pervaded the material
conditions of concrete life, psychic survival, and the values that were the
meaning of life for the subjects. It seems relevant to recall that, despite
the psychopathological consequences described, we are not dealing here
solely with psychopathology, but also with concrete expressions of political violence that have marked and destroyed individual bodies, lives, and
social interactions by means of the violations of human rights (Lira,
1988).

A description of psychopathology, although it may help to determine the severity of the problem, still does not indicate the specific
nature of the trauma. Different traumatic situations often produce similar symptomatology. Therefore, trauma can be understood only with
direct reference to the traumatic situation. Thus, our diagnostic conceptualization of the traumatic experience includes a characterization of the
specific repressive situation. In this sense, we have defined torture as a
specific psychological trauma because of the intensity of the physical
aggression that is experienced, the dire threat to life that is encountered,
and the degree of passivity and impotence created in the victims (Weinstein et al., 1987).

We have emphasized the distinctions between the traumatic and the
pathogenic elements in the specific psychological consequences of torture. The conceptual amplification that begins with the "trauma" and
leads to the "traumatic situation" is potentiality dangerous because of
the possible adulteration of the concept of *trauma* and the drawing of an
equation between "traumatic situation" and "pathogenic situation."
Anna Freud, and others, correctly refused to equate *traumatic* with *pathogenic* to preserve a certain specificity for the traumatic (Baranguer, Baranguer, & Mom, 1988). But what specificity do we indicate here? This
question is fundamental to the efforts to conceptualize a psychotherapeutic approach and a psychosocial approach that complement
each other. This differentiation has remained a very important clue to
the "social working through" when democracy has been constituted
within the authoritarian institutional framework.

Situations such as the discovering of clandestine graves in 1990 and
1991 underline that perspective. We observed that these findings affected former victims so that they suffered a reactivation of their psychic
distress. We spoke of this as a "retraumatization" process for some of
them. The most shocking of these cases were the Pisagua graves. In a
deep, oblong grave were 19 bodies, stacked in rows and layers, not yet
skeletal because the desert soil had preserved them intact. Some still

wore blindfolds; the hands behind their backs were still held with their rope intact. Entry and exit wounds were easily visible, and some faces, though no longer recognizable, retained expressions of panic and protest. A Santiago newspaper published the photograph of one such face, on its front page, with the headline, "Look at me—I am a disappeared person." Other media publicized the discovery, too, and the nation began a visceral confrontation with the crimes of the past. The devastating impact of the Pisagua discovery was not surpassed by any other excavation, but each of the nearly 20 clandestine graves opened during 1990 contributed to a portrait of the months following the coup (Americas Watch Report, 1991). Those events deeply affected all the victims. The possibility of "retraumatization" leaves many questions unanswered about the aftereffects of these traumatic experiences.

The following case reported by a therapist in 1991 illustrates some of these elements:

> I had a patient for three years. During the first year, I began to suspect that she had been raped, but she never told me so. Her somatic symptoms did not improve. I came to feel that it was probable that rape, which she had hinted to me, could be the main issue in her life connected to her symptomatology. One day I told her, "I suspect that you were raped." She reacted by saying, "What?" I said, "It is probable, because all women, if they were in the hands of the secret police, were raped." She said, "Yes, but I have decided not to speak about it."
>
> I discussed this case with my supervisor. When I could voice my feelings about this to the patient, I said, "I feel it is very difficult for you to speak about this." Then, she left the state of consciousness, she fixed her eyes at a certain point, and she did not say anything, but she moved as if she were living through something. She tried to vomit. She had a terrified expression in her face. I tried to describe in words to her what I was seeing. I said, "I think that you feel very threatened." I preferred to speak and not do anything else—and suddenly she said, "I am very tired; I need to rest," and she lay down. She did not sleep, but it was like sleep for a few minutes. When she woke up, she asked me, "What happened?" I said, "You moved in a strange way. I felt you were very threatened by something. I think it was related to torture." Later, this sequence was repeated: She replaced words for this type of movement. The following times, I observed the process and put into words what was happening. Only very slowly was it possible for her to go into her experience. Afterward, she improved a lot. She can speak about her rage because she had been tortured.

This case illustrates different aspects of the problem. One of them is the repetition of dissociation in therapy. Dissociation is a coping mechanism during and after torture which implies splitting and repression. Dissociation had allowed this patient to survive then and now, establishing partial disintegration of her ego to avoid the overwhelming anxiety that would risk total disintegration. Through splitting, she had survived when she was forced to face the impossible choice between bodily and emotional integrity. This patient could put a part of her experience into words and feel some anguish that had invaded her whole life and relationships. Horror was impossible to put into words, but it was possible to contextualize this experience as a part of political repression and not as a private experience.

In therapy, it is important to uncover the meaning that the individual has given to his or her traumatic experience. Another fundamental dimension is the need to think historically, to "historicize" these traumatic experiences. Patients and therapists are unable to give meaning to such experiences without linking them to particular and concrete circumstances. As time passes, especially in the case of tortured people, screen memories are made up of fragments of images. The images are fragments of memories. These fragments of fragments are the first attempts to historicize," to put every segment in a personal historic perspective.

Sometimes, these segments appear as partial reconstructions of what may have happened, but for the patients, they are not easily recognizable as his or her own experience because of the coping mechanisms that he or she has developed throughout time in the sheer attempt to survive psychically. Strong emotions are frequently associated with these fragments. As time passes and the therapeutic process continues, the reconstruction of the gaps in the patient's own history are eased. Historical reconstruction of the traumatic experiences can be integrated about the past and the present. At that point, the patient develops the possibility of returning to the present and working through these experiences.

DEVELOPING RESOURCES TO SUPPORT THERAPISTS IN THEIR THERAPEUTIC WORK

An effort to integrate clinical practice, psychosocial perspective, and the struggle to protect life and human rights in Chilean society has been a defining feature of therapists working with victims of political repression. In this specific context, one of the resources developed by therapists to deal with their own anguish was the attempt to describe the patients' situation in detail, and to denounce violations of human rights from the perspective of mental health. They wrote scientific papers, documents, and articles in which they developed their perceptions of both the individual and the collective consequences of political repression. By formulating these ideas and situating these experiences in a conceptual framework, we circumscribed our anguish. Through words, we gave conceptual order to the horrifying reality of the victims, thereby enabling them to express our anxieties and confusions.

We were able, during the dictatorship, to build the basis of a therapeutic approach. Our writings dealt with patients; they lacked references to the difficulties of therapists. The subjective impact of the violence, aggression, and anguish that the patients brought to the sessions was hardly mentioned. During the first 10 years, the demand for assistance was too immediate to allow a proper consideration of the impact on therapists. Only after the dictatorship was it possible to start reflecting collectively on the hatred and rage connected with these issues.

THE CONFLICTS AND ANXIETIES OF THE THERAPIST

Therapists faced a very difficult professional challenge when they started working with victims of human rights violations in their own society under a threatening situation. They engaged themselves in this work because of ethical as well as sociopolitical commitment. The values and concerns they shared with the patients permitted the kind of bond that we have called a "bond of commitment" (Lira & Weinstein, 1984), and that made therapy possible under those conditions. This bond gave the patients the necessary confidence to consult and, at the same time, allowed for the "translation" of meanings between the different contextual levels implied in the suffering of the subjects.

It is important to make a difference between the period when therapists worked under the dictatorship (1973–1990) and afterward. Therapists did not immediately recognize the full implications of this type of concern in the permanent threat affecting everyday life. This general threat was sometimes addressed to therapists, generating such deep anguish in them that it invaded their lives beyond the therapeutic field. However, the impact of this threat was not sufficiently registered to elicit adequate psychological support for them.

During the military rule, the anxiety caused by this type of problem was expressed in different ways. One of them was placing anxieties and fears onto the training and abilities needed to work in this field. Therapists realized that they did not have sufficient theoretical knowledge and practical experience to deal with this type and intensity of social and political violence. The impotence and frustration experienced in everyday life, and in therapeutic work, were attributed to the dictatorship and to the lack of appropriate knowledge for such a difficult therapeutic challenge.

Therapists were really overwhelmed. The political nature of the problems encouraged some type of overinvolvement, hidden under their "commitment." This type of psychological pressure (internal and external) came from different places and built an ideological approach for the people involved in this type of work. "Commitment" has its roots in Christian values. Every human being is a brother or sister because he or she has the same father, God. This implies the radical perspective of fighting for human life. Another perspective is political involvement in a party or in "the cause," which can have different meanings. All these elements have existential values that increase in a threatening situation, affecting therapists in their professional work as in their everyday life.

In spite of its ethical value, "commitment" also implied a possible dangerous perspective both for therapists and for their therapeutic work. Human rights workers most often did not put limits in their job. They worked long hours and did not take adequate care of their own problems and health. They postponed their personal needs because they were working in an "emergency" situation and apparently against something more important that their own lives. They lived with a threatening and traumatic perception of the present. The present was the dictatorship, and it was very difficult to imagine the future. The "future" referred only to the end of the dictatorship. Therapists lived this process of both internal and external pressures, mainly without any possibility of distancing themselves to think about it, and therefore, anxieties remained in the therapeutic teams without any legitimacy and possibility of facing them.

One of the teams' characteristics was personal isolation inside the team. This separation was aggravated by the need to protect sensitive and vulnerable collective ties. We had great difficulties discussing differences and facing conflicts because our main problem—accepting and recognizing our own limitations, anxieties, and impotence—was implicitly forbidden. We were dealing with an institutional and political situation in which omnipotence was an expression of "commitment"; it implied the denial of any kind of anxiety. We also had difficulties with aggressive feelings, as if they were a kind of legacy of the dictatorship inside the team. These intense anxieties and emotions coexisted with the dilemma shared by the opposition to the Pinochet regime: defining a method to end the dictatorship. This added another difficulty because intolerance appeared as a reaction against people who did not share the same political position. Nevertheless, the existence of the team depended on its cohesion. Under these conditions, to accept differences and to remain together appeared an impossible challenge. Therapists had political differences, and they projected anxieties and rage into their political differences. It seemed easier to discuss those differences than to confront feelings and anxieties. How can a team of therapists be protected if they express their bad feelings against one another and are not aware that such feelings are a consequence of dealing with political violence and death? This type of problem appeared clearly at the end of the military rule.

Therapists have also to deal with the anxieties and destructive feelings of patients. They were affected both by the patients' suffering and by political threats but were not aware of their own reactions as individuals or as members of a group. All those elements generated ambivalent feelings, which ranged from total omnipotence to total impotence, and which circulated among them without a real "holding," in the sense that Winnicott gave to this concept. Winnicott (1965, p. 240) referred to "the holding function" as the one between analyst and patient. He wrote that "this often takes the form of conveying in words, at the appropriate moment, something that shows that the analyst knows and understands the deepest anxiety that is being experienced, or that is waiting to be experienced."

SOCIAL AND POLITICAL SIGNALS IN THE FIELD OF HUMAN RIGHTS AFTER THE DICTATORSHIP

In most of the Latin American countries, the first steps in the political transition period have consisted of initiating discussions about truth, justice, social reparation, reconciliation, impunity, memory, and forgetting. To face the past abuses, "truth" had to be converted from what had been an officially sanctioned knowledge about what had happened into an actual knowledge of what had really occurred.

One of the most important things is to reestablish or build a fair political order (Zalaquett, 1990) that provides an ethical, political, and subjective framework for dealing with all of these problems in the long run. When torture and other repressive situations can be placed in their social and political context, societies are able to face the aftereffects not as private ones, but as the consequences of a repressive policy. Such a perspective allows the prevention of future similar outcomes.

Breaking the silence at the social level implies truth. The humiliation and pain produced by torture are not easy to put into words. As difficult as it is to talk about torture privately, it becomes an even larger problem when one tries to talk about it publicly because of people's unwillingness to listen, including the survivors.

The suffering of patients has been closely linked to a political "working through" of the human rights issues. This process involved three interrelated public tasks: public validation of "the truth" (i.e., that human rights violations had actually taken place), the setting up of measures of reparation,[3] and efforts to bring those accused of human rights violations to justice.

The elected government faced numerous difficulties in following human rights policies. The dictatorship had constrained the political transition with a new constitution that also increased the power of the military in politics. For many reasons, the processes of the indictment and trial of those accused of violations of human rights have been slow. Probably, trials and punishment will never occur because of the 1978 amnesty law and the lack of sufficient evidence, as well as the political restraints on the judiciary. This is a problem that will continue beyond the current government and will affect both patients and therapists.

Nevertheless, the Report of the National Commission of Truth and Reconciliation (1992) built a bridge between private suffering and social policies, when it tried to develop proposals for reparation. As the report notes, "During all these years, these testimonies, these pains, have been little listened too" (pp. 769–770). Now people offered testimony to official representatives who, for the first time, neither scoffed at it nor harassed the relatives for having brought it forward, and who, on the contrary, listened, were moved, and showed respect for the pain being exposed. This experience, as relatives said publicly and privately, has been a step toward healing.

For families of disappeared detainees, the uncertainty has become a permanent pain. For relatives who imagined or experienced somehow the torture of their dead loved ones, the pain is like a nightmare:

> "I could hear his sobs and screams of pain. When I stopped hearing them, I knew he had died."

> "When they took my father, they took my husband and me, too. A whole group that guarded me raped me. I never told my husband. It's been 15 years."

Each of these glimpses suggests that the entire life of those victims has been permanently affected. It implies a continuation of pain in the lives of the following generation: "Our children are different from the rest. We hid the truth for them so that they would not suffer, but then they

---

[3]This word is the translation of the Spanish word *reparación*, which has different meanings, such as compensation and an expiatory offering. Probably the English word *atonement* brings a better meaning of the intentions, if not of the results, of these measures. The real military power and the political limitations of the Aylwin government restricted the social and political impact of these reparation measures.

were pointed at in school for being the children of an executed prisoner (fusilado)." Survivors feel "like pariahs in our own land" (Americas Watch Report, 1991).

FINAL COMMENTS

How does the political reality affect healing of patients? Under the dictatorship, the continuation of disorders often corresponded to the adaptation to the threat, the fear, and the apparently open-ended character of the repression process. Therapists thought that the end of state terrorism would contribute significantly to the healing of their patients.

The experience with patients since March, 1990 and the character of the political transition has challenged therapists to go over their concept of trauma in depth and to revise their therapeutic aims. Nowadays, their objectives are more specific and more differentiated, oriented to particular psychodynamic processes as well as to family processes. More attention is paid to the pre-traumatic situations of the patients and to deeper-lying psychodynamic issues. Consequently, they have come to view the dictatorship within a broader context, focusing, for example, on themes such as authoritarianism and alienation in Chilean culture and history, as well as the roots of the political repression (Mishler, 1992).

All these elements have contributed to clarify their work at both clinical and psychosocial levels. They are more aware and concerned with the holding process (in the sense of Winnicott) of the therapists and the therapeutic team, including themselves as part of a complex psychosocial process linked to Chilean political and social history. However, the full psychological implications of the political transition for victims of human rights violations, and therapists dealing with these patients, are not yet clear. What is clear is that the political circumstances of transition will have consequences for patients and therapists alike a parallel psychological also political "working through" interacts to influence the therapeutic process.

ACKNOWLEDGMENTS. I am indebted to María Isabel Castillo, who contributed very clever observations to the first version of this paper. I am also indebted to Brian Loveman, who contributed his time and knowledge to refocus and rethink many ideas of this paper.

REFERENCES

Americas Watch Report. (1991). *Human rights and the "politics of agreements": Chile during President Aylwin's first year.* New York: Human Rights Watch.

Baranguer, M., Baranguer, W., & Mom, J. M. (1988). The infantile psychic trauma from us to Freud: Pure trauma, retroactivity and reconstruction. *International Journal of Psycho-Analysis, 69*, 113–128.

Becker, D., Castillo, M. I., Gómez, E., Kovalskys, J., & Lira, E. (1989). Subjectivity and politics: The psychotherapy of extreme traumatization in Chile. *International Journal of Mental Health, 18*, 80–97.

Bettelheim, B. (1981). *Sobrevivir: El Holocausto una generación después*. Barcelona: Ed. Crítica.

Castoriadis, C. (1975). *L'institution imaginaire de la societé* (The imaginary institution of the society). Paris: Du Seuil.

Cienfuegos, A. J., & Monelli, C. (1983). The testimony of political repression as a therapeutic instrument. *American Journal of Orthopsychiatry, 53*, 43–51.

Lira, E. (1988). Consecuencias psicosociales de la represión política en Chile (Psychosocial consequences of political repression in Chile). *Revista de Psicología de El Salvador, 28*, 143–159, El Salvador, UCA Editores.

Lira, E., & Weinstein, E. (Eds.). (1984). *Psicoterapia y represión política* (Psychotherapy and political repression). Mexico City: Siglo XXI Editores.

Lira, E., Becker, D., & Castillo, M. I. (1990). Psychotherapy with victims of political repression in Chile: A therapeutic and political challenge. In *Health services for the treatment of torture and trauma survivors*. Washington, DC: American Association for the Advancement of Sciences (AAAS).

Loveman, B. (1993). *Constitution of tyranny: Regimes of exception in Spanish America*. Pittsburgh, PA: University of Pittsburgh Press.

Martin Baró, I. (1984). Guerra y salud mental (War and mental health). *Estudios Centroamericanos (ECA), 429–430*, 503–514, San Salvador, El Salvador. See also *Writings of a liberation psychology*. Cambridge, MA: Harvard University Press, 1994, pp. 108–121.

Martin Baró, I. (1988). La violencia política y la guerra como causas del trauma psicosocial en El Salvador (Political violence and war as the causes of psychosocial trauma in El Salvador). *Revista de Psicología de El Salvador, 28*, 123–141. San Salvador, El Salvador: UCA Editores.

Martin Baró, I. (1989). *Prologue for the book "Derechos humanos: todo es según el dolor con que se mira"* (Human rights: Pain is in the eye of the beholder). Santiago, Chile: ILAS.

Martin Baró, I. (1990). Guerra y trauma psicosocial del niño salvaroreño (War and the psychosocial trauma of Salvadoran children). In *Psicología social de la guerra* (Social psychology of war, pp. 234–247). San Salvador, El Salvador: UCA Editores. See also *Writings of a liberation psychology*. Cambridge, MA: Harvard University Press, 1992, pp. 121–135.

Mishler, E. (1992, February 19). *Chile: The politics of therapy with victims of violence*. Department of Psychiatry, Harvard Medical School, Massachusetts Mental Health Center Grand Rounds. Conference manuscript.

National Commission of Truth and Reconciliation. (1992). *To believe in Chile: Summary of the Truth and Reconciliation Commission Report*. Santiago, Chile: Ministry of Foreign Affairs.

Weinstein, E., Lira, E., Becker, D., Castillo, M. I., Gomez, E., Neumann, E., et al. (1987). *Trauma, duelo y reparación* (Trauma, grief and reparation). Santiago Chile: FASIC Editorial Interamericana.

Winnicott, D. W. (1965). *The maturational processes and the facilitating environment*. London: Hogarth, New York: International Universities Press.

Zalaquett, J. (1990). Confronting human rights violations committed by former governments: Principles applicable and political constraints. In *Persona y Sociedad* (Vol. 6, No. 2–3). Santiago, Chile: ILADES.

8

Cultural Analysis of Findings on the Political Instability in the Philippines

ISABELITA Z. GUIAO

INTRODUCTION

The continuing incidence of political instability, conflict, or unrest worldwide has prompted me to investigate the effects of political instability, if any, on mental health. Because I was born, raised, and lived in the Philippines for over 25 years, and because my family lives there, I chose to do a study on the political instability in the Philippines in regard to its effects on the mental health of women.

The aim of this chapter is to analyze and to interpret the findings of a study of the impact of political instability on Filipino women from the viewpoint of Filipino culture. Essential in this endeavor is the combination of this general cultural analysis with a stress and coping theoretical perspective. First, I describe the political instability in the Philippines. The terms *political instability, political conflict,* and *political unrest* are used interchangeably. Then follows a brief presentation of the research and its findings. Subsequently, central findings of the study are presented, such as the important role of education and the considerable stress tolerance and resilience of the women. Finally, future recommendations for studies on political unrest in other areas of the world are examined.

ISABELITA Z. GUIAO • University of Texas, Health Science Center at San Antonio, San Antonio, Texas 78284-7951.
Beyond Trauma: Cultural and Societal Dynamics, edited by Rolf J. Kleber, Charles R. Figley, and Berthold P. R. Gersons. New York, Plenum Press, 1995.

POLITICAL INSTABILITY IN THE PHILIPPINES

The stressful condition studied was the 18-year political instability in the Philippines. Political instability is a state or condition characterized by events or situations indicating political unrest, for example, demonstrations, riots, frequent changes in government officials, war, and coups d'état (Feierabend & Feierabend, 1966). This condition is stressful because it creates demands that may exceed the resources of the people involved.

The Philippines was classified as a politically stable nation in the early 1960s (Feierabend & Feierabend, 1966). But since President Ferdinand Marcos declared martial law in 1972, the world has known the opposite about the Philippines (Ruiz, 1986). Political killings occurred almost daily from 1972 until Marcos was overthrown by the People Power Revolution in 1986 (Mercado, 1986). Many civilians, including suspected communist insurgents, were killed by the military, and some military persons were murdered for political reasons by civilians (Bacho, 1987). Protests, demonstrations, and rallies against Marcos's repressive dictatorship were staged frequently by students and non-students alike (Kessler, 1989). Every time local and national elections were held, cheating was rampant in order to keep Marcos and his men in office. It is generally known that Marcos got "reelected" as president of the Philippines in the national election of February 1986 because of fraud (U.S. Congress, 1987b).

Guerrilla warfare, in the form of communist-inspired insurgency, blossomed in the 1970s and 1980s in the fight for agrarian reforms and in the revolt against repression (Bacho, 1987; Kessler, 1989; Ruiz, 1987). Consequently, suspected and known communist leaders and inspirers were detained one after another until none of them could be seen in public anymore, as they sought refuge and hid in the mountains (Gregor, 1984). Noncommunistic leaders who were staunch opponents of Marcos were detained as well, if they did not choose political exile or stopped their open criticism (Raul Manglapus, personal communication, November 23, 1983). Torture and murder were commonly employed to punish those who insisted on democracy. The assassination in 1983 of Benigno Aquino, the number one critic and opponent of Marcos, is a case in point (Gregor, 1984; Ruiz, 1986).

Six coups d'état have been attempted from the time President Corazon Aquino took over the presidency in February 1986 until December 1989 (U.S. Congress, 1987a, 1991). Because of voluntary and involuntary resignations due to ideological conflicts, the Aquino cabinet went through frequent changes (U.S. Congress, 1987a).

In spite of Aquino's crusade for human rights protection, ambushes, mass gunning, and assassinations continued (Bacho, 1987; Ruiz, 1987). The assassinations of Jaime Ferrer, a cabinet man; Orlando Olalia, a national labor leader; and Leandro Alejandro, a leftist; and the massacre of peasant farmers while demonstrating—all made international news on this issue (White, 1989).

Between 1988 and 1991, the brutal murder of civilians was in the headlines in Philippine newspapers. A person would be murdered, and the body would be chopped into parts. The chopped parts were separated from the head and thrown in different places. The murderer and the motive for the murder were generally unknown.

Finally, the rebel situation in the Philippines needs to be noted. Peace talks and negotiations for a cease-fire with the communist rebels by the Aquino government failed (Bacho, 1987; Ruiz, 1986, 1987; U.S. Congress, 1988, 1991). The same applies to the Muslim rebel situation (Che Man, 1990; George, 1980; U.S. Congress, 1987b).

In conclusion, the quest for national survival and peace continues and remains to be a stressful process for many Filipinos. The general population is exposed continually to this environment. Political instability, given its stressful nature and worldwide incidence, poses a major challenge for researchers and health professionals to investigate and to be responsive to the ill effects, if any, of continued exposure to political unrest.

THE STUDY IN BRIEF

Assuming that political instability is stressful and can have negative effects on the mental health of those continually exposed to it, the theoretical perspective on cognitive appraisal and coping was used (Lazarus & Folkman, 1984) to formulate the research questions and to select the instruments. The stress and coping theory (Lazarus & Folkman, 1984) proposes that coping with stress is preceded by cognitive appraisal. Cognitive appraisal is an "evaluative process that determines why and to what extent a particular transaction or series of transactions between the person and the environment is stressful" (p. 19). Coping is defined as "the constantly changing cognitive and behavioral efforts to manage specific demands that are appraised as taxing to the person" (p. 141). Two modes of coping have been distinguished by Lazarus and his associates: (1) emotion-focused coping, which regulates emotional responses to the problem, and (2) problem-focused coping, which manages or alters the problem concerning the distress.

The central research questions were: (1) What is the degree of negative impact of political instability that Filipino women report? (2) What coping methods do Filipino women use to deal with the political instability in the Philippines? and (3) What are the relationships among negative appraisal of and coping with political instability, socio-demographic characteristics, depression, and the life satisfaction of Filipino women in the Philippines?

The instruments used were the Bryce Life Events Inventory (Bryce & Walker, 1986), the Jalowiec Coping Scale (Jalowiec, 1979), the Beck Depression Inventory (Beck, Rush, Shaw, & Emery, 1979), the Cantril Self-Anchoring Life Satisfaction Scale (Cantril, 1963), and the Guiao Socio-Demographic Data Questionnaire. The measures on the life events and coping were both modified to fit the needs of the study. To augment the Jalowiec Coping Scale (JCS), after its administration, for instance, an open-ended question was added: "In addition to the coping strategies listed in the coping scale, what other coping methods do you use to deal with the stress of the political event or situation that you identified?"

The foregoing noted scales are reported to have moderate to very satisfactory psychometric properties (Beck, Steer, & Garbin, 1988; Bryce & Walker, 1986; Cantril, 1963; George & Bearon, 1980; Jalowiec, Murphy, & Powers, 1984; Palmore & Kivett, 1977). They were determined to be culturally sensitive and lacking in cultural bias against Filipinos (Guiao, 1990, 1994). All instruments were researcher-administered in Tagalog, the national language of the Philippines.

Thirteen political events or situations characteristic of the political instability in the Philippines were mixed with the common life events listed in the Bryce Life Events Inventory (BLEI). These political events or situations were: (1) detention in jail; (2) street demonstrations; (3) family member being kidnapped; (4) someone you know being ambushed; (5) not being able to go out because of the political violence situation; (6) frequent changes in the president's advisers or department secretaries; (7) activities of government rebels; (8) the assassination or "liquidation" of important people or government officials; (9) rioting in your neighborhood or at your place of work; (10) coup d'état attempts; (11) not having a safe place to go during rioting or a coup d'état attempt; (12) fighting between the military and the communist insurgents (NPA or NLF); and (13) seeing or hearing people being brutally murdered (a murdered person's body was chopped into parts).

The separate negative impact of each event and the mean negative impact of all political events or situations on the life of the respondents were assessed through the BLEI. As part of the JCS, the respondent was asked to identify, from the list of 13 political events or situations, the one event or situation which she considered most stressful to her.

The purposive nonprobability sample consisted of Filipino women ($N = 200$), as women are generally known to be more vulnerable than men to the depressogenic effects of stress (Weismann, 1987). They were recruited from the general population. They were between 25 and 50 years old (mean age = 36), and 37% were married with children (mean number of children = 2.7). A large share of the respondents reported having a baccalaureate degree or more (49.5%). Some had at least some college credits (24%), and the rest had a high school diploma only (26.5%). The majority (50.5%) were in high-stability occupations, 10% were in medium-stability occupations, and 25% were in low-stability occupations. All were residents of the metropolitan area of Manila. None of the respondents reported having been a survivor of a potentially traumatic political event or a situation like jail detention, a kidnapping, a demonstration, a riot, a coup d'état-related injury, or a murder attempt.

The data were collected in June 1989 in Metro Manila, Philippines, the capital and center of government activities in the Philippines. The general condition of political instability is more visible and appreciated in Metro Manila than anywhere else in the country.

Data analysis was done with descriptive statistics to calculate the mean scores on the various measures. Stepwise multiple regression was used to identify the variables with the most predictive power on depression and life satisfaction. The qualitative data on the open-ended question on coping were content-analyzed.

MAIN STATISTICAL FINDINGS

The main statistical findings of the research can be summarized as follows (for an elaborated description of the results, see Guiao, 1990). First, descriptive statistics demonstrated that (1) the political instability in the Philippines had a mild negative impact on the respondents; (2) the respondents' depression was mild; (3) the primary coping style of the participants was problem-focused; and (4) the life satisfaction of the participants was moderate (see Table 1). Content analysis of the qualitative data on coping showed that the respondents used primarily problem-solving behavior.

Second, stepwise multiple regression showed *positive* relationships

Table 1. Mean Scores: Major Variables and Scales Used

Variable/scale	Mean	Std. dev.	Interpretation
1. Collective negative impact of *all* 13 indicators of political instability (modified Bryce Life Events Inventory)	1.5	.41	Mild negative impact
2. Affective-focused coping (AFC) (Modified Jalowiec Coping Scale)	59.4	10.8	Below the required AFC mean of > 75 to consider the sample as AFC users
3. Problem-focused coping (PFC) (modified Jalowiec Coping Scale)	45.5	9.6	Above the required PFC mean of ≥ 45 to consider the sample as PFC users
4. Depression (Beck Depression Inventory)	13.2	8.6	Mild depression
5. Life Satisfaction (Cantril Self-Anchoring Life Satisfaction Scale)	5.15	1.7	Moderate life satisfaction

between (1) annual individual income and life satisfaction; (2) educational achievement and life satisfaction; and (3) affective-focused coping and depression. A *negative* relationship was shown between (1) annual individual income and depression; (2) educational achievement and depression; (3) impact of "brutal murders" and life satisfaction; (4) impact of "frequent changes in the president's cabinet" and life satisfaction; and (5) problem-focused coping and depression (see Tables 2 and 3).

Table 2. Predictor Variables with Significant Regression Coefficients with Life Satisfaction

Predictor variables	B	Beta	T	Significance
Annual income of individual	2.54	.3	3.8	.0002
Educational achievement	.4	.22	2.7	.007
Frequent cabinet changes	−.26	−.15	−2.4	.02
Brutal murders in news	−.23	−.14	−2.2	.03

Table 3. Predictor Variables with Significant Regression Coefficients
with Depression

Predictor variables	B	Beta	T	Significance
Annual income of individual	−9.18	−.19	−2.5	.015
Educational achievement	−2.5	−.24	−3.1	.002
Affective-focused coping	.30	.38	4.9	<.0005
Problem-focused coping	−.19	−.21	−2.8	.006

AN INTERPRETATION FROM THE PERSPECTIVE OF FILIPINO CULTURE

In this section, the main findings are analyzed and interpreted from the perspective of the Filipino culture. Other perspectives beyond culture are also offered.

Analysis of the Descriptive Findings

The negative impact of the political instability in the Philippines was appraised to be mild. This is not surprising. Filipinos are known to have an existential belief system (Church, 1986) as evidenced by the frequent use of "pray and trust in God" to cope with political unrest. Indeed, trust in God has been identified as one of the strongest Filipino values (Porio, Lynch, & Hollnsteiner, 1978; Sechrest & Guthrie, 1978). This value is rooted in the teachings of Roman Catholicism, which has been the predominant religion in the Philippines since the Spaniards brought Christianity to the Philippines in 1521 (Agoncillo & Guerrero, 1977). Ninety percent of the participants reported being Roman Catholics. Existential beliefs, such as faith in God, may have a neutral effect on emotions and may enable individuals to create meaning and maintain hope in difficult situations (Lazarus & Folkman, 1984, p. 80).

Filipinos, women in particular, are adaptable and accepting of their environment (Bonifacio, 1977). Given the 18-year duration of political unrest in the country (at the time of the study), the respondents may have adapted well to a political state that had become a way of life. Finally, the appraisal of mild negative impact is consistent with the fact that the participants came from the general population, which had not been traumatically victimized by any of the political events or situations studied.

The finding that the respondents mainly use problem-focused coping supports reports that confrontive approaches predominate in some Filipinos' coping repertoire, exceeding fatalism and optimism (Guthrie, 1970; Sechrest & Guthrie, 1978). My findings are definitely contrary to previous reports about Filipinos that (1) they use blaming or blame shifting (Lapuz, 1974); (2) they endure problems with patience (Guthrie & Jacobs, 1966); (3) they are fatalistic rather than manipulative (Andres, 1981); (4) they function more in a receptive mode than in an active cognitive mode (Church, 1986); and (5) they are passive (Fernandez, 1989). Bulatao (1986) proposed that the Filipino is changing from being accepting to exerting control over his or her situation and future. The indices of political instability, such as riots, demonstrations, protests, coup d'état attempts, communist insurgency, and the people's revolution that brought President Marcos down, illustrate and support, indeed, that some Filipinos are not tolerant and will carry out even drastic means to resolve their problems and indicate their dissatisfaction. Further, the problem-focused coping finding supports the political and social consciousness activities of the Filipino middle class started in the late 1960s to the early 1970s by college students on school campuses.

The mild depression finding is consistent with reports on psychopathology in Filipinos (Duff & Arthur, 1967; Escudero, 1972; Lapuz, 1973; Sechrest, 1969), although it may be relatively high with regard to a group from the general population. Likewise, the moderate life-satisfaction finding supports the findings of previous life-satisfaction studies on Filipinos (Bulatao, 1973; Cantril, 1963). It is remarkable to note that my study's findings are similar to the findings of Cantril (1963) in a study that was conducted when the Philippines were still politically stable (Feierabend & Feierabend, 1966) and those of Bulatao (1973) in a study that was conducted about six months before the declaration of martial law by President Ferdinand Marcos in 1972. My study was conducted 18 years after the 1972 martial law was declared. Despite the decline in both political and economic stability in the Philippines since 1972, it appears that the mental health of some Filipinos relative to depression and life satisfaction had not decompensated.

Based on this study's findings on depression and life satisfaction, a highly relevant question can be formulated: What, then, protects Filipino women from severe depression and life discontent? To answer this question with scientific certainty would probably take another systematic study, but the following assumption can be stated here: The Filipino culture may be *protective* in nature. There are cultural reasons for this mild depression and moderate life satisfaction.

First, Filipinos are known to be receptive and accepting of their environment (Bonifacio, 1977). An environment that is stressful is not one that an individual can reverse quickly. The respondents had been exposed to this environment for at least 18 years. Some of them had not even known the Philippines when it had been better. They must have learned to deny, ignore, or accept the political environment because they had and/or knew of no effective means of changing or leaving it. To deny, ignore, or accept something that one cannot personally change or improve is not problem-focused coping. However, these non-problem-solving processes are appropriate and could be effective in preventing negative adaptational outcomes. Lazarus and Folkman (1984) proposed that, in general, affective-focused coping is more likely to occur following a secondary appraisal that nothing can be done to modify harmful, threatening, or challenging events.

Second, Filipinos have a strong cultural tendency to endure, suppress, or deny depression (Lapuz, 1973). The stress of political instability may be denied to maintain comfort and well-being. Likewise, depressed feelings may be denied to maintain a cheerful outlook on life, as optimism for the future is a valued cultural trait (Fernandez, 1989). Filipino women possess "inner strength" (Lantican, 1987, p. 275). This inner strength may enable women to focus on the good and ignore the bad to resist feeling depressed and dissatisfied with their lives.

Third, Filipinos value and pursue education in the belief that education will better their lot and will improve their place in society. Filipinos have a literacy rate of approximately 83% (Emmanuel, Pelaez, personal communication, 1987). Two findings in this study support this cultural value: (1) When asked about their aspirations in life, 65% of the respondents stated "having children complete college education"; this aspiration was ranked as the number one hope and aspiration, even higher than restoration of peace and order in the Philippines (Guiao, 1990). And (2) 49.5% of the 200 participants had at least a baccalaureate education, 24% had some college credits, and 26.5% had a high school education only. It has been found that more educated individuals have a wider social support network than do their less-educated counterparts (Griffith & Villavicencio, 1985; Ortiz & Arce, 1984). Social support has been repeatedly reported as mediating psychological distress (Hourani, Armenian, Zurayk, & Affifi, 1986; Murphy, 1977; Steinglass, De-Nour, & Shye, 1985). Thus, it can be conjectured that more educated people report being less depressed and dissatisfied with life than do their less-educated peers not because of their educational achievements, but because of their social networks. Filipinos, in general, are known for their extensive social support, irrespective of education, due to their group orientation and the valued and strong kinship system (Sechrest & Guthrie, 1978).

The fourth factor may be social desirability needs. Filipinos, like members of most cultures, present the best image possible. The collection of data through face-to-face interviews might have encouraged the reporting of information that would present or maintain a good image to the interviewer.

Analysis of the Regression Findings

The positive relationship between annual individual income (AII) and life satisfaction suggests that persons with higher personal incomes tend to be more satisfied with their lives. Because the direction of the relationship is unclear, it is also possible that persons with better life satisfaction tend to earn more. Perhaps because the Philippines has generally been economically depressed, Filipino women, whether single or married, customarily earn money either through other-employment or self-employment. They work to help the family "make both ends meet" and to save for a "rainy day." The AII mean is P19,726. which is a considerable contribution to the mean annual family income of P47,568. The U.S. dollar–Philippine peso exchange rate was approximately $1:P28 in 1989. The respondents must have been content with their respective incomes as these earnings were within the standard range of incomes for their occupations.

The positive association between educational achievement (EA) and life satisfaction suggests that the more schooling one has, the higher the life satisfaction may be. Filipinos, in general, believe that education is wealth because education *is* the means of getting a better-paying job. To have an education is also a status symbol in the Philippines. Parents aspire to and take pride in being able to send their children to school (Guiao, 1990). Because unemployment and underemployment are so high in the Philippines, only those prepared for jobs through college education can expect to have decent employment. Thus, education is highly valued and pursued in the Philippines. Life satisfaction is possibly elevated by realistic hopes of having a job and a higher income because of education. The positive relationship between EA and life satisfaction may also suggest that those with higher life satisfaction tend to achieve higher education.

Finally, it is to be noted that the strong positive relationship of annual individual income and educational achievement with life satisfaction may be due to the colinear effects of these two variables on life satisfaction. Because of this colinearity, it is uncertain which of these two variables is more important in predicting life satisfaction.

In the respondents, "frequent changes in President Aquino's cabinet" and the "news of unexplained brutal murders of civilians" were negatively associated with life satisfaction. Why? Perhaps because the Filipino's outlook in life is becoming more global and analytical (Bulatao, 1986) as to how extrapersonal forces affect his or her future. Constant shifts of government officials could be seen as detrimental to the welfare of the country, in general, and to the welfare of the citizens, in particular. Shaken optimism and faith in government due to perceptions of graft and corruption in the government could well demoralize those who are governed.

News of brutal murders is relatively new in Philippine daily life in comparison to riots, assassinations, and ambushes, which are "old" news. Because of the novelty and personal threat of the murders, they are played up by the media. The murders, therefore, are anxiety-producing to civilians, who think they cannot employ enough precautions to be safe. Events that can be negatively personalized can be more threatening (Lazarus & Folkman, 1984).

Of the 11 sociodemographic variables, personal income and education were found to have a negative relationship with depression. This finding suggests that persons with higher personal incomes and education tend to be less depressed than those with lower personal incomes and education. As the direction of the relationship is not clear, this finding may also suggest that euthymic individuals tend to acquire more education and money.

The high value Filipinos place on education and on family welfare may provide insight into this finding. Traditionally, Filipino parents take the full responsibility of sending their children to school from the elementary grades to college. Filipino children are socialized to acquire a college education and to have a stable job, help the family, and improve the family's lot. If the parents are wealthy, they fund every child's education; if not, they use every means possible to finance the firstborn child's college education. The firstborn child, after completion of a college degree, is expected to help with the family expenses and to help finance the secondborn sibling's education. When the secondborn gets a job after college, he or she takes responsibility for the thirdborn's college education. The expectation carries through until the lastborn child completes a college degree. This is how poor families in the Philippines get to have college-educated sons and daughters. It is then plausible to find educational achievement and personal income as antidepressant factors, despite a very stressful political environment, because these two factors promote and maintain self-esteem and self-respect. Because education and kinship are valued in the Philippines, they are cultural expectations, if not obligations, and once they are fulfilled, one feels very accomplished and can expect recognition by society.

Additionally, individuals with more education and income have more personal resources and therefore better access to more coping alternatives, when feeling distressed, to prevent or minimize depression. Finally, the possible colinear effects of education and personal income on life satisfaction should not be ignored.

The positive relationship between affective-focused coping (AFC) and depression suggests that women who mainly use AFC strategies tend to be more depressed and that those who use problem-focused coping (PFC) methods tend to be less depressed, as indicated by the negative relationship between PFC and depression. These findings support the Bryce and Walker (1986) study findings on the West Beirut political situation: (1) The use of an affective coping style was positively correlated with high levels of depression among West Beirut women, and (2) a problem-solving style was negatively associated with high levels of depression in the same women. Although neither problem-focused coping nor affective-focused coping is inherently better than the other (Folkman, 1982), the former type showed a mediating effect on depression in both the West Beirut (Bryce & Walker, 1986) and this study's samples. This finding strengthens the current notion that problem-focused coping is more associated with mental health than is affective-focused coping. Perhaps the mere employment of problem-oriented coping strategies, regardless of the outcome, mediates depression development, as an initiative to problem-solve promotes self-esteem and hope. Because the direction of the relationship between coping styles and depression is not clear, the findings may also suggest that women who are less depressed tend to employ PFC methods more frequently and those who are more depressed tend to use AFC methods more frequently.

GENERAL DISCUSSION AND CONCLUSION

The interaction between stress and coping is indeed complex. Diversities in the appraisal of a situation and coping possibilities influence the outcomes of coping, which may vary from one individual, group, and/or community to another.

In this study, the assumption that stress does not always produce distress (Selye, 1976) was validated. Negated was the proposition that exhaustion, the third stage of the general adaptation syndrome, follows the stage of resistance to continued exposure to stress (Selye, 1976). Rather, stress tolerance or resistance may increase as the individual becomes coping-proficient, so that she or he is more resilient and hardy in dealing with constant hardships and therefore in achieving comfort and balance.

The stress tolerance of the Filipino women studied was considerable, as evidenced by the mild depression and moderate life satisfaction findings in the midst of political and economic instability. Two factors in the political conflict may have facilitated building up stress tolerance: (1) the familiarity of the situation and (2) the universality (shared experience) of the political environment. Being used to a (familiar) situation allows for a less complex view of the situation; it is thus easier to manage. If the situation is difficult to manage in spite of its familiarity, it becomes an opportunity for the individual to develop hardiness and resiliency. A universally shared difficult situation is less likely to be personalized, so that the individual accepts the situation more readily. Acceptance promotes adaptation to stress, although it does not decrease the problem that causes the stress.

Finally, the influence of culture on stress and coping is significant in the context of adaptational outcomes. Culture-bound means of coping may mediate illness and may protect communities from feeling general discontent and unhappiness.

RECOMMENDATIONS FOR FUTURE STUDY

There are three reasons that warrant this final section of the paper. First, the cultural perspective used to analyze and make the findings understandable may be too simplistic for the complexity of the questions studied. Second, this study was exploratory; it does not clarify what was discovered, nor does it give all the possible answers. And third, several questions came to mind after the analysis of the results of the study. The following questions are proposed for further study.

1. If this study were to be replicated in Somalia, Bosnia-Herzegovina, Rwanda, Haiti, and Cambodia, to name a few currently politically unstable regions, would the results vary because of cultural differences? What factors besides culture would make the results different? Assuming that the cultures in these places are different, different results may be expected. The apparent severity of the political unrest in these places, as evidenced by war and the presence of famine, point to

traumatic stress. The presence of famine is a confounding variable that may seriously influence the results. The relative youth of the political conflict in these regions (in comparison to the Philippine situation) would also affect the results.

2. The results of this study may not have to do with culture. They may have to do with the gender of the respondents. Or they may be related to both the culture and the gender of the respondents. Would the results vary if men were the target population? I believe so, but only on the outcome variables of depression and life satisfaction. Men would score similarly on the relationship between coping, depression, life satisfaction, education, and personal income. However, Filipino men would score much lower on depression and life satisfaction because they are more stoic and less emotional than Filipino women and because of their strong provider role. My personal anecdotal observations suggest that Filipino husbands in the Philippines are less content with their lives than are their spouses.

3. What is the role of religious behavior? When does a victim start praying, and what does he or she pray for? How does religious behavior such as praying mediate traumatic stress? "Pray, trust in God" is an affective-focused coping item in the coping measure used and was reported as almost always used as a coping behavior by all the respondents in the study. The following propositions about "praying" are submitted for support and validation: (a) Praying presumes a belief and faith in a supernatural power who or which can keep or change the situation about which one is praying; (b) it involves asking the supernatural power to keep one in a desirable state or to change an undesirable condition; (c) the victim of traumatic stress starts praying as soon as he or she recognizes a threat of danger; (d) victims pray for different things at different stages of the general adaptation syndrome (Selye, 1976); in the alarm stage, the victim prays for the "unreality" of the threat of danger; in the resistance stage, the victim prays for personal safety, situation reversal, and/or the situation not to get worse; and in the exhaustion stage, the victim prays to be kept alive or to bear or end pain and suffering; and, finally, (e) praying mediates stress because it provides hope, which allows one to hold on and to continue resisting.

4. What is the role of optimism? Can it be measured? This study showed the resilience of women in circumstances of political unrest. Optimism has been described as "an inclination to put the most favorable construction upon actions and events or to anticipate the best possible outcome" (Merriam-Webster, 1984, p. 829). To be optimistic requires being both realistic and hopeful about a problem situation. It mediates traumatic stress because problem-solving strategies are in-

volved in an optimistic outlook. It presupposes that the problem has been appraised and that all possible interventions have occurred, but because there is no assurance of problem resolution from the interventions, the individual can only hope for positive results. Personality factors may also influence optimism about a difficult situation. One approach to developing a measure of optimism would be to present a vignette video of a problem situation to a group of research participants, then to ask the participants to list and describe all the factors that made them feel optimistic or not optimistic about the situation. Responses should be content-analyzed, and themes or categories of responses should be developed from the content analysis. From here, a series of reliability and validity tests of the instrument should follow to develop a reliable and valid quantitative measure of optimism.

5. What measures are there to quantify denial, minimizing, dissociation, hardiness, and endurance as coping processes? There is a well-known measure of hardiness (Kobasa, 1983), but there are not published instruments that measure the other concepts.

6. What does it mean for women in other cultures to have an education and their own personal income? Which one of these variables is more important to women and why? Which variable is more predictive of women's mental health? Having an education and having one's own personal income have different meanings to women in diverse cultures. It may therefore be proposed that education, more than personal income, would be predictive of women's mental health in general.

In sum, although conjectural at this point, the role and significance of culture as a buffer to the potential negative impact of political instability in a country on its citizens are underscored. For the sake of science and its goal of providing direction to those who use the knowledge embodied in it, further validation of the buffering effects of culture on stress is in order.

REFERENCES

Agoncillo, T., & Guerrero, M. (1977). *History of the Filipino people*. Quezon City: R. P. Garcia.

Andres, T. D. (1981). *Understanding Filipino values: A management approach*. Quezon City: New Day.

Bacho, P. (1987). Rural revolt in the Philippines: Threats of stability. *Journal of International Affairs, 40*(20), 257–270.

Beck, A. T., Rush, A. J., Shaw, B. F., & Emery, G. (1979). *Cognitive therapy of depression*. New York: Guilford Press.

Beck, A. T., Steer, R. A., & Garbin, M. G. (1988). Psychometric properties of the Beck depression inventory: Twenty-five years of evaluation. *Clinical Psychology Review, 8,* 77–100.

Bonifacio, M. F. (1977). An exploration into some dominant features of Filipino social behavior. *Philippine Journal of Psychology, 10*(1), 29–36.

Bryce, J., & Walker, N. (1986). *Family functioning and child health: A study of families in West Beirut.* Final Report to UNICEF.

Bulatao, J. C. (1986). *Another look at Philippine values.* Unpublished paper.

Bulatao, R. A. (1973). Measures of happiness among Manila residents. *Philippine Sociological Review, 21,* 229–238.

Cantril, H. (1963). A study of aspirations. *Scientific American, 208*(2), 41–45.

Che Man, W. K. (1990). *Muslim separation: The Moros of southern Philippines and the Malays of southern Thailand.* Singapore: Oxford University Press.

Church, A. T. (1986). *Filipino personality: A review of research and writings.* Manila: De La Salle University Press.

Duff, D. F., & Arthur, R. J. (1967). Between two worlds: Filipinos in the U.S. Navy. *American Journal of Psychiatry, 123,* 836–848.

Escudero, M. M. (1972). Mental disorders in a Philippine community: An epidemiological survey. In W. P. Lebra (Ed.), *Transcultural research in mental health* (pp. 137–147). Honolulu: University Press of Hawaii.

Feierabend, I. K., & Feierabend, R. L. (1966). Aggressive behaviors within polities, 1948–1962. *Journal of Conflict Resolution, 10,* 249–272.

Fernandez, D. G. (1989). *What's wrong and what's right with the Filipino?* Unpublished paper.

Folkman, S. (1982). An approach to the measurement of coping. *Journal of Occupational Behavior, 3,* 95–107.

George, L., & Bearon, L. (1980). *Quality of life in older persons: Measuring and measurement.* New York: Human Services Press.

George, T. J. S. (1980). *Revolt in Mindanao: The rise of Islam in Philippine politics.* Kuala Lumpur: Oxford University Press.

Gregor, A. J. (1984). *Crisis in the Philippines: A threat to U.S. interests.* Washington, DC: Ethics and Public Policy Center.

Griffith, J., & Villavicencio, S. (1985). Relationships among acculturation, socio-demographic characteristics and social supports in Mexican-American adults. *Hispanic Journal of Behavioral Science, 7*(1), 75–92.

Guiao, I. Z. (1990). *Filipino women's morale and mood: Their relationships with appraisal of and coping with the political instability in the Philippines.* Ann Arbor, MI: University Microfilms.

Guiao, I. Z. (1994). Predictors of mental health in women of a politically unstable country, the Philippines. *Health Care for Women International, 15*(3), 197–211.

Guthrie, G. M. (1970). *The psychology of modernization in the rural Philippines.* Quezon City: Ateneo de Manila University Press.

Guthrie, G. M., & Jacobs, P. J. (1966). Child rearing and personality development in the Philippines. University Park: The Pennsylvania State University Press.

Hourani, L. L., Armenian, H., Zurayk, H., & Affifi, L. (1986). A population-based survey of loss and psychological distress during war. *Social Science and Medicine, 23*(3), 269–275.

Jalowiec, A. (1979). *Stress and coping in hypertensive and emergency room patients.* Master's thesis, University of Illinois, Chicago.

Jalowiec, A., Murphy, S. P., & Powers, M. J. (1984). Psychometric assessment of the Jalowiec coping scale. *Nursing Research, 33,* 157–161.

Kessler, R. J. (1989). *Rebellion and repression in the Philippines.* New Haven, CT: Yale University Press.

Kobasa, S. C. (1983). Type A and hardiness. *Journal of Behavioral Medicine, 42,* 168–177.

Lantican, L. S. M. (1987). Social support among Filipino pregnant women in an atmosphere of socioeconomic political uncertainty. *Health Care for Women International, 8*(4), 261–276.

Lapuz, L. V. (1973). *A study of psychopathology.* Quezon City: University of the Philippines Press.

Lapuz, L. V. (1974). The changing Filipino personality. *Philippine Journal of Mental Health, 5*(2), 97–99.

Lazarus, R. S., & Folkman, S. (1984). *Stress, appraisal and coping.* New York: Springer.

Mercado, M. A. (1986). *People power: The Philippine revolution of 1986.* Manila: James B. Reuter, S. J. Foundation.

Merriam-Webster. (1984). *Webster's ninth new collegiate dictionary.* Springfield, MA: Author.

Murphy, J. M. (1977). War stress and civilian Vietnamese: A study of psychological effects. *Acta Psyhciatrica Scandinavia, 72,* 92–108.

Ortiz, V., & Arce, C. (1984). Language orientation and mental health status among persons of Mexican descent. *Hispanic Journal of Behavioral Science, 6*(2), 127–143.

Palmore, E., & Kivett, J. (1977). Change in life satisfaction: A longitudinal study of persons aged 46–70. *Journal of Gerontology, 32,* 311–316.

Porio, E., Lynch, F., & Hollnsteiner, M. R. (1978). *The Filipino family, community, and nation: The same yesterday, today, and tomorrow?* (IPC Paper No. 12). Quezon City: Ateneo de Manila University Press.

Ruiz, L. E. J. (1986). Philippine politics as a people's quest for authentic political subjecthood. *Alternatives, 11*(4), 505–534.

Ruiz, L. E. J. (1987). On the post-Marcos transition and popular democracy. *World Policy Journal, 4*(2), 333–351.

Sechrest, L. (1969). Philippine culture, stress, and psychopathology. In W. Caudill & Y. T. Lin (Eds.), *Mental health research in Asia and the Pacific* (pp. 306–333). Honolulu: East–West Center Press.

Sechrest, L., & Guthrie, G. M. (1978). Psychology of, by and for Filipinos. In V. Enriquez (Ed.), *Readings in Filipino personality: A preliminary compilation* (pp. 397–418). Manila: Centro Escolar University Graduate School.

Selye, H. (1976). *The stress of life.* Philadelphia: McGraw-Hill.

Steinglass, P., De-Nour, A. K., & Shye, S. (1985). Factors influencing psychological adjustment and forced geographical relocation: The Israeli withdrawal from the Sinai. *American Journal of Orthopsychiatry, 55*(4), 513–528.

U.S. Congress House of Representatives Committee on Foreign Affairs Subcommittee on Asian and Pacific Affairs. (1987a). *Implications of recent developments in the Philippines: Hearing before the Subcommittee on Asian and Pacific Affairs of the Committee on Foreign Affairs, House of Representatives, Ninety-Ninth Congress, Second Session, December 1, 1986.* Washington, DC: U.S. Government Printing Office.

U.S. Congress House of Representatives Committee on Foreign Affairs Subcommittee on Asian and Pacific Affairs. (1987b). *Philippine elections: Hearing before the Subcommittee on Asian and Pacific Affairs of the Committee on Foreign Affairs, House of Representatives, One Hundredth Congress, First Session, May 19, 1987.* Washington, DC: U.S. Government Printing Office.

U.S. Congress House of Representatives Committee on Foreign Affairs Subcommittee on Asian and Pacific Affairs. (1988). *The current situation in the Philippines: Hearing before the Subcommittee on Asian and Pacific Affairs of the Committee on Foreign Affairs, House of Representatives, One Hundredth Congress, First Session, December 2, 1987.* Washington, DC: U.S. Government Printing Office.

U.S. Congress House of Representatives Committee on Foreign Affairs Subcommittee on Asian and Pacific Affairs. (1991). *The situation in the Philippines: Hearing before the Subcommittee on Asian and Pacific Affairs of the Committee on Foreign Affairs, House of Representatives, One Hundredth First Congress, Second Session, January 30, 1990.* Washington, DC: U.S. Government Printing Office.

Weismann, M. M. (1987). Advances in psychiatric epidemiology: Rates and risks for major depression. *American Journal of Public Health, 77,* 445–451.

White, M. (1989). *Aquino.* London: Word Publishing.

9

Psychotherapeutic Work with Refugees

GUUS VAN DER VEER

INTRODUCTION

In 1986, the author of this chapter started to work as a psychotherapist at the Social Psychiatric Service for Refugees[1] in Amsterdam, Netherlands. The staff of this service had years of experience with the use of psychotherapeutic techniques with refugees, but very little of it had been documented. Therefore, the author started to make reports of all therapeutic interviews he conducted, and to collect written material about the problems of refugees and other victims of trauma and the experiences in treating them. At the same time, the author consulted a selection of the available literature on psychology and psychiatry to find possibilities for making extrapolations that could help to enlarge the insight into the problems of refugees. The confrontation between the author's six years of practical experience,[2] the knowledge he found in the professional

---

[1]Now the Pharos Foundation, Health Service for Refugees, Department of Mental Health.
[2]The practical experience was described in reports of 3,387 therapeutic sessions, divided over 120 clients of 20 different nationalities, with very divergent cultural, religious, and ideological backgrounds.

GUUS VAN DER VEER • Pharos Foundation, Health Service for Refugees, Department of Mental Health, Prins Hendrikkade 120, 1011 AM Amsterdam, The Netherlands.
Beyond Trauma: Cultural and Societal Dynamics, edited by Rolf J. Kleber, Charles R. Figley, and Berthold P. R. Gersons. New York, Plenum Press, 1995.

literature, and the knowledge and experience he encountered in numerous discussions with colleagues working in the same or a closely related field resulted in a body of practical know-how[3] (Van der Veer, 1992, 1993).

In this chapter, the reader will be introduced to this know-how through the discussion of three main assumptions:

1. For refugees, traumatization is not a relatively isolated incident or set of events, but a cumulative, ongoing process.
2. Overcoming cultural differences is an important ingredient in working with traumatized refugees.
3. Psychotherapy with refugees is a matter not of inventing completely new techniques, but of creatively adjusting a variety of existing techniques. However, psychotherapy with refugees makes special demands on the professional attitude of the psychotherapist.

TRAUMATIZATION AS A CUMULATIVE ONGOING PROCESS

For refugees, traumatization is usually not a specific traumatic event in the sense of an isolated incident or a set of events which have left painful scars. More often, it is an enduring, cumulative process that continues during exile because of distinct new events, both in the native country and in the country of exile. It is a chain of traumatic and stressful experiences that confront the refugee with utter helplessness and interfere with her or his personal development over an extended period of time.

---

[3]This practical know-how includes (a) an overview of the diverging traumatic events that refugees report (e.g., political repression, detention, torture, terror, battlefield experiences, disappearance of relatives and friends, separation and loss of families and friends, hardships during the flight or in refugee camps, and exile and (b) descriptions of behavioral and emotional reactions to these traumatic experiences—analyzed in terms of diverging theoretical approaches, discussed in relation to various individual characteristics (e.g., commitment to an ideology or the presence or absence of protective factors) and transformed in lists of relevant diagnostic questions—as well as information about their reactions to being uprooted from their familiar surroundings and having to adapt to a new and different cultural environment; (c) concrete descriptions of techniques useful in counseling and psychotherapeutic work with refugees; (d) notes on the prescription of psychotropic medication; (e) discussions of the problems of special groups of refugees, like children, adolescents, and both male and female victims of sexual violence, and (f) a discussion of the consequences of working with refugees for the helping professional.

A typical example is the following case. A client reported that he first was arrested and tortured; during his detention, he witnessed the execution of his father; later, he underwent a mock execution; after three years of hardships in prison, he escaped; after his escape, he went into hiding for three month while living in constant fear; during the flight from his country, he suffered from hunger and cold; in exile, he received the news that his sister had died; and later, he suffered very much from receiving a negative answer on his request for political asylum. Detention and torture took place while the client was 16 years old. When he was seen by the therapist, he was 22. His main complaints were intrusive memories of traumatic experiences, panic attacks, and nightmares. During the therapeutic interviews, it became apparent that this client, regarding the development of social cognition and the self-concept, was functioning partly at an early-adolescent level. Also, he seemed to have a problem in dealing with his aggressive impulses, which made him feel as if he had become a different person.

Refugees suffering from posttraumatic symptoms often attribute their suffering primarily to recent events that have been experienced as traumatic (e.g., a racist incident, a negative answer to their request for asylum, receiving bad news from their native country, insufficient housing conditions, failure to get a job, or not succeeding in making friends in the country of exile). Only a minority of them mention a change in their character resulting from less recent traumatic experience (by saying something like, "I have become weaker," "I have become very impatient," "I became a bad person"). Later, it may become clear that the recent experiences that most refugees see as the main cause of their suffering, on top of being unpleasant and stressful in themselves, have brought back memories of traumatic experiences of a less recent date. The recent events then seem to be interpreted as proof of the refugee's implicit conviction that his or her flight has brought neither freedom nor an end to suffering resulting from organized violence, but a never-ending accumulation of hardships and pain.

R., a 28-year-old refugee from an African country, had been detained for political reasons and tortured. After his release, he was conscripted for military service. He was sent to the front in an ethnic civil war and witnessed many bloody scenes and atrocities. During the two years he spent at the front, he saw many of his buddies die. In his first interview with the therapist, he complained about being depressed and fearing a loss of control over his suicidal ideation. At first, he mentioned an immediate cause for his complaints: He had been denied admission to three different institutes of education on grounds he considered unjust. He was unemployed and felt that all possibilities of giving his life meaning had been obstructed. In the discussion that followed, he mentioned that he had experienced a similar feeling in his native country, at the time that his education had been interrupted by his detention and forced military service. He said that his flight had not given him any relief but had resulted only in a prolongation of his suffering from frustrating and painful experiences; the only difference was that, in Europe, the pain was not inflicted by brute force, but by more sophisticated forms of humiliation and discrimination.

UPROOTING

In addition to traumatization, refugees have experienced uprooting: the experience of being forced to leave one's familiar surroundings and to settle in a new and unfamiliar environment for an indefinite period. Uprooting brings additional, ongoing stress because it involves at least three forms of loss (cf. Coelho, 1982):

1. The loss of love and respect experienced in the relationships with family and friends; this may include, for instance, the loss of respect that was experienced in connection with companions in distress during detention and combat.
2. The loss of social status, which may be accompanied by discrimination; in the country of exile, most refugees have to start at the bottom of society. The students among them also experience a decline in social status through a decline in their academic achievements due to language difficulties and the necessity of adapting to a different educational system from the one they were used to, which often does not recognize the diplomas achieved in the native country. Also, refugees requesting assistance from a therapist take the risk of losing the respect of their compatriots just because they are seeing a mental health professional.
3. The loss of a familiar social environment, with its mutual obligations and dependencies, which gave meaning to life. This loss is experienced, for instance, through the ignorance and lack of interest of the people in the country of exile with regard to the situation in the refugee's country.

Uprooting can cause various long-lasting adjustment problems, such as language problems, problems in adjustment to alien cultural values, and homesickness.

PHASES IN THE EXPERIENCES OF REFUGEES

Analogous to the way in which Keilson (1979) distinguished three phases in the traumatization experienced by Dutch Jewish children during and after World War II, the experiences of refugees can be ordered by distinguishing three phases:

1. The phase of increasing political repression.
2. The phase of major traumatic experiences, including experiences like detention, torture, terror, combat experiences, the disappearance of relatives or friends, and hardships suffered during escape or in refugee camps. These experiences are connected with a variety of emotional reactions, including guilt and self-blame, mortal fear, disgust, bereavement, the feeling of having been deceived, and anger.
3. The phase of exile, including stressful experiences such as receiving bad news from the native country, difficulties in cultural adjustment, language problems, social isolation, uncertainty related to the request for political asylum, and problems in finding housing or work.

OVERCOMING CULTURAL DIFFERENCES

Unfamiliar, Diverging Cultural Backgrounds

Therapy with refugees often entails meeting people from cultural backgrounds with which the therapist is not familiar. Therapists have to face the fact that they cannot be sure in which way and how much the specific cultural background of a refugee has influenced her or his personality development. Also, therapists are not sure how culturally determined differences in family life and child development may be reflected in specific ways of coping with stress, specific psychological problems, or specific forms of transference. On the other hand, there is no reason to let oneself be intimidated by cultural differences in personal development as long as there are strong indications that, above all cultural differences, the needs, the feelings, and the vulnerabilities we experience as people are the same the world over.

Everyone who seeks assistance for mental problems would like to be treated by an expert whom he or she considers trustworthy (cf. Pederson, 1981). But the criteria by which someone is judged an expert and trustworthy are not the same in all cultures. The same is true of specific therapeutic techniques: What is considered useful and credible in one culture may be thought of as stupid or immoral in another culture. On the other hand, sometimes, a refugee has more confidence in the helping professional because the latter belongs to a different culture. For instance, the refugee may think the professional is more objective, more trustworthy, or better educated.

The therapist has to be attentive to cultural differences and flexible in the use of therapeutic techniques. For instance, therapists who want to use the discussion of dreams as a therapeutic technique must inform themselves of the ways in which dreams are interpreted in the refugee's cultural background.

Beliefs about Mental Problems and Their Treatment

Because of this difference in cultural background, helping refugees means also dealing with the condition of refugees having divergent ideas about mental problems and the way they should be treated. The kind of help a Western therapist can offer to a refugee does not always correspond to what a doctor or healer in the refugees own culture can offer (Kinzie, 1978). For example, the refugee may expect to be cured quickly. The idea that the complaints will disappear if the refugee learns more about himself or herself through a long series of talks is both strange and difficult to comprehend.

In the eyes of the Western therapist, the distinction between "madness" and "normality" may be much less strict than it generally is in some African or Asian culture (Kortmann, 1986). Some refugees come from cultures where visiting a psychiatrist is a proof of madness.

Beliefs about the Causes of Illnesses

There are also cultural differences in the causes people ascribe to illnesses. For instance, in Cambodian culture, illness is thought to be the consequence of coming into contact with dangerous spirits, witchcraft, or sorcery (Eisenbruch & Handelman, 1989). The same belief is found in India (Srinivasa & Trivedi, 1982), in some Caribbean cultures (Cancelmo, Millán & Vasquez, 1990), and in some African cultures. Occasionally, this kind of explanation may be mentioned by refugees. However, it is the author's experience that traumatized refugees do not usually have much trouble in considering the idea that there may be a relationship between their symptoms and their traumatic experiences.

Moreover, cultural differences are present in the ideas people have about the cause of traumatic experiences. In this connection Mollica and Son (1988) reported that Cambodian refugees who have been tortured relate the torture to the Buddhist concept of *karma*. Because of their karma, they feel responsible for their suffering. This view is opposed by the Western conception that torture is something done to the individual for political reasons. More generally speaking, it is important for the therapist to understand the cultural framework within which certain symptoms are evaluated, as well as the causal explanations implicit in any cultural framework (Lee & Lu, 1989).

Differences in Manifest Behavior

Refugees from non-Western cultures may express their complaints in a manner unfamiliar to the Western therapist. The psychiatrist Giel (1984) described the moaning and sighing of patients in an Addis Ababa outpatient department. Initially, he found this behavior theatrical, but his interpreter was impressed by the patients' suffering. Further investigation revealed that these patients were not suffering from a hysteric complaint but were really sick. Giel concluded, "The generally reserved Ethiopian apparently loses his armour of impassivity during illness" (p. 40).

The same apparently theatrical behavior can also be observed sometimes in refugees, especially those who have gone into exile recently.

Differences in Norms

In addition, the refugee may be accustomed to different norms relating to what counts as morally responsible or healthy behavior, for example, with regard to taking care of relatives (e.g., refugees from the Middle East often have a negative opinion of adolescents who want to live independently of their parents, or of adults who allow their elderly parents to go to a nursing home) or to sexuality. In such cases, it is useful to explore these norms (cf. Agger, 1988; Brown, 1986).

> A. O., a 25-year-old refugee from the Middle East, was very worried about his younger brother, who had come into exile with him and for whom he felt responsible. He had caught his brother masturbating and was worried about the consequences for his health. The therapist asked A. O. what he thought about the physical consequences of masturbation and how he viewed it morally. Also, the therapist explained that research in the West had shown masturbation to be a common form of sexual behavior. It was seen as preparation for other forms of sexuality, and the majority of the population did not view masturbation as morally objectionable.

Readiness to Talk about Personal Matters with a Stranger

Another cultural difference directly influencing contact with the therapist is a readiness to talk about personal matters with someone outside the family. Kabela (n.d.) reported that Chinese and other East Asian patients, like those from the Middle East, are not used to talking about feelings of dejection or loneliness, or about sexual problems, because they feel guilty or are ashamed. In some cultures—Japan, for example—personal feelings are discussed, but only through symbolic terms derived from nature, such as *rain, dark, misty, cloudy* (Kabela, n.d.). Denley (1987) noted that refugees from Indochinese cultures mask their personal suffering by politeness and smiles. In general, Asian clients often seem to avoid expressing their emotions. They tend to express psychic distress through physical complaints. In the first contacts, the therapist may mistakenly perceive them as passive; this passivity, however, should be seen as a cultural expression of respect for authority (Tsui & Schultz, 1985).

According to the author's observations, people from Middle Eastern countries may begin by talking about trivial matters, even a bit tediously, before they are ready to discuss what is really bothering them. Therefore, an inexperienced or impatient therapist may underestimate the seriousness of their problems.

> V. S., a refugee from a Middle Eastern country, started the first interview with a lengthy and minute discussion of last week's weather report. The therapist listened for a while and then mentioned that V. S.'s family doctor had called him, saying that V. S. was suffering from nightmares and panic attacks. V. S. reacted by amply discussing the abilities of his family doctor, which he considered outstanding, even more if one took into account that this doctor was a woman with a colored skin. The therapist confirmed that the family doctor was a good one and then asked about the frequency of the nightmares and the ways in which V. S. usually reacted to having them. Only after half an hour was he able to discuss the content of the nightmares.

Gifts

Another cultural difference has to do with donating gifts. In some cultures, it is normal for the client to give the therapist small gifts. Some refugees maintain this habit in their contacts with Western therapists. If the latter are not in the habit of accepting gifts, they will have to make this clear in a tactful manner.

Corrective Feedback or Adjustment from the Therapist

Corrective feedback from the therapist can help the refugee to understand what kinds of behavior are acceptable or unacceptable in particular situations (De Anda, 1984). In some situations, however, it is desirable for the therapist to conform to the expectations of the client.

> B. O., an Islamic refugee, always drank a cup of coffee during the weekly therapeutic sessions. During ramadan, the therapist offered him his usual cup of coffee, but he refused. The therapist asked B. O. about how he

celebrated Ramadan and, as a result, did not offer B. O. any more coffee that month.

It is important for the therapist to be continuously aware of the communication problems that may arise as the result of cultural differences. For example, the therapist should be aware that people from particular cultures (e.g., Micronesian), and under certain conditions, may experience eye contact as threatening or disrespectful.

Sometimes, the therapist may decide to accommodate a bit to the refugee. For example, the therapist may consider how her or his clothing will be viewed by refugees from various cultural backgrounds (cf. Vontress, 1981) or may examine the magazine covers in the waiting room from the point of view of an orthodox Muslim.

Recognizing Misunderstandings

In the author's experience, a therapist cannot always recognize when a misunderstanding has arisen. The consequence may be that the refugee interrupts treatment. Whenever a refugee misses an appointment, the therapist should inquire into whether some communication problem may exist without his or her being aware of it. In such cases, the misunderstanding is sometimes cleared up if the therapist takes the trouble to invite the refugee to come again by phoning her or him, for example, or writing a personal letter.

Whatever the cultural background of the refugee, however, there is no need for the therapist to bargain his or her professional attitude. Genuine interest, respect, and tolerance of the anxiety in the client are basic conditions for counseling and therapy. Of course, the therapist has to make sure these features are recognized by the refugee, and this may be more difficult as a consequence of language problems and cultural misunderstanding.

Final Remarks on Cultural Differences

The importance of the cultural factor in communication problems with refugees should not be overestimated. Communication problems may have diverging causes, of which cultural differences are only an example. One cannot avoid communication problems with refugees through merely informing oneself about their various cultural backgrounds.

Moreover, culture should not be conceived of as a complete package of meanings fully determining all behavior and thinking of any individual who grew up in this culture (cf. Knudsen, 1991). An alternative is understanding cultural background as one of the factors contributing to the process of the identity development in each individual refugee. Meeting a refugee does not mean that one encounters a sort of representative of an exotic world; rather, one meets an individual with a personal identity. The communication problems that the therapist may encounter while working with this individual should be analyzed in relation to the unique personality of this individual.

ADJUSTING THERAPEUTIC TECHNIQUES

On the level of treatment techniques (cf. Sundberg, 1981), the therapist should be careful in using a nondirective approach. Many refugees are unfamiliar with this approach and misinterpret it as a sign of inadequacy or a lack of interest. More generally, it is important that the therapist take the time to explain again and again how her or his treatment works, why she or he is asking certain questions, what she or he expects from the refugee, and so on. In this connection, therapists and counselors may compare their services to those of a bank. Although at first it may seem complicated to explain all the ins and outs of plastic cards and PIN codes, most refugees learn how to cash a check. And it does not usually make much difference whether the employee of the bank is white or black, male or female.

DEVELOPING CULTURAL EMPATHY

In order to overcome communication problems resulting from cultural differences, the therapist must become informed about cultural differences in order to develop cultural empathy (Dahl, 1989). On the other hand, the therapist has to be aware that cultural sensitivity may become cultural stereotyping when the therapist underestimates the individual differences between people from the same culture.

The helping professional can inform herself or himself about the cultural background of refugees by studying anthropological and other relevant sources about the cultures in question, or by contacting local experts. Of course, the refugee may also be an important informant. Many refugees are aware that communication problems may develop and are ready to explain things as soon as the therapist shows some interest. For her or his part, the therapist can prevent compounding the communication problems by explaining rules and standards common to Western society.

LANGUAGE PROBLEMS

It is often thought that, in the ideal therapeutic situation, both therapist and client speak the same language fluently. Unfortunately, this is not always true; sometimes it is easier to discuss a private matter or a taboo in a second language, rather than in one's native tongue (cf. Sundberg, 1981). However that may be, psychotherapy with refugees often means that the therapist has to work with people who have grown up speaking very different languages. Refugees with personal problems often have difficulty concentrating or cannot remember what they have been taught. This usually has a negative effect on their efforts to learn the language of the country in which they are in exile.

In the case of refugees who do speak the therapist's language, it is necessary to realize that they are likely to have just a limited vocabulary of common terms. They do not know or understand many of the terms which they need to describe or express their emotions. Thus, they are limited in their ability to articulate their problems. The therapist must take care that what he or she says comes across in the intended manner. He or she must be constantly alert for misunderstandings stemming from the use of a unfamiliar language. In such cases, therapeutic sessions will be slower than usual and often cannot be limited to the standard 45 minutes.

CULTURAL BIAS AND DIAGNOSIS

Cultural bias can be an obstacle to diagnosis. Diagnostic errors are easily made in misinterpreting behavior that impresses the Western clinician as theatrical, manipulative, troublesome, or avoidant. Observations of such behavior may tempt the practitioner to diagnose a refugee as suffering from a personality disorder, as described in DSM-IV (American Psychiatric Association, 1994). In some cases, that may be correct. It is also possible that the refugee's behavior would be completely adequate in his or her specific cultural background.

Moreover, the aforementioned types of behavior can sometimes be explained as the result of a learning process. Behaviors belonging to an adequate pattern of coping responses in an enduring traumatizing situation have become habitual. If the clinician fails to identify these behaviors as red herrings and diagnoses a personality disorder, his or her attention will be distracted from cues referring to posttraumatic symptoms.

It is the experience of the author that posttraumatic symptoms themselves, however, appear to be more-or-less the same in refugees from divergent cultural backgrounds (see also Alexander, Klein, Workneh, & Miller, 1981). Most of the refugees the author has attended who suffered from posttraumatic symptoms, like nightmares and flashbacks, quickly understood the connection between these symptoms and their traumatic experiences. A few of them initially ascribed their symptoms to some evil ghost or djinn, but it was never difficult to awaken their interest in the possible relationship between their symptoms and traumatic experiences.

Often, the refugees whom the author and his colleagues (Vladar Rivero, 1992) attended to seemed to be fully aware of this cultural bias. They could live with it. In that sense, they did not seem to be narrow-minded at all.

USING INTERPRETERS

When the language barrier between therapist and client is so great that they cannot communicate adequately, an interpreter should be used. Using an interpreter leads to an unusual situation: Communication proceeds through a third person, who is usually not trained to give assistance, but who nonetheless makes a personal contribution in the course of the encounter. The interpreter's attitude toward the client determines the atmosphere in which the encounter will take place. This attitude does not always conform to what the therapist considers desirable. A sympathetic, businesslike, or authoritarian, patronizing attitude on the part of the interpreter may facilitate or impede the development of a relationship of mutual trust between the therapist and the client. The extent of the interpreter's knowledge of the client's culture may also facilitate the process.

The interpreter's behavior may evoke certain feelings in the client. If the interpreter is a compatriot, the client may be comforted by his or her presence. But the client may also be ashamed of problems considered a sign of madness or a cause for contempt in their common culture. Sometimes, refugees distrust compatriot interpreters for political reasons. If the interpreter has the same political ideology as the client, the latter will be inhibited in expressing doubts about her or his own political convictions.

The interpreter's gender may also influence the client's frankness, particularly about sexual problems. Various transference phenomena also may be present in the relationship with the interpreter. For example, a client who feels that the therapist does not understand his or her problems may direct his or her irritation at the interpreter, accusing the interpreter of not translating properly. Also, the therapist may vent her or his irritation at the client by directing it at the interpreter.

Sometimes, the client places the interpreter in a difficult situation, by telling him or her something and then asking him or her not to inform the therapist.

Finally, the interpreter may make translation mistakes that result in a negative effect on the therapeutic process. Some of these mistakes can be attributed to words not having an exact translation (Sue & Sue, 1987). For example, it is difficult to find a completely satisfactory equivalent for *disappointment* in Persian. Price (1975) conducted research on the mistakes made by three Hindustani interpreters working in a psychiatric practice in Australia. He found that translation mistakes very rarely led to a wrong diagnosis, but they did increase the time needed to make a diagnosis. According to Price, more mistakes were made in translations of the patients' answers (at most 15.5%) than in translations of the doctors' questions (at most 7.4% when they were talking to psychotic patients, 4.2% when they were talking to neurotics). In translating the answers of patients who had been diagnosed as acutely psychotic or chronically psychotic, the interpreters made more mistakes (15.5%) than with neurotic patients (5.2%).

The most common mistakes that interpreters made in translating doctors' questions were that they changed open questions into leading questions, they altered the content of questions, and they added their own comments. Their mistakes in translating patients' answers included leaving out part of the answer, adding something to the answer, and making mistakes because of their limited knowledge of English.

Various authors have formulated recommendations concerning the use of interpreters in a therapeutic context. Pentz-Moller, Hermansen, Bentsen, and Knudsen (1988) claimed that it is important for the interpreter to speak in the first person whenever the person speaking does so. Also, they considered it of vital importance that the interpreter feel empathy for the refugee, but this should not lead the interpreter to intervene in the treatment without the consent of the therapist. They considered it important that the interpreter have some knowledge of such relevant topics as the different forms of torture. Baker (1981) claimed that it is important to inform interpreters about the basic principles of the therapist's approach, for example, that she or he assumes the client has to make decisions himself or herself, that the topics discussed during sessions are confidential, and that silence during sessions may be meaningful. In addition, Baker regarded it necessary that the interpreter feel involved with the client, even if interpreter and client are from a different social class or background. Baker preferred interpreters who did not suffer from psychological problems themselves; they provided an adequate identification approach for the client and were less likely to lose their objectivity during sessions.

Putsch (1985) also considered neutrality and objectivity important characteristics of a good interpreter. Often, the client brings along friends or relatives to interpret. Putsch considers them unsuitable. They have the advantage of being familiar with the client, but the disadvantage of not being objective. This lack of objectivity affects their translations. For example, they may exaggerate or minimize the client's complaints. In the case of children (who often learn the new language faster than their parents), playing the role of interpreter can disturb the existing family hierarchy. Also, Marcos (1979) considered relatives less suitable as interpreters because often they answer the therapist's questions without even putting them to the client.

Therefore, a preferable interpreter is one who does not know the client, but who is somewhat familiar with the procedures used by the therapist. But even then, the therapist must be aware of the possibility of incorrect translations and the loss of information, specifically information pointing to thought disorders or covert depression (Sabin, 1975). Incidentally, cultural differences may also hinder the contact between therapist and interpreter. Because of their own cultural values, interpreters may feel uncomfortable with some questions about sex (Rendon, 1989).

Another problem with interpreters is that they may have experienced traumatic events similar to those of the refugee. In this case, the interpreter may want to avoid unhappy memories for herself or himself by not translating accurately, evading certain topics, changing the subject, informing the therapist that the interview is too stressful for the refugee, and so on (Westermeyer, 1989).

The following procedure has sometimes been used by the author. One way of maintaining the client's anonymity, and thereby increasing the chance that he or she will discuss problems openly, is to use a loudspeaker telephone and the services of external interpreters. Then, there is no need for the interpreter to meet the refugee personally; the interpreter does not know what the client looks like and need not even know his or her name. The disadvantage of this method is that gestures and other nonverbal aspects of communication are lost.

When an unfamiliar interpreter is to be present, the client's embarrassment or suspicion may be reduced if the interpreter introduces himself or herself to the client before the session so that they have a chance for an informal chat. It may also be very worthwhile for the therapist to have a preparatory conversation with the interpreter. It may be very enlightening to find out whether certain questions (e.g., about sexual behavior) can be expressed at all by this interpreter in the client's language. In spite of the language barrier, eye contact between the therapist and the client facilitates the client's understanding of what is being said without the intervention of the interpreter. Keeping questions and remarks concise also helps to improve communication. Long questions mean that the therapist has to direct more of his or her attention to the interpreter than to the client. Sessions should be prepared beforehand, if necessary in consultation with the interpreter. Sometimes, it is useful for the therapist to explain to the interpreter why she or he is saying, or asking, certain things.

Using an interpreter from the same country or region as the refugee has an advantage. Not only do they share the same language, but they also share the same cultural background. Also, working regularly with the same interpreters increases the therapist's understanding of other cultures.

The emotional reactions of interpreters during therapeutic sessions are sometimes a useful source of information. If the therapist sees that the interpreter is embarrassed or surprised or shows some other emotional response, he or she may interrupt the session to consult the interpreter about the reasons for this reaction.

Sometimes, it is useful to ask the interpreter for an opinion of the client's emotions. Such interventions break the conventional boundaries of the interpreter's role, and she or he becomes a bicultural cotherapist. Proper training is necessary to enable an interpreter to fulfill this role adequately.

In the United States, much experience has been gained in the cooperation between American and Vietnamese or Cambodian cotherapists, and in providing special training programs for the latter (see, for example, Teter, Maudlin, Nhol, Conkin, & Sum, 1987).

THE ATTITUDE OF THE PSYCHOTHERAPIST

Does helping refugees with psychotherapeutic techniques and methods require a specific attitude from the helping professional? The author's experiences suggest that psychotherapy with refugees is a matter not of inventing a totally new method, but of creatively adapting a variety of existing methods and techniques and procedures.

The goals of psychotherapy with refugees are as varied as the goals of psychotherapy in general. However, they always include two very concrete objectives: supporting the refugee with regard to his or her daily functioning and creating a future in the country of exile. The various goals, methods, techniques, and procedures can be described in terms of diverging theoretical approaches. Up to this point, psychotherapy with refugees does not seem to be very special.

However, on a different level of analysis, psychotherapy with refugees does have some special features. First, it includes a risk for the therapist, a risk of becoming overwhelmed by feelings of powerlessness as a result of being confronted with clients suffering from ongoing traumatization. The ongoing traumatization of a refugee may obstruct a progressive development in his or her functioning or may result in a regressive development. Ongoing traumatization may have this result even when the therapist does his or her work adequately and the refugee does all he or she can to use the opportunities the therapy is providing. That is not encouraging for either party. Suggestions for dealing with overwhelming feelings of powerlessness have been given elsewhere (Van der Veer, 1992).

Second, the specific quality of the problems of refugees makes special demands on the professional attitude of the practitioner. Because of their experiences with perpetrators who did not leave them any self-determination or control over their situation and their own body, and who were not interested in their well-being and humiliated them, some refugees may be extremely sensitive. As a result of traumatization, many refugees have a generalized feeling of being powerless, humiliated, and not taken seriously. In exile, this feeling is often reinforced by daily experiences (like receiving bad news from the native country, receiving a denial of political asylum, or being confronted with a negative attitude toward refugees).

As a result, some refugees are allergic to anything in the behavior of the therapist and her or his co-workers, or in the procedures of the institute in which they are employed, that resembles, however slightly, humiliation, indifference or abuse of power. For example, an individual refugee may feel extremely offended by such questions as "What kind of help do you expect from us?"; by an insufficiently explained postponement of a therapeutic interview, by a psychiatrist prescribing psychotropic medication hurriedly, or by a snappy sound in the voice of a receptionist.

Therefore, in order to be effective, the behavior of the therapist and her or his co-workers should express respect, interest, willingness to give the refugee control over his or her situation, and hospitality. Because of the possibility of cultural misunderstandings, all this should be expressed in a way that is understandable to people of diverging cultural backgrounds.

This attitude of respect, interest, willingness to give the refugee control over his or her situations, and hospitality can be expressed in many different ways, by various persons, and in many situations (e.g., in the waiting room, during telephone calls by the receptionist, during the discussion of traumatic experiences with the therapist, or during a discussion of the possible prescription of medication with the psychiatrist). More generally, it can be communicated by a willingness to deviate, if necessary, from fixed procedures by everybody who is in any way involved in the treatment, including the administrative personnel.

Any client, no matter what his or her background, deserves respect, interest, and the opportunity for self-determination, but it may be a bit more difficult to convey this attitude to refugees. The example of a waiting, nondirective approach that may be considered a sign of lack of interest and of incompetence by refugees from non-Western backgrounds has already been mentioned. In the same connection, other therapeutic conventions should be open to reconsideration. For instance, psychotherapists, often for good reason, do not give priority to listening to the political opinions of their clients. But in therapy with refugees, it is often a very important subject.

In order to be able to express the aforementioned attitudes, alertness for cultural misunderstandings, as well as alertness to one's own reactions that are the result of ethnocentrism or xenophobia, is needed. Also, the therapist needs patience and perseverance, like the patience and perseverance of a counterclerk who has to explain the intricacies of the public transport system of a city to a lost tourist.

The combination of the aforementioned features reflects the specific characteristics of counseling and psychotherapy with traumatized refugees. When these specific characteristics have to be summarized in a few words, it could be stated that therapy with traumatized refugees is an ongoing effort to help or stimulate the client to regain his or her liberty, in the sense of acquiring control over posttraumatic symptoms that interfere with present psychological functioning and the opportunities for future psychological development. In that sense, it is very concrete. For example, the therapeutic interviews can be structured as opportunities for the client to make well-considered concrete decisions that have important consequences for her or his future: the decision to talk or not to talk about traumatic experiences, the decision to use or not to use psychotropic medication, and the decision to change or not to change daily routines. The aforementioned attitude requires flexibility

in the therapist; it will be demanding to combine such a viewpoint with
the bureaucratic tendencies in some organizations for mental health and
with a rigid adherence to particular therapeutic procedures.

> N. N., a 42-year-old refugee, found a job, which made it impossible for him to
> continue therapeutic sessions within the usual office hours. The therapist was
> ready to give him a weekly appointment early Monday evening, but this
> resulted in problems with the security officer of the office building.

FINAL REMARKS

At first a little stunned by the horror in the stories of his clients,
intimidated by the invalidating character of their symptoms, and also
impressed by the strength of their coping skills, the author of this paper
now has an essentially optimistic view of the possibilities of helping
refugees with psychotherapeutic techniques. Even with limited resources, it is possible for a psychotherapist to build up expertise with
regard to this category of clients. Psychotherapy with refugees appears
to be within the reach of the average professional in the mental health
sector, assuming that he or she is ready to plunge into the backgrounds
of the patients and to listen to the stories of refugees and is allowed to
adapt procedures and organizational structures in a way that meets their
specific needs.

REFERENCES

Agger, I. (1988). *Psychological aspects of torture with special emphasis on sexual torture: Sequels and treatment perspectives.* Copenhagen: Institute of Cultural Sociology.
Alexander, A. A., Klein, M. H., Workneh, F., & Miller, M. H. (1981). Psychotherapy and the foreign student. In P. B. Pederson, J. G. Draguns, W. J. Lonner, & J. E. Trimble (Eds.), *Counselling across cultures* (rev. and expanded ed., pp. 226–243). Honolulu: University Press of Hawaii.
American Psychiatric Association (1994). *Diagnostic and statistical manual of mental disorders* (4th ed.). Washington, DC: Author.
Baker, N. G. (1981). Social work through an interpreter. *Social Work, 26,* 391–397.
Brown, L. S. (1986). From alienation to connection: Feminist therapy with posttraumatic stress disorder. *Women Therapy, 5,* 101–106.
Cancelmo, J. A., Millán, F., & Vazquez, C. I. (1990). Culture and symptomatology—The role of personal meaning in diagnosis and treatment: A case study. *The American Journal of Psychoanalysis, 50,* 137–149.
Coelho, G. V. (1982). The foreign students sojourn as a high risk situation: The "culture-shock" phenomenon re-examined. In R. C. Nann (Ed.), *Uprooting and surviving* (pp. 101–107). Dordrecht: D. Reidel.
Dahl, C. (1989). Some problems of cross-cultural psychotherapy with refugees seeking treatment. *American Journal of Psychoanalysis, 49,* 19–32.

De Anda, D. (1984). Bicultural socialization: Factors affecting the minority experience. *Social Work, 29,* 101–107.

Denley, J. (1987). Personal communication, cited in J. Reid & T. Strong. *Torture and trauma* (p. 96). Sydney: Cumberland College of Health Services.

Eisenbruch, M., & Handelman, L. (1989). Development of an explanatory model of illness schedule for Cambodian refugee patients. *Journal of Refugee Studies, 2,* 243–256.

Giel, R. (1984). *Vreemde zielen: Een sociaalpsychiatrische verkenning in andere culturen.* Meppel, The Netherlands: Boom.

Kabela, M. (no date). *Transculturele aspecten van depressie.* Haarlem, The Netherlands: Elizabethsgasthuis.

Keilson, H. (1979). *Sequentielle Traumatisierung bei Kindern.* Stuttgart, Germany: Ferdinand Enke Verlag.

Kinzie, J. D. (1978). Lessons from cross-cultural psychotherapy. *American Journal of Psychotherapy, 32,* 110–120.

Knudsen, J. C. (1991). Therapeutic strategies and strategies for refugee coping. *Journal of Refugee Studies, 4,* 21–38.

Kortmann, F. (1986). *Problemen in transculturele communicatie.* Assen, The Netherlands: Van Gorcum.

Lee, E., & Lu, F. (1989). Assessment and treatment of Asian-American survivors of mass violence. *Journal of Traumatic Stress, 2,* 93–120.

Marcos, L. R. (1979). Effects of interpreters on the evaluation of psychopathology in non-English speaking patients. *American Journal of Psychiatry, 136,* 171–174.

Mollica, R. F., & Son, L. (1988). *Cultural dimensions in the evaluation and treatment of sexual trauma: An overview.* Unpublished study.

Pederson, P. B. (1981). The cultural inclusiveness of counselling. In P. B. Pederson, J. G. Draguns, W. J. Lonner, & J. E. Trimble (Eds.), *Counselling across Cultures* (rev. and expanded ed., pp. 22–58). Honolulu: University Press of Hawaii.

Pentz-Moller, V., Hermansen, A., Bentsen, E., & Knudsen, I. H. (1988). *Interpretation in the rehabilitation of torture victims at the RCT.* Copenhagen: International Research and Rehabilitation Center for Torture Victims.

Price, J. (1975). Foreign language interpreting in psychiatric practice. *Australian and New Zealand Journal of Psychiatry, 9,* 263–267.

Putsch, R. W. (1985). Cross-cultural communication: The special case of interpreters in health care. *Journal of the American Medical Association, 254,* 3344–3348.

Rendon, M. (1989). Discussion of "some problems of cross-cultural psychotherapy with refugees seeking therapy," by Carl-Ivar Dahl. *The American Journal of Psychoanalysis, 49,* 45–50.

Sabin, J. E. (1975). Translating despair. *American Journal of Psychiatry, 132,* 197–199.

Srinivasa, D. K., & Trivedi, S. (1982). Knowledge and attitude of mental diseases in a rural community of South India. *Social Science and Medicine, 16,* 1635–1639.

Sue, D., & Sue, S. (1987). Cultural factors in the clinical assessment of Asian Americans. *Journal of Consulting and Clinical Psychology, 55,* 479–487.

Sundberg, N. D. (1981). Research and research hypotheses about effectiveness in intercultural counselling. In P. B. Pederson, J. G. Draguns, W. J. Lonner, & J. E. Trimble (Eds.), *Counselling across cultures* (rev. and expanded ed., pp. 304–342). Honolulu: University Press of Hawaii.

Teter, H., Mauldin, D., Nhol, S., Conkin, D., & Sum, S. (1987). *Treatment through training: A Cambodian mental health workshop.* San Francisco: International Institute of San Francisco.

Tsui, P., & Schultz, G. L. (1985). Failure of rapport: Why psychotherapeutic engagement fails in the treatment of Asian clients. *American Journal of Orthopsychiatry, 55,* 561–569.

Van der Veer, G. (1992). *Counselling and therapy with refugees: Psychological problems of victims of war, torture and repression.* New York: Wiley.

Van der Veer, G. (1993). *Psychotherapy with refugees: An exploration.* Amsterdam: Stichting voor Culturele Studies.

Vladar Rivero, V. (1992). The use of psychotropic medication. In G. van der Veer (Ed.), *Counselling and therapy with refugees: Psychological problems of victims of war, torture and repression.* New York: Wiley.

Vontress, C. E. (1981). Racial and ethnic barriers in counselling. In P. B. Pederson, J. G. Draguns, W. J. Lonner, & J. E. Trimble (Eds.), *Counselling across cultures* (rev. and expanded ed., pp. 87–107). Honolulu: University Press of Hawaii.

Westermeyer, J. (1989). Cross-cultural core for PTSD: Research, training, and service needs for the future. *Journal of Traumatic Stress, 2,* 515–536.

10

The Prevalence, Trauma, and Sociocultural Causes of Incestuous Abuse of Females
A Human Rights Issue

DIANA E. H. RUSSELL

INTRODUCTION

"I just did what he told me to do," declared Irma Viljoen (pseudonym), a white South African incest survivor who was sexually abused by her stepfather from the age of 8 to 13. Irma, now 25 and recently divorced, has attempted suicide eight times. She was 13 years old when she first tried to kill herself. Her stepfather, Piet Viljoen, succeeded in silencing her until she was almost 16—three years after his marriage to her mother broke up. This is how Irma described his method of silencing her:

> He threatened to hit me if I ever spoke about it. He used to sit there in the afternoons with his gun and threaten me. At a later stage when I went to boarding school, he threatened to kill me. When I was about 10 or 11, he

DIANA E. H. RUSSELL • Emerita Professor of Sociology, Mills College; and Russell Research on Sexual Assault, 2432 Grant Street, Berkeley, California 94703.   This chapter is an edited version of a keynote speech delivered at the World Conference on Trauma and Tragedy held in Amsterdam in 1992, and sponsored by the International Society for Traumatic Stress Studies. For this reason, there is a greater focus on the author's own work and less documentation than is customary for papers specifically prepared for scholarly publication.
Beyond Trauma: Cultural and Societal Dynamics, edited by Rolf J. Kleber, Charles R. Figley, and Berthold P. R. Gersons. New York, Plenum Press, 1995.

made me watch two movies and then do what the women did in them. In one
of the movies a lot of men raped a woman and did whatever else they wanted
to her. The other movie showed a woman being cut up alive after the men
had sex with her. My stepfather threatened to do the same to me if I told
anyone what he was doing to me. That is why I would rather have died than
tell anyone. The movies pumped into my head that "this is my life." (Russell,
1993a, p. 10)

This is how Irma described what it was like to live with her stepfather:

I was always petrified of him because he was so strict. I just did what he told
me to do. He used to send my sisters and my brother to their friends. He
allowed them to play and take part in sports—anything to get them away
from the house. Then he abused me. He wanted me to touch his penis. I must
have been about nine when the intercourse started. He also did it behind
[sodomized her]. He used to give me presents of money and sometimes food
if I did what he wanted. Later on the abuse was sometimes every day, sometimes every two days. Every time he did it he told me it was because he loved
me and because my Mom couldn't give him a child [she had had a hysterec-
tomy]. . . . The main thing I can remember is that I used to get so sick—
vomiting and bleeding [from oral sex and vaginal rape]—and because I
vomited, he gave me a hiding. (Russell, 1993a, p. 10)

Irma was also sexually abused and raped by her older brother. "He
used to call me a whore and he threatened to tell others that I was a whore
because I was having sex with him. That cracked me up." In addition,
several other relatives sexually assaulted Irma: "By that time, I could not do
anything," she explains. "I just let them do what they wanted to. . . . I was
broken." After another suicide attempt and an emotional breakdown,
Irma confides, "I was very furious that I wasn't dead."

Irma's story is one of many that reveals what some fathers are doing in
the privacy of their homes. Piet Viljoen was a petty dictator who fashioned
his home into a hell reminiscent of a mini-concentration camp. His threats
to murder his daughter were intended to ensure that his secret life of sexual
torture would go to the grave with her. It almost did.

The purpose of this chapter is to document the prevalence and
effects of incestuous abuse, to suggest some of its major structural and
cultural causes, and to note that it qualifies as a form of torture in many
instances and should thus be treated as a massive gender-related human
rights issue.

DEFINITIONS AND TERMINOLOGY

In most Western societies the legal definition of incest has been
limited to sexual intercourse between blood relatives. Most clinicians and
researchers have expanded this narrow definition to include sexual

abuse by non-blood-relatives and sexual acts such as oral and anal sex, as well as genital fondling.

Broader definitions of this kind necessitate a further distinction between abusive experiences and nonabusive sex play between relatives who are peers. Hence, I have defined *incestuous abuse* as *any kind of exploitive sexual contact or attempted contact that occurs between relatives, no matter how distant the relationship, before the victim turns 18 years old* (Russell, 1986). Experiences involving sexual contact that are wanted *and* that occur with a peer are considered nonexploitive. A "peer relationship" is defined as one in which the age difference between the participants is less than five years. Because of the power relationship inherent in age differences of five years or more, it is assumed that sexual contact in such situations are abusive, whether or not they are wanted. The term *incestuous abuse* is preferred over *incest* to distinguish exploitive and non-exploitive sexual contact between relatives.

Some researchers prefer the term *intrafamilial child sexual abuse* to *incestuous abuse*. These terms are used synonymously in this chapter.

Many of the women who have been victimized by incest prefer to refer to themselves as incest survivors rather than as incest victims. The term *survivor* will be used in this chapter except where the term *victim* is more appropriate, for example, when I am discussing incestuous abuse at the time of its occurrence. It is also important to remember that an unknown number of incest victims do *not* survive. Some are murdered, suicide is quite common, and many suffer such incapacitating trauma that the term *survivor* is unsuitable.

This chapter focuses on the *prevalence* of incestuous abuse rather than on its *incidence*. *Prevalence* refers to the percentage of people—in this case, females—who have been victimized by incest at some time in their lives. *Incidence* refers to the number of cases that occurred within a specified period of time—usually one year. Focusing on prevalence better conveys the magnitude of this problem.

THE PREVALENCE OF INCESTUOUS ABUSE

David Finkelhor (1994) reviewed nearly two dozen prevalence surveys of child sexual abuse that were "conducted on large nonclinical populations outside of North America" (p. 410) (only four of which were easily accessible in English-language journals or books). In those countries where more than one such study had been conducted, he selected the study that was largest in its geographical scope and population, and hence the closest to being national, for the purposes of comparison. He noted that these studies are "extremely variable in their scope and quali-

Table 1. A Comparison of Prevalence
Rates of Incestuous Abuse of Female
Children in 16 Countries[a]

Country	Prevalence per 100
Australia	10
Austria	9
Belgium	6
Canada	8
Costa Rica	14
Denmark	6
France	2
Great Britain	2
Greece	5
Netherlands	16[b]
New Zealand	12
South Africa	10
Spain	4
Sweden	2
Switzerland	6
United States	8

[a] Extrapolated from Finkelhor (1994, Table 2, p. 412).
[b] Finkelhor reported a 15% prevalence rate for the Netherlands, but according to Nel Draijer's raw figures (1990), the prevalence rate was 16% when rounded to the nearest whole number (164 of the 1,054 women in Nel Draijer's sample reported at least one experience of incestuous abuse, which amounts to 15.56% of the sample).

ty," ranging from "sophisticated national probability samples and household interview studies to local convenience sample studies of university students using self-administered questionnaires" (p. 410). They were also largely confined to English-speaking and northern European countries (see Table 1).

Most of these studies included males as well as females in their samples and reported prevalence data for extrafamilial and incestuous abuse combined. Fortunately, the majority of them also provided information on incestuous abuse as a percentage of child sexual abuse in general, making it possible to extrapolate separate prevalence rates for incestuous abuse. Since this chapter focuses on the incestuous abuse of females, the comparisons reported in Table 1 are confined to those studies reported by Finkelhor that pertain to this form of child sexual abuse.

Table 1 shows that the prevalence rates range from a low of 2% in France, Great Britain, and Sweden, to a high of 16% in the Nether-

lands. Finkelhor (1994) suggested that Nel Draijer's high 16% prevalence figure for the Netherlands (1990) "almost certainly stems from
the numerous detailed screening questions and sensitive interviewing"
(p. 411) that she did, revealing the key role that methodology plays in
these studies. Indeed, Draijer partially modeled her study on my San
Francisco survey (Russell, 1986), in which a prevalence figure for incestuous abuse of 16% was also found. (Note that Finkelhor chose a
U.S. survey that was national in scope rather than my one-city survey
for his international comparison.) Since Draijer's prevalence figure applies to females under the age of 16, whereas mine applies to females
under the age of 18, the Dutch prevalence rate is slightly higher than
the rate I found in San Francisco.

Even though Draijer's and my 16% prevalence rates for incestuous
abuse are considered high, I believe that this figure significantly underestimates the magnitude of the problem in San Francisco. Because my
study was based on a household sample, some of the populations with
the highest rates of incestuous abuse were excluded, for example, mental hospitals, prisons, brothels, residential alcohol and other drug rehabilitation programs, battered-women's shelters, and homeless women. In
addition, many women are known to repress traumatic experiences of
incestuous abuse; for others, the abuse happened when they were so
young that they cannot remember it. And other women in my study
undoubtedly chose not to confide their experiences to the interviewer.
Presumably, a prevalence rate of 16% constitutes an underestimate of
the occurrence of incestuous abuse in the Netherlands for some of the
same reasons.

It seems reasonable to conclude that the prevalence figures reported in Table 1 probably understate the magnitude of the incest problem in all the other countries listed even more significantly than our 16%
prevalence rates for San Francisco and the Netherlands. Finkelhor
(1994) cautioned readers that "the variation in rates between countries
probably does not reflect variation in true prevalence," noting that "similar wide variations in rates have been found in studies within the U.S.,
and these have been shown to be explained by methodological factors,
such as the survey methodology, the questions asked, and the definition
of sexual abuse" (p. 411). Nevertheless, Finkelhor concluded:

> In every country where researchers have asked about it [child sexual abuse],
> they have found that an important percentage of the adult population—
> measurable in simple surveys of adults—acknowledges a history of sexual
> abuse. These include countries where there has been a great deal of publicity
> about the problem as well as those where publicity has been limited. This
> suggests the scope of the work that remains for those who wish to understand

the hidden sufferings of children in cultures all around the world as well as for those who wish to change it. (p. 413)

THE TRAUMA OF INCESTUOUS ABUSE

The research and clinical literature has documented many serious immediate and long-term consequences of incestuous abuse, ranging from depression to multiple-personality disorder. Angela Browne and David Finkelhor (1986) concluded their classic review of the empirical literature on consequences by noting that child sexual abuse "is a serious mental health problem, consistently associated with very disturbing subsequent problems in a significant portion of its victims" (p. 163). In a more recent review, Finkelhor (1990) noted that later studies have continued "to establish the connection between a history of sexual abuse and a variety of mental health symptoms and pathologies" demonstrating that "sexual abuse has a noxious impact both initially and in the long term" (p. 325). In his comparison of international epidemiological studies, Finkelhor (1994) pointed out that "all the studies that looked at long-term effects also found a history of sexual abuse associated with adult mental health impairments" (p. 411).

Defining the initial effects of child sexual abuse as "the reactions occurring within two years of the termination of the sexual abuse," Browne and Finkelhor (1986, p. 144) cited empirical studies demonstrating reactions of fear, anxiety, depression, anger, hostility, guilt, shame, and inappropriate sexual behavior, such as open masturbation, excessive sexual curiosity, and frequent exposure of the genitals.

With regard to the many long-term effects of incestuous abuse that have been documented by empirical studies, Browne and Finkelhor pointed out that these studies succeeded in identifying significant differences between survivors of child sexual abuse and others, despite the fact that the abuse had occurred from 5 to 25 years previously: "Moreover, all these studies used fairly broad definitions of sexual abuse that included single episodes, experiences in which no actual physical contact occurred, and experiences with individuals who were not related to or not emotionally close to the subjects" (pp. 163–164). These effects, as well as those mentioned by other researchers (e.g., Briere, 1989; Courtois, 1988; Finkelhor & Browne, 1986: Finkelhor, 1990), are summarized in Table 2.

Research has also shown that father–daughter incestuous abuse (both biological and stepfathers) is significantly more traumatic than other forms of incestuous or extrafamilial child sexual abuse by male

Table 2. Some of the Confirmed Consequences of Child Sexual Abuse

Psychological manifestations

Depression, "the symptom most commonly reported among adults molested as children" in the clinical literature (Browne & Finkelhor, 1986, p. 152).

Anxiety, for example, anxiety attacks, nightmares, insomnia, and extreme tension.

Chronic and acute somatizing, for example, psychosomatic illnesses, as well as aches and pains.

Dissociation, such as "out-of-body experiences," and depersonalization.

Feelings of isolation, stigma, or alienation, especially common in incest survivors.

Negative self-image and poor self-esteem.

Interpersonal problems, for example, relationships impeded by difficulty in trusting others, a sense of betrayal, fear, and hostility. These problems manifest in survivors having difficulties relating to men and women in intimate relationships (with a spouse or a sex partner) and nonintimate relationships; difficulties with parents, especially mothers in cases of father–daughter incest; and conflicts with parenting.

Sexual maladjustment, such as sexual dysphoria, impaired sexual self-esteem, and sexual dysfunctions, for example, flashbacks, difficulty with arousal, difficulty achieving orgasm, sexual guilt, lack of sexual pleasure, negative associations with sexual activities and arousal sensations, and aversion to sex or intimacy.

Mental illness, for example, dissociative identity disorder and borderline personality disorder.

Physical symptoms ranging from headaches to nonorganically caused epilepsy.

Gynecological problems, for example, problems with premenstrual tension and menstruation, endometriosis, persistent bladder infections, and cystitis.

Attention deficit disorder.

A sense of being different from others.

Confusion of sex with love and caregetting and caregiving.

Extreme dependency.

An impaired ability to judge the trustworthiness of others.

A perception of oneself as a victim.

Identification with the aggressor.

Phobias.

Behavioral manifestations

Self-destructive behavior, such as a history of suicide attempts, a desire to hurt oneself, deliberate attempt at self-harm, and suicide.

Eating disorders, for example, anorexia, bulimia, and obesity.

Substance abuse, including alcoholism and other drug addiction, as well as abuse of tranquilizers and other medications.

Sexual effects, for example, avoidance of, or abstention from, sexual activity, precocious sexual activity, sexual preoccupation and compulsive sexual behavior, promiscuity,[a] aggressive sexual behavior, inappropriate sexualization of parenting, and phobic reactions to sex acts used by the perpetrator.

Prostitution.[b]

Self-mutilation.

Hypochondria.

Giving birth at a younger age than non-incest-survivors.

Antisocial acting out, for example, delinquency, criminal behavior, and truancy.

(continued)

Table 2. (*Continued*)

Poor school performance and underachievement.
Employment problems, often as a result of attention deficit disorder.
Becoming a perpetrator of child sexual abuse (particularly common in male survivors).

Other manifestations

Revictimization; that is, child sexual abuse survivors are far more likely to be raped by
    another perpetrator, and to be raped and/or beaten by a husband.
Own children become sexually victimized.
Record of unnecessary surgery often due to chronic somatizing.
Defection from religion of upbringing (in Protestants and Catholics).

---

[a] I use the pejorative terms "promiscuity" and "prostitution" rather than "multiple sex partners" and
    "sex worker" to emphasize the lack of choice on the part of incest survivors who become promiscuous
    and/or enter prostitution.
[b] See previous footnote.

perpetrators (Briere & Runtz, 1985; Browne & Finkelhor, 1986, p. 168; Russell, 1986). Mother–daughter incestuous abuse will probably be found to be more traumatic as well, since sexual abuse by a parent typically involves a greater sense of betrayal for the victim than does abuse by more distant relatives. The fact that such victims are usually trapped in these abusive relationships presumably compounds the trauma. Therefore, many of the effects listed in Table 2 are likely to be significantly more serious in cases of parent–child sexual abuse.

Although most experiences of incestuous abuse are not as extreme as in Irma Viljoen's description at the beginning of this chapter, it is clear that incestuous abuse is frequently a traumatic and severely damaging experience.

SOME SOCIOCULTURAL CAUSES OF INCESTUOUS ABUSE

There are two major facts that any theory on the etiology of incestuous abuse has to address. The first is the high prevalence rates, particularly in studies with methodologies that are appropriate for gathering data on taboo experiences. The second is that the perpetrators are predominantly male. For example, in his comparative international study of over 20 epidemiological studies discussed above, Finkelhor (1994) noted that "all the studies reporting such information showed offenders against girls to be disproportionately male (above 90%)" (p. 411). Finkelhor noted elsewhere (1984) that the sexual abuse of boys or girls by female family members is "extremely rare" in comparison to their abuse by male family members.

The preponderance of male perpetrators of incestuous abuse requires that the issue of gender be given a central place in causal explanations, a fact often overlooked by theorists. For example, some theorists maintain that the majority of male incest perpetrators were themselves sexually abused in childhood (e.g., Groth, 1979). Frequently, their sexually assaultive behavior is seen as being caused by this abuse. However, girls are far more subject to this form of victimization than are boys (Finkelhor, 1994), yet far fewer females than males become incest perpetrators.

Clearly, both women and men have the biological capacity to sexually abuse children. Even if one were to concede that testosterone may account for a stronger sex drive in males than in females, it is very clear that many sociocultural factors play a significant role in males' greater willingness than females to act out this drive. Incestuous abuse of children, rape, and sexual harassment of females would be rare if males were simply socialized to be uninterested in having sexual contact with unwilling partners.

Male Sex-Role and Sexual Socialization

Finkelhor and I (Russell & Finkelhor, 1984) have argued that many sex-role socialization practices common in patriarchal societies contribute to males' greater willingness to incestuously abuse females. For example:

1. Males are taught the importance of developing qualities regarded as masculine: aggression, power, strength, toughness, dominance, fearlessness, and competitiveness. These notions of masculinity frequently result in a predatory sexuality geared to proving manhood and establishing dominance over females (Russell, 1975, 1984). Hence, aggression and sexuality are often closely related in males.
2. Males are trained that being hypersexual is vital to proving their virility and that it is important to "score" sexually—the more women, the better. Masturbation is not regarded as a satisfactory outlet. When opportunities for sex with appropriately-aged females are lacking, men may more readily turn to children.
3. Males are encouraged to split feelings of respect, love, tenderness, and caring from sexual desire. This split enables many of them to treat females as sexual objects to conquer and control, by sexual and nonsexual means. Since females, in contrast, are

raised to value romance, love, and commitment, males often have
to seduce, manipulate, or con them into having sex.

4. Males are socialized to prefer partners who are younger, smaller,
   weaker, more innocent, more vulnerable, and more dependent
   than themselves. Sexual interest in children is highly compatible
   with these qualities.

5. As a result of being socialized to be hypersexual, males are more
   apt than females to define all affectionate contact as sexual, and
   thus to become aroused by it. This confusion may facilitate men's
   sexual interest in family members.

6. Males are expected to take the initiative in sexual relationships,
   and to overcome resistance, sometimes even to perceive resistance as a cover for sexual desire. Hence, coercive sexuality has
   become normative male behavior.

Male Supremacy and the Power Imbalance in the Family

Judith Herman (1981) maintained that male supremacy creates the
social conditions that favor the development of father–daughter incest.
This is her theory:

> Male supremacy invests fathers with immense powers over their children,
> especially their daughters. The sexual division of labor, in which women
> nurture children and men do not, produces fathers who are predisposed to
> use their powers exploitatively. The rearing of children by subordinate wom-
> en ensures the reproduction in each generation of the psychology of male
> supremacy. It produces sexually aggressive men with little capacity to nur-
> ture, nurturant women with undeveloped sexual capacities, and children of
> both sexes who stand in awe of the power of fathers.
>
> Wherever these conditions obtain, father–daughter incest is likely to be
> a common occurrence. In any culture, the greater the degree of male su-
> premacy and the more rigid the sexual division of labor, the more frequently
> we might expect the taboo on father–daughter incest to be violated. . . . The
> same logic applies to particular families within any one culture. The greater
> the domination of the father, and the more the caretaking is relegated to the
> mother, the greater the likelihood of father–daughter incest. (pp. 62–63)

The fact that men are typically the primary breadwinners also
makes it extremely difficult to deal with the small minority of father–
daughter incest cases that are reported. When father perpetrators are
convicted for their crimes, the family loses their primary breadwinner.
This loss frequently has dire economic consequences for the mother and
the children, which discourages mothers from believing and supporting
their abused daughters in these circumstances. Hence, the economic
power of males serves to protect them from receiving the punishment
they deserve. This usually results in greater betrayal of these victimized

daughters, the intensification of their feelings of powerlessness, and the increased duration of the sexual abuse.

Cultural View of Children as Property

Just as females are viewed as the property of males, children are almost universally seen as the property of their parents. Some fathers assume that this gives them the right to sexual access, especially to their daughters.

Here are two cases that illustrate this particular sociocultural contributor to the occurrence of incestuous abuse:

> A step-father perpetrator said to his 14-year-old stepdaughter: "I've been your father since you were three. I've been a good father. You owe it to me." (Russell, 1984, p. 248)

> An adoptive father who molested his daughter when she was 13 years old said: "I resisted, but he said, 'You do what you're supposed to do because I'm the parent and you're the child.'" (Russell, 1984, p. 261)

Male Entitlement

Because of male supremacy and the feelings of superiority that males typically have vis-à-vis females in such cultures, males frequently feel entitled to dominate females and to have their sexual and other needs met by them. As Herman (1981) states:

> Implicitly the incestuous father assumes that it is his prerogative to be waited upon at home, and that if his wife fails to provide satisfaction, he is entitled to use his daughter as a substitute. It is this attitude of entitlement—to love, to service, and to sex—that finally characterizes the incestuous father and his apologists. (p. 49)

This sense of male entitlement is one of the reasons why father–daughter incestuous abuse is particularly likely to happen when mothers are unavailable for some reason, whether they are in the hospital giving birth, ill, out at work for long hours, or for some other reason. Many representatives of the family dynamics approach to incestuous abuse appear to believe that wives who do not sexually service their husbands are partially responsible for their daughter's sexual abuse. This sexist notion is one of many examples of mother-blaming typical in patriarchal cultures that contribute to letting the incest perpetrator off the hook. Many survivors of father–daughter incest also feel more intense rage and resentment against their mothers than against their fathers. Presumably, this rage reflects an expectation common in patriarchal societies, that a primary responsibility of mothers is to protect their children from harm.

Exposure to Mass Media That Encourage Child Sexual Abuse

Many people would probably like to help themselves to merchandise in stores without paying for it. However, most would be inhibited from so doing because they have been taught that stealing is wrong (internal inhibition), and because they fear they will be caught (social inhibition). Similarly, although there is evidence that many males are predisposed to sexually assault females, many refrain from doing so because they think it wrong, cruel, shameful, and so on.

However, the more messages males get from the culture that female children enjoy sex with adults, and/or that they deserve it because they are inferior creatures, and/or that they are not really human, the more men's internal inhibitions will be undermined. For example, Edward Donnerstein and Daniel Linz have conducted numerous experiments in which they found that the viewing of woman-slashing films results in males' trivializing rape, blaming the victim, and becoming more accepting of rape myths and interpersonal violence (Donnerstein, Linz, & Penrod, 1987). These changed perceptions are likely to undermine the internal inhibitions of males who would like to rape a woman.

Female children are frequently eroticized in the mass media, such as in movies, ads, newspapers, and magazines and on records. One has only to remember the 12-year-old Brooke Shields being named in the United States as the most beautiful woman in the world to realize how female children are held up as an erotic ideal for women. And because what happens in the United States is broadcast all over the world, the effects are not confined to that country. The more females are eroticized and objectified, the easier it is for males to overcome whatever internal inhibitions they may have against acting out their sexual desires with children, including with children to whom they are related.

Exposure to Pornography[1]

Most Western nations have embraced pornography, and the nations of eastern Europe and the former Soviet Union are rapidly following in their footsteps. Although certain forms of child pornography are typically banned, some forms rarely are (for example, pornographic novels

[1] I define *pornography* as material that combines sex and/or the exposure of genitals with abuse or degradation in a manner that appears to endorse, condone, or encourage such behavior. *Erotica* refers to sexually suggestive or arousing material that is free of sexism, racism, and homophobia, and that is respectful of all the human beings and animals portrayed (Russell, 1993b, p. 2). For a detailed description and analysis of my theory of the causal relationship between pornography and rape, see Russell (1993b, pp. 120–150).

that glorify child–adult sex), and the banned material is often quite easily available under the counter, via the cottage industry of men's private collections, or by ordering from abroad as well as through national and international computer networks.

A simple application of the laws of social learning suggests that viewers of pornography may develop arousal responses to children. Viewing pornography may also intensify or reinforce such desires in those who already have them (Russell, 1993b, Chap. 14). Masturbation to such pornography reinforces the association between sexual excitement and sexual assault. This is an example of masturbatory conditioning.

The pervasive sexual objectification of females in pornography dehumanizes them, thereby undermining some males' internal inhibitions against acting out their desires to sexually abuse girls and women (Russell, 1993, p. 135). We have seen that during war men find it easier to act aggressively toward those they perceive as objects or nonpeople than toward those they perceive as human beings (Brownmiller, 1975). It is important to point out that the use of adult women in pornography does not preclude girls from becoming targets of its consumers.

Pornography also tends to undermine men's internal inhibitions by increasing their beliefs in myths about children's sexuality, by increasing their acceptance of interpersonal violence and the trivialization of sexual assault, by increasing their sex-callous attitudes and hostility toward females, by increasing their acceptance of male dominance in intimate relationships, and by desensitizing them to the horror of rape and child sexual abuse, including incestuous abuse (Russell, 1993b, p. 139).

In an experiment by Dolf Zillmann and Jennings Bryant (1984), for example, male students who were exposed to 4 hours and 48 minutes of typical nonviolent pornography per week over a period of six weeks (the so-called heavy-exposure condition) were significantly more inclined than a control group to minimize the suffering caused by sexual assault, for instance, "an adult male having sexual intercourse with a 12-year-old girl" (p. 132).

The Ineffectiveness of Institutions of Social Control

Males who want to commit incestuous abuse and whose internal inhibitions have been undermined by one or more of the factors described above may still refrain from acting out their desire because of fear of arrest and conviction. However, since men make the laws and control the legal and law enforcement institutions, they have ensured that they will very rarely be held accountable for incestuous abuse. The tiny minority of incestuous abuse survivors who report the abuse are rarely believed and are frequently accused of making false charges. Therefore, the perpetrators are absolved of responsibility for their behavior.

Only a minute fraction of incest perpetrators ever serve time in prison. Hence, the fear of being caught does not serve as an effective mechanism of social control. Furthermore, there is a singular lack of success in treatment and rehabilitation efforts for the few incest perpetrators who experience them, as judged by the recidivism that frequently occurs. Nevertheless, incest perpetrators in treatment and rehabilitation programs are often released either by naive and wishful-thinking professionals or because they received inappropriately brief prison sentences enabling them to continue their destructive behavior on the same or other children.

In summary, notions of masculinity and femininity are components of the sexist ideology of patriarchal societies. The values responsible for the different socialization of males and females, the portrayal of females in the media and in pornography, and the male bias in the political, legal, and law enforcement institutions are all manifestations of a sexist social structure and culture. Sexual abuse is a direct outcome of this pervasive sexism. In a nonsexist society, sexual abuse would be an aberrant rather than a normative behavior.

CONCLUSION

Amnesty International (1973), an organization whose aim is to protect the rights of political prisoners worldwide, defines torture as follows:

> The systematic and deliberate infliction of acute pain in any form by one person on another, or on a third person, in order to accomplish the purpose of the former against the will of the latter. (p. 31)

This definition makes it clear that many cases of incestuous abuse—particularly those in which the victim is trapped in a long-term relationship with the perpetrator—qualify as torture.

The authors of the Amnesty International *Report on Torture* (1973) stated that "Under every relevant international legal document torture is prohibited" (pp. 31–32). After citing many of these legal documents, Amnesty International concluded that

> It can safely be stated, accordingly, that under all circumstances, *regardless of the context in which it is used,* torture is outlawed under the common law of mankind [*sic*]. This being so, its use may properly be considered to be a crime against humanity. (p. 36; italics added)

Yet when this crime against humanity takes the form of incestuous abuse, the victims are not perceived by policymakers or public opinion as equally deserving of rescue, treatment, or preventive efforts as are the more readily recognized victims of torture. For example, international outrage has frequently been expressed for Western hostages in Middle Eastern countries whose treatment is defined as torture. Many female children are routinely subjected to much worse treatment by their fathers or other male relatives in homes all over the world. But the screams of these children are rarely heard, and when they are, they are frequently greeted with apathy and blame. No matter how brutal the treatment of incest survivors, it has never before been conceptualized as torture. Might it be that conceptualizing the more severe cases as torture would induce societies to take this ubiquitous crime more seriously instead of dismissing it as a private and nonpolitical matter?

To answer this question, it may be helpful to understand people's reluctance to perceive incestuous abuse as a significant and widespread crime against humanity. Could it be that, because incestuous abuse is typically inflicted on females by their male relatives, men—the major power holders in and out of the home—prefer to discount or minimize the abuse of this power over their female relatives? Whether or not this is the case, there seems to be little to prevent incest perpetrators from continuing to trap their victims in a state of sexual torture and to train them (not necessarily intentionally) to sexually service and serve men when they grow up. Despite Amnesty International's definition of torture, this organization appears to be unwilling to try to assist females who are tortured in their homes. Nor have they seen fit to recognize the widespread problem of incestuous abuse as a political crime.

Incestuous abuse of females by males *must* be recognized as a political offense that both reflects and perpetuates the unequal power relations between males and females. The so-called sanctity of the family must no longer be used as a rationale for ignoring the pain and trauma resulting from the sexual abuse of women and children.

Some people will reject this analysis because it emphasizes that society's conception of masculinity is a key to understanding the incestuous abuse of females. While men are not responsible for their socialization, they *are* responsible for their unwillingness to embrace the changes necessary to diminish and ultimately to eradicate their assaultive behavior. This fact must not be denied because some people, particularly men, are offended by it. We have seen the tragic consequences of Sigmund Freud's turning away from the reality of child sexual abuse because his colleagues could not face the fact that adult men were sexually abusing young girls, particularly their own daughters (Herman, 1981; Masson, 1984; Rush, 1980). We must endeavor not to repeat this infamous cover-up. We must face the fact that males are being socialized from the cradle to develop the attitudes and characteristics that will keep girls and women subordinated, on both an individual and a collective level. The enormity of the cost to females, and ultimately to males, requires our urgent attention.

ACKNOWLEDGMENTS. I would like to thank Mary Armour and Ronel Alberts for their editorial assistance in the preparation of this article.

REFERENCES

Amnesty International (1973). *Report on torture.* London: Gerald Duckworth.

Briere, J. (1989). *Therapy for adults molested as children.* New York: Springer.

Briere, J., & Runtz, M. (1985). *Symptomatology associated with prior sexual abuse in a non-clinical sample.* Paper presented at the annual meeting of the American Psychological Association, Los Angeles.

Browne, A., & Finkelhor, D. (1986). Initial and long-term effects: A review of the research. In D. Finkelhor & Associates (Eds.), *A sourcebook on child sexual abuse* (pp. 143–179). Beverly Hills, CA: Sage.

Brownmiller, S. (1975). *Against our will: Men, women, and rape.* New York: Simon & Schuster.

Courtois, C. (1988). *Healing the incest wound: Adults survivors in therapy.* New York: Norton.

Donnerstein, E., Linz, D., & Penrod, S. (1987). *The question of pornography: Research findings and implications.* New York: Free Press.

Draijer, N. (1990). *Seksuele traumatisering in de jeugd.* Amsterdam: Uitgeverij Sua.

Finkelhor, D. (1990). Early and long-term effects of child sexual abuse: An update. *Professional Psychology: Research and Practice, 21*(5), 325–330.

Finkelhor, D. (1994). The international epidemiology of child sexual abuse. *Child Abuse and Neglect, 18*(5), 409–417.

Finkelhor, D., & Browne, A. (1986). Initial and long-term effects: A conceptual framework. In D. Finkelhor & Associates (Eds.), *A sourcebook on child sexual abuse* (pp. 180–198). Beverly Hills, CA: Sage.

Groth, N. (1979). *Men who rape: The psychology of the offender.* New York: Plenum Press.

Herman, J. (1981). *Father-daughter incest.* Cambridge: Harvard University Press.

Masson, J. (1984). *The assault on truth: Freud's suppression of the seduction theory.* New York: Farrar, Straus & Giroux.

Rush, F. (1980). *The best kept secret: Sexual abuse of children.* Englewood Cliffs, NJ: Prentice-Hall.

Russell, D. E. H. (197⁵). *The politics of rape.* New York: Stein & Day.

Russell, D. E. H. (1984). *Sexual exploitation: Rape, child sexual abuse, and workplace harassment.* Beverly Hills, CA: Sage.

Russell, D. E. H. (1986). *The secret trauma: Incest in the lives of girls and women.* New York: Basic Books.

Russell, D. E. H. (1993a). The divine right of the father: Incest in the white Afrikaner tribe. *Off Our Backs, 23*(3), 10–11.

Russell, D. E. H. (1993b). *Making violence sexy: Feminist views on pornography.* New York: Teachers College Press.

Russell, D. E. H., & Finkelhor, David. (1984). The gender gap among perpetrators of child sexual abuse. In D. E. H. Russell (Ed.), *Sexual exploitation: Rape, child sexual abuse, and workplace harassment* (pp. 215–231). Beverly Hills, CA: Sage.

Zillmann, D., & Bryant, J. (1984). Effects of massive exposure to pornography. In N. Malamuth & E. Donnerstein (Eds.), *Pornography and sexual aggression* (pp. 115–138). New York: Academic Press.

11

What Went Wrong?
Diagnostic and Ethical Problems in Dealing with the Effects of Torture and Repression in South Africa

MICHAEL A. SIMPSON

"Tell me, what went wrong?
Born like I was, good and murky,
Bred like you were, human and odd . . .
Can't you see you've been killing the dead?
Sending me to pastures grey, when pastures green abound?
Have you said I'm good, when dead?
Born like I were, dead as a grave . . .
Born like I am, great and murky,
Bred as I am, human and wise,
Have you said it? Dead.
No, Alive!

From a poem by Donald Madisha, who died as a political prisoner in South Africa in June 1990; found during a psychological autopsy (Simpson, 1993d).

No category of crime has been so extensively and widely condemned as crimes against humanity and abuses of human rights. But beyond doubt, there is no category of criminal so certain to escape punishment or even serious inconvenience, or so likely to retire on a pension at the expense of his or her victims. Trauma is an inevitable consequence of such of-

MICHAEL A. SIMPSON • Centre for Traumatic Stress, P.O. Box 51, Pretoria 0001, South Africa.
Beyond Trauma: Cultural and Societal Dynamics, edited by Rolf J. Kleber, Charles R. Figley, and Berthold P. R. Gersons. New York, Plenum Press, 1995.

fenses, and accordingly, clinicians and researchers working with trauma are provided with both opportunities and responsibilities to understand these phenomena.

This chapter briefly outlines how trauma in South Africa is affected by the social-political-cultural context and by prevalent belief systems. I argue that the political context of trauma has been comprehensively neglected, although it is essential for a full understanding of trauma and its effects. I then review diagnostic and forensic problems arising from this neglect and, finally, examine the ethical problem of how some health professionals become involved in facilitating torture and political trauma.

These themes are explored in relation to my experiences in South Africa in the 1980s and 1990s. It is a society which has suffered the chronic trauma of apartheid and the effects of its acute events. This system of repression and discrimination was designed with the significant use of behavioral science expertise, to enable a very small cultural minority within the country to exert complete political, social, cultural, economic, and personal control over the great majority of its inhabitants who are racially and/or culturally or linguistically different from the ruling caste. It has become abundantly clear that both acute and chronic trauma were deliberately planned, designed, and administered in order to achieve this aim, rather than that they were simply by-products or side effects of the process. The apartheid system has been recognized as a series of crimes against humanity, and the suffering it caused was integral and was in no way regretted by its perpetrators and profiteers.

THE NATURE OF APARTHEID AND ITS RELATED TRAUMA

Apartheid may not have reached some of the grisly genocidal excesses of the Holocaust, but this was not due to scruples on the part of the perpetrators. Rather, it was inhibited by the practical realities of the limits of sustainable repression in more recent decades, and by the need of the regime's favored caste to exploit the labor of the majority. As a result, apartheid was able to endure far longer than the Nazi era. Apartheid is not yet dead: I have not found its grave. The only initial change has been that it is no longer required by law and enforced by the State Department of "Justice." It is not yet effectively prevented or even discouraged, let alone penalized, by law, and its effects on the average citizen have not substantially altered. Just as the effects of the Holocaust still reverberate within direct survivors and within surviving generations and communities, so the effects of apartheid will long outlive the hateful system itself. Elaborate arrangements have been made to preserve and guarantee the wealth and earnings of the bureaucrats who built and ran apartheid. But those so carefully neglected by health care and education are still largely neglected. The hungry are still hungry; the homeless still lack shelter.

Chronic discrimination, poverty, landlessness and homelessness, lack of freedom and civil liberties, and denial of political power and human rights were imposed on all who were outside the ruling caste. In addition, very large numbers suffered acute and sequential trauma arising from the calibrated cruelty of "forced removals" and ethnic cleansing, migrant labor, internal deportations and external exile, torture, political harassment and killings, and chronic social unrest. An unplanned dimension of trauma arose, secondary to these primary causes: a uniquely high degree of social pathology, with higher rates of divorce, rape, intra- and extra-familial abuse, suicide, white-collar and violent crime, motor vehicle accidents, and murder than in most other countries. The usual societal traumas are increased as an indirect result of the extent to which political trauma weakens the body politic and the capacity of a social system to defend and heal itself. In much the same way, HIV leads to the occurrence of opportunistic infections, which would not have been able to thrive but for the effects of the virus. The effects of this array of sources and types of trauma are seen both in the surviving targets of officially administered or sanctioned trauma, and in its perpetrators and beneficiaries, as discussed elsewhere (Simpson, 1993a,e).

THE EFFECTS OF BELIEF SYSTEMS ON TRAUMA AND RESPONSES TO IT

A variety of cognitive framing systems coexist. The perpetrators were nominally Christian (though their actions contradicted every tenet of Christianity), and their political ideology was avowedly right-wing, conservative, authoritarian, rigid, and paternalistic, and was based on a narrow and exclusionary nationalism limited to members of the ruling elite. Faced with an increasingly critical and hostile world, the elite focused more and more inwardly, convincing itself that it was a noble bulwark of those very Western values it so comprehensively degraded, and justifying all its actions as being required by what was repeatedly called a "total onslaught" by a worldwide "communist" conspiracy bent on its destruction.

The majority was initially characterized by a very wide diversity of ethnicity, culture, religion, and ideology, a diversity that the regime sought to exploit by fostering divisiveness and separation by all available means. In earlier decades of the system, many victims responded with a degree of passivity and reluctant acceptance of what seemed inevitable, similar to learned helplessness (Seligman, 1975) and keenly cultivated by the regime. But increasingly, especially in younger generations, awareness of the political dimensions of apartheid came to dominate. One of the social effects of repression was, via an experienced unity of suffering, to forge an increasingly unified liberation movement. Broad consensus developed, a mirror image of that of the regime. Politically, it ranged from center to left-wing; its ideology was determinedly democratic, participatory and inclusive, and nonracial (rather than multiracial, thus embracing all groups without striving for a racially determined balance and without an obsessive focus on racist classifications).

These widely different ideologies affected how people reacted to the trauma of change (Simpson, 1993b). The regime's worldview served it well during its era of dominance. The monopoly of power and profit was justified, both paternalistically (as being ultimately beneficial to the majority, so sadly ungrateful for being deprived) and as regrettably essential to withstand the "onslaught" of the fantasized international plot to destroy it. The mythical external enemy allowed sufficient projection and deflection of all fears and responsibility for evil actions. But the theory disastrously failed to provide sustenance when apartheid imploded, and when the Soviet Union—the focal point of that essential external projection—disintegrated. For those who have not been able to adapt by adopting some version of the majority ethos, the prospect of democracy has been terrifying. Without guaranteed continuance of the excessive and unearned privileges they had so long assumed to be inevitably ordained by nature, normality seems like loss. When the entire sense of self-worth was based on the essentially meaningless fact of skin color, democracy was seen as devaluing that congenital distinction, while offering no equivalent prizes they could comprehend. Extremist groups showed collective dissociative responses, making untenable demands for modes of independence within which they could maintain discriminations favorable to them, though inevitably doomed to fail to meet even their own demands.

On the other hand, the majority and liberation culture contributed positively to coping with the oppressive government. It was helpful to have a widely shared political interpretation of the traumatic events, which accounted for them and validated the value, self-esteem, and courage of those who suffered for opposing Apartheid, and which convincingly predicted the inevitable failure and demise of the hated system. Having a clear, close, and real enemy, obviously directly responsible for negative events, discouraged survivor guilt. Strong community support following trauma has been notable, especially in black communities. A cultural tradition, ancient and modern, of honoring participants in the struggle for freedom, and of valuing storytelling and review, has facilitated the support and resolution of trauma. The liberation belief system is also more compatible with the democratization process, though there are some areas of concern. The leadership of the liberation movement became preoccupied with preparing for the first-ever democratic elections and the likelihood of forming the government. Violent threats by the most conservative black and white minority groups who fear democracy led to extensive steps to placate them, which have seriously compromised the duty to attend to the urgent needs of the needy majority and of those who fought for liberation, returning political exiles, former political prisoners, and the millions of victims of apartheid's trauma. These survivors have felt offended by being ignored and aggrieved that their trauma-related needs have had to compete both with the very real needs of the majority, and with their own other major needs. When you need aid for severe effects of traumatic stress—and also housing, and education, and a job, and clean water, and security from further trauma—the need to prioritize or choose creates further stress. Seeing all these needs subordinated to the selfish and greedy demands of the already overprivileged compounds the offense.

There is an often overlooked difference from, for instance, postwar Europe. The situation would have been far easier had apartheid been defeated militarily. A defeat, a surrender, and a formal date of liberation allow a relatively fresh start. In contrast, South Africa has experienced a sort of negotiated revolution, in which the regime that caused such massive damage to others for generations is negotiating an end to that system. But it has been able to enforce a total and secret amnesty for its worst perpetrators, and to require extensive appeasement, not of the majority or of the victims, but of the minority and of the perpetrators (Simpson, 1992d).

The trauma survivors in South Africa find that the world keeps congratulating them on a good fortune they have not experienced, and on great changes they have not seen. The trauma continues, with minor variation. As an example, during the worst periods of repression, the torture survivors I saw were politically active participants in the liberation struggle. Since negotiations began, many political prisoners have been freed. But now I see ordinary citizens, often wholly innocent and arrested in error for nonpolitical offenses such as theft, who now complain of physical and psychological torture, including electric shock. With the guaranteed availability of amnesty, it seems that old habits die hard.

PROBLEMS OF PSYCHIATRIC DIAGNOSIS IN TORTURE VICTIMS

Is There a Posttorture Syndrome?

There has been much debate about whether there is a specific posttorture syndrome seen in survivors of such experiences, but there is no evidence of the existence of such a discrete syndrome, reliably different from the syndrome of posttraumatic stress disorder (PTSD) seen after all other varieties of extreme traumatic stress, and widely described and diagnosed in torture survivors.

We must distinguish between our wistful wish that there were such a specific, unique posttorture syndrome—a psychological fingerprint whose existence would establish firmly the fact that a person had been tortured (how useful that could be, in practice!)—and the scientific question of whether such a syndrome can be shown to exist. While there is room for further research, the answer to the question seems to be no. Just as earlier decades saw descriptions of a KZ syndrome following concentration camp experience (Schmolling, 1984; Sjaastad, 1986; Thygesen, 1980), and a war sailor syndrome (Askevolde, 1980; Sjaastad, 1986), and a rape trauma syndrome (Burgess & Holmstrom, 1974), and other such entities, none of these have proved to be consistently or usefully different from the currently understood entity of PTSD.

Is PTSD an Adequate Broad Diagnostic Concept?

PTSD is not, of course, the only diagnosis seen in such survivors. Depression, generalized anxiety disorder, and other conditions are also common. There are other more particular sequelae, not as yet fully articulated or broadly accepted, such as the range of responses described rather clumsily as DESNOS (disorders of extreme stress not otherwise specified; proposed for, but not included in, the DSM-IV; American Psychiatric Association, 1994) and better called complex PTSD (Herman 1992a,b). There is also partial PTSD, in patients who consistently suffer from severe symptoms of PTSD without fully meeting the American Psychiatric Associations *Diagnostic and Statistical Manual of Mental Disorders* (DSM) criteria for PTSD in regard to the number of symptoms present at one time. Furthermore, there is an inadequately studied category of "enduring personality change after catastrophic experience" are acute stress reaction in the ICD-10 (World Health Organization, 1992). Finally, there are adjustment disorders; dissociative disorders, including both acute dissociative states and more chronic disorders as late sequelae to childhood trauma, such as self-mutilation and the munchhausen syndrome; and somatization, personality, and other disorders.

Of course PTSD does not describe *all* the phenomena that will be seen in any single patient, but that is not, of course, the function of a diagnostic system. To the extent that one wants a diagnostic system to reliably identify a recurrent cluster of symptoms and/or signs which usefully predict the likely prognosis and course of the illness, and to help to select therapies likely to do more good than harm, the broad concept of PTSD has proved reasonably robust and helpful.

Some would argue that one should not take the diagnosis of PTSD too literally, that it is just a diagnostic concept, and not an entity in itself. The particular organization of criteria may describe a theoretical and practical construct without literal reality in itself (but no different from the literal reality of any other diagnosis), but a common body of symptoms and experiences following severe trauma is a genuine, real entity in external reality. The criteria are satisfactory if they help us to reliably identify real people with consistent characteristics so as to enable us to assist them more efficiently.

General Problems with the DSM Diagnostic Criteria for PTSD

> "What's the use of their having names," the Gnat said, "if they won't answer to them?"
>
> "No use to *them*," said Alice, "but it's useful to the people that name them, I suppose."
>
> Lewis Carroll, ALICE THROUGH THE LOOKING GLASS (1965)

There are some problems, however, with the diagnostic criteria of the DSM (American Psychiatric Association, 1987, 1994), which have entered into wide international use. As such usage was predictable and expected, it is unfortunate that its authors (and especially those preparing the DSM-IV; American Psychiatric Association, 1994) have so persistently failed to facilitate adequate field testing of the criteria and their revisions in settings that would truly test their adequacy, rather than simply suit the convenience of the testers, or to consult those experienced in their use in transcultural settings. In regard to PTSD and other trauma-related states, it is particularly regrettable that they failed to consult effectively with those of us who work with the results of torture and political violence (which often constitute the deliberate induction of such disorders) and who see them soon after the causative events, rather than years or decades later.

Unless such projects are explicitly limited to local usage, it behooves their authors and publishers to test their validity and applicability within the world community that will use them, and where they are energetically marketed. Where there is a significant potential for abuse of the system in undemocratic or oppressive settings, it is ethically important to consider and to try to thwart potential abuses. The producers of the DSM industry have failed to do so. Similarly, researchers whose work may be applied in torture chambers that they never personally enter, or whose published opinions may be used to promote or hide torture, have some responsibility to consider such possible abuses when choosing their words.

As Kirk and Kutchins so eloquently demonstrated in their book *The Selling of DSM: The Rhetoric of Science in Psychiatry* (1992), the DSM has served multiple functions within medical and health care politics and has been markedly shaped by such forces, masked by a rhetoric of science, but often leaving much to be desired in the scientific nature of its construction and field testing. Such testing as was done served the purpose of helping to gain acceptance and marketability but, where it occurred at all, was generally done in such a way as to enhance the likelihood that the criteria would look adequate, and to support the grand claims being made for them, rather than, as a truly scientific approach would require, testing its potential weaknesses and allowing for disproof and refutation of its hypotheses. The backing for the DSM-IV may be more substantial in volume, but it has still ignored many of these needs.

Problems in the Forensic Application of the PTSD Criteria in Relation to Torture and Human Rights Abuses

In South Africa, political detainees were held without trial and without access to lawyer, independent doctor, or family, usually for lengthy periods in solitary confinement, and with protracted interrogation. They have often alleged that they were tortured during their detention. No unbiased but informed observer can doubt that such torture occurred in many instances. The courts have tended strongly to accept the testimony of the police that there was no maltreatment and have placed the onus of proof of torture or coercion to confess on the detainee, failing to recognize that the fact that victims could not bring independent witnesses to support their allegations had no possible logical implication to suggest that their story might not be true but was actually required by the repressive laws.

The issue of whether any evidence suggests that such allegations may be true in any particular case is obviously important. Rarely, a victims seeks damages. More often, the outcome of a trial (and thus, the patient's life or death) could hang on the issue of whether a confession made during the period of incommunicado detention was made under undue pressure, threat, or duress. In addition, just as the uncertainty imposed by political "disappearances" causes severe trauma and suffering, so it may be of primary therapeutic importance to enable a victim to prove what actually happened. So often, victims have been taunted by their captors and have been told that, in the unlikely event of their survival, no one will ever believe them.

Where victims have been held incommunicado, when torture could easily have occurred, where the setting was designed to make it impossible for them to prove what did occur, and where they show a full range of the classical features of PTSD, including nightmares, exaggerated startle responses, and flashbacks, and show definite disturbance on meeting stimuli that recall the events described, are we not entitled to make the diagnosis of PTSD? And does such a diagnosis not lend some credibility to the patient's allegations of prior ill treatment, especially when torture seems to be prominent in the content of the dreams and flashbacks?

Some of the criteria are specifically difficult to assess and to apply to individuals within such settings and circumstances. Symptoms of reex-periencing and those of increased arousal are often seen. Avoidance symptoms can be harder to assess. For instance, if individuals were tor-tured by their interrogators in the prison system within which they are still being held, avoidance of activities or situations that arouse recall of the trauma may be impossible for them to achieve (they are still held by those who caused the trauma and in the place where it occurred). Con-versely, if the trauma happened elsewhere, someone in prison may be effectively (though inadvertently) protected from meeting such stimuli. A patient who in a natural state would probably meet this criterion may in this situation be unable to demonstrate it.

Markedly diminished interest in significant activities may be more difficult to demonstrate in solitary confinement or similar settings in which "significant" activity is prevented. It is not always easy to assess change in normal and close human relationships, a "feeling of detach-ment or estrangement from others," or a restricted range of affect in someone in solitary or high-security confinement. How do you assess the extent to which a person who has been condemned to hang, or a prison-er daily threatened with death, has a significant "sense of a foreshort-ened future"? In such a setting, the *lack* of such a perception might be more odd and noteworthy.

In circumstances where some criteria are not readily assessable, how should one proceed? It could be argued that, unless every listed criterion is fully assessable, one simply cannot make a diagnosis. In relation to general research, where one can simply seek another subject, there is no necessary problem, although this circumstance could exclude significant numbers of actually typical individuals from studies that could benefit them directly. Epidemiologically, this approach could in some settings lead to serious underestimations of the extent of significant posttrauma-tic pathology. Such a position could also have serious implications in forensic settings and could also deny a patient needed treatment, if ruthlessly and insensitively applied.

Simply ignoring the problem item effectively alters the diagnostic threshold among patients who would in different circumstances show an identical extent and severity of psychopathology. A patient unencumbered by this problem needs, for example, only three of seven items to meet Criterion C. But if two of these items are situationally excluded, such a patient would need to demonstrate three out of the remaining five items. One could, for instance, rather accept two of the remaining five items. The basic need is not necessarily to revise the diagnostic criteria, but to develop agreed-on conventions as to how to modify procedures to maintain comparable thresholds of caseness.

Problems with the Stressor Criterion

Although criticisms of the criteria defining whether a stress is traumatic have acquired widespread acceptance in practice since I and others first articulated them soon after the DSM-III and the DSM-III-R were published, they have not yet been adequately reflected in the DSM, nor in modern textbooks. Only recently has the issue begun to be effectively discussed in the literature (March, 1993; Simpson, 1993e). The misleading interpretations are especially mischievous in relation to victims of torture and political violence and thus merit further discussion in print.

The DSM has been (and remains) consistently ambivalent in both recognizing and denying the essential component of subjective perception within the construct, and about how to allow for the obviously relevant issue of the individual's specific and general vulnerabilities, while wishing to exclude patently trivial stresses from recognition as traumatic.

We seem satisfied to assess the traumatic impact of a physical trauma in terms of the physical damage and distortion it induces, without feeling bound to use the instrumentation of physics to estimate the intensity of the stimulus. Lacerations, bruises, and fractures are accepted as sufficient criteria of the traumatogenicity of the stimulus. Yet some authors seem to feel strangely queasy in treating psychological trauma analogously and would prefer to ignore any number of signs and symptoms of the psychological impact of events, in favor of a feeble pretence at "objectivity," referring to the assessor's imaginative assumptions about the likely impact of the event "in most people," or "within the range of usual human experience." Even more absurdly, some have mistakenly claimed that, in diagnosing PTSD, one must assess the severity of the stressor with regard to a guess about how severely it would affect a mythical "average person," while resolutely ignoring the authentic effects on the actual individual involved.

Such exercises in no way introduce objectivity; they substitute the irrelevant subjectivity of the examiner for the relevant subjectivity of the patient. What masquerades as an objective assessment becomes a projective test, more revealing of the nature of the examiner than of the nature of the examined. The more assessors try to ignore the actual person before them, and to invent an "average person," the more the result will be influenced primarily by the imagination and fantasy of the assessors.

Ridiculously and contradictorily, the DSM, while asking us to rate the stress that this "average person" would feel, asks us to invent one "in similar circumstances and with similar sociocultural values," and considering the desirability of the event and the amount of life change it induces, to attend to the "sociocultural values" and "circumstances" of the patient! So, I must ignore how this actual recently divorced Catholic Croatian immigrant laborer experienced the trauma, but I must assess how an *average* recently divorced Catholic Croatian immigrant laborer would experience it. Surely this is simply very silly indeed?

The stressor is defined as being "outside the range of usual human experience," and this definition can cause problems in cynical hands. A state psychiatrist in South Africa has testified that, because political detentions without trial, solitary confinement, and police assaults have been common in the black community, these experiences are therefore not exceptional and thus cannot meet Criterion A! Presumably, he would also argue that the routine horrors of a concentration camp, by their commonness and routinization, would lose the capacity to traumatize.

Surely, the central issue is never the epidemiological frequency of an experience, but whether the occurrence was sufficiently outside the patient's capacity to cope with it to have been traumatic, with some concern to exclude obviously trivial experiences. Once again, the individual response cannot be ignored. A leg is none the less broken because a fall from the same height would not have broken the leg of *most* "average" people and thus was not "outside the range" of human falls?

There is accumulating evidence (March, 1993) that significant numbers of patients show the clinical phenomenology of PTSD following stressors that do not meet the DSM criteria for severity. There is insufficient evidence for the presumption of a major significant difference in the clinical impact of "catastrophic" and more everyday stressors, or for the exclusion of bereavement as a potential cause of PTSD.

The DSM-IV Options Book (American Psychiatric Association, 1991) offers three options. One requires the stressor to be "exceptional" (which depends on the assessor's subjectivity); another emphasizes characteristics of the event (involving "actual or threatened death or injury, or a threat to the physical integrity of oneself or others"); and a third combines these options with recognition of the patient's subjective response (involving "intense fear, helplessness, or horror").

The ICD-10 (World Health Organization, 1992) refers to a stressful event "of an exceptionally threatening or catastrophic nature, which is likely to cause pervasive distress in almost anyone," a description that may also exaggerate the severity of trauma required to produce the relevant symptoms, although it does move toward an appropriate recognition of the role of vulnerability.

Inappropriate Unease about Recognizing the Causal Sequence in PTSD

Some authors have raised a peculiar concern about the diagnosis of PTSD, saying, like Engdahl and Eberly (1990), that "it is curious that in a diagnostic manual that purports to eschew etiologic considerations (on grounds of insufficient knowledge) PTSD is the lone companion of the organic mental disorders in having a pinpointed causal sequence." (Oddly, they forgot about the whole very analogous section of psychoactive-substance-use disorders). Why on earth should the failure to be able to determine the etiology of *other* psychiatric disorders make anyone hesitate to define it when we can? Should we eschew etiological considerations where sufficient knowledge *does* exist? We do not feel coy about describing alcoholism as being related to alcohol consumption. How could we contemplate an alcohol-free definition of alcoholism? No one has qualms about diagnosing posttraumatic leg fractures in relation to the "purported" causative trauma. No other mental or physical insult to the human being is assessed thus.

The extent to which the DSM-III-R can be abused in regard to torture is seen when, as in the Cele case (Simpson, 1989), a person was detained without trial, held in solitary confinement for months, interrogated for lengthy periods, and eventually produced a confession. When in court facing the resultant charges, he repudiated the confession, saying he had been tortured. There was medical evidence supporting his story. On careful clinical examination, he had all the features of PTSD and met the DSM-III-R criteria, and the defense psychiatrist made that diagnosis. A psychiatrist working for the South African government insisted that it was impossible to make the diagnosis because, he argued, one cannot ever diagnose PTSD unless there is "objective, collateral proof" of the existence of the stressor (a requirement invented by him and highly convenient in hiding the effects of torture). This cynical proposition would mean that PTSD could be diagnosed only in victims of torture and rape, with the active consent and assistance of the torturer and the rapist. The state psychiatrist in this case also argued that solitary confinement, an incommunicado detention of indefinite duration, was not severe enough to meet Criterion A and suggested that even assault, interrogation, and torture might not be sufficient to qualify. This is obviously untrue. It is clear in unbiased experience that such stressors are often sufficient to cause PTSD.

Are the Phenomena Listed in the Criteria Always Symptoms?

There are features which we appropriately describe as criteria and as symptoms in a patient in a stable, generally safe community, who has survived a discrete, single, distant traumatic event well in the past (like a burg amid the placid community life). Yet the same features, while still relevant as criteria in reaching the diagnosis, may be necessary survival skills in other communities and circumstances. In repressive societies, what would otherwise be hypervigilance may be adaptive: Hypovigilance can kill. It may still be a characteristic sequel to trauma, but not necessarily a symptom, while it is still functional and useful. Similarly, some of the avoidance symptoms, to the extent that they avert disruption by emotional responses and by avoiding reexposure to danger, may be adaptive during continuing trauma.

Posttraumatic Social Disorders

We should also recognize the extent to which posttraumatic disorders can be interpersonal and more broadly social phenomena. Denial, numbing, and avoidance do not occur solely within the direct victims. It has been repeatedly confirmed that they often suffer from the denial, numbing, and avoidance responses of others, as their need to discuss and explore their reactions to traumatic events is matched by the reluctance of others to hear or comprehend them.

The possibility that the individual experience of abuse may lead to later abusive conduct is recognized and debated. Within the community and society, a similar recursive cycle can occur. At this level, trauma can indeed generate further trauma. Where no attempts by normal and peaceful means are allowed to improve the situation, some of those survivors of continuing repression and trauma, frustrated by the certainty of lack of progress, may take action involving force or violence. They are usually condemned unreservedly, while the violence of repression is largely ignored and exonerated. Repression usually claims to be justified on the basis of the violence to which it gave rise, the trauma of which it was a substantial cause.

Most of the literature on posttraumatic disorders has focused on the effects of conventional warfare on combatants (with a limited focus on the impact on noncombatant civilians, and with limited attention to the effects of nonconventional, guerrilla warfare). There is a largely separate literature on the effects of terrorism, mainly looking at nonstate terrorism. The literature on torture and state terrorism is very limited and is excessively concentrated on the atypical experiences of distant centers profitably treating refugees and largely rather obsessively engaged in cataloguing the categories of cruelty and the associated symptoms, while avoiding serious study of or engagement with the universal political element in such trauma, or in work realistically likely to help prevent such events. Only recently have realistic studies of the context and culture of such processes begun to appear (e.g., Kelman, 1993; Staub, 1993).

An increasingly common cause of both planned and side-effect trauma is a newer variety of political warfare, sometimes called *low-intensity conflict*. Such methods are far from "low-intensity" in their impact on the victims of such conflict but avoid the set-piece, dramatic, and widely recognized ordinance-oriented battles fondly recorded by historians. South Africa has been one good example of this method of state terrorism. In such strategies of conflict, the noncombatant community is the primary target of state activity, with the result that increased numbers of individual casualties of traumatic stress arise, as well as the development of communities with a climate of chronic political violence and other consistent patterns of posttraumatic community stress disorders.

ETHICAL ASPECTS OF TORTURE, HUMAN RIGHTS ABUSES, AND THE PARTICIPATION OF HEALTH PROFESSIONALS

All I maintain is that on this earth there are pestilences and there are victims, and it's up to us, as far as possible, not to join forces with the pestilence.

ALBERT CAMUS, *The Plague*

Another dimension is the participation of health and mental health professionals in torture and human rights abuses. This is not merely an ethical problem but contributes greatly to the frequency with which such trauma is inflicted, and to the skill and efficacy with which its practitioners inflict traumatic stress disorders.

Although there is a large literature deploring such involvement, mainly written by people with no direct personal experience of such abuses, there have been no really comprehensive models of the ways in which health professionals can be involved and of the conditions which facilitate their involvement. Thus, I discuss below my general model of these varieties of unethical conduct and then illustrate it with some briefly described local examples. To propose detailed solutions to this currently intractable problem lies beyond the scope of this chapter and lies elsewhere in my writings, but before one can contemplate realistic solutions, one needs to understand the nature of the pathology of such unethical behaviors.

Comparing the Situations in South Africa and Nazi Germany

There are significant similarities between the South African experience and that of Nazi Germany, and major figures in the formation of the ruling South African Nationalist Party, which created apartheid, were for years unabashed admirers of German National Socialism. There were not such gross examples of abuses of medical science as the pseudoscientific experiments of the Nazi doctors, which senior and academic figures in German medicine condoned and in which many participated (Pross, 1991). Yet the research uses of black subjects in South Africa and the creation of discriminatory and damaging health services (De Beer, 1984) deserve close scrutiny and serious concern. But while Nazi atrocities used and abused addled anthropology and physiology, South Africa saw especially the perversion of the social and behavioral sciences in the design, creation, and administration of apartheid. Prime Minister Hendrik Verwoerd, its prime architect, was a qualified sociologist and psychologist, a former professor of applied psychology (Fisher, 1969; Hepple, 1967), whose doctoral thesis had been on "The Blunting of the Emotions."

Much malignant creativity was shown, for example, in the evolution of interrogation techniques which involved the careful and deliberate induction of acute traumatic stress disorders. This strongly suggests professional involvement in helping to make more efficient the politicians' permanent "solution" to the "problem" of its people (even South African schools and universities gave lessons dealing with "the Indian problem" and "the African problem"). Of the Afrikaner doctors in South Africa, one could echo the comment of Pross (1991): "It is striking how willingly German doctors were prepared to cover up for their criminal colleagues with false medical diagnoses and on the other hand how fussy and reluctant they were in acknowledging the severe illnesses of Nazi victims, for whom they had to provide expert opinions in compensation trials" (p. 14). (See also Pross, 1988.)

Lifton (1986) explored the issue of how the Nazi doctors were able to participate in genocide and medical killing. He developed the concept of "doubling," a Faustian bargain in which such doctors, having made a choice for evil, split the self into two functioning wholes, each able to act as an entire self. One would be the "Auschwitz self," fully capable of the dirty work of taking part in the diabolical deeds in the camps, and the other would be the "prior self," able to retain his or her formerly humane conduct at home. Thus, the doctor could do dreadful things and yet still see himself or herself as essentially unchanged and decent. Such a shift in moral consciousness presupposes the existence of a significantly different "prior self," which would not have been capable of bad deeds, and an initial perception of the prejudicial activities as profoundly wrong. In the case of the South African doctors who participated in human rights abuses, it is far from clear that they ever perceived such deeds as other than their correct and patriotic duty, or that there was any prior self not equally capable of such deeds and not already considering the victims as sufficiently nonhuman as not to be considered worthy of more humane treatment. Some did, though, show the sort of "derealization" which the Mitscherlichs (1975) described as divesting oneself of the actuality of what one is part of, not choosing to recognize the impact or extent of one's acts as part of a larger system of oppression. These doctors also showed a refusal to contemplate any of their very real alternatives to resist or at least not to participate, using such mechanisms to avoid recognizing their accountability in a manner very like that discussed by Rosenbaum (1993) in his study of the prosecution of Nazi war criminals.

The Nature of the Problem

Torture is a common practice internationally, and there is consistent clear evidence of the frequent involvement of health professionals, especially doctors and psychologists, in the process (Amnesty International, 1992; British Medical Association, 1992; Stover & Nightingale, 1985). As I have discussed elsewhere (Simpson, 1992b), existing international laws and codes of professional conduct are seriously inadequate, and means of specifically discouraging this conduct are entirely lacking. A mechanism for investigating such complaints, and for excluding from professional activity all those who compromise codes of conduct, is much needed. Currently, some of the doctors, lawyers, and others who were involved in the commission of human rights abuses, and in the protection of perpetrators, have been freely emigrating to Europe, America, and Canada, and the ease with which such people are able to emigrate and gain registration and employment in other countries when their protective regimes fail adds nothing to the promotion and protection of human rights.

Torture, like all convenient abuses of power, is addictive both to individuals and to governments. Protection, amnesty, and care for the torturers and their assistants have always been far more effective, and much better funded, than any provision for their victims (Simpson, 1992a). The major weakness of current international conventions and declarations is that they specifically exclude major human rights abuses not occurring in the context of formally declared aggressive war, and/or actions against a nation's own citizens (almost certainly the largest category of victims), and/or suffering arising from "low-intensity conflict" or from "legal sanctions," thus effectively evading the problem of the many states which have passed laws allowing inhuman and degrading treatment.

Torture and the Prevention of Traumatic Stress Disorders

If one has any concern for the prevention of traumatic stress disorders, then the prevention of human-made disorders can be more effective than attempts to prevent earthquakes or other acts of God. There is, therefore, a need to identify and study those circumstances which facilitate the practice of torture. Just as bacteria flourish when exposed to situations ideally suited to their growth needs, so torture thrives within environments that meet the torturer's needs.

Characteristics of settings hospitable to the successful practice of torture include giving any officials the power to seize and detain people in secret, without having to show clear proof of sufficient cause to a court of justice not fully controlled by the state; allowing the secret holding of detainees incommunicado, and without access to family and friends, or to independent lawyers and doctors of their choice; allowing circumstances of detention in which there will be no independent witnesses of the conduct of those holding the detainee, or of the potential results of torture and maltreatment; not allowing for independent and public investigation of reports of torture and related maltreatment or having such investigations conducted by the police and security or prison authorities themselves; and allowing the use in court of statements extracted in situations in which torture is alleged or possible, as in South Africa, while placing the onus on prisoners held incommunicado to prove the truth of their allegations of torture, rather than requiring the state to prove that such statements were made voluntarily and free of coercion. The final ingredient which greatly encourages torture and abuse is the availability of amnesty for such actions (Simpson, 1992a).

As the South African experience has shown, such circumstances will allow the practice of torture with impunity, or, at least, with a minimum risk of discovery or interference with its practice. Such existing agreements and codes also err by overemphasizing physical methods of torture and mere physical damage. Torture is rarely carried out simply to achieve its physical effects as such (except when meeting the psychopathological personal needs of torturers themselves) but is used for the psychological effects these have (Simpson, 1993e). Skillfully used psychological pressures can break almost anyone. Coercive interrogation and related psychological torture constitute a specific form of antitherapy: the deliberate and expert production of posttraumatic stress disorders in the service of repression.

Similarly, instruments such as the United Nations *Principles of Medical Ethics Relevant to the Role of Health Personnel, Particularly Physicians, in the Protection of Prisoners and Detainees against Torture* (United Nations,

1982) have concentrated on forbidding the direct physical involvement of health professionals in the conduct of torture, while ignoring the many indirect ways in which they far more frequently assist in torture.

Analysis of the Ways in Which Health Professionals Assist in Torture

Those who use torture, apart from their political aims, usually also want to achieve deniability: to be able to prevent the victims from proving what happened to them and who did it to them. Doctors have been especially active in helping torturers achieve this unworthy aim. Understanding these modes of assistance is an essential step in seeking to prevent this common cause of traumatic stress.

Health professionals can be involved in abuses of human rights in different phases:

1. Prior to torture:
   a. Their expertise may help to identify and select appropriate target victims. In state terrorism, like any other terrorism, the targets are chosen in order that their suffering or danger will have a maximum impact on others in the local or international community (Simpson, 1987; 1988).
   b. They may help to design and select the most effective methods, especially of psychological torture, and can assess the weaknesses and vulnerabilities of the victim, so that techniques of torture and coercive interrogation can be matched to these, for maximum effect. This is often done in the name of providing health care to detainees, but with sharing of information with the captors, rather than maintaining the confidentiality of medical records.
   c. They may certify that the victim is fit for interrogation and torture or fit for execution (a South African psychiatrist, for example, has boasted of how many men he has sent to hang, often for political offenses).
   d. Drugs may be prescribed and/or administered to assist in softening up victims and in reducing their capacity to resist, such as the use of benzodiazepines to induce disinhibition and to affect memory.
2. During torture:
   a. By their presence before, during, and/or after torture, they can give it an air of respectability and of due process, helping the torturers to feel more secure, while also frightening the

victims with an awareness that sophisticated knowledge of body and mind is being used by their captors.

b. Drugs may be prescribed or administered to damage or hurt the patient, or to facilitate the processes of coercion and torture.

c. By monitoring the progress and effects of torture, they can advise the interrogators when to pause and revive the subject, to enable to process to be cruelly prolonged; similarly, by providing acute resuscitation, they may enable torture and interrogation to be prolonged.

d. Detainees' capacity to resist their captors can be undermined by providing inadequate medical treatment of their health problems.

3. Following torture:

a. They can provide treatment not purely for the patient's benefit, but to enable torture and interrogation to continue over extended periods.

b. Treatment can be provided, not so much for the patient's benefit, but so as to help to reduce or remove telltale signs of torture, so that such signs will not be found, by the courts, inspectors, or potential independent witnesses, of what has been done to the victim.

c. They can advise the captors as to when it is safe to allow the victims to be seen by others, without showing signs of what has happened to them.

d. There are many ways in which they can hide evidence of torture: by keeping no medical records; by omitting or falsifying relevant details in such records; by giving cynical or false evidence in court or at inquests or inquiries, denying the facts; by misrepresenting scientific knowledge in interpreting such evidence in favor of the official denials of abuse; or by explaining away the facts so as to enable or encourage the court to ignore evidence strongly suggestive of torture.

e. By using knowledge gained in the confidentiality of the doctor–patient relationship, they can assist the state or security police in their interrogation or in the prosecution of political prisoners; discuss the patient's confidential medical affairs with the security police or similar authorities; share clinical decisions as to diagnosis, treatment, and referral with the police; and even defer to police or security needs and judgments in making such clinical decisions.

Illustrative Examples from Recent South African Experience

A doctor from the department of psychiatry at a major Afrikaans university took part in the treatment of a political detainee suffering from PTSD arising after his interrogation in solitary confinement, referred to him by the prison doctors. Without revealing his intentions to his patient, and without obtaining his consent, the doctor then worked closely with the state prosecutor, advising him, even in court, when the state challenged the diagnosis and the necessary management of the patient, but without himself testifying, as this would have opened him to cross-examination about his conduct.

Another psychiatrist in Pretoria, associated with the same department, worked extensively with the security police in opposing expert evidence of damage to political detainees. In various trials, he testified that interrogation conducted with the subject kept standing for 10 to 14 hours without rest would not be highly stressful; that PTSD cannot be diagnosed unless there is absolute, external, independent, irrefutable, and objective proof of the facts and nature of the trauma (though this would invalidate almost every diagnosis of PTSD ever made and would forbid the use of the diagnosis without the collaboration of the torturer); and that it was impossible for the defense psychiatrist to diagnose PTSD after examining the patient for a total of only 12 hours, but that he could authoritatively diagnose that the man had no possible psychiatric disorder whatever, without ever examining the patient, but solely on the basis of having watched him listen to some other evidence in court.

In the case of a political prisoner kidnapped in another country and brought to South Africa under duress, the man developed very severe psychiatric symptoms after interrogation and torture. A prison doctor decided to arrange to transfer his patient to the psychiatric department of the local university hospital for observation and expert treatment. His clinical decision was intercepted and countermanded by a more senior doctor, who did not examine the patient but discussed the case with senior security-police officials and, jointly with them, decided instead to transfer his colleague's patient to solitary confinement in another city, providing no facilities whatsoever for expert observation or treatment. Instead, he arranged for access by a forensic specialist working with the security police, who specialized solely in preparing court reports, and who has not been known to agree that any black political prisoner has ever suffered from any serious clinical state.

Finally, let us consider the example of a professor of forensic medicine who was appointed as assessor (a role which is designed to enable such a specialist to advise the court on highly technical evidence, and which also gave him an equal status with the judge or magistrate in deciding the verdict) in an inquest into the sudden death of a political prisoner in highly ambiguous circumstances. Among the evidence heard and accepted by the court acting with his expert assistance, and not seriously challenged or questioned by him in court, were the following assertions, all of which are totally contrary to scientific knowledge and to the professor's own textbook on forensic medicine: that the patient had received a large intravenous injection of diazepam some 12 hours before he was found dead of asphyxia, but no trace of any drug was found in his blood after death; that the police surgeon had been able to reliably establish, when called to the scene, that the man had been dead for exactly 20 minutes (this timing being of critical importance in averting suspicion from certain police officers) and that he had achieved this assessment, with such precision previously unknown to the world of forensic science, simply by guessing the body temperature by placing his hand on the man's forehead; and that there was no significant contradiction or problem in the discovery that a police doctor had sworn in his affidavit and had recorded in the prison records that the patient had never had any medical complaints nor had ever received any treatment, while his own personal records of their consultations showed that there had been significant medical complaints, diagnoses, and treatments by him. With the assistance of this professor, the court found nothing suspicious or irregular in the facts of the case, the likely cause of death, or the standard of the care the detainee had received.

Modes of Political Abuse of Psychiatry

There has been a great deal of worldwide publicity about the political abuses of psychiatry and of mental health services, concentrating on the former Soviet Union almost entirely, to the exclusion of recognizing political abuses elsewhere. The Soviet experiences have been promoted, not as an example of what can happen, but as if the Soviet Union were the sole exemplar of it. In South Africa, equally serious abuses of psychiatry occurred, but in a mirror image of the Soviet abuses that have been so well described (e.g., Cohen, 1989; Gluzman, 1989; Van Voren, 1987).

In the Soviet Union, for a period, the publicly promoted political myth was that there was complete political freedom and that the reason for the lack of a significant and organized opposition was that there was really no successful or popular competing political viewpoint. It was felt to be undesirable to incarcerate political dissidents for being political dissidents; in such an ideal state, there should simply be no dissidence. Instead, significant numbers were declared to be psychiatrically unfit, and to be suffering from specially devised political "psychiatric" diagnoses, so that they could be held in psychiatric facilities without public trial or open legal process. Thus, healthy dissidents were dealt with by being given a nonexistent psychiatric diagnosis, against the interests of their mental health.

In South Africa, the regime had no compunction about seizing political dissidents and punishing them, with or without trial, for holding and supporting alternate political views. But it wished to maintain a public political myth that it provided caring, compassionate treatment of all the huge numbers of people in its prisons and institutions, and it had laws that would have been embarrassing to remove, which stated that the health of prisoners and detainees must be maintained in excellent condition. When, as a result of torture, coercive interrogation, brutality, and sheer neglect, political prisoners became ill, the regime did not want this fact to be acknowledged, both because to do so would confirm the common knowledge of how cruelly detainees were treated, and because it could be argued in court that such ill and traumatized detainees should be released.

There was no lack, in South Africa, of white Afrikaans doctors and psychiatrists who were happy to assist by skillfully and emphatically finding nothing wrong with political detainees, no matter how severe their symptoms, and by testifying that they were perfectly fit, no matter how damaged they might be. There was also an almost total lack of doctors willing to take the risk of working with human rights lawyers to testify as to the facts of such trauma.

Thus, there was widespread political abuse of medicine and psychiatry, but in the mirror image of the Soviet abuses. In South Africa, unhealthy and traumatized dissidents were dealt with by being denied real psychiatric and physical diagnoses, and by a denial of the existence of their genuine illnesses and suffering, against the interests of their mental health.

CONCLUSION

Other authors in this book have written about the importance of taking sociocultural factors more closely into account in seeking to understand the effects of traumatic stress. I would add that it is equally important to understand the political context of the events and individuals. Just as no one speaks except by using linguistic and grammatical structures of which we generally have little or no conscious awareness, so no one acts except within a political context—political in the sense of power relationships and social governance, and not of party politics.

Much trauma has directly political causes, and almost all trauma has politically relevant effects and dimensions. Some trauma is obviously highly political in causation, like assassinations (Simpson, 1993c), warfare, Holocaust, and persecution. But all trauma arising from human agency—human actions or inaction—is at least in part determined by political forces, effects, and motives. Even the effects of natural disasters, so-called acts of God, are usually significantly affected by political factors and are not equal-opportunity destroyers. When the floods, the earthquakes, and the fires come, the families in the flimsy wooden shacks, who are unemployed and have very few material or social resources, are often at higher risk of exposure to trauma and its effects, both in the course of the disaster event and in its aftermath. Similarly, as the trauma literature is gradually beginning to explore effectively, rape and child and marital abuse are essentially acts within sexual and gender politics and family and interpersonal politics and are pathologies of power relationships. Not only does politics cause trauma, but in a relevant sense, trauma causes politics. Individual, group, and societal responses to earlier trauma form a substantial substrate for the violence, pain, and conflict that pervade the world (Simpson, 1993b; De Zulueta, 1993).

The human potential for violence and injustice to others lies in all of us. Internally, individuals need to defeat the tyrant within by the personal exercise of reason and a will to justice. Because not everyone can or will choose to defeat or control this inner tyrant consistently, we need the external structure of law, like a moral exoskeleton, to allow all to enjoy their human rights within a framework that is just; to protect the weak from the strong, the scrupulous from the unscrupulous; and to enable genuine freedom to occur. In South Africa, a society was created in which, with marvelous consistency, very few good deeds go unpunished, and very few bad deeds go unrewarded. We are trying to recover from a situation in which the laws protect the strong from the weak, and rather than serving justice, these laws often required injustice.

A common variety of denial among workers in the field of trauma is the fallacy of neutrality. Within secure and established democracies, there are many issues and debates from which a professional caregiver can remain aloof. But with regard to torture and repression, doing nothing, or behaving as if nothing is happening, is *not* neutral; it is pathological denial and is usually effective assistance to the perpetrators. As Montaigne wrote some 400 years ago, "Science without conscience is but the death of the soul." No doctor feels bound to be neutral toward cancer. We proudly oppose it and feel no need to balance evenly the needs of the patient and the needs of the cancer. Why should we treat torture, the cancer of freedom, any differently?

210

MICHAEL A. SIMPSON

POSTSCRIPT

This chapter was written in early 1994. As of this writing, 18 months have passed of what has been called the "New South Africa." The world has congratulated the nation and its people for achieving "peaceful transformation." But it has been a weird form of peace, causing death and damage in political violence fully equivalent to a modest-scale war, yet this is called "unrest," as if merely minor turbulence. Sadder still is the disillusionment among those who suffered in the struggle for freedom, who have seen their needs and wishes ignored. The perpetrators have not only avoided all penalties, but great care has been taken to spare them embarrassment or inconvenience. Many millions of rands have been spent on lavish pensions for their care. In contrast, no realistic provision has been made for their victims, who will be heavily taxed to pamper them. In a supreme insult, the law set up a "Truth and Reconciliation Commission" to provide formal amnesty for all crimes perpetrators may admit. This denies victims of apartheid the right to seek civil damages or reparation from those who injured them. Leaders of the liberation movement now in government show a variation of "identification with the aggressor," by pandering to the perpetrators. Those who coped with apartheid, aided by hopes for a just and fruitful victory, are now bitterly disaffected (Simpson, 1996).

Most international funding, the only source of support for the defense of human rights and the care of victims, stopped after the election, and the new government fails to make any provision for these continuing and urgent needs. South Africa has given history an example, not of how peace is attained by peaceful negotiation, but how skillfully a repressive minority can retain their benefits and ensure the continued neglect of their victims. Those who dreamed of freedom and recognition for their contribution to attaining it have been trampled, and express no hope for the future: a situation far worse than their state under apartheid, for no one will liberate them from the Liberation that failed to set them free.

This is a basis for severe, continuing, and evolving postraumatic problems. The new Political Correctness forbids victims to speak of their experiences. In the name of reconciliation, they must be silent about their anguish—The Silence of the Lame—as those who are responsible for the new suffering are admired international icons. The future for survivors of apartheid has never been bleaker.

REFERENCES

American Psychiatric Association. (1987). *Diagnostic and statistical manual of mental disorders* (3rd ed., rev.; DSM-III-R). Washington, DC: Author.

American Psychiatric Association (1991). *DSM-IV options book.* Washington, DC: Author.
American Psychiatric Association. (1994). *Diagnostic and statistical manual of mental disorders* (4th ed.; DSM-IV). Washington, DC: Author.
Amnesty International. (1992). *Amnesty International Report: 1992.* London: Author.
Askevolde, F. (1980). The war sailor syndrome. *Danish Medical Bulletin, 27,* 220–223.
British Medical Association. (1992). *Medicine betrayed: The participation of doctors in human rights abuses.* London: Zed Books.
Burgess, A. W., & Holmstrom, L. L. (1974). Rape trauma syndrome. *American Journal of Psychiatry, 131,* 981–986.
Carroll, L. (1965). *Alice through the looking glass.* London: Penguin.
Cohen, D. (1989). *Soviet psychiatry: Politics and mental health in the USSR today.* London: Paladin.
De Beer, C. (1984). *The South African disease: Apartheid health and health services.* Johannesburg: Southern African Research Service.
De Zulueta, F. (1993). *From pain to violence: The traumatic roots of destructiveness.* London: Whurr.
Engdahl, E. E., & Eberly, R. E. (1990). The effects of torture and other captivity maltreatment: Implications for psychology. In P. Suedfeld (Ed.), *Psychology and torture* (Chap. 3). New York: Hemisphere.
Fisher, J. (1969). *The Afrikaners.* London: Chappell.
Gluzman, S. (1989). *On Soviet totalitarian psychiatry.* Amsterdam: International Association on the Political Uses of Psychiatry.
Hepple, A. (1967). *Verwoerd.* London: Penguin.
Herman, J. L. (1992a). Complex PTSD: A syndrome in survivors of prolonged and repeated trauma. *Journal of Traumatic Stress, 5,* 377–392.
Herman, J. L. (1992b). Sequelae of prolonged repeated trauma: Evidence for a complex posttraumatic syndrome (DESNOS). In J. R. T. Davidson & E. B. Foa (Eds.), *PTSD: DSM-IV and beyond* (pp. 213–228). Washington, DC: American Psychiatric Press.
Kelman, H. C. (1993). The social context of torture: Policy process. In R. D. Crelinstein & A. P. Schmidt (Eds.), *The politics of pain: Torturers and their masters* (pp. 21–38). Leiden, Netherlands: COMT.
Kirk, S. A., & Kutchins, H. (1992). *The selling of DSM: The rhetoric of science in psychiatry.* New York: Aldine de Gruyter.
Lifton, R. (1986). *The Nazi doctors: Medical killing and the psychology of genocide.* New York: Basic Books.
March, J. S. (1993). What constitutes a stressor? The "Criterion A" issue. In J. R. T. Davidson & E. B. Foa (Eds.), *Posttraumatic stress disorder: DSM-IV and beyond* (pp. 37–55). Washington, DC: American Psychiatric Press.
Mitscherlich, A., & Mitscherlich, M. (1975). *The inability to mourn.* New York: Grove Press.
Pross, C. (1988). *Wiedergutmachung: Der Kleinkrieg gegen die Opfer.* Frankfurt: Atheneum Verlag.
Pross, C. (1991). Breaking through the postwar coverup of Nazi doctors in Germany. *Journal of Medical Ethics, 17* (Suppl.), 13–16.
Rosenbaum, A. A. (1993). *Prosecuting Nazi war criminals.* Boulder, CO: Westview Press.
Schmolling, P. (1984). Human reactions to the Nazi concentration camps: A summing up. *Journal of Human Stress, 10,* 108–120.
Seligman, M. E. P. (1975). *Helplessness: On depression, development and death.* San Francisco: Freeman.
Simpson, M. A. (1987, November). *Psychological findings in eight accused of murder by "common purpose" in the course of a township riot: Report to the court in the case of State vs. M. Ncaphayi,*

V. Jack, B. Sonamzi, S. Booysen, E. Nelani, M. Sgoko, R. Yebe, and N. Madolo. Supreme Court of South Africa (Eastern Cape Division), Grahamstown.

Simpson, M. A. (1988, June). *Psychological and psychiatric findings in three men accused of terrorist bombings: Report to the Court in the case of State versus Nthunzi Tshika, Thembinkosi Nkosi, and Zwellinjani Mathe.* Supreme Court of South Africa, Pietermaritzburg.

Simpson, M. A. (1989, January). *Traumatic stress problems in a patient alleging prolonged solitary confinement, prolonged interrogation, and torture: Report to the court in the case of State versus P. Sibankulu, T. Nkgati, and M. P. Cele.* Natal Regional Court, Newcastle and Utrecht, South Africa.

Simpson, M. A. (1992a, December). Amnesty means never having to say you're sorry. *Critical Health* (Johannesburg), *41,* 23–25.

Simpson, M. A. (1992b, June). *Ethical aspects of torture and health professionals.* Paper presented to the ISTSS First World Conference on Traumatic Stress, Amsterdam.

Simpson, M. A. (1993a). Bitter waters: Effects on children of the stresses of unrest and oppression. In J. P. Wilson & B. Raphael (Eds.), *The international handbook of traumatic stress syndromes* (pp. 601–624). New York: Plenum Press.

Simpson, M. A. (1993b, June 10). *Changes as trauma: Challenges in the transition to democracy in South Africa.* Closing Plenary Address, Third European Conference on Traumatic Stress, Bergen, Norway.

Simpson, M. A. (1993c, June 10). *On surviving assassination attempts.* Paper presented to the Third European Conference on Traumatic Stress, Bergen, Norway.

Simpson, M. A. (1993d). Poems and notes by Donald Madisha, South African detainee. *Torture, 3*(4), 125–130.

Simpson, M. A. (1993e). Traumatic stress and the bruising of the soul: The effects of torture and coercive interrogation. In J. P. Wilson & B. Raphael (Eds.), *The international handbook of traumatic stress syndromes* (pp. 667–684). New York: Plenum Press.

Simpson, M. A. (1996). The second bullet—Intergenerational impacts of trauma: The South African experience. In Y. Danieli (Ed.), *Multigenerational legacies of trauma: An international handbook.* New York: Plenum.

Sjaastad, O. (1986). The war sailor and KZ syndrome. *Functional Neurology, 1,* 5–19.

Staub, E. (1993). Torture: Psychological and cultural origins. In R. D. Crelinstein & A. P. Schmidt (Eds.), *The politics of pain: Torturers and their masters* (pp. 109–123). Leiden, Netherlands: COMT.

Stover, E., & Nightingale, E. O. (1985). *The breaking of bodies and minds: Torture, psychiatric abuse, and the health professions.* San Francisco: Freeman.

Task Force on DSM-IV. (1991, September 1). *DSM-IV options book: Work in progress.* Washington, DC: American Psychiatric Association.

Thygesen, P. (1980). The concentration camp syndrome. *Danish Medical Bulletin, 27,* 224–228.

United Nations. (1982). *Principles of medical ethics relevant to the role of health personnel, particularly physicians, in the protection of prisoners and detainees against torture.* New York: Author.

Van Voren, R. (Ed.). (1987). *Koryagin: A man struggling for human dignity.* Amsterdam: Second World Press.

World Health Organization. (1992). *The ICD-10 classification of mental and behavioural disorders: Clinical descriptions and diagnostic guidelines.* Geneva: Author.

12

Health Problems in Areas Contaminated by the Chernobyl Disaster
Radiation, Traumatic Stress, or Chronic Stress?

JAN VAN DEN BOUT, JOHAN M. HAVENAAR, and
LUDMILLA I. MEIJLER-ILJINA

INTRODUCTION

On April 26, 1986, one of the four blocks of the Ukrainian nuclear power plant at Chernobyl exploded as a result of human error. The fatal accident sequence was initiated by the decision of the plant's management to shut down all safety mechanisms in the reactor in an overnight experiment to test the generator under extreme conditions. That night, at 01.24 hours, eyewitnesses outside Chernobyl Unit 4 observed two explosions, one after the other. Burning debris and sparks shot into the air above the reactor, some of which fell on the roof of the machine room and started a fire. The explosions left a gaping hole in the roof, exposing the reactor core to the outside air (Medvedev, 1990; Mould, 1988). Fire-fighters from the nearby town of Pripyat made heroic efforts to control

JAN VAN DEN BOUT • Department of Clinical and Health Psychology, Utrecht University, 3584 CS Utrecht, The Netherlands.   JOHAN M. HAVENAAR and LUDMILLA I. MEIJLER-ILJINA • Department of Psychiatry, Utrecht University, 3584 CS Utrecht, The Netherlands.
Beyond Trauma: Cultural and Societal Dynamics, edited by Rolf J. Kleber, Charles R. Figley, and Berthold P. R. Gersons. New York, Plenum Press, 1995.

the fires. Even after rescue workers had entered the Unit 4 building, the operating crew reacted with disbelief to the reported devastation of the reactor's core. Disbelief and outright denial also characterized the first official response. The authorities had only recently proclaimed that the Chernobyl reactor was so safe that one could have built it on Red Square in Moscow. Only when alarming background readings of radioactivity in the Scandinavian countries made it apparent that a large-scale nuclear accident was occurring somewhere in the Soviet Union did the first public announcements appear in the Soviet press. The state press agency, TASS, issued a four-line statement that an accident had occurred at the Chernobyl nuclear power plant and that every measure had been taken to limit the damage.

Meanwhile, hundreds of tons of radioactive dust were released and dispersed over Europe (see Figure 1), and even over the whole world. Elevated levels of radiation, especially due to short-lived radioactive iodine contamination, caused anxiety in large parts of Europe. Governments had to impose protective measures for the safety of the population in areas as remote from the reactor site as the Netherlands and Italy. The Chernobyl disaster was the largest civil nuclear disaster ever. The efforts made by the governments of three former USSR republics (Belarus, Ukraine, and Russia) to assess and monitor the consequences of the accident and the resources allocated to this assessment were probably one of the greatest operations ever created in response to a human-made environmental disaster (Shigematsu, 1991). The disaster has affected and will continue to affect the lives of millions of people, especially those of the more than 4 million people who are still living in contaminated areas.

The first two authors have visited the contaminated areas in the three republics more than a dozen times since 1991. During these visits, many patients were seen and medical doctors, psychiatrists, authorities and activists were interviewed, as well as inhabitants of the contaminated areas and "liquidators" (i.e., the emergency response and recovery workers, including those who extinguished the fire, entombed the destroyed reactor, helped decontaminating and cleaning up the surroundings of the nuclear power plant after the disaster, and assisted in the evacuation operation). The third author, a Byelorussian citizen, worked at the time of the disaster as a psychiatrist in Minsk. For the past few years, she has worked with the first two authors on several projects in the contaminated regions.

This chapter gives a general overview of the psychological reactions following the Chernobyl disaster as they were encountered in inhabitants living in or near the contaminated areas. A prominent reaction of

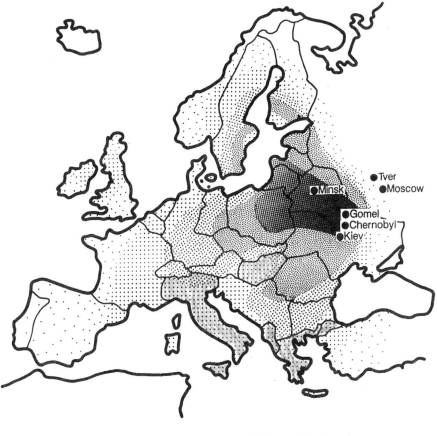

Extent of radiation dispersal May 3, 1986

▒▒ 10^{-2}-1 x background dose rate
■■ >100 x background dose rate

Figure 1. The extent of radiation dispersal by the Chernobyl disaster. (Adapted from J. H. Gittus et al., 1989.)

the people in these areas is massive health concern. People fear their health has deteriorated since the disaster and will get worse in the future. Epidemiological information about the health status of the population is incomplete, but their health status appears to be rather poor (Shigematsu, 1991). We present here arguments for the hypothesis that the health problems of the population are the result not of radiation, but of identifiable psychosocial stressors (Darby & Reeves, 1991), and identify ways in which these stressors may result in health concerns, health problems, and illness behavior. Also, we deal with the question of whether a psychotrauma model or a psychosocial stress model better fits the health problems encountered in the affected populations.

At the present time, empirical data about the psychological and psychosocial consequences of the Chernobyl disaster based on systematic research are scarce. Our account of the situation is therefore based mainly on observations and interviews. Some preliminary empirical evidence based on research that was recently carried out by the authors in Belarus is presented.

THE DISASTER AND ITS AFTERMATH: SOCIAL, CULTURAL, AND SOCIOECONOMIC ASPECTS

In order to really understand the reactions of the inhabitants to the Chernobyl disaster, it is essential to understand the *social and cultural situation* in the former USSR in that period. Although, at the time of the disaster, the era of the *glasnost* ("openness") and *perestroika* ("restructuring" or "renovation") had been officially declared by Mikhail Gorbachev, a substantial part of the population had a severe distrust in the government. People had lost their trust in the communist system. Hardly anybody, however, dared to criticize the government openly in the official public media. Instead, many people discussed the social and political problems privately with relatives or among friends. Information favoring the government in the public media was received critically and with disbelief. So, among the inhabitants of the former USSR, a somewhat paradoxical attitude had arisen: People trusted rumors more than official reports. The manner in which the government of the Soviet Union and the official press handled the Chernobyl disaster confirmed the inhabitants' skepticism, as the following account amply demonstrates.

Following the explosion at the plant, the initial reaction of the authorities was to keep silence and to fix the problem by all possible means. With the exception of a small group of workers at the site and governmental officials, the inhabitants of the nearby settlements were told nothing about the explosion and the release of radioactive material. During the first day, life went on as usual. In some nearby towns and villages, evacuation started on April 27, but the inhabitants of neighboring regions, such as Kiev (Ukraine), Gomel (Republic of Belarus), and Novozybkov (Russian Federation), were kept ignorant in the first weeks following the accident. After some days, rumors began to appear, but in the public media only scarce information was given about the incident. It was stressed that there was no danger to the population. To convince people of this, a farmer was interviewed on television who lived next to the nuclear plant and who continued working his fields. Also, the government did not cancel the First of May parade in Kiev, the USSR's third largest city (with nearly 3 million inhabitants). Kiev is the capital of the former Soviet republic and now independent country Ukraine, situated 160 kilometers from Chernobyl. The parade was held as if nothing unusual was going on, and a considerable number of children attended the parade to prove this.

In the meantime, the Soviet army and civil services deployed one of the largest peacetime operations imaginable to stop further contamination and to evacuate people from the 30-kilometer zone. Thousands of people were recruited to help. The initial period after the accident created an atmosphere of determination and perseverance reminiscent of the struggle of the Soviet people during World War II. However, when it became evident after quite some time that the children of the elite had been evacuated, a small exodus of women and children fleeing from Kiev took place (Park, 1989).

Only after about a week following the disaster did the public media release information about precautionary measures which the inhabitants had to take, such as staying inside as much as possible and eating only canned food. Still later, information was given on how the accident had taken place, and on the size and the number of victims of the disaster after the explosion.

In the following two or three years, hardly any information was provided about the consequences of the disaster. It was acknowledged that many of the 200 firefighters who had had to clean the nuclear reactor suffered from radiation disease. In contrast, thousands of "liquidators," who had participated in the cleaning activities in the first three months were left in doubt about whether any complaints they developed were a result of radiation. Frequently, it was stated that their complaints were not radiation-caused. A characteristic example is the story of a colonel of 45 years who, originally in good health, became ill a year after the cleaning activities. Radioactive cesium was found in his body during a radio-isotopic investigation. He was told that he was contaminated by cesium but that there was no relation between his disease and his cleaning activities, which of course he disbelieved. Other stories recount the distribution of contaminated food mixed with clean products and the sale of furniture looted from evacuated villages on markets all over the USSR. We have no way of knowing to what extent stories like these—and there are numerous such stories—are based on reality.

Till 1989, the main message of the government was that there was really no problem and that matters were under control. *Glasnost* was practiced to only a very limited extent: The authorities had maps on the levels of radioactive contamination of the soil, but these were not made publicly available. Instead, officials simply declared that adequate measures had been taken and would be taken in the future. The *Wall Street Journal* (April 27, 1987, p. 29) christened the nuclear accident a "test for *glasnost*," which the Soviet government had failed. In the meantime, more contaminated areas were discovered, and as a result, further evacuations and relocations became necessary. People were even evacuated to 'safe' areas that, after some time, appeared to be contaminated as well.

This policy of only partially telling the truth and assuring people that there was nothing to worry about led to more unease in the population. About 1989, the inhabitants became more and more upset about the delayed consequences of the disaster. There were rumors about high numbers of miscarriages. It was also reported that calves with monstrous eyes were being born. This commotion resulted in large demonstrations in many cities. The fact that the inhabitants had the courage to hold these sort of demonstrations was undoubtedly a consequence of the *glasnost* and *perestroika* policies, which became quite important during these years (Young & Launer, 1991). On the other hand, the Chernobyl accident had developed into a major issue, and in this sense, it had a catalytic effect on these policies. The government had no other choice than to change its approach and started to release factual information on the consequences of the disaster. Maps showing the extent of contamination of the land were made publicly available. However, this policy had hardly any effect because distrust of the government and the official press was far too great. The fact that the attempts to cover up the consequences of the Chernobyl disaster had been repeatedly followed by reassuring evidence was conceptualized by people as a confirmation of the untrustworthiness of the official sources of information.

For a good understanding of the reactions of the people of Belarus, Russia, and Ukraine, it is further necessary to pay attention to other social, cultural, and political problems, some of which are not related to the Chernobyl disaster itself. Soviet society has gone through a turbulent phase of political instability and economic crises, the onset of which almost coincided with the Chernobyl disaster. Old ideals and ideology have been demolished, but there is a lack of new ones. Many persons have adopted the Western ideology. There is a huge identification, especially among the young people, with Western lifestyles, shown for example by the immense popularity of Western sportswear and drinks, such as Pepsi Cola and Coca-Cola. At the same time, there is a deep sense of disillusion about the lack of economic recovery.

The Chernobyl accident had enormous *socioeconomic consequences*, which have lasted up to today. Some 130,000 people have been evacuated, and an additional 200,000 are to be evacuated in the future, although conflicting views with respect to the criteria for evacuation make it doubtful whether this will indeed happen. Between 600,000 and 1 million people were involved in the cleanup of the nuclear plant site and the surroundings. The 30-kilometer zone around the nuclear plant is now still a forbidden area, although the government allows older people to stay there, who want to live and to die in the villages in which they have lived all their life. Nearly 300,000 persons are living in "strict control zones," where continuous monitoring of the level of radioactive contamination takes place. Although the accident took place in Ukraine, Belarus has suffered the most severe consequences, as the contaminated clouds moved northward. Of all the territory that was contaminated by radioactivity following the accident, 70% is situated in Belarus (38,000 square kilometers, which equals 18% of the land area of this republic). In this now independent republic, 300,000 hectares of farmland were taken out of agricultural use. Some 1 million acres of the forests were contaminated to varying degrees (Shigematsu, 1991). In addition to losses in agricultural production, there has been a loss of the market for food products from the region and loss of tourism as a source of income in some districts.

PSYCHOSOCIAL STRESSORS AFTER THE CHERNOBYL ACCIDENT

The central and perhaps most important stressor for the inhabitants of the contaminated areas is the threat of having been exposed—and still being exposed—to dangerous levels of radiation, possibly resulting in current or future damage to the body. However, as the foregoing account already suggests, in the case of the Chernobyl disaster several other severe stressors were chronic in nature. In our opinion, these stressors are at least as important as the threat of having been or being exposed to radiation. In this section we discuss these chronic stressors, which were mostly an indirect consequence of the disaster and could also be characterized as a sequence of severe stressors.

Evacuation and Discrimination

Shortly after the accident, some 130,000 people were evacuated. This evacuation caused severe psychosocial stress. In many cases, rural people were evacuated to cities, where they now live in flats. In addition, in the years immediately following the disaster, government policy was to evacuate families and individuals rather than whole communities. The result was a severe loss of social structure and social ties. Thus, many of those evacuated became socially uprooted. Furthermore, they were far from welcome in "clean" areas and frequently experienced outright discrimination.

> *Case vignette 1:* A woman 54 years old is referred to a medical specialist for evaluation of cholecystitis (gall-bladder infection). She lives in a village about 60 kilometers from Gomel in an area contaminated by less than 5 Curie radiocesium per square kilometer (i.e., mild contamination). She was a liquidator; she helped with the evacuation of cattle from the 30-kilometer zone around Chernobyl. Except for uneasiness in the upper abdomen and a dislike of fat food, complaints which are consistent with the gall-bladder problems, she reports a number of complaints such as dryness of the mouth, obstipation, and pain in urinating. Although she acknowledges that her complaints started years before the disaster, the patient insists that her health has deteriorated since the Chernobyl disaster. She believes that she was exposed to dangerous levels of radiation when evacuating the cattle. She now is forced to live together with other liquidators and evacuees from contaminated areas and work together with them, which she does not like at all because she is afraid that the evacuees are full of radiation. Also, she is afraid of the contaminated agricultural machines and materials they brought with them. She fears that her current complaints are caused by cancer from Chernobyl.

On one hand, the hostile reception in "clean" areas was due to the fact that people were afraid to be contaminated with radiation through contact with the evacuees. Children in particular seem to have become targets of discrimination. On the other hand, the unfriendly reception stemmed from the fact that evacuees were treated with priority concerning the assignment of newly built houses, thus decreasing the prospects of the local people of moving to a new house.

As a result of evacuation, people also frequently experienced loss of contact with relatives. Especially in the very first weeks or months after the accident, people were often evacuated quite unexpectedly. Suddenly, they found themselves separated from their loved ones. Families were separated from each other according to seemingly rational, but not psychological, guidelines. In one republic, for example, people were evacuated according to the lifetime doses they would accumulate if they stayed in the contaminated areas. Consequently, the young people had to leave, and the older people had to stay.

Confusion about Safe Dose Limits

Two basically different concepts were used to calculate permissible radiation doses: the degree of contamination per square kilometre and the total dose a person accumulates during a lifetime. The three republics adopted different safety concepts, and even within one single concept, they used different criteria. Moreover, these criteria changed within republics as time passed. These confusing safety concepts and criteria led to distrust, anxiety, and indignation. People asked themselves, "Why have the people in Belarus been evacuated, and we in Russia not? Are we that unimportant?" These different conceptions of safety thus enlarged the stress of the evacuations and also gave rise to a commotion among nonevacuees.

Departure of People with High Socioeconomic Status

A lot of educated people moved to clean areas. In particular, medical doctors left. As the vice mayor of a small town put it, "How can you explain to people that you can live here safely when the doctors are the first to leave?" Migration was probably not due solely to the disaster. Emigration restrictions were lifted during the same period, and the result was an emigration wave in the whole former USSR (e.g., to Israel). An unknown number of people who had migrated came back disillusioned after a few years. There was also an influx of refugees from other trouble-stricken areas in the former Soviet Union, reportedly even to some abandoned villages in contaminated areas.

Changes in Lifestyles, Especially for Children

Before the Chernobyl disaster, people living in the area had spent much time in the woods and by the rivers for recreation. After the disaster, many of these activities were discouraged and, in some areas, even forbidden. Children especially were affected by these changes. Because of the contamination of the surroundings, children in some areas had to spend their recess in the classroom for a long time. This confinement may have resulted in deteriorated physical condition and in developmental delay. In some areas, there are still restrictions on playing outside. In addition, there have been many prohibitions in the contaminated areas, especially in the first years after the disaster. For example, it was forbidden to eat home-grown fruit and vegetables. Cows had to be milked, and the milk had to be thrown away. One can imagine the dilemma created by such decrees in times of economic hardship and food shortages.

Insecurity about the Level of Contamination of Food

An additional stressor stems from insecurity about the level of contamination of food. There are a number of radiohygienic precautions that people know they should take, such as not eating fish from certain rivers or untested home-grown foods. The newspapers publish extensive lists with the results of radiation measurements in food products every week. If people do not follow these instructions—which in these times of economic hardship may become a dire necessity—they know that they run a health risk.

CHARACTERISTIC REACTIONS OF THE INHABITANTS

Based on in-depth conversations and interviews, the following reactions of the inhabitants of the contaminated areas can be distinguished as characteristic.

Loss of Trust and Pervasive Distrust

As already mentioned, the fact that the authorities withheld a great deal of information about the Chernobyl accident during the first three years after the disaster led people to become suspicious. All official information is distrusted, even if it is factually correct or in accordance with Western reports. This applies to information about the contamination of food and soil, as well as to information about the dose of radiation people received. It looks as though people are constantly seeking reliable information but, at the same time, disqualify every piece of information that is presented. Reassuring information only triggers the search for more reassuring information.

These feelings of distrust and insecurity concerning the consequences of the Chernobyl disaster stem from several sources. Seventy years of communist government have undermined general trust in the authorities. Distrust was augmented by the ideological and economic bankruptcy of the communist state. Although, undoubtedly, the socialist ideology was not supported by all of the inhabitants, it gave most of them some "anchor point," for better or for worse. People now lack a unifying frame of reference, and many feel betrayed by the former system. People have become cynical and do not trust anyone or anything.

Loss of trust is a universal characteristic among the inhabitants. For example, after the disaster, numerous experts arrived to carry out all sorts of investigations. These experts stayed in the contaminated areas for only a short time. Many of the inhabitants thought—falsely—that the cause of the short stay of these experts was the danger of the radiation. The inhabitants asked themselves why living in the contaminated areas was evidently considered safe for them, while it was not for other people (such as these experts).

Anxiety and Depression

Anxiety was the core negative emotion of the inhabitants in the first years after the disaster. People are especially anxious about the amount of radiation to which they (and especially their children) have been, still are, or will be exposed, and about the extent of contamination of the soil and their food (Giel, 1991). In past years, Russian investigators have reported a gradual shift toward depression as the core negative emotion (G. M. Rumyantzeva, personal communication, September 1992). Many people have become apathetic and hopeless about their future, but especially about the future of their children. Typically, inhabitants are not really interested in information about the future consequences of the disaster, because "we know what will happen—we will die in a few years."

Psychotraumatic Consequences

In comparison to natural disasters like earthquakes and floods, technological disasters such as the Chernobyl accident have a number of specific characteristics. One characteristic of "natural" or "classical" disasters is that they are beyond human control, whereas in most technological disasters humans can no longer master the systems they thought they had under control (Baum, 1987). Another important difference is that "classical" catastrophes typically have a clear "high point" and "low point" (Baum, Fleming, & Davidson, 1983): When the terrors of a flood subside, the damage can be assessed, and the actual disaster is over. After a nuclear disaster like Chernobyl, the consequences are not visible or tangible. There is no high point and no low point. Characteristic of this type of technical disaster, which is sometimes referred to as a *diluted disaster* (Bertazzi, 1989), is the fact that it seeps gradually into awareness and holds a threat mainly for the future.

After an earthquake or a flood, posttraumatic stress reactions of intrusion are typically reported, that is, images that directly or indirectly imply the reexperiencing of the event (for example, feelings of being back in the traumatic situation or nightmares concerning the event) (Kleber & Brom, 1992). During the Chernobyl accident, however, only a few outward signs of the event were visible, even within the range of some kilometers. The absence of intrusive reactions that we encountered with respect to the accident proper is probably related to the absence of a high-impact phase. The psychotraumatic consequences of the Chernobyl disaster thus refer less to experiences with the disaster proper (i.e., the explosion itself). Intrusive memories may occur in people who underwent immediate evacuation in the early days after the disaster, which certainly had an acutely psychotraumatic quality for many. Similar reactions occur in people directly involved in combating the disaster at the time of the explosion of the nuclear unit. Together, however, these two groups make up only a relatively small proportion of the population. The incident itself left hardly any psychological impression on the majority of the population, which was kept ignorant at the time.

In our view, a nuclear disaster like the Chernobyl accident reveals some limitations of the concept of posttraumatic stress reactions and especially of the rigid definition of the posttraumatic stress syndrome as it is defined in the DSM-III-R (American Psychiatric Association, 1987). This syndrome requires the presence of intrusive as well as avoidance symptoms. Our observations in the contaminated areas point to the presence of avoidance, but to the presence of intrusion to only a much smaller extent.

Characteristic of the Chernobyl accident is that, apart from the destruction at the nuclear power plant itself, nothing concrete seemed to have happened. The millions of people in the contaminated areas witnessed no actual destruction in their neighborhood. Probably, many people living in the smaller villages did not even see the television broadcast or read the minimal newspaper coverage about the terrible accident that had happened far away. It was only gradually that they realized something terribly wrong had happened which affected their lives. The threat of future destruction and damage to the body is augmented by several factors. People know that the soil on which they live is contaminated to a certain degree and is a potential health hazard. In addition, there is always the chance that the food is contaminated. Finally, the threat of future destruction is strengthened by the fact that two blocks (and now three) of the Chernobyl nuclear power plant are still functioning and that the exploded block repeatedly gives rise to severe problems.

Psychologically speaking, the Chernobyl disaster is therefore more comparable with a situation where a person is informed that she or he has HIV infection or incurable cancer than with a disaster like a flood. And with this statement, we arrive at the fourth—and in our opinion, most important—characteristic reaction of the inhabitants.

Health Problems and Attribution of These Health Problems to Radiation

Perhaps the most prominent characteristic of many inhabitants in the contaminated areas is the extent to which they are concerned about or even preoccupied with their health. They experience all kinds of health problems (headaches, gastrointestinal complaints, common infections), some of which (hypertension, sleeplessness, tiredness) seem to be of a clearly psychosomatic nature. The complaints mentioned are to a very large extent attributed to radiation. For example, two old women told about the lethal heart attack of their nephew at the age of 43. They commented, "All our family members become very old. He must have died from radiation." Or a young mother commented on the eye problems of her 5-year-old child: "I was pregnant with her when the accident took place. I'm sure this is the result of radiation." Frequently, parents of teenagers state, "In our young days, we were quite active. Our sons and daughters are so apathetic and always tired. We are afraid they will not become very old. What future do they have?" Even people who at first glance do not appear to be preoccupied with their health live with a deep-down expectation of imminent lethal disease.

> *Case vignette 2:* A man 31 years old, living in Gomel, comes to his physician for a yearly checkup, which is compulsory because in 1986 he worked for three weeks as a liquidator in Chernobyl. Shortly before the end of his study to become an engineer, he was drafted into the army and sent immediately to Chernobyl. In 1987, he worked again for several weeks at Chernobyl. He says he feels well and has no complaints. Except for some slight fatigue, which he attributes to stress at work, he says he feels fine. When asked about his thoughts about the consequences of Chernobyl, he answers that he believes it is better not to worry now because he knows he will die from a radiation-related disease within some years.

This preoccupation with health problems, combined with the attribution to radiation, is quite understandable. It is similar to that observed in the survivors of the atomic bombs in Hiroshima and Nagasaki. Lifton (1971) stated that these survivors tended "to associate the mildest everyday injury or sickness with possible radiation effects" (p. 138).

Strictly speaking, we do not know whether this increase of all kinds of health problems reported by the population reflects an actual increase in morbidity in the population, because reliable epidemiological data from the period before the disaster are lacking. In addition, after the disaster, the inhabitants were screened extensively, and this screening possibly resulted in an increase in medical diagnoses. Thus, the interpretation of health statistics is difficult. The clinical importance of the complaints by inhabitants of the areas near Chernobyl therefore remains uncertain.

HEALTH ATTRIBUTIONS: SOME ILLUSTRATIVE DATA

The observation that inhabitants in contaminated areas largely attribute poor health to radiation can be illustrated by preliminary data from a study which was carried out by us in the Gomel region in 1992. This region is situated in the southeastern part of Belarus (the former By-elorussian Socialist Soviet Republic) and has a population of 1.5 million people. It was one of the most contaminated regions following the Chernobyl accident. The city of Gomel (500,000 inhabitants) lies at a distance of 100 kilometers to the northeast of Chernobyl. Although Gomel was only mildly contaminated, the city and the surrounding districts harbor many of the thousands of people who have been evacuated thus far.

In an effort to get a representative sample of inhabitants, we decided to draw from a sample of factories, schools, and other working sites. As unemployment in the former Soviet Union is extremely low (according to official statistics, less than 1%), this procedure seemed warranted. In the study, 1,617 inhabitants were asked to fill in self-report questionnaires, including five items about health attributions. People were asked to rate each of five factors as being a possible hazard to their own health. The potential health hazard was rated on a scale ranging from 1 ("hardly at all") to 5 ("very much"). The factors were deficiencies in essential *nutritional* elements; biological effects of *radiation;* nervous tension (*stress*) related to the *Chernobyl* disaster (such as fear of radiation and stress related to evacuation); the *political situation* in the country; and *economical problems.* As is shown in Table 1, biological effects of radiation were rated the highest of all health hazards.

Not only inhabitants, but also medical doctors are inclined to attribute health problems to radiation. This was found in a small study of 30 medical doctors (general practitioners, medical specialists, and psychiatrists), who were asked to rate the five factors mentioned above according to their contribution to health problems in the Gomel region. Also from Table 1, it can be seen that they rated radiation as the main health hazard.

This empirical evidence illustrates that inhabitants and medical doctors perceive radiation as the most important cause of health problems.

Table 1. Possible Hazards to Health According to Inhabitants (N = 1,617) and Doctors (N = 30) in the Gomel Region[a]

	Inhabitants	Doctors
Radiation	3.9	3.6
Economic problems	3.7	3.1
Nutrition	3.6	3.3
Stress because of Chernobyl	3.4	3.2
Political situation	3.3	1.9

[a]Mean scores may vary from 1 ("hardly at all") to 5 ("very much").

Undoubtedly, the inhabitants' belief is intensified by the fact that medical doctors hold the same view.

RADIATION, TRAUMATIC STRESS, AND CHRONIC STRESS IN RELATION TO HEALTH PROBLEMS

Above, we stated that inhabitants tend to think that their ailments and illnesses are caused by radiation. What is scientifically known about the medical (biological) consequences of the exposure to the doses of radioactivity that the population was exposed to as a result of the Chernobyl accident?

Experts disagree on this question to some extent, but there is an absolute consensus that radiation causes a limited number of discrete medical problems and is not related to any or all kinds of medical problems. For instance, it has been found that cancer is clearly related to high doses of radiation. It is, however, hard to establish such a relationship with the much lower doses that the population in contaminated areas was exposed to. Morbidity and mortality rates are influenced by a large number of factors (McCally, 1990). According to a recent scientific report (Ivanov & Tsyb, 1993), no excess leukemias can be attributed to the Chernobyl radiation, not even in the most affected populations. On the other hand, according to the same report, in the Gomel region thyroid cancer in children rose from 1 or 2 cases in 1986–1989 to 39 in 1992 (cf. Kazakov, Demidchik, & Astakhova, 1992). There is hardly any doubt that this increase is a direct consequence of radiation. Radiation experts generally share the view that, with the exception of this rise in the incidence of thyroid cancers in children, a direct link between radiation and other ailments is highly improbable. The results of the first international study on the medical effects of the Chernobyl accident (Shigematsu, 1991) are in agreement with this view. The study, held in 1989, was financed by six United Nations agencies and by the International Atomic Energy Agency (IAEA). The main conclusion of the study was that the accident had not resulted in any measurable radiological effects on the health of the local population. No evidence was found of an increase of radiation-related illnesses such as leukemia and birth defects.

What is known about the effect of the *traumatic stress* of being exposed to radiation or, in the words of Stiehm (1992), exposure to "psychological fallout" (i.e., living in the constant fear that health effects will inevitably appear soon or later)? Studies of the accident at the Three Mile Island (TMI) nuclear plant in Harrisburg, Pennsylvania (United States) provide invaluable information for understanding the stress-effects of the Chernobyl disaster. In 1979, severe problems arose at the TMI nuclear plant, resulting in intense feelings of anxiety and panic among the inhabitants. Despite a very limited evacuation advice, for only pregnant women and young children within a five-mile radius of the reactor, thousands of inhabitants fled to safer regions. Ultimately, the radioactive release appeared to be very small, namely, 13-millionths of a Curie, which is a negligible quantity, especially when compared to the 50 million Curie which was released in the Chernobyl accident. Considering this negligible radioactive release at TMI, it is certain that effects of the TMI incident have to be attributed to psychological stress, that is, to the immense fear of being exposed to radiation. There have been several controlled studies in which the long-term effects of this stressor were clearly established. Years later, TMI inhabitants still exhibited stress symptoms on a variety of indices, ranging from psychological and behavioral to biochemical and physiological (e.g., Baum, Gatchel, & Schaeffer, 1983; Bromet & Schulberg, 1986; Davidson & Baum, 1986; Davidson, Fleming & Baum, 1986). These TMI studies show that the threat of being exposed to radiation can lead to long-lasting effects on people's health. These findings strongly suggest that at least some of the psychological and somatic problems of the inhabitants of areas near Chernobyl may be related to the traumatic experience of the disaster.

Should the health problems of the inhabitants in the contaminated areas be interpreted as the result of more mundane *chronic stress* (e.g., the above-mentioned psychosocial stressors, such as evacuation, different conceptions of safety, and the loss of their traditional way of life)? In the absence of systematic research in the contaminated areas of the former USSR, no definitive answers to this question can be given. However, considering the number and severity of these stressors, it seems safe to conclude that the health effects of these stressors must be considerable.

We conclude, in terms of the subtitle of this chapter, that the massive health problems of the inhabitants of the contaminated areas are only to a very small extent the result of the exposure to radiation. The various health problems are the consequence of the combined effect of the traumatic stress of being exposed to radiation (a stress which is still going on) and of the chronic stress of a number of factors that arose in the aftermath of the Chernobyl accident.

A PSYCHOSOCIAL STRESS MODEL FOR THE DEVELOPMENT OF HEALTH PROBLEMS AND ILLNESS BEHAVIOR

How may Chernobyl-related stress lead to health problems and illness behaviors, such as seeking medical care? In Figure 2, we have ten-

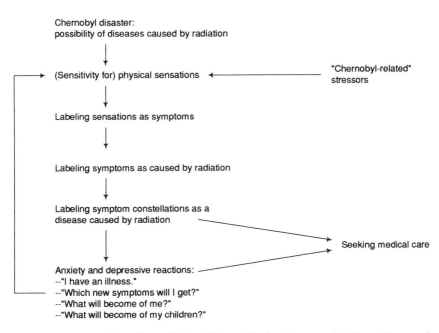

Figure 2. Psychological pathways linking Chernobyl-related stress to health problems and illness behavior.

tatively tried to specify these processes (using a adaptation of the model by Cohen & Williamson, 1991).

First of all, having been exposed to radioactive contamination means that people will monitor themselves more closely with respect to all sorts of physical sensations. They will be more sensitive to bodily sensations. Uncertainty about whether one has been exposed to dangerous levels of radioactivity will probably worsen this situation. The psychological significance of radiation, which is a rather incomprehensible phenomenon to most people and which is associated with dreadful health consequences, further contributes to this state of affairs. Furthermore, the Chernobyl-related stressors discussed in the preceding section trigger physiological arousal.

The physical manifestation of this arousal state may be interpreted as symptoms (Pennebaker, 1982), and symptom constellations may be interpreted as radiation-related. It is quite conceivable that this interpretation leads to anxiety and depressive reactions. For example, people are worried about their future ("What will become of me?"). In addition, they view themselves as having a disease, as "sick persons," and this view is likely to lead to a higher sensitivity to physical symptoms, which in turn feeds on their anxieties concerning contamination. The result may be the development of stress-related syndromes (somatic or mental) and/or changes in illness behavior, such as seeking medical care more frequently.

CONCLUDING REMARKS

The hypothesis that the many health problems in the contaminated areas are stress-related needs further systematic investigation. Concluding that the problems are stress-mediated does not, of course, mean that they are imaginary. Stress-related diseases are quite real from a quality-of-life point of view and may have considerable public health consequences because they increase medical consumption. Neither does the hypothesis imply that direct radiation-caused disorders do not or will not occur in the contaminated areas. As mentioned earlier, in the case of thyroid cancer in children, such a direct relationship is very likely. However, and this is the main point of our argument, it seems unlikely that all or even the majority of the current health problems and illnesses are caused by radiation, as the inhabitants of these regions tend to think. Other factors are likely to be involved as well. In these, Chernobyl-related stress factors may play an important role.

Many of these additional factors consist of a sequence of measures which have been taken by authorities. In this sense, the authorities have inadvertently made matters much worse by adding stress to the disaster itself. Their policies (or sometimes lack of them) are classic examples of factors causing stress and thereby causing poor health, such as providing conflicting information or misinformation, breaking up social networks, and depriving people of their feeling of personal control.

The assertion that a considerable number of the health problems is stress-related may not be spectacular or amazing to some readers of this book. It should be remembered, however, that this view is based only on hypotheses, which await scientific verification. For example, it has yet to be shown that people in the contaminated regions suffer from mental health problems more often then those in noncontaminated areas. On the other side, we can testify that the view that the health problems are to a large extent stress-related is quite astonishing to the inhabitants of the contaminated areas, including the medical doctors and other health care professionals who work in these areas. Or to put it more strongly, it is a view that is so controversial that one can hardly state it publicly without eliciting strong emotional reactions in the people affected by the disaster. The worries and fears (and even panic) concerning radiation and radiation-related diseases have probably been greater than the actual risk, either immediately after the disaster or in the present. People themselves, however, appraised the situation as a real death threat.

It is open to debate how much cultural factors have kindled fear of radiation and fear of severe health problems among the inhabitants of the affected republics. Young and Launer (1991) described a film by Shevchenko showing mine workers tunneling under the foundation of the damaged reactor without any form of protection; in the film, there are many other details of the enormous struggle of the army and others to prevent the spread of radiation. The whole atmosphere of the film echoes the remarkable endurance of the Russian people and the sacrifices that they made to save their homeland during World War II.

Some of our informants have pointed out the glorification of suffering, which is not limited to the majestic war monuments built in the Soviet era. It is also a popular theme in many children's stories and fairy tales. An example is the story of a crippled child who is despised by everyone but who behaves heroically and saves all the other children at the moment of danger. Naturally, the cultural context illustrated by such cultural symbols and stories and the entire social situation at the time have influenced the victims' process of ascribing meaning to the disaster. However, there are incontestably many aspects in the reactions of the inhabitants which they share with other people exposed elsewhere to similar dangers. Reports on the victims of the atomic bomb in Hiroshima and Nagasaki (Lifton, 1971) and on the public reactions on near accidents with nuclear power plants (e.g., TMI in the United States and Sellafield in the United Kingdom) suggest that cultural factors have a limited impact. Psychological reactions to radioactive contamination are quite similar throughout different cultures. Underlying this pattern is probably the phenomenon of radioactivity itself. Radioactivity is potentially very harmful to the human body, but it cannot be detected directly through the senses. Radioactivity is perceived to be treacherous because many of its most serious health effects will appear only after a long latency period. After years, many thousands of extra deaths may ensue without even leaving a detectable trace in the health statistics. All these qualities contribute to the mythical quality and the sense of dread which surround the Chernobyl accident. It is not radioactivity itself but the psychological impact of radioactivity which matters. It may be exactly this almost mythical quality, with its implicit reference to human survival in the age of pollution, which may give the Chernobyl accident a psychological significance beyond trauma.

ACKNOWLEDGMENT. This study was conducted in the framework of a Byelorussian-Dutch humanitarian aid project to alleviate the negative consequences of the Chernobyl disaster. The project was sponsored by the Dutch government and executed by the National Institute of Public

Health and Environmental Protection in cooperation with the Utrecht
University Hospital, The Netherlands.

REFERENCES

American Psychiatric Association. (1987). *Diagnostic and statistical manual of mental disorders* (3rd ed., rev.). Washington, DC: Author.

Baum, A. (1987). Toxins, technology and natural disasters. In G. R. Vandenbos & K. B. Bryant (Eds.), *Cataclysms, crises and catastrophes: Psychology in action* (pp. 5–53). Washington: American Psychological Association.

Baum, A., Fleming, I., & Davidson, L. M. (1983). Natural disasters and technological catastrophe. *Environment and Behavior, 15*, 333–354.

Baum, A., Gatchel, J. R., & Schæffer, A. (1983). Emotional, behavioural and physiological effects of chronic stress at the Three Mile Island. *Journal of Consulting and Clinical Psychology, 51*, 565–572.

Bertazzi, P. (1989). Industrial disasters and epidemiology. *Scandinavian Journal of Work Environmental Health, 15*, 85–100.

Bromet, J. E., & Schulberg, C. H. (1986). The Three Mile Island disaster: A search for high risk groups. In J. H. Shore (Ed.), *Disaster stress studies: New Methods and findings* (pp. 1–19). Washington, DC: American Psychiatric Press.

Cohen, S., & Williamson, G. M. (1991). Stress and infectious disease in humans. *Psychological Bulletin, 109*, 5–24.

Darby, S. C., & Reeves, G. K. (1991). Lessons of Chernobyl: Psychological problems seem to be a major health effect at present. *British Medical Journal, 303*, 1347–1348.

Davidson, L. M., Fleming, I., & Baum, A. (1986). Post traumatic stress as a function of chronic stress and toxic exposure. In C. Figley (Ed.), *Trauma and its wake* (Vol. 2, pp.57–77). New York: Brunner/Mazel.

Davidson, M. L., & Baum, A. (1986). Chronic stress and post-traumatic stress disorders. *Journal of Consulting and Clinical Psychology, 54*, 303–308.

Giel, R. (1991). The psychosocial aftermath of two major disasters in the Soviet Union. *Journal of Traumatic Stress, 4*, 381–392.

Gittus, J. H., et al. (1989). *The Chernobyl accident and its consequences.* London: UKAEA.

Ivanov, E., & Tsyb, A. (1993). Cited in *Nucleonics Week, 34*(16), p. 1.

Kazakov, V. S., Demidchik, E. P., & Astakhova, L. N. (1992). Childhood thyroid cancer after Chernobyl. *Nature, 359*, 21.

Kleber, R. J., & Brom, D. (1992). *Coping with trauma: Theory, prevention and treatment.* Amsterdam: Swets & Zeitlinger.

Lifton, R. J. (1971). *Death in life: Survivors of Hiroshima.* New York: Random House.

McCally, M. (1990). What the fight is all about. *Bulletin of the Atomic Scientists, 46*, 10–14.

Medvedev, Zh. (1990). *The legacy of Chernobyl.* New York: Norton.

Mould, R. F. (1988). *Chernobyl: The real story.* New York: Pergamon Press.

Park, C. C. (1989). *Chernobyl: The long shadow.* London: Routledge.

Pennebaker, J. W. (1982). *The psychology of physical symptoms.* New York: Springer-Verlag.

Shigematsu, I. (Ed.). (1991). *The International Chernobyl Project—Technical report.* Vienna: International Atomic Energy Agency.

Stiehm, E. R. (1992). The psychological fallout from Chernobyl. *American Journal of Disease in Childhood, 146*, 761–762.

Young, M. J., & Launer, M. K. (1991). Redefining Glasnost in the Soviet media: The recontextualization of Chernobyl. *Journal of Communication, 41*, 102–124.

III

Ethical Considerations

Ethical considerations and dilemmas take a significant place in the consequences of traumatic stress as well as in the treatment of trauma-related disorders. By definition, traumatic stress signifies an exceeding of the existing boundaries and limits. A victim is confronted with a drastic disruption of her or his assumptions and expectations. Existing norms and values are not applicable anymore. They are not as certain as one thought they were. The person's belief in the goodwill of other people and in the benevolence of the world is shattered. An aggressor abuses another individual. Property is lost. The victim doubts and wonders whether he or she can still believe in what he or she trusted before. His or her basic values are at stake, and there is a fundamental breach of confidence. What is the sense of this all? Why are people behaving this brutally and inhumanely?

Such a dramatic exceeding of limits touches not only the victims and their direct surroundings, but also the therapist and the researchers who work with people victimized by war, violence, repression, disaster, and loss. The therapist is no longer the neutral, independent expert but gets involved in questions and perplexities that touch her or him personally. Of course, this is rather obvious in the case of human rights violations, where norms have been disrupted. Several chapters in Part II have already pointed to this issue. Infringements of basic rights pose ethical questions that have to be dealt with. The horrors of the events require a commitment of a therapist. His or her own values and norms as a human being are also upset. He or she is appalled by the atrocities told by the patients but is also confronted with uneasy questions: What would I have done in such a situation? Would I myself have behaved in a acceptable way? Does my contribution make any sense in the case of such overwhelming terror?

It is therefore not surprising that therapists or counselors are often inclined to avoid feelings and thoughts related to the terror and to seclude themselves from the possible implications for themselves as human beings. On the one hand, therapists cannot be indifferent to human suffering. Dedication to the plight of the patient is an imperative requirement. Therapists feel compassion and attempt to understand the misery. On the other hand, total commitment is a contradiction of professional standards. Therapists and researchers should be independent and even, to some extent, detached. Nonindependent experts are not trustworthy anymore; they become interested parties. They have to sympathize and to identify with the concerns of the patient, but they should not equate themselves with the patient. In such a situation, the experts may ignore certain phenomena and will lose their credibility. Undoubtedly, any professional has to deal with this dilemma in one way or another, but the dilemma is more conspicuous in the case of traumatic events such as war, violence, disaster, and violations of human rights. The expert is required to find a careful and painstaking balance between distance and involvement, detachment and dedication, and independence and compassion.

Unfortunately, ethical reflections are repeatedly overlooked even in traumatic stress research and treatment. Because of this neglect, we have included here three chapters dealing with ethical considerations from different angles. The first chapter pays attention to the difficult decisions of the therapist in a situation of conflicting interests. The second chapter deals with the necessity of teaching later generations about the violence and crimes of their immediate ancestors. The last chapter emphasizes the necessity of using our expertise in traumatic stress for the prevention of war and other insufferable situations.

Posttraumatic stress disorder is a reaction to an external threatening situation and to the individual's inability to integrate it within her or his internal world. In general, it is considered an inadequate way of coping with extreme stress. The disorder may also be considered, however, an expression of a conflict between the values of the individual and those of the surrounding environment.

In the chapter by Brom and Witztum, a case is described and discussed in which the therapist was confronted with ethical dilemmas concerning the goals and means of the treatment. An Israeli man was referred to a psychiatric outpatient clinic three years after he had served his reserve duty as a medic in a prisoners' camp on the West Bank during the Intifada. He witnessed the physical abuse of prisoners and was caught in an unconscious moral dilemma. The posttraumatic stress disorder he was suffering expressed both his moral dilemma and his conflict in dealing with aggression and loyalty. The moral and ethical issues involved are discussed by the authors on the basis of the hypnotherapeutic treatment of this patient.

The issue that Brom and Witztum discuss is not specific to their case or to the Israeli situation of war. In many instances of posttraumatic stress disorder, therapists should be aware of confrontations and struggles in society which are parallel to the conflicts expressed by their patient. As therapists or counselors living with these frictions, we cannot pretend that we are not involved in these conflicts, and our choices in these conflicts determine our treatment strategies to a certain extent.

In a creative analysis of interviews with young people in Germany, Brendler portrays the relevance of the knowledge of the crimes of their immediate ancestors in World War II to their self-esteem and their perception of reality. Most of those interviewed were still trying to cope with the psychic ballast related to the moral bankruptcy of their progenitors. If one expects this generation to have gained in moral sensibility from their attempt to come to terms with the mistakes and crimes of their ancestors or to have developed a sense of responsibility, it is clear that only a few have learned from history. Most families have failed their children in this respect. Instead of seeing their children's questions as an opportunity to develop their conscience, most parents and grandparents set a negative example: a perfect model, as Brendler argues, of self-deceit, a search for scapegoats, and an aggressive way of dealing with their narcissistic tendencies. Brendler's analysis of successful learning processes proves, however, that it is not being burdened but being not burdened that becomes the obstacle in the process of overcoming one's shadows in matters of identity and possible relief. The narratives of the young people demonstrate that nobody increases his or her moral insight without going through a period of mental suffering and personal bewilderment.

It is not a exaggeration to state that the ultimate goal of traumatic stress studies is prevention: prevention of the consequences of war, violence, disasters, and other events (secondary prevention) as well as the prevention of the noxious events themselves (primary prevention). Of course, the last goal is often an illusion; nevertheless, it is worthwhile and necessary to strive for this perhaps unreachable goal.

Sidel, Gersons, and Weerts argue that primary prevention is a responsibility of everyone who works in the field of treating and counseling the victims and the survivors. Those who deal with the consequences of trauma have special knowledge of its depredations and therefore a special sense of the urgent need for its prevention. Health professionals as individuals and particularly in groups have a responsibility to help to prevent trauma by education: by contributing to public and professional understanding of the nature of traumatic stress; of the health consequences of abuse, calamities, and destruction; and of the nature and effectiveness of intervention. The authors discuss these issues in particular in relation to war. They stress the responsibility of advocating specific measures that will promote arms limitation and collective security and of actions that will lessen tensions and reduce the gaps between the "haves" and the "have nots" that lead to war. They suggest avenues for the involvement of health professionals in the primary prevention of traumatic stress caused by war. They conclude that the responsibility of trying to prevent the wounds of war is at least as important as the responsibility of binding up the wounds after they have been inflicted.

13

When Political Reality Enters Therapy
Ethical Considerations in the Treatment of Posttraumatic Stress Disorder

DANIEL BROM and ELIEZER WITZTUM

INTRODUCTION

Most literature on the treatment of posttraumatic stress disorders deals with the reactions of victims to the hardships they have gone through. Much less attention has been paid to the fate of people who belong to the side of the perpetrators.

This chapter presents some thoughts about ethical and professional dilemmas in the treatment of posttraumatic stress disorder, especially when the disorder can be said to express a conflict with clear moral or political implications. Kinzie and Boehnlein (1993) described the difficulty for therapists when patients make choices about which the therapist feels strongly. This issue will be discussed through the description of one case example within the framework of the Israeli situation, that is, the Intifada. It should be kept in mind, however, that the issue is not specific to this case or to a situation of war, but that, in many instances of PTSD, we should be aware of conflicts in society which are parallel to the

DANIEL BROM • Latner Institute for the Study of Social Psychiatry and Psychotherapy, Herzog Hospital, Jerusalem 91351, Israel. ELIEZER WITZTUM • Jerusalem Community Health Center, Ezrath Nashim, Jerusalem 91001, Israel.
Beyond Trauma: Cultural and Societal Dynamics, edited by Rolf J. Kleber, Charles R. Figley, and Berthold P. R. Gersons. New York, Plenum Press, 1995.

conflict expressed by our patients. As therapists of these conflicts, we cannot pretend we are not involved in these conflicts and our choice in these conflicts determines, to a certain extent, our treatment strategies.

ISRAEL AND THE INTIFADA

It is intriguing to begin the discussion of this issue with a quotation of the famous historian Barbara Tuchman (1967/1981) after Israel conquered the West Bank and the Gaza Strip in 1967: "What they will make of it and what conquest will make of them is the question that remains" (p. 187).

The Intifada, yet another chapter in the Arab–Israeli conflict, began in December 1987 and consists of an uprising of the Palestinian population of the West Bank and the Gaza Strip. Violence on the Palestinian side and counterviolence by the Israeli army in attempts to quell the uprising have led to the daily killing and wounding of citizens and soldiers. In the first stages, there was a lot of denial and a lack of will on the Israeli side to admit that the Intifada was a form of war. Great amounts of soldiers were sent to the areas to suppress demonstrations and fulfill other tasks, which are mostly thought of as police tasks.

In a parallel process, the Israeli public began to be exposed to unpleasant violent scenes on television. Seeing Israeli soldiers hit Palestinian citizens brought up in some Israelis associations with Jews being hit in Europe, and these associations increased the denial and repression of the subject.

In a later stage, articles in papers and magazines started to appear about the doubts and perplexities of reserve soldiers and officers and their bitter experiences with the Intifada. An Israeli general, responsible for the antiterrorist activities in the Gaza Strip, declared that the real danger to Israel was not the terrorist activities or explosions, but the threat to the moral standards of Israeli society. All this shows the gradual awareness in Israel of the national impact of the Intifada.

As clinicians in the public mental health system, we began to see reserve soldiers after their yearly service who had posttraumatic stress disorders as a result of their experiences in the West Bank and Gaza. Feelings of guilt and shame about the role they had felt forced on them were a prominent phenomenon.

THEORETICAL CONCEPTIONS OF PTSD AND THE PLACE OF THE THERAPIST

Posttraumatic stress disorders are considered reactions to external situations, which involve an existential shock to the individual. The internal structure of the individual is threatened by an overwhelming event. Most authors contend that the nucleus of an unprocessed traumatic experience is an unconscious conflict within the individual (Breuer & Freud, 1895/1952; Horowitz, 1976). This conflict develops when information contained in an experience clashes with the preexisting information in the person and thus leads to unbearable emotions. The psychodynamic theory of coping with traumatic events sees the disorder as a response to the inability to process and integrate the information.

The view of Janet (Van der Kolk, Brown, & Van der Hart, 1989) is fairly similar. He sees dissociative symptoms as being the result of a failure to store an event and its meanings in memory. But unlike in more classical psychodynamic theory, in this view memory is split up and traumatic memories become inaccessible. In more severe cases, one or more splits in the whole personality organization, and not only in memory, may occur under the pressure of unbearable information, so that a multiple personality disorder may be the consequence.

Yet another approach, that of Janoff-Bulman (1989), gives us a more precise insight into the cognitive conflicts that may arise after traumatic events. Generally, people live with basic assumptions, which together form the cognitive "schemata" of the individual. Primary categories of such assumptions are

1. The perceived benevolence of the world (i.e., the extent to which the world is viewed positively or negatively).
2. The meaningfulness of the world (i.e., people's beliefs about the distribution of good versus bad results according to the preceding events or behavior).
3. The worthiness of the self (i.e., how people evaluate themselves).

Coping with traumatic events can be understood as a struggle of the individual to reconcile her or his basic assumptions with the ideas raised by the events (Kleber & Brom, 1992). How can one feel safe after experiencing an assault? How can one trust one's body after a heart attack? How can one restore one's self-esteem after making a mistake that was fatal to another human being?

From the above perspective, the aim of psychotherapeutic treatment is to integrate the conflicting information. In order to promote the integration, the unconscious conflict has to be allowed into consciousness, and new meanings have to be constructed (McCann & Pearlman, 1990), which can contain both the old and the new information.

An unwritten assumption in the above-mentioned literature on coping with trauma is that the intrapsychic conflict is of a neurotic nature; that is, the conflict has to do with the individual and his or her developmental phase more than with reality. The cognitive schemes that have to be adapted to integrate the new information are considered part of personality. The flexibility or inflexibility of these schemes is thought to determine the difficulty of the person in coping with highly distressing events. The rage of crime victims is accepted as a "normal" reaction in the first few months after the crime, but if it persists, we tend to look for a cause in the individual's developmental history. For this reason, therapists are warned against identification with the conflict and against taking sides. Taking conflicts on their societal value and meaning is seen as a personal (countertransferential) reaction on the part of the therapist.

Newberry (1985) described different levels of countertransference that he observed in the treatment of Vietnam veterans. These levels ranged from a more general adoption of societal attitudes toward veterans and their problems to more individualized emotional responses of the therapist toward his or her work with one specific veteran. The main issue that Newberry was writing about, however, was the way therapists identify with or refrain from identifying with patients with posttraumatic stress disorder. In his discussion of these issues, the implicit assumption is present that the therapist is not a part of the traumatizing system. If there is a clear connection between the intrapsychic conflict of a patient and problems in reality, we are warned to monitor our countertransferential reactions (Haley, 1974) or antitherapeutic defenses (Kirshner, 1973).

There are, however, situations in which patients struggle with conflicts that are directly related to reality and to their behavior and that require working through. In the case we will describe, we felt that emotional and moral conflicts were interconnected, and that we should acknowledge both if we are to avoid countertransferential mismanagement of the treatment. The title of this chapter could have been: What if the patient's unconscious conflict, which is at the basis of the symptoms she or he is presenting, is also a real-life conflict and, in the opinion of the therapist, should not be interpreted solely as an expression of a neurotic personality?

At this point, the clinical material of a man suffering from posttraumatic stress disorder, with a strong emphasis on symptoms connected to a narcissistic injury, may illustrate the dilemma. Afterward, we will formulate some issues facing the therapist when confronted with a patient like this. Finally, some of the solutions used in the therapy will be discussed.

Clinical Material

Robert came to the Jerusalem Community Mental Health Center complaining about having gone through a traumatic period and since then suffering from anxiety. Robert, 38 years old when he came for help, is married, has one child, and works in a publishing company. He came to Israel from a Spanish-speaking country about 10 years ago. Since there are quite a number of people who come to the clinic to try not to serve their yearly reserve army duty, the intake worker had the impression that Robert was trying to get out of his yearly army reserve duty through a mental health record. Robert did not look as if he suffered very much. His words were very general, and he smiled a lot. On the intake form under the heading of "diagnosis" the intake worker had written: "Maybe PTSD."

What did Robert tell the intake worker about his "traumatic event"? He had served his reserve duty as a medic in a prison camp on the West Bank in December 1987 (these were the first weeks of the Intifada). The camp consisted of a prisoners' department and a department of investigations. It was the beginning of the Intifada, and the situation was tense and overcrowded. Because the Intifada was a relatively new phenomenon (i.e., the massive scale of the events was new, not the incidents themselves), the authorities did not give clear instructions about its handling. Every night, dozens of Arabs were brought in for questioning and detention. Because the place was overcrowded, the smell was sharp and repulsive. Robert served in this camp three weeks, day and night, and did not get any time off during this period.

After this period, he suffered a period of depression, but this was not recognized by him, nor by the physicians he consulted. He had intestinal problems and lost 10 kilos in three months, he suffered from nausea and a lack of desire to function at all. Since this period, he has functioned on a lower level, has not worked full days, and has had a variety of medical check-ups, all negative.

When asked for more detail about his symptoms, he reported difficulties in concentration, sleep disturbances, nightmares, and frequent intrusive memories of the prison camp. He felt overly alert. What upset him most was the estrangement from his environment, the feeling of being alone, of not belonging. He recounted an incident during the week before, in which a colleague criticized a piece of work. He could not take the criticism and wanted to cry and disappear but was silent instead. This pattern of reaction had been unknown to him until his specific army duty.

The diagnosis was posttraumatic stress disorder. The specific form of Robert's symptoms, such as his feelings of inadequacy and his heightened vulnerability, recalled what Goldberg (1973) termed a "narcissistic regression." Further anamnestic data did not reveal prior psychopathology. The differential diagnosis of "malingering" could be discarded in the course of the first few sessions.

Commentary

Case histories in general at this point would discuss the personal background of Robert, his personality, and his development. Alternatively, one could choose to focus on the meaning of his army service and the experiences he had gone through in the prison camp. Although, of course, the two of them are connected, the choice of focus reflects the way in which we see the problem. What are the possible conflicts here? What is the connection between reality and the problem presented? Are we talking about neurotic tendencies of the person, or about the way in which people can be trapped in difficult situations? We will come back to this issue later.

> Our choice was to go into the meaning of Robert's stay in the prison camp. As mentioned, Robert came from a Spanish-speaking country, and from his first visit to Israel, he felt very much at home. His father is an M.D., though he himself never made it through university education. He was very proud to join the army as a medic, because this connected him to his father, and through his service, he felt part of the country.
>
> As a medic in this prison camp, he felt like a football between the guards and the prisoners. The prisoners knew they could get some extra care and attention by complaining about pains, and the guards would not trust *any* of their complaints. Robert was caught in between and had to decide what was real and what not. He did not want to be part of either side. He might have tended to feel more sympathy for the Arab men, but several circumstances prevented this: The homosexual acts which were openly conducted in the heavily overcrowded cells repelled him strongly. Furthermore, he saw that placebo medication got rid of most symptoms, and this fact reduced his trust in the prisoners. His relationship with the guards was ambivalent. On the one hand, he knew they were "on his side"; on the other, he was repelled by the sadistic attitude of some of them.
>
> The most difficult assignment for Robert was strip-searching the prisoners, who were brought in during the nights. Writing down all existing wounds and scars would prevent the prisoners from claiming they had been maltreated. The degradation of the strip-search procedure was clearly felt by all. Robert also knew the fallacy of the procedure because he had been a witness to the physical abuse of prisoners.
>
> A meaningful moment occurred when Robert, after a week, found himself one evening walking around one of the prisoners he was checking and noticed that he was enjoying it. His sudden awareness of this pleasure frightened Robert intensely. His first association was: I am a Nazi. (This association once more points to the intricate dynamics between traumas on all sides of the Arab–Israeli conflict.) Robert was so much disturbed by this incident that he asked for a leave, which was refused. From this moment, he was very tense, suffered from frequent nausea, but did serve his full duty.
>
> Back home, he slept for days and nights on end and over the following few months lost 10 kilos. He suffered from nausea, had no appetite, and thought something was wrong with his stomach. This seems a metaphoric representation of his difficulty in digesting his experiences. He felt alienated from his environment and did not function at work or at home.

THE CONCEPT OF DISORDER

Let us think of different models to conceive of the presented material. The most common conception of posttraumatic stress disorder

(American Psychiatric Association, 1987; Peterson, Prout, & Schwarz, 1991) is that it is a disorder with psychological and biological roots, which has to be cured. It interferes with normal functioning. This fits the case description and conforms with the research findings on the relation between the exposure to atrocities and the occurrence of post-traumatic stress disorder (Yehuda, Southwick & Giller, 1992).

This viewpoint fits into the medical model, in which there is no societal meaning to the disorder, other than that the individual suffers and should recover. The medical model uses as its keystone the term *disease*, or *disorder*, and a physiological correlate is assumed to be at its basis. The implicit assumption of the use of the term *disorder* is that it is an objective state, and that there is a universal meaning to that state. Psychiatry has tried to pull away from the medical model at some point when theory started to include the environment as an important part of the pathogenesis. With the strengthening of biological psychiatry and of counseling as a profession, the wish to define "treatable entities" has strengthened.

In the antipsychiatry movement of the 1960s and 1970s, we find authors who write about the conception of disease as a form of communication (Leifer, 1969). A symptom, in this view, is not merely an undesirable phenomenon, but a response of the individual to her or his environment. The individual has found her or his particular way of expressing dissatisfaction. Halleck (1971), for example, wrote, "Much of the behavior that psychiatrists consider symptomatic is at least partly an effort on the part of an individual to communicate with others in order to change something in his environment" (p. 118).

In this line of thought, the symptoms of Robert can be seen as a compromise in his struggle with the unbearable conflicts created in the prison camp. This struggle is obviously connected to the actual moral problem he experienced, but it is also connected to the personal meaning of "belonging to" and of "loyalty."

In the case of Robert, conflicts were present on two levels of conceptualization:

1. The most basic psychodynamic theme, which has accompanied Robert through his life, is the theme of belonging and loyalty. This theme most clearly has its roots in the developmental difficulties of Robert. He always felt that his mother did not really love him, and the theme of belonging became a central issue for him. In his childhood, he desperately tried to belong to groups of children and was disappointed over and over. His solution was to build a narcissistic world of his own, in which he did not need other people. Withdrawing into this world prevented Robert from feeling the pain and rage of being rejected. From this theme, we can also understand his problem with experiencing and expressing aggression.

2. On the level of the reality of the prison camp, Robert was torn between the poles of his conflict about the cruelty of the prison camp. On the one hand, he was appalled by it and objected to the methods used. On the other hand, he saw the hopelessness of the situation and the "game" which the Arabs and the Israelis were playing together. His moral condemnation of the situation remained on a level of consciousness that did not allow him to take a public stand on the issue. The reason was the entanglement of the moral issue in the developmental conflict of belonging, as described above.

Lifton (1976) observed the difficulties for therapists in working with soldiers who oppose the war they are fighting in. The help which is offered by chaplains and psychotherapists may be perceived by both helpers and patients as a rationalization and justification of "an absurd and evil situation."

One treatment approach, which we assume to be the most accepted, would be to look in the direction of developmental problems. For Robert, the State of Israel functioned as a self-object; that is, it gave Robert a substitute for a failing or unavailable psychic structure. Early deprivation had led to arrests in his development and can be considered a cause of his poor identity formation. Treatment could have been based solely on this conception. In the light of the above, this would be a neglect, if not a denial, of the importance of the moral conflict.

Szasz (1970) wrote about the therapist as an agent of the established social culture. Therapy is used to close up the cracks in a system under pressure. Lifton (1976) formulated this problem as a "double agent" problem, because he saw the therapist as an agent of both society and the patient. Leifer (1969) called the social function of psychotherapy "ethnicization," which is defined as "the molding and polarizing of behavior so that it conforms to prevailing cultural patterns" (p. 158).

Psychotherapy, an activity which is characterized by selective attention and selective neglect, always implies the making of choices. The therapist chooses the contents on which she or he focuses and also the conceptualization of the solution she or he offers to alleviate the presented problem.

Posttraumatic stress disorders, most clearly in our example of Robert, are expressions of conflicts (Horowitz, 1976). Our contention is that these intrapsychic conflicts may at the same time be a struggle with the existing order. Because of external and internal pressures, expression of these conflicts may not occur. The choice of the therapist is on what level he or she conceptualizes the problem and what kind of expression he or she is striving for. Is he or she striving to restore the broken bond of the individual with the environment? And does this mean, in our case, that we should help Robert to feel part of the army and restore his pride and his Jewish and national identity?

Are we striving for the uncovering of the underlying under-developed self, which is so vulnerable because Robert experienced parenting which was not sensitive to his needs? Or are we striving to uncover the acute conflict in Robert between belonging to Israel and the army in all its meanings and at the same time participating in acts which he morally condemned? Could we say that the expression of his moral judgment was entangled in a conflict of loyalty?

TREATMENT APPROACH

Different and equally effective treatment methods are available for the treatment of posttraumatic stress disorder (Brom, Kleber, & Defares, 1989). An explorative hypnotherapeutic approach was used to treat Robert. After two intake session, hypnotic inductions were started, and Robert was presented with evocative imagery, such as walking up a hill and not knowing what he would be able to see over the top of the hill. As expected with such a method (Kleber & Brom, 1992), images started to appear which bore a similarity to the original traumatic events and their meanings. Robert came up with comforting scenes from a previous military duty he had fulfilled, but also with conflict-laden images, for example, of a childhood scene in which he had willfully hurt a cat and felt guilt and shame afterward. A scene in which he had beaten his father in a game of chess was followed by a dream in which he met his army superiors, turned them away, and told them he had no time to see them. The images more and more approached the original traumatic scenes, until he could relive these scenes and feel and express his disgust and hurt. In a later stage, age regression techniques were used to explore Robert's difficulties connected to the issues of belonging and loyalty and his resulting problems in the expression of anger.

The treatment lasted 23 sessions, and a full recovery was reached both on the level of daily functioning and on the symptom level.

The conflictual situation for therapists in Israel is even more complicated: As a therapist in a Community Mental Health Center in Israel, you know in advance when treating male patients that you will get a form from the army asking whether the patient is fit to serve his reserve duty. In the beginning of the treatment, it was clear that Robert was not able to function. Toward the end, there was no medical reason for him not to serve, but in that period, Robert decided he did not want to serve anymore.

In the treatment of Robert, a dual approach was adopted concerning the different aspects of his problem. Time was spent in exploring his trapped situation in the army, which led to the much clearer expression of his opposition to the situation in the prisoners' camp. He expressed his feelings of degradation by the army for the assignments that he had to fulfill. At the same time, however, we focused on the dynamic conflicts that had prevented him from feeling or expressing the emotions at the time of his service. Robert quite easily connected these conflicts, which centered mainly on the issues of aggression and guilt and of loyalty and authority, with his developmental difficulties.

Concerning the army, we decided to recommend a postponement of his reserve duty in order to make the treatment possible. When this postponement was over, we discussed the issue with Robert and told him that we would like not to take sides in his personal moral conflict with the army. We would intervene, however, if we expected retraumatization to occur, that is, if he would have to serve under the same conditions. The limits of this approach are unclear, and the personal judgment of the therapist is the crucial factor here. Our ideal is that the patient will fight his own moral fights, but we are aware that societal systems may cause (re)traumatization.

DISCUSSION

In psychiatry there is a considerable debate about how we choose a therapeutic modality (Sider, 1984). This dilemma concerns not only the pros and cons of treatment methods, but also the value considerations that are intrinsic in every choice of therapeutic intervention. Robert presented us with posttraumatic psychopathology which, in our opinion, was based both on a moral conflict and on a developmental difficulty. His disorder can be seen as a compromise solution between the different sides of his conflicts.

When political reality enters the therapeutic space (Lipsedge, 1993), it is very easy to slide into countertransferential attitudes, in particular when conflicts of the patient are so easy to share or reject. In our case, it does not matter whether one chooses to disregard the current conflict in reality or the individual developmental background of the problem: both are clear instances of countertransferential mismanagement.

Social scientists often try to refrain from involvement in social conflicts, and psychotherapists have tried to develop a mode of working without expressing their own value system. The therapist is described as a blank mirror for the patient's perceptions, which are considered distorted. It has been understood by many, however, that implicit choices in all fields of social sciences do express our values (Becker, 1967). Every choice in the treatment of Robert had its implications and reflected how the therapist participates in the sociopolitical reality.

The case of Robert made the different traps in treatment very clear. In many other cases, where the actual conflicts are less clear-cut, therapists are inclined to neglect the social and moral meaning of their intervention. This may be true of combat experiences and equally so of experiences in organizations, where employees are exposed to or are put in charge of handling violence or other traumatic events as part of their job. The moral involvement of therapists requires us to be able to see all aspects of the conflicts with which the patients present us. Selective attention and selective neglect imply choices with far-reaching moral and sometimes political implications.

How specific are the issues we raised in this chapter to the situation in Israel, or even to a military situation? Can we find parallel situations in other circumstances? Warlike situations make most clear the moral dilemmas of people who do things they would condemn under different circumstances. The entanglement of real-life conflicts in emotional conflicts, in our opinion, is not specific to war situations. The rage of victims of traffic accidents about the way they are treated by insurance companies is an example that therapists do encounter. Another example of a similar dilemma occurs when victims of violence consider starting legal procedures in the course of treatment. The question of our aims as therapists cannot be avoided. Do we want to free the aggressive impulses so people will fight their personal wars, or do we want to repair the breach in the confidence that the patients have in the systems that have harmed them so they can live with them in peace?

Like Robert, others may see their (pretrauma) world as all good and as the fulfilling of their ideals, while the traumatic events may drastically change the way they perceive their environment. Therapists mostly choose not to be involved in choices between different sides of the conflicts of their patients. They also tend to translate the conflicts into a metaphorical language, such as the developmental psychoanalytic language. Emphasis then shifts away from reality and toward the internal world, often not to return to the incurring events. Therapy with patients who have acute traumatic states can teach us the risks of this approach.

As therapists, we are confronted with the way we see our own place in the actual world. Do we see ourselves as an active part of society, or do we consider the therapeutic space a "nonpart" of society? Work with trauma victims confronts us with questions of social involvement that are inescapable, even if we are not always aware of them.

REFERENCES

American Psychiatric Association. (1987). *Diagnostic and statistical manual of mental disorders* (3rd ed., rev.; DSM-III-R). Washington, DC: Author.

Becker, H. S. (1967). Whose side are we on? *Social Problems, 14*, 239–247.

Breuer, J., & Freud, S. (1952). *Studien über Hysterie. Gesammelte Werke* (Vol. 1). London: Imago. (Original work published 1895)

Brom, D., Kleber, R. J., & Defares, P. B. (1989). Brief psychotherapy for post-traumatic stress disorders. *Journal of Consulting and Clinical Psychology, 57*(5), 607–612.

Goldberg, A. (1973). Psychotherapy of narcissistic injuries. *Archives of General Psychiatry, 28*, 722–726.

Haley, S. A. (1974). When the patient reports atrocities. *Archives of General Psychiatry, 30*, 191–196.

Halleck, S. L. (1971). *The politics of therapy.* New York: Harper & Row.

Horowitz, M. J. (1976). *Stress response syndromes.* New York: Jason Aronson.

Janoff-Bulman, R. (1989). Assumptive worlds and the stress of traumatic events: Applications of the schema construct. *Social Cognition, 7*, 113–136.

Kinzie, J. D., & Boehnlein, J. K. (1993). Psychotherapy of the victims of massive violence: Countertransference and ethical issues. *American Journal of Psychotherapy, 47*(1), 90–102.

Kirshner, L. A. (1973). Countertransference issues in the treatment of the military dissenter. *American Journal of Orthopsychiatry, 43*, 654–659.

Kleber, R. J., & Brom, D., in collaboration with P. B. Defares (1992). *Coping with trauma: Theory, prevention and treatment.* Amsterdam: Swets & Zeitlinger International.

Leifer, R. (1969). *In the name of mental health: The social functions of psychiatry.* New York: Science House.

Lifton, R. J. (1976). Advocacy and corruption in the healing professions. *International Review of Psychoanalysis, 3*, 385–398.

Lipsedge, M. (1993). Cultural influences on psychiatry. *Current Opinion in Psychiatry, 6*, 274–279.

McCann, I. L., & Pearlman, L. A. (1990). *Psychological trauma and the adult survivor.* New York: Brunner/Mazel.

Newberry, T. B. (1985). Levels of countertransference toward Vietnam veterans with post-traumatic stress disorder. *Bulletin of the Menninger Clinic, 49*(2), 151–160.

Peterson, K. C., Prout, M. F., & Schwarz, R. A. (1991). *Posttraumatic stress disorder: A clinician's guide.* New York: Plenum Press.

Sider, R. C. (1984). The ethics of therapeutic modality choice. *American Journal of Psychiatry, 141*, 390–394.

Szasz, T. (1970). *The manufacture of madness.* New York: Harper & Row.

Tuchman, B. W. (1981). Israel's swift sword. In B. W. Tuchman, *Practicing history.* New York: Knopf. (First published in *The Atlantic,* September 1967)

Van der Kolk, B. A., Brown, P. A., & Van der Hart, O. (1989). Pierre Janet on posttraumatic stress. *Journal of Traumatic Stress, 2*, 365–378.

Yehuda, R., Southwick, S. M., & Giller, E. L. (1992). Exposure to atrocities and severity of chronic posttraumatic stress disorder in Vietnam combat veterans. *American Journal of Psychiatry, 149*(3), 333–336.

14

Working through the Holocaust
Still a Task for Germany's Youth?

AOR. KONRAD BRENDLER

APPROACH AND AIM

In an analysis of interviews with young people in West Germany, it is shown here that the legacy of silence within the family and confrontation with the documentation of the Holocaust may have a traumatizing effect on the psyche of the generation of the grandchildren.

So far, there have been no empirical inquiries into the perception of the history of Nazism by the third generation and its effects on current behavior. General claims about a "psychic inheritance" among today's youth (Giordano, 1987; Mitscherlich, 1987) have remained vague and speculative, as they have been supported only by sporadic case histories of individual or family therapy (Hecker, 1983; Heimansberg & Schmidt, 1988; Müller-Hohagen, 1988, 1989; Stierlin, 1982), or as they have merely been extrapolations from findings related to the generation of perpetrators and their children (Massing & Beushausen, 1986; Mitscherlich, 1987; Mitscherlich-Nielsen, 1992). The research project de-

AOR. KONRAD BRENDLER • Department of Educational Sciences, University of Wuppertal, 42097 Wuppertal, Germany.
Beyond Trauma: Cultural and Societal Dynamics, edited by Rolf J. Kleber, Charles R. Figley, and Berthold P. R. Gersons. New York, Plenum Press, 1995.

scribed in this chapter presents the first systematic investigation of a nonclinical sample.[1] This project was based on the following assumptions:

1. For adolescents nowadays, as opposed to the children of the generation directly involved, the problems of coming to terms with Nazi history no longer focus on the dynamically connected problems of distancing themselves from their guilt-ridden parents (Bar-On, 1989). Almost all the parents of the young people studied in this chapter grew up during the war or were not born until after the Nazi period.

2. For young people who are in their 20s and 30s and grew up in the former West Germany, it is not possible to avoid taking note of the Holocaust. Unlike their parents, they did not grow up in a social atmosphere of suppression and silence (Müller-Hohagen, 1989). Since the 1960s, Nazi history has been an essential part of the history syllabus in schools.

3. As a result, young persons have to cope with moments of conflict because they are involved in a conflict of wants. On one hand, they want to ignore the consequences and the burden of history, and on the other hand, they feel the need to discover the whole truth about the moral bankruptcy of their ancestors.

The term *working through* is used here for the gradual assimilation of overwhelming conflicttype experiences which the psychic organism initially rejects and in the long run suppresses if there is no adequate psychic basis and support for processing the impressions.

We initially gained information on the effects of the Nazi period on the minds of young people from a quantitative survey in 1989. The surprising results of this research with 1,130 pupils and students concerned the relevance of the "quality of the coping process" and the attitudes of today's youth. For instance, 70% have problems identifying positively with their nationality. They can not establish deeper feelings of attachment or bonding with their own country and background.

An overall look at the most striking results of the scale "emotional reactions in memorizing the Holocaust" showed that

- 65% feel ashamed when they hear about the mass murder by their ancestors.

---

[1] It was a binational research project which took place from 1989 to 1992, carried out by a team of researchers from Wuppertal, Germany, and the University of Beer-Sheva, Israel. The financial resources came mainly from the German-Israeli Foundation (GIF). The conceptual remarks on this empirical research are to be found in Bar-On, Beiner, and Brusten (1988, pp. 214–221).

- 41% have feelings of guilt even though they were not involved in any of those crimes.
- 50% feel somehow paralyzed.
- 68% feel threatened, are afraid of punishment, or are afraid of the future, while thinking of the Holocaust.[2]

These results illustrated not only that most of today's young people are in no way indifferent to those crimes, but also that their self-esteem is afflicted by feelings of guilt and shame. This might be seen as a hint that the young people have not managed to draw a clear line between themselves and the crimes of their immediate ancestors.[3] From a sociopsychological point of view, these feelings of shame and guilt are not good prerequisites for the development of individual responsibility. Rather, they keep alive aggressive mechanisms of defense and compensation (Hultberg, 1987; Jacobi, 1991).

The next period of our qualitative research aimed at deeper insights into the origin, meaning, and effect of the outlined psychological burden. Instead of assuming a hypothetical connection between previously outlined phases of working through and models of attitude, as we did in the quantitative study, our qualitative research focused on the following clusters of questions:

1. What is the relevance of the knowledge of the crimes of their immediate ancestors to the self-esteem and the reality perception of our young people?
2. Which different levels of history perception and adaptation can be elicited from their reports? Do these have a significant impact on their behavior?
3. How were the aforementioned levels of dealing with history achieved? Which different specific stimuli in their social environment affected pseudolearning or significant processes of learning?

METHODOLOGY

In line with these questions, we aimed at two levels in the narrations of our population. By use of the method of "narrative interviews," descriptive data were gained. This material may help to explain how processes of learning or gathering information were either hindered or encouraged. It also provides a detailed insight into the internal patterns

---

[2]For a survey of all results, see Brusten (1992) and Brusten and Winkelmann (1992).
[3]According to the Jewish philosopher Ernst Tugendhat, this reaction points to "irrational working through of collective guilt."

of the "working-through" process itself and what effects these had on the youth's self-concept. Here we used the method of the "phenomenological dialogue" (Sommer, 1987), in the sense of client-centered counseling (Rogers, 1972).

Ten main questions served to evoke memories of the relevant situations. Here are some examples:

- Can you remember situations in which your parents or grandparents told you something about the period of Nazi fascism?
- What did they tell you about the Holocaust?
- Can you remember impressions of how this topic really affected you?
- Do you remember further talks or events, which you could say helped you to see clearly the real meaning of Nazi fascism?
- Can you remember situations in which you felt uneasy being German?

To evaluate these interviews, we used the behavioral psychology concept of the *partial-relevance approach* that Bar-On (1989, 1991, 1992) transferred to a psychoanalytical context. His basic assumption can be illustrated as follows: Failures in the process of "working through" the Holocaust can lead to two extreme tendencies in the behavior of German and Israeli people: Some individuals perceive that their environment is not influenced by these events at all ("The present time has nothing to do with the past, and so we can forget it"). The other category applies to those for whom today's reality seems to be overdetermined by Nazi history ("Everything has its origin in the Past"). Both of these patterns can be seen as inadequate tendencies of behavior. First, those individuals who underestimate the relevance of their Nazi past may ignore their characteristics as a historically generated species, although their behavior may be influenced by hidden or ignored aspects of the same reality. These types of suppression and defense strategies can cause irrational behavior, for example, when German youths cannot understand the negative reactions they may get from older Dutch or Jewish people abroad. Second, individuals who overestimate the relevance of the past may find it difficult to establish a realistic perspective on the present. Overreactions may result, as all aspects of life seem to be overshadowed by the past.

In contrast to these patterns, there are those individuals whose knowledge and experiences of this aspect of our past is well integrated into their concept of the world and themselves: They consider these events realistically and are generally neither obsessively ignorant nor oversensitive. Their sense of the past and its moral implications for today can be described as elaborated. Bar-On referred to this attitude toward the past in relation to the present subjective experience as the "partial relevance of the Holocaust."

The interpretation of the data follows cyclic processes of evaluation and reconstruction, so that we are able to identify which quality or significance the reported experiences have in the mind of the interviewee. We can therefore describe different patterns of "working through the Holocaust" in detail and can link these with four different levels of coping quality, with reference to the "partial-relevance approach."

THE SAMPLE

Our sample consisted of 22 participants: 2 schoolgirls aged 17, 13 student teachers and 7 students from various faculties of Wuppertal University, all of whom were in an initial period of studies. Of the students, 15 were in their early 20s, and 5 were between 25 and 28. In the questionnaire of the quantitative period, 6 participants stated that they were willing to take part in an interview. For the other 16, the interview was obligatory for an optional seminar on the "methods of teaching Nazi history." The schedule included a sponsored trip to Israel. It is significant that the sample was not representative and did not necessarily show the overall interest of students in studying Nazi history.

The fathers of four students (Paul, Sigurd, Olga, and Werner) had been born in or before 1927. They had been actively involved as Wehrmacht soldiers in World War II combats. Five (Angelika, Tina, Beate, Renate, and Ulla) participants noted that at least one of their grandparents had been a member of the Nazi party NSDAP. When interviewing five other students, we found that members of their families must have been more than just Nazi sympathizers. For example someone with a top position on an administration staff must have had means of collaboration with the Hitler regime. This level of acceptance was not seen by the interviewed persons, and in two cases, it was persistently denied.

Olaf's family consisted of resistance fighters and therefore takes a special position in our sample. His grandfather had rejected military service and had been imprisoned until the end of war. A great-uncle had fought in the communist resistance. He had survived two years in a concentration camp and "the notorious punishment battalion 999" afterwards.[4] In contrast to his maternal grandfather, who had been enthusi-

---

[4]Passages in quotation marks are phrases literally quoted from the interview.

astic about the war, his paternal grandfather and great-uncle had, according to Olaf's report, "hardly told anything" about their experiences.

RESULTS

Classification of "Working-Through" Levels

With reference to the theoretical concepts of "working through" and the "partial-relevance approach," we used the following criteria to identify the different levels concerning the quality of working through the Holocaust:

1. General appearance
2. Quality of knowledge and understanding
3. Level of moral consequences taken from the past
4. Manner of transferring the relevant experiences into behavior
5. Identity diffusion and coping strategies

For our participants, we can identify four different levels of rating. Nineteen of the 22 who were asked could be unequivocally assigned to one of these working through levels. Three participants were on the border between Levels III and IV, as they had only partially come to terms with the psychological impact of the subjects.

Level I: Aggressive Defense of the Shadows of the Past

This level could be found in Paul, aged 27, economics student, and Olaf, aged 22, student teacher in history.

General Observations. The way these students reported shows all the aspects of ignorance and defense strategies mentioned in the literature referring to the perpetrators' generation. Toward the criminal side of this epoch, they reacted with resistance but they were well informed and interested in other details.

During the interviews, they showed a diffusion of personality: On the surface they acted decently, educated, and capable of remembering. Behind this, there was a layer of resentment due to narcissistic offenses and suppressed emotions. This frustration could be seen in their selective and perverted perception and interpretation.

On the one hand, Olaf was enraged by "those people who explain everything that happens here, everything that happens anywhere, in terms of National Socialism." Here he meant such "catastrophic cases" as

- "Fanatical anti-Fascists" who made it difficult for him to gain access to one of Schönhuber's Republican meetings.
- "People who are oversensitive in the way they react and get upset about skinheads and the like."
- Fellow students and teachers who comment on his choice of language if he "uses a wrong word . . . which happens subconsciously and can happen very quickly" because, as he said, "The terminology is part of your vocabulary if you read very much about this subject."

On the other hand, Olaf complained that "everything that happened in the Nazi period—and I mean everything—is somehow taboo nowadays." He clarified this statement by giving as examples his experiences during his military service: "In the army, you are disciplined for every wrong word you say. If you step out of line there, then it's very dangerous. Everything that was ever part of the army system under the Nazis had to be changed. Everything, even the tiniest little things, has been avoided. Lots of things are made more complicated as a result, simply because the easier solution is avoided. . . . If you look the way I do, you have to be careful what haircut you have. . . . People don't bother to find out what the person is really like. No. 'That's how it was in the Third Reich, and it's not different now. Piss off, I don't want to have anything to do with your kind.'"

Paul's selective readiness to recall was also symptomatic of these distorted views. On one hand, he saw National Socialism nowadays as "no more than an awkward topic" and went on to say, "You have to come to terms with it and express your views on it as well." On the other hand, he felt that "the topic of the Holocaust is especially burdensome." He asked, "What's the sense in raking over the whole business again and again and reminding generations of it who had nothing to do with it . . . going so far that you feel hounded by it for the rest of your life, that you constantly have to come to terms with it, something I think is no longer important? In my opinion what we have seen of it and done about it is quite enough."

When asked when and how his personal "coming to terms" took place, all he could think of was "the Nazis, who are still being hunted down all over the world." But instead of coming to terms with the guilt of the criminals, he sympathized with them and speculated about revenge motives on the part of the hunters: "In the long run the man in question has lost everything for something about which there is still no agreement whether he even did what he's supposed to have done. . . . On the other hand, you might ask what is the point of it all? Do the Jews get a sort a of satisfaction when they track another one down? Or do they really get such a kick out of being able to organize another trial and being able to say, 'We are going to put you behind bars now for two hundred years'?"

Characteristic Behavioral Aspects of Defense Structures. In the narratives, the nomenclature of the Nazi period and the repertoire of terms associated with the instruments of death were reproduced: the Führer, the Jews, the Frenchmen, and so on. The Jews were simply "taken away." Those in power, with their "orders" and "special measures," "incidentally cleaned up rather brutally."

There was sympathy for right-wing leading figures of the present day. Receptiveness to neofascist thoughts and ideas was strongly denied or suppressed.

There were strong aversions to Germany's political commitments abroad. Residual encumbrances resulting from the Nazi past were blown up out of all proportion into "stifling restrictions imposed by the victorious allies."

The generation responsible was exculpated by relativizing the Nazi atrocities and comparing them with others. One had "respect for older people who lived through the period" and one could sympathize with them and understand them.

Level of Moral Consequences. Results of the past were seen as handicaps imposed from the outside. There was not even a mention of consequences resulting from recognition of historical guilt and informed by principle.

Hints about special obligations and residual commitments on Germany's part were interpreted as blackmail or an unfair burden on those no longer responsible. When these subjects were in fact asked to express their opinion, they trotted out the amoral cynicism of the technician of death, who characterizes as a victim of his or her environment the culprit unlucky enough to be caught. The following example is an illustration. When Paul was asked about his attitude toward the arrest of seven people for supplying gas-warfare components to Iraq and about the hostility this caused toward the Germans, he failed to see the moral or historical relevance of the scandal: "I don't think that it is a problem where you can say 'the Germans of all people!' If we were allowed to sell weapons officially, the question would not arise."

Identity Conflicts and Strategies for Overcoming Them. Because they were unable to get around the consequences of the Hitler period, these subjects saw themselves as victims of the allied victors and those who survived. Here is one example: When asked whether the political consequences of the Nazi period had affected him personally, Olaf assured us vehemently, "Yes, personally I feel that to some extent I'm a victim. Because the actual culprits no longer have to pay for what they did, but like the victims of original sin, those who come after. . . . That's how it is today. Every German has to pay the price for things he played no part in." *Hedrich*

They were unable, however, to distance themselves from the generation that had actually been responsible and thus continued to identify subconsciously with their guilt. In answer to the question of what views he would pass on to his children, Paul clearly showed how he was still harnessed to guilt complexes: "I would say, so that they develop the attitude that they should not have any feeling of guilt anymore, that they can live freely, not to have to live with this guilt feeling, to have to make amends for something or be made responsible for something you can do nothing about. . . . You handicap yourself, because you are not free to make decisions, whether they are political, commercial, or private. If I always have to say to myself when I'm making a decision, 'Stop, remember you are German!' that's a restriction of my freedom."

Quality of Knowledge and Comprehension. There was a lot of knowledge of the spectacular events of the Nazi period, but only partial knowledge of the actual crimes. Impressions gathered from the documentation of the atrocities were nevertheless suspended in the consciousness. When these subjects were repeatedly questioned, "Certain scenes reappear. The pictures are imprinted and are always there, ready, in the back of the mind, because you simply can't forget them."

There was no recognition of the fact that the so-called little people, those without power but nonetheless observers, had failed in their duty and had been involved in the guilt. The Holocaust was distanced, becoming a "secret operation" carried out by exceptional people and having no connection with the everyday world of ordinary people: "The majority of the people were not even aware. . . . People who lived very close to a concentration camp, who could see the smoke rising, who maybe even had the smell of it in their nose, they probably knew what was going on. But remember they were positioned on purpose in such a way that not all that many people came close to them."

The well-documented facts about the abuses of the Nazi regime have produced neither moral nor political consequences. Paul was "aware of the fact that things didn't go all that well," but the concept of fascism still fascinated him. "Whether this mass hysteria and a dictatorial system is really all that great an advantage still remains to be seen," as he said. For him, "this herd instinct is somehow part of human nature. . . . It's absolutely fascinating to see how people will follow one personality or one person and regard everything that person does or says as good."

Level II: Rejection and Rationalization of Bewilderment

To this group belonged Beate, Monika, Gunhild, Renate, and Lisa. Most of the group came from families with a Nazi background.

General Remarks. These young people had heard only one version of the Holocaust. They were shocked by the moral bankruptcy of their progenitors but had rejected or suppressed the suffering of the victims. Explanations and mental constructs ensured, however, that they suffered no serious anxieties and that their view of the world was relatively "normal." The topic of Nazism was ignored as much as possible, on the grounds that "it is no use rummaging around in it over and over again." Their marked unease at being forced to recall evoked self-pity. They wanted to forget but could not. Those who issued warnings were countered with the accusation that they were being "unfair." The same resentment was directed at teachers who, with their "brutal and unbelievable cheek," had actually "taken innocent students by surprise with these atrocities."

Characteristic Behavioral Aspects of Defense Structures. Reports of experiences with the topic of the Holocaust were couched in objectifying categories of an emotionally neutral language without signs of outrage or bewilderment. Common strategies were used to relativize Nazi crimes. Questions about whether relatives had possibly been involved or had partaken in the guilt were ignored or vehemently dismissed. Sometimes, hidden resentment toward peripheral groups and foreigners could be heard. If these suggestions were mentioned, they were corrected contritely.

Viewing the Holocaust from the perspective of the victims or of the consequences for the survivors did not concern these young people. Beate was asked by a friend in a bus in Israel to keep her voice down because there were "still people in Israel who despise the Germans." When asked how she would have reacted if an elderly Israeli had asked her to do the same, she replied, "I would have been angry. Can I help it that I'm German? It's not my fault."

Level of Moral Consequences. Taboo subjects and concrete consequences resulting from the Nazi period were accepted on the grounds that society required this, but they were neither internalized nor accepted on the basis that they were moral commitments. History was not taken into consideration spontaneously, in the light of current events, but reactively, out of fear of social sanctions and censure, as described in Kohlberg's Stage 1 of moral development (Kohlberg & Thriel, 1978).

An example of this type of moral reasoning was that the scenario to honor the SS dead at Bitburg was seen merely as an inopportune political mistake: "They just were not aware that they were doing any wrong."

Identity Conflicts and Strategies to Overcome Them. Declaration of national identity abroad was regarded as "embarrassing." If the subject of the Nazi past came up, they felt a sense of shame and tried to change the subject. Attempts to consider themselves "more as Europeans" helped them to escape from this identity conflict. Hints at a special responsibility on the part of Germans as a result of the Nazi past were interpreted as a they-are-responsible attitude. They then insisted on the right of later generations not to be associated with the events of the past.

Level of Knowledge and Comprehension. Although the Holocaust was regarded as the fault of the whole German people, the concrete questions of who was responsible or partly responsible have never been closely analyzed. Real anxieties about the manifestation of human bestiality were responded to with pseudoexplanations of ideological thought systems or anthropological dogmas, for example, the existence of an inborn human depravity or reflections on "God's plan of saving his chosen people."

Level III: Resigned Acceptance of Guilt and Suffering from the Past

To this group belonged Anna, Robert, Sigurd, Katrin, Susanne, Anke, and Ulla.

General Remarks. These young people were deeply affected psychologically by the pictures of those who had suffered and had experienced the horror of the crimes perpetrated against human beings. But the associated impressions and shocks had not been properly processed. When they talked about the events, sadness and perplexity were evident in their tone of voice. What was missing, however, was anger and revulsion toward those responsible. What made this group different from the others already described in their dealing with the problem was a deep-rooted destabilization of their basic trust. The syndromes caused by pressure due to suffering can be divided into two experiential areas in terms of traumatic experiences that these young people had not come to terms with:

1. *Traumatization of the feeling of identity (narcissistic trauma).* The enormous guilt of the ancestors was combined, in these young people's concept of themselves, with their own identity as Germans and either children or grandchildren of the actual culprits. The vague suspicion that members of their families had involved and knowledge that these crimes had been committed by Germans were self-deprecating.
2. *Traumatization of the basic trust (existential trauma).* The impressions of the immeasurable sufferings caused by the factorytype killings and the frightening brutality of those involved produced real trauma. Pictures had become imprinted in the mind. The unprocessed fright at realizing what human beings are capable of shattered any trust there was in the human condition. It had further consequences as a devitalizing factor in the general attitude toward life and fear of what lay ahead.

The narcissistic trauma was indicated by the following phenomena. National identity was perceived as a negative stigma. For these young people, being German was a "defect within oneself" and a cause of shame (Wurmser, 1990; see also Erikson, 1981). There was also distrust of themselves due to the suspicion that they were sociogenetically imprinted with fascist leanings. As a result, a split personality developed and inner impulses were suppressed because they were suspected of being potentially fascist: nationalist feelings, aggressive feelings, hostility toward foreigners and asylum seekers, and so on. Finally, the narcissistic trauma was indicated by marked feelings of guilt about the Holocaust that could not be eradicated by rational argument. Parallel to these feelings, there was a potentiated sense of shame in the presence of the victims of Nazi crimes, because there was the fear that one would be "stood in the culprit's corner."

The two following examples illustrate the narcissistic trauma. Ulla (26) accused the non-German world around her of expecting from her a contrite feeling of guilt because of Nazi war crimes: "I find that terrible when we meet. . . . They don't understand that we suffer simply because of the fact that we were born in Germany. What can I do about that? (pause) Nevertheless, I'm held partly responsible for it. . . . These are the times when I feel ashamed to be German. (pause) I can remember that there were moments like these, and that, in fact, it is always like this." Robert (22) stated, "But then the point is whether you can forgive it. What I mean is, whether we Germans will ever be able perhaps to forgive ourselves or whether the other side will ever be able to forgive us for what we did. . . . You always seem to be responsible over and over again and to defend yourself for the things that were done. For me, that is a concrete burden which is constantly there. . . . I want to be rid of the stigma of being German, because that's a form of discrimination as well."

An existential trauma is indicated by the following phenomena:

- Helplessness and fear in the face of the possible repetition of such crime: "I don't know if I could do anything to counter it!"
- Fear of human bestiality, which is ultimately uncontrollable, and which seems to be inherent.

Examples of this durable existential bewilderment are the following: Sigurd said, "It is totally incomprehensible to me how human beings can treat other human beings in that way. . . . I'm very afraid, too, of something like that happening again. . . . I really don't know if we can do anything about it. Yes, I must admit I live in permanent fear. . . . I see how things are changing at present. You must be prepared for escalations like this. I would be even more frightened if I belonged to a minority group."

Ulla said, "I have seen pictures of concentration camps, those that show Jews being shot and (pause) showing the atrocities of the Holocaust. (pause) That was enough for me! (pause) How unbelievably pitiless it all was! (pause) That they could no longer see people as people. . . . That human beings can do that, do a thing like that, that undermines my trust in humankind. I really have doubts! What are we actually that we can turn into such beasts? . . . For a while I had this terror of other people and of myself. It was a phase where I was afraid of other people and of myself."

Characteristic Behavioral Aspects of Defense Structures. There were marked fears of such crimes' being repeated. Some subjects did nothing about it; other became involved in antineofascist activities but nevertheless had a bad conscience for not doing enough in this direction.

Some tried to improve the image of the German abroad by behaving in an exemplary manner themselves and became angry at the behavior of fellow Germans.

The ability to sympathize with the victims and their relatives was blocked to some extent in these young people because of their inhibitions. Expectations arising from the bewilderment of the progeny of the victims were frequently inadequately or wrongly anticipated. Where there was otherwise a marked desire to make up for the past, such failures caused them deep shame.

Level of Moral Consequences. The consequences of the crimes committed were internalized, but only as a diffuse reparation and evasion ethos in the face of social conventions and taboos. Acceptance of concrete responsibilities resulted from the need for social acceptance. There were no signs of principled insights and their integration into an autonomous court of conscience (Kohlberg's Stages 3 and 4). They expected a high level of moral sensibility from themselves, but since they had internalized only global postulates and taboos, they were quite blind when it came to the concrete requirements of the situation. Failure to meet their own demands repeatedly triggered further feelings of shame.

Quality of Knowledge and Comprehension. Statements about the Nazi war crimes were charged with emotion, indirect as well as diffuse. The Holocaust, which, like an ancient myth, touched personal feelings, was an "incomprehensible affair." Similar global formulas were used to describe the political and personal results of it.

The Holocaust was recognized as a moral failure and a "collective monstrous guilt" on the part of their ancestors. Possible involvement in this guilt of their own relatives was never mentioned, though. Even if they knew that their grandparents had been puppets of the Nazi regime, their contributory guilt was never discussed. The ethical problem "How could people do such a thing or allow it to happen?" was a painful question, because to answer it there could be no recourse to ideological consolation and apparent solutions (see Level II).

Level IV: Moral Responsibility and Autonomy by Learning from History

To this group belonged Arthur, Christian, Olga, Angelika, and Werner.

Level of Moral Insight and Consequences. This group "understood" what the Holocaust meant for the victims, and they had also come to terms with the guilt of the generation responsible for it. They could name concrete situations in the lives of the actual culprits and their fellow travelers in which they had displayed moral weakness, and they complained about the continued reluctance of their relatives to justify their actions. This was not done, though, in a spirit of arrogant self-assurance, the implication being that they would have done better.

Olga, for example, criticized her father: "My father still says, 'We knew nothing about what was going on.' . . . Nobody can make me believe that they knew nothing about it! Where people were disappearing in droves, you can't tell me that nobody noticed. That simply doesn't hold water. Good God, you can't shut your eyes to that sort of thing! . . . Then there were a lot who somehow just became involved in some way or other, got in and then couldn't get out again. . . . But then they should not go around behaving as they do. On the other hand, I can understand the fear. That I can well understand, how people were afraid when the bullyboys came. Can I point the finger at anyone? How would I have reacted if I had been there?"

They had discovered "the Eichmann in themselves" and recognized the role of rationality in the machinery of death. Diffuse shattering of their self-trust caused by an uncontrollable mechanism of evil had been replaced by critical self-reflection.

They had developed a general moral sensorium for inhumanity. The degraded and tortured victim of the concentration camp machinery had become part of the meaning of the term *tortured humankind*. Because it was understood how it had all started in 1933 at the very latest, there was no longer a need for normative stereotypes to put up resistance. From a structural point of view, the level of integration of insights and emotions into the moral consciousness corresponded to postconventional, principle-guided morality, in Kohlberg's sense. Where real bewilderment had been worked through to an advanced level, the quality of the moral consciousness went beyond the formalism of Kantian ethics. This was then completed by a "morality of fellow-feeling."[5]

Consciousness of Identity. National identity was no longer considered a stigma but had become a central marker of political commitment into which its shadows had been integrated. Arthur described this change from defense to critical acceptance in the following way: "Through the developments with the German Democratic Republic (DDR), for the first time I have felt German. I saw that nothing has happened to what is called the Fatherland. At first, this was a bit suspicious, the fact that I felt this way, because I hold thoughts about the Fatherland being partly responsible for the outbreak of war and the development of Nazism. . . . It became quite clear to me what it means to other nationalities when I say I'm German. . . . That's why I think that, as a German, I am forced to come to terms with this period between 1933 and 1945. And that means that I come to terms in a different way from the way other nations do."

[5]The psychological precondition for this high level of morality is described in the late work of H. E. Richter. The philosopher A. Schopenhauer defended this modus of morality against I. Kant.

When the shadows were worked through, the narcissistic fear of shame, with its fantasies of exposure, vanished, too. Olga described the acceptance of the inevitable for her as follows: "I acknowledge the fact that I am German. That is something that cannot be changed, and for that reason, I can understand when I am attacked because of this. I know what the people suffered at that time. I really am very sorry about it, but I feel no sense of my shame. I would feel shame if I had been directly involved myself. . . . I would never say I will not talk about it again. One of the reasons for that is that I am German. . . . As a German, it is part of my culture and my past. That's something I cannot discard."

Level of Knowledge and Comprehension. All those questioned at this stage described striking examples of confrontation. They emphasized that these experiences had opened new dimensions of incomprehensibility. Arthur, for example, described this qualitative leap from meaningless knowledge to real comprehension as follows: "Previously, I had known that people had been tortured and killed and that millions had been gased. But the term *gasing* at first conveyed nothing to me. The horror involved still had no reality for me. I first realized it in Buchenwald, where it was like a thump in the stomach. . . . Out of a historical date something comprehensible evolved. No, actually something incomprehensible and which had something to do with me." In Werner's case, the change came about as a result of his personal contact with concentration camp survivors, burnt-out cases. In Angelika's case, it was the children's drawing in Theresienstadt; in Christian's, the reconstruction of the fate of individual Jews in his hometown.

Reconstruction of the process of their successful working through makes one thing clear in all cases: Learning through the Holocaust culminates in self-confrontation, because one is then no longer willing to accept determinist explanations but recognizes one's own shadows in the failures of one's forefathers.[6]

EXPLAINING THE DIFFERENT LEVELS OF COPING WITH NAZI HISTORY

To explain in depth the formation of the above-characterized levels, it is necessary to consider a variety of views. While we believe that the effects of peer pressure, television, and books have their impact, family

---

[6]An example for this kind of learning is the American curriculum, Stern Strom & Parsons (1982). For examples and a scheme of phases of the working through process for German youth see Brendler (1992).

and school must be seen as more influential agencies of socialization. Here we focus on such influences.

Biographical data—highlighting the active involvement of family members in Third Reich politics or the fact that some fathers of the interviewed students had fought in World War II—provide little explanation of the different means of coping with the Holocaust in our sample. Participants with such a background were found in equal proportions at all levels (Angelika, Tina, Ulla, and Regina). Students whose fathers had been World War II soldiers achieved Level I (Paul), Level III (Sigurd), and even Level IV (Olga and Werner).

Intergenerational Communication in Families

Within the family, serious discussions about the Nazi period had usually occurred after this issue was taught in school. Four subjects of our sample related that they had never talked about Nazi crimes in their family. At this juncture, we have to realize that, from an early stage, subtle statements and implicit messages had been communicated through rare remarks, the effects of which should not been underestimated. Consequently, we shall distinguish in our analysis of family communication two distinct types of interaction.

First, the level of explicit conversation may be referred to as *officially accepted communication*. Generally, this type of communication was found in connection with specific questions by the children based on their experiences at school. Second, there was an informal stream of communication that was stressed when actualities—for example, in newspapers or on television—were commented on, and at a deeper stage, they could evoke spontaneous talk of personal experiences, painful or irrelevant, dating back to that historical period.

Analysis of Informal Communication

Older family members' unintentional remarks during family talks were not meaningless for the children. Their intuition responded with a subtle feeling about the crime, in the context of their own family. They established a certain awareness and suspicion of older family members which they could develop by studying this issue in a formalized school setting.

For instance, there were the "good-natured" jokes and anti-Semitic stereotypes of Olaf's maternal grandparents, or his grandfather's enthusiasm when he praised the "beautiful experiences" in the Wehrmacht during the "desert operation," or when he recalled the "Führer's visit to Wuppertal." Olaf always sensed a "certain similarity" in those talks but also recognized a taboo at the same time: "Everything meant to be political was clearly excluded. . . . Grandpa just told personal stuff, especially in the presence of us kids."

Having two prominent antifascists in his family, Olaf was an exception in our sample. The quietness of the two communist resistance fighters in his father's family may have irritated Olaf. He subsequently developed a type of counteridentity to offset the "resistance fighter" element in his family, as we can see from the material shown above.[7]

The communication pattern in Anna's (22) family can be characterized as a meaningful silence. She was often rejected by her mother. Whenever Anna—obviously "moved"—challenged her family about things she had seen or heard by chance, she received "no reply." Her family "just wants to live peacefully. . . . They avoided this topic." On the other hand, they simply assured her, "Not everything was bad. Eventually, they got the unemployed away from the streets to build the motorways."

At the time of this study, Anna was surprised by the negative connotations she associated with the term *Jew*. Indeed, the term *Israeli* seemed so much easier to say. Abroad, she felt so threatened by "exaggerated suspicion" that she always felt the need to behave properly.

Anna's grandfather "must have been pretty high up in the ranks." It still took Anna by surprise "how often he could take time off." Her mother explained how much he had helped during their flight from Danzig in 1944. What Anna knew was that "he was some sort of construction engineer," but she did not know "what he really did during the war."

Other families in our sample demonstrated a similar attitude. Although they had explained or given more information to their children, they had shown through their concrete behavior what they really thought about this period of history. As Beate (21) estimated, these topics "appeared often enough" in the media. Her family had developed specific ways of expressing little interest: "Shown on television, it does not effect you all that much, because you can talk or do other things at the same time. . . . Perhaps you talk a little about it afterward. Then my parents usually said, "An end must be put to all that. We live in different times today. We have to carry on.'"

Analysis of Intended Communication

First attempts aimed at specific information had usually taken place in the 14 to 15 age range. This correlates with the start of history lessons

---

[7]It has to be considered, too, that communist resistance had been discriminated against and put under taboo in the anticommunistic atmosphere of postwar Germany.

in school on the Nazi period. Most of the teenagers had gathered their first detailed information about Nazism from these lessons. This information had been significant enough for them to challenge the older generation about the Holocaust. Four interviewees mentioned their teacher as encouraging them to ask their parents or grandparents about the persecution of the Jews.

Attempts to classify the intentional communication within families led us to four modes in the family members' "readiness" for conversation about Nazi issues:

1. Silence or appeals for consideration, because "horrible things" had happened and "precious memories of that time" should not be spoiled.
2. Resistance or defense, because "those" questions were considered disturbing. Here we can find the usual symptoms of repression and denial, as they have been described in the works of Mitscherlich & Mitscherlich (1967) and Giordano (1987).
3. Reactions showing helplessness: admitting the incomprehension you feel in facing what happened. Though superficially curious, we found a basically "neutral attitude." Personal statements had been avoided, and the person's own involvement or responsibility had been denied. His or her private experiences had been changed into impersonal facts and abstract descriptions. Some of the interviewed students regretted how their family members had "refused to speak out for themselves."
4. Unrestrained cooperation, which we found in only two cases. In this context, suggestions were given for appropriate literature, movies, or magazines. The importance of listening openly to each other's experiences and showing an awareness and readiness to console was also emphasized in these cases.

Examples of Refusal of Children's Questions

In our sample above, Modes 1, 2, and 3 were mainly found in parents' and grandparents' communication. A broad spectrum of defense strategies had been used. The older generations had often asked for consideration: "Yes, if you had gone through all that, you would understand that we do not want to talk about it." Other means of appealing had been: "It has to be forgotten sometimes." There had also been aggressive refusal. The curiosity of the children had been interpreted as reproach. Although the children's questions were meant to be "harmless," the relatives "quickly had the feeling of being attacked."

In nine families, it was noticeable that the parents had adopted their own parents' justifications. Except for one case, we found this modus in all families with Nazi relatives. Ulla's mother, for example, had adopted the role of an advocate for her own parents against the grandchildren's "attacks." Ulla declared "My father and mother always look at it as an offense, which is strange, because I keep on telling them, 'Mama, I do not mean to offend you. Surely, you were only a child yourself in those days.'" Asked straightforward by Ulla "What was the matter with your father?" the mother reacted offensively: "Do you really believe you would behave better? They did not know it. It was not their fault."

Family Communication and "Double-Wall" Disturbances

Frustration of the child's curiosity obviously had an impact on later attitudes and approaches to other people. Moreover, both sides came with negative preconditions for neutral dialogue, the children and their elders. Most of the latter had suppressed guilt feelings as result of their Nazi experience; the children got upset by what they had heard in school or on television and were looking for explanations. By going through these different modes of the mutual blocking of true communication, we can distinguish four main types of mutual hindrances:

1. The third generation had suppressed questions in order to avoid conflicts within the family.
2. Witnesses of the events had held back information. They did not want to speak out, as this would contradict the expectations of their grandchildren and children. They had had experiences of being criticized and being rejected.
3. Conversations with relatives had been avoided, as the children had realized or had been told that it was painful for the witnesses to be reminded.
4. Exploring the past had been avoided because of the fear of discovering that loved ones had been involved. This would have had fatal implications for the individuals' self-esteem, being blood-related.

Examples and Explanation. After having learned the facts of the Holocaust in school, many children had challenged their parents and grandparents. Their resentment of the facts they had just learned may have been noticeable to their relatives. Their attempts to gather information at firsthand were often rejected rather abruptly. To avoid further trouble, the children had simply stopped making further inquiries.

On the other hand, the witnesses of that time had been rejected as well. If they had started to talk about ordinary situations of the everyday life in the Nazi era, their relatives might overreact. The Holocaust over-shadowed the opportunities for mutual understanding, shown in the following example. Ulla reported, "There was one situation that really shocked me. My grandma told us, 'Sure, in the times of Hitler, a lot of things were different. The economy was not as bad, and we had fewer criminals.'" Ulla had immediately become suspicious that her grand-mother might be biased. Being upset she had criticized and reproached her grandmother: "Listen, what happened, then, to the Jews?"

Other students as well assured us that they had quickly realized having said something unpleasant when referring to Nazi fascism. They sensed that perpetrators, bystanders, Wehrmacht soldiers, and even children who had observed this era had not coped with it and therefore did not want to be reminded. Ulla, for example, had detected aspects of guilt in her parents deeds, even if they (born in 1937 and 1949) could not have been involved: "I believe they always transfer the guilt to themselves. In fact, they want to get rid of this guilt because they do not know how to cope with it."

Surprisingly, we found this general "wall of silence" even among those witnesses of the time whose attitude during the Hitler years could cause little moral suspicion today. Even active fighters in the resistance had not spoken out freely. Olaf's grand-uncle had never spoken of his torture in the concentration camp or about his experiences in the punishment brigade: "Though he suffered the most, he kept quiet about it. . . . As a matter of fact, I have never asked persistently. They did not want to talk about it, which I realized easily. Then I kept quiet."

Others, like Judith (17), had not asked because they felt threatened by what they might discover. She was "afraid, that I will sometimes find out something. . . . My grandpa loved me dearly. I never saw him doing any harm. I believe I could not carry on if I had found out anything. . . . My world would have fallen in ruins if I had discovered something. . . . I would not have been able to cope with myself anymore, . . . since my grandfather's blood is also in my veins—symbolically. I simply could not come to terms with it."

Caring and Authentic Communication

In only two families of our sample (those of Judith and Tina) did we find substantial support for attempts of family members to work through these walls of silence. These young women's relatives had not only answered questions but had even encouraged their children at an early stage—in fact, while still at primary school—to learn about the Holocaust.

Though Judith's grandparents had been quiet, she could always ask her mother. Judith recalled one situation especially, which must have happened when she was 6 or 7: "There was something on television which I found really horrible. So my mother told me what happened . . . the way you can talk to a child, but she told as well how cruel and horrible it was."

Being realistic and careful at the same time, Judith's mother had helped her to get over that shock. The same thing happened later on, when they discussed films on Nazi history for a long time. In a similar way, they dealt with Anne Frank's diary, which Judith read when she was 13. The essential question of "how human beings can do or allow such things to happen" has not left Judith since then.

Tina had received similar support from her family. Her maternal grandparents had been Nazis: "Grandpa was a judge, and grandmother was looking after the kids." The other grandparents' politics, too, "still today are rather right-wing-oriented." This grandfather had had privileges in the Wehrmacht and had always been "a bit against the Jews" and biased against the blacks in South Africa.

When we looked deeper into the attitude of criticism in this family and the intellectual distance they kept from the grandparents, we found that they dealt intensively with the guilt, in which the elders were involved. Similarly to Judith, Tina had had the opportunity to learn about the Holocaust at a fairly early stage. She had learned early "that Jews were gased." She remembered a quarrel with a girlfriend in the primary school, who had told her, "Hitler was good."

DISCUSSION OF RESULTS

Most of those interviewed were still trying to cope with the psychic ballast related to the moral bankruptcy of their progenitors. Some continued to fight against the consequences of the past or tried to ignore them (Levels I and II). Still inhibited, at least for the present, by social conventions they represented a recruiting potential for right-wing movements and the new "anti-Semitism as a result of Auschwitz" (Bergmann & Erb, 1991).

Others suffered from the stigma of their identity and from existential trauma (Level III). Because they stared in disbelief at the last bestial link in a chain of events that had begun for all initially with banal envy, self-deception, and moral blindness, they neither comprehended how the culprits had ended up in the abyss of their own guilt nor where the joint responsibility of the average citizen had begun and was beginning again in the present. If one expects this later generation to have gained in moral sensibility from their attempt to come to terms with the mistakes and crimes of their ancestors or to have developed a sense of responsibility, it is clear that only very few have learned from history. Why had only a minority of those interviewed accomplished this?

Most families have failed their children. Instead of seeing children's questions as an opportunity to develop their conscience, with two known exceptions, all the grandparents involved in the study set a negative example, a perfect model, we might say, of self-deceit, a search for scapegoats, and an aggressive way of dealing with their narcissistic traits. In 9 out of 10 families with known Nazi backgrounds, the parents as well as the grandparents had adopted defense mechanisms. Instead of showing solidarity with the psychic needs of their children, they had stood by their own parents and protected them. All those questioned at working-out Levels I and II came from families with such repressive traditions. Even the fathers who had been actively involved in the war never became constructive speech partners for their children (Olga, Sigurd, Paul, and Werner).

The role played by the schools had been just as meager. All of the subjects who had reached an advanced working level had either had discussion partners in their families (Tina, Judith, and Angelika) or had had their most salient key experiences outside school. At school, the Nazi period had been treated in a purely objective way, like every other subject. As a result, the preconceptions and personal problems of the students had simply been passed over. The attempt to explain this period objectively was bound to fail. Instead of first working on defensive attitudes, in the end the teachers had relied on the shock effect of documented atrocities. Using materials in this way for moral intimidation had led to confrontations that had been counterproductive and inhuman. The factual material had triggered the adolescents' rigid defense mechanisms or had inflicted deep psychic shock.

First, there had been the actual shock of a possibility that contradicted all rationality and faith in humankind. Then, there was the spontaneous impulse to protect oneself from the shocking realization that there is no guarantee of human survival. Knigge (1992) called it the "tendency to look after yourself," associated with the realization that the Holocaust "cannot be avoided" (p. 255).

There had also been the phenomenon of narcissistic defensiveness, as one did after all belong to those people who had committed the crimes. We were able to show that, because of their nationality and family connections, the grandchildren were still so affected by the moral bankruptcy of the generation responsible for Nazi crimes that they were in danger of stigmatizing themselves. Every teacher must be prepared for his or her students to be deeply shocked, regardless of their nationality. Coming to terms with and overcoming narcissistic defensiveness, on the other hand, is a problem which poses a special task for German educationists and teachers, since it involves massive impediments to learning and the danger of aggressive attempts to compensate for the "stigma of being German."

Both these problems have been ignored up to now in the classroom, an omission that has reinforced the existing defensive mechanisms or has traumatized the view of life of the young people concerned. Instead of noticing what the pictures trigger in the children, teachers merely repeat the mental cruelty and indifference of the relatives who have left their children stranded with their frightening questions or have saved themselves by offering harmless, neutral explanations. Instead of discussing the self-defense reactions of the children, they ignore them or sanction them. In view of the emotional stress syndromes, it could be argued that these children should be spared any confrontation with the brutality of the Holocaust pictures and that the treatment of the subject should be confined to a sober analysis of facts.

Our analysis of successful learning processes proves, however, that it is not being *burdened* but rather being *not burdened* that becomes the obstacle in this process of overcoming one's shadows in matters of identity and possible relief. The narratives of those interviewed who had reached the advanced stage of Level IV demonstrate that nobody increases her or his moral insight without going through a period of mental suffering and personal bewilderment.

There is no enclave in Germany where a later generation can flee from the shadows cast by the memory of the crimes against humankind. Even outside the school, there are items such as films, pictures, and memorials for the victims, all of which are occasions for recall and which trigger personal anguish. The world around Germany will never forget. Confrontational experiences in schools were an opportunity to integrate resistance to learning, for it is through these experiences that the psychic burden inherited by the grandchildren can be lightened. The children require dialogue and emotional support as well. Otherwise, there is the danger that they will be scarred or socialized to be latent fascists like Paul and Olaf.

To prevent traumatization, which is demonstrated at Level III, our analysis of teaching in schools leads to the following didactic requirements:

1. Children should be prepared before being forced to see docu-

mentation of the cruelties of the Holocaust. They should have sufficient time afterward to grieve and to comprehend the facts.

2. Teachers should then deal with the youngsters' emotional and existential bewilderment. Confrontation with the brutal reality without working it through is superficial moralizing by means of intimidation. It acts as a deterrent to the observance of fragile social taboos, but not as moral education via insight and understanding.

3. If children show opposition to the topic of the Holocaust, this should be neither ignored nor reproached by the teacher. The impulse to reject the unbelievable facts should not be a cause of censure or taboo. Censure can cause those concerned to become outsiders with neofascist sympathies. Ignoring resistance can lead to a fixation on the so-called Auschwitz lie.

4. The administrative decision in Germany to teach the topic of the Holocaust to children aged 14 and 15 needs to be discussed. Since the topic is to be taught in the critical preadolescent phase, the danger of identity trauma is particularly acute (Erikson 1981).

EPILOGUE

Being a German, I dare not draw generalizing conclusions about the transfer of perpetrators' trauma from one generation to the next and coping with the consequences. But the question is whether drawing any conclusions is valid at all?

Something like those facts described here has never occurred before, and let us hope that they will never take place again. As the epitome of dehumanization of victims and a collective national crime, the Holocaust is unique and incomparable, for both sides.

The identity of French or American citizens is built up by an awareness of belonging to a nation which has, by espousing human dignity and human rights, gained something essential for civilization. The identity of young Germans is affected by succeeding the generation that caused the "break with civilization called Auschwitz" (Diner, 1988), that deprived humankind of the assurance of survival based on human relations, and that also destroyed forever a fundamental confidence in culture and civilization.

Something happened that, on the secure ground of civilization, appeared to be unimaginable: a civilized people perverted into a mass of murderers and bystanders. This is the proof that it might happen over and over again. And so the possibility of identifying with their nation without inner struggle is lost forever to all following generations in Germany.

As long as today's generation fights against instead of accepting the narcissistic insult of belonging to this kind of nation, they will remain predisposed to similar actions and will have to depend on regulation from outside to avoid the compulsive repetition caused by this defense.

The awareness of menace is universal, a problem of humankind; the trauma of perpetration belongs to the Germans. And it must be worked through anew with every generation; that is what we owe to humanity forever. Only by doing this may we achieve reconciliation with ourselves and the world. On that score, the results of our investigation can convey only a glimmer of hope.

REFERENCES

Bar-On, D. (1989). *Legacy of silence: Encounters with children of the Third Reich.* Cambridge: Harvard University Press.

Bar-On, D. (1994). Partial relevance of the Holocaust for our reality: Learning and pseudolearning from a psychological perspective. In K. Brendler & G. Rexilius (Eds.), *Drei Generationen im Schatten der NS-Vergangenheit* (pp. 7–13). Wuppertal: University Press.

Bar-On, D. (1992). Begegnung mit dem Holocaust. Israelische und deutsche Studenten im Prozess des Durcharbeitens. In G. Hardtmann (Ed.), *Spuren der Verfolgung: Seelische Auswirkungen des Holocaust auf die Opfer und ihre Kinder* (pp. 167–197). Gerlingen: Bleicher.

Bar-On, D., Beiner, F., & Brusten, M. (Eds.) (1988). *Der Holocaust: Familiale und gesellschaftliche Folgen.* Wuppertal: University Press.

Bergmann, W., & Erb, R. (1991). *Antisemitismus in der Bundesrepublik Deutschland: Ergebnisse der empirischen Forschung von 1946–1989.* Opladen: Leske.

Brendler, K. (1988). Von den Schwierigkeiten, aus der Geschichte zu lernen. In D. Bar-On, F. Beiner, & M. Brusten (Eds.), *Der Holocaust: Familiale und gesellschaftliche Folgen* (pp. 147–157). Wuppertal: University Press.

Brendler, K. (1991). Die Unumgänglichkeit des "Themas" Holocaust für die Enkelgeneration. In K. Brendler & G. Rexilius (Eds.), *Drei Generationen im Schatten der NS-Vergangenheit* (pp. 220–258). Wuppertal: University Press.

Brusten, M. (1992). Die Bedeutung des Holocaust für die Einstellung der deutschen Jugend zu aktuellen sozialen und politischen Fragen. In U. Ewald et al. (Eds.), *Entwicklungsperspektiven von Kriminalität und Strafrecht* (pp. 289–331). Bonn: Forum.

Brusten, M., & Winkelmann, B. (1992). Understanding of the Holocaust and its influence on current perspectives of German youth. *Soziale Probleme, 1,* 1–27.

Diner, D. (Ed.). (1988). *Zivilisationsbruch: Denken nach Auschwitz.* Frankfurt: Fischer.

Erikson, E. H. (1981). *Jugend und Krise.* Stuttgart: Klett.

Giordano, R. (1987). *Die zweite Schuld oder Von der Last Deutscher zu sein.* Hamburg: Rasch & Rührig.

Hecker, M. (1983). Die deutsche Nachkriegsfamilie: Lernerfahrungen in einem Familientherapieseminar auf dem Hintergrund der eigenen Familiengeschichte. In E. J.

Brunner (Ed.), *Eine ganz alltäglich Familie: Beispiele aus der familientherapeutischen Praxis.* München: Kösel.

Heimannsberg, B., & Schmidt, C. J. (Eds.). (1988). *Das kollektive Schweigen: Nazivergangenheit und gebrochene Identität in der Psychotherapie.* Heidelberg: Ansager.

Hultberg, P. (1987). Scham—Eine überschattete Emotion. *Analytische Psychologie, 18,* 84–104.

Jacobi, M. (1991). *Scham-angst und Selbstwertgefühl.* Olten: Walter.

Knigge, V. (1992). Abwehr-Aneignen: Der Holocaust als Lerngegenstand. In H. Loewy (Ed.), *Holocaust: Die Grenzen des Verstehens* (pp. 248–259). Hamburg: Rowohlt.

Kohlberg, L., & Thriel, E. (1978). Moralische Entwicklung und Moralerziehung. In G. Portele (Ed.), *Sozialisation und Moral.* Weinheim: Beltz.

Massing, A., & Beushausen, U. (1986). "Bis ins dritte und vierte Glied"—Auswirkungen des Nationalsozialismus in den Familien. *Psychosozial, 28,* 27–42.

Mitscherlich, A. (1987). *Erinnerungsarbeit: Zur Psychoanalyse der Unfähigkeit zu trauern.* Frankfurt: Fischer.

Mitscherlich, A., & Mitscherlich, M. (1967). *Die Unfähigkeit zu trauern.* München: Piper.

Mitscherlich-Nielsen, M. (1992). Die (Un)fähigkeit zu trauern in Ost- und West-Deutschland: Was Trauerarbeit heiszen künnte. *Psyche, 46,* 406–418.

Moser, T. (1992). Die Unfähigkeit zu trauern: Hält die Diagnose einer Überprüfung stand? Zur psychischen Verarbeitung des Holocaust in der Bundesrepublik. *Psyche, 46,* 389–405.

Müller-Hohagen, J. (1988). *Verleugnet, verdrängt, verschwiegen: Die seelischen Auswirkungen der Nazizeit.* München: Kösel.

Müller-Hohagen, J. (1989). Folgen und Spätfolgen des Nationalsozialismus in Beratung und Therapie. In R. Cogoy, R. I. Kluge, & B. Meckler (Eds.), *Erinnerungen einer Profession: Erziehungsberatung, Jugendhilfe und Nationalsozialismus* (pp. 241–249). Münster: Votum.

Richter, H. E. (1987). *Die Chance des Gewissens: Erinnerungen und Assoziationen.* Hamburg: Hoffmann & Campe.

Rogers, C. R. (1972). *Die klientenzentrierte Gesprächspsychotherapie.* München: Kindler (Work, *Client-centered therapy,* first published 1942)

Sommer, J. (1987). *Dialogische Forschungsmethoden: Eine Einführung in die dialogische Phänomenologie, Hermeneutik und Dialektik.* Weinheim: Psychologie Verlags Union.

Stern Strom, M., & Parsons, W. S. (1982). *Facing history and ourselves: Holocaust and human behavior.* Watertown, MA.: International Education.

Stierlin, H. (1982). Dialog zwischen den Generationen über die Nazi-Zeit. *Familiendynamik, 1,* 13–48.

Tugendhat, E. (1991). Der Golfkrieg, Deutschland, und Israel. *Die Zeit,* 22(2).

Wiedemann, P. M. (1986). *Erzählte Wirklichkeit: Zur Theorie und Auswertung narrativer Interviews.* Weinheim: Psychologie Verlags Union.

Wurmser, L. (1990). *Die Maske der Scham: Die Psychoanalyse von Schamaffekten und Schamkonflikten.* New York: Springer.

15

Primary Prevention of Traumatic Stress Caused by War

VICTOR W. SIDEL, BERTHOLD P. R. GERSONS, and JOS M. P. WEERTS

Dear Professor Freud,
. . . This is the problem: Is there any way of delivering mankind from the menace of war? . . .

A. Einstein, 1932

Dear Professor Einstein,
. . . You have taken me by surprise, however, by posing the question of what can be done to protect mankind from the curse of war. . . . Our mythological theory of instincts makes it easy for us to find a formula for indirect methods of combating war. If willingness to engage in war is an effect of the destructive instinct, the most obvious plan will be to bring Eros, its antagonist, into play against it. . . .

S. Freud, 1932 (Freud & Einstein, 1932, pp. 199, 212)

VICTOR W. SIDEL • Montefiore Medical Center, Albert Einstein College of Medicine, Bronx, New York 10467-2490.   **BERTHOLD P. R. GERSONS** • Professor of Psychiatry and Chairman, Academic Medical Center, University of Amsterdam, 1105 BC Amsterdam, Netherlands.   **JOS M. P. WEERTS** • Consultant for Research and Strategy, BNMO-Centre (Veterans Center), Doorn, Netherlands.
Beyond Trauma: Cultural and Societal Dynamics, edited by Rolf J. Kleber, Charles R. Figley, and Berthold P. R. Gersons. New York, Plenum Press, 1995.

INTRODUCTION

Prevention of health problems is conventionally described as having two levels. Primary prevention is the prevention of the underlying illness or trauma itself by intervention to eliminate one or more of its causes. Encouragement of abstinence from cigarette smoking, for example, is an important method of the primary prevention of lung cancer in both the smoker and the nearby inhalers of the sidestream smoke. Secondary prevention is the prevention of one or more of the consequences of illness or trauma by intervention after the illness process has begun or the trauma has occurred. The early detection and treatment of lung cancer—preferably during the asymptomatic phase before the illness has risen "above the clinical horizon"—has been demonstrated to be effective in limiting the consequences of the illness in a significant number of patients. A third level, sometimes called *tertiary prevention* but more commonly known as *treatment* or *rehabilitation,* seeks to prevent the progression of the disease after the symptoms appear (Last, 1992). Figure 1 indicates the "windows" (time periods during which opportunities exist) for prevention during the progression of an illness.

A similar schema can be applied to the prevention of the conse-

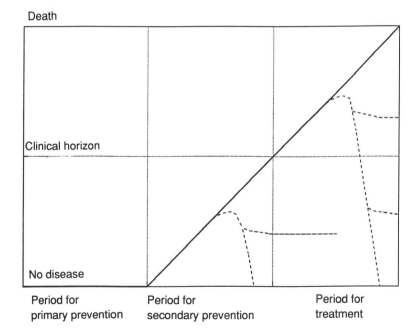

Figure 1. Windows for prevention and treatment.

Table 1. Levels of Prevention of Health Consequences of Traumatic Stress

Primary prevention: Prevention of the traumatic event or prevention of the exposure of individuals or groups to the trauma.

Secondary prevention prior to the occurrence of the traumatic event: Intervention before a predictable event occurs among individuals or groups who cannot be spared exposure to the event.

Secondary prevention after the occurrence of the traumatic event: Intervention among individuals or groups who have been exposed to an event as quickly as possible after the event, preferably before the onset of symptoms.

Treatment and rehabilitation ("tertiary prevention"): Amelioration or reversal of the symptoms and signs of traumatic stress syndrome after the symptoms or signs have become clinically apparent.

quences of trauma (V. W. Sidel, Onel, Geiger, Leaning, & Foege, 1992). Primary prevention involves prevention of the trauma itself; secondary prevention involves intervention, preferably as early as possible after the trauma or even, when a traumatic event is predictable but not preventable, before the trauma occurs. As an example, the prevention of fires by the construction of fireproof structures or the removal of flammable materials is primary prevention. Constructing effective fire escapes and preparing the population in advance of a possible fire to understand that it may happen and how to escape from its consequences are secondary prevention *before* the occurrence. Intervention with the victims as soon as possible after the fire to lessen its traumatic effect is secondary prevention *after* the occurrence. (See Table 1.)

Most of the prevention efforts of those concerned with the consequences of traumatic stress, insofar as prevention is addressed at all, lie in the area of secondary prevention after the occurrence of trauma, although there is indeed some attention given to secondary prevention before the trauma occurs.

The primary prevention of traumatic stress caused by war requires the prevention of war. Relatively little attention has been given to the role of health professionals in the primary prevention of the health consequences of war. The purpose of this chapter is to emphasize the importance of, and to suggest avenues for, the involvement of health professionals in the primary prevention of traumatic stress caused by war.

THE ROLE OF HEALTH PROFESSIONALS IN PREVENTION OF HEALTH PROBLEMS

It is widely accepted that professionals concerned with the management and treatment of individual clients or patients have an obligation to provide advice on methods of secondary prevention of the consequences of health problems. An example is screening by cervical smear in order to detect and treat cancer of the uterine cervix before it becomes clinically apparent. Health professionals, we believe, also have an obligation to advise primary prevention. In work with individual clients or patients, this obligation is often accepted. Many professionals, for example, routinely counsel their patients about the risks of smoking. But if primary prevention is to be applicable to cervical cancer, prevention of which may require changes in community sexual patterns, or to be applicable to reduction of smoking exposure—both active and passive—for everyone in the community rather than simply for the individual patient, community-based techniques are needed. The obligation to be involved in communitywide primary prevention is nonetheless questioned in many fields of medicine. Does the health professional have a duty not only to urge smoking cessation for his or her patients who smoke but also to work for the reduction of smoking in the entire community? Does the professional who treats patients with hepatic cirrhosis have an obligation not only to counsel individual patients but also to attempt to limit the consumption of alcohol by everyone in the community?

Perhaps more important than the question of the professional's obligation to work for primary prevention is the question of his or her competence—requisite knowledge and skills—to do so. Does a physician, for example, have any special knowledge or skills that would permit effective work to prevent fires, change sexual patterns, reduce cigarette smoking, or limit alcohol use in the community? Is the work better left to public health workers, educators, mass communication specialists, sociologists, political activists, government officials, or others who may have greater knowledge and skill in such work or who have greater access to effective community-based methods?

We believe that primary prevention is a responsibility of everyone who works in the treatment or the rehabilitation of the victims of health problems. The basis for our argument is that those who deal with the consequences of health problems—in this case, the consequences of trauma—have special knowledge of its depredations and therefore a special sense of the urgent need for its prevention.

THE HEALTH CONSEQUENCES OF MODERN WARFARE

One example of attempts to apply primary prevention to the health consequences of war has been the effort by many physicians around the world to prevent nuclear war. In 1962, a small group of physicians in

Boston prepared a series of articles for the *New England Journal of Medicine* on the medical consequences of thermonuclear war (Physicians for Social Responsibility, 1962). The analysis led to the conclusion that, once the bombs had been detonated and tens of thousands, if not hundreds of thousands or millions, of people were injured by the blast, heat, and radiation, there was relatively little that those responsible for the management of the injured could do to relieve or reverse the injury. Those responsible for care of the injured, the authors argued, had a special responsibility to prevent the use of such weapons—in other words, had a special responsibility for primary prevention. This was the basis for the formation of the Medical Association for the Prevention of War (MAPW) in the United Kingdom in 1952, Physicians for Social Responsibility (PSR) in the United States in 1961, and the Nederlandse Vereniging voor Medische Polemologie (NVMP) (Netherlands Medical Association for Peace Research) in 1969.

The International Physicians for the Prevention of Nuclear War (IPPNW) was formed in 1980. Groups similar to MAPW, PSR, and NVMP have now been organized in 80 countries and are affiliated with IPPNW. The work that IPPNW and its national affiliates have accomplished was recognized by the award of the Nobel Peace Prize in 1985 (Lown, 1986). The Nobel citation summarized the work of IPPNW and its national affiliates:

> [IPPNW] has performed a considerable service to mankind by spreading authoritative information and by creating an awareness of the catastrophic consequences of nuclear warfare. . . . This in turn contributes to an increase in the pressure of public opposition to the proliferation of nuclear weapons and to a redefining of priorities, with greater attention being paid to health and other humanitarian issues. Such an awakening of public opinion . . . can give the present arms limitation negotiations new perspectives and a new seriousness. (IPPNW, 1986, p. 3)

But it was clear at the time of the Nobel ceremony in 1985, and it remains clear now as control over the nuclear stockpiles of the former USSR has changed dramatically, that the work of the prevention of nuclear war has barely begun. The world still has tens of thousands of nuclear weapons with an explosive equivalent of billions of tons of TNT, over a ton of TNT for every human being on the planet. The agreements between Russia, Ukraine, Kazakhstan, Belarus, and the United States, all of which possess nuclear weapons, as well as the recent decision by the United States to place a moratorium on nuclear testing, are extremely important, but even if they are fully and permanently implemented, the world will still be left with sufficient nuclear weapons to cause unprecedented injury, death, and ecological damage.

Nuclear weapons are, in military terms, an extraordinarily efficient and effective method of creating massive amounts of injury and death. But they are not the only method of accomplishing such a military objective. Other weapons of indiscriminate mass destruction exist, and some of them may be even more selectively dangerous than nuclear arms to civilian, noncombatant populations. Well-trained and disciplined military personnel can largely be protected against known forms of chemical weapons. Nonetheless, since protective gear reduces the efficiency of troops, and chemical attack (or even its threat) may, despite effective protection, reduce the will to fight, chemical weapons may still be used against troops. It is virtually impossible, on the other hand, even with a massive investment in protective measures, to protect an entire civilian population. The very young, the very old, and the sick are particularly vulnerable. And even the threat of the use of chemical weapons can cause civilian deaths from the faulty use of protective methods or can cause the consequences of traumatic stress. The same is even more true of biological weapons (V. W. Sidel, 1989).

The 1972 Biological Weapons Convention banned the use of biological weapons, and the 1993 Chemical Weapons Convention banned the development, manufacture, stockpiling, transfer, and use of chemical weapons. Much work remains to be done to make these arms control agreements effective and to develop methods of verification of these agreements. Again, professionals responsible for treating the victims have a special responsibility for primary prevention of the use of such weapons by supporting effective arms control and verification measures.

A similar argument can of course be made for war itself. Great progress has been made in the prevention of mortality among wounded combatants, from a 20% mortality rate in the Crimean War to 3% mortality among U.S. troops in the Korean and Indochina wars. (See Table 2.)

Table 2. Wounded Combatants Who Died of Wounds, by War[a]

War	Years of warefare	Wounded combatants who died of wounds (%)
Crimean War	1854–1856	20.0
U.S. Civil War (North)	1861–1865	14.1
Franco-Prussian War	1870–1871	13.6
Spanish-American War	1898	6.7
Boer War	1899–1901	8.8
World War I	1914–1918	6.1
World War II[b]	1941–1945	4.5
Korean War[b]	1950–1953	2.5
Vietnam war[b]	1965–1973	3.6

[a]Garfield and Neugut (1991).
[b]Data for U.S. troops only.

Table 3. Estimated Annual Military Deaths in War, Worldwide, by Century[a]

Century	Mean annual number of military deaths	World midcentury population in millions	Mean annual no. of deaths per million population
17th	9,500	500	19.0
18th	15,000	800	18.8
19th	13,000	1,200	10.8
20th	458,000	2,500	183.2

[a]Garfield and Neugut (1991).

But despite this success in treating physical trauma, deaths among combatants have nonetheless risen sharply during the 20th century, from under 20,000 annual deaths in the 17th century to almost 500,000 annually in this century (Garfield & Neugut, 1991). (See Table 3 and Figure 2.) The net result of the improved care for physical trauma is that many more wounded combatants have been left to suffer postwar disability, including posttraumatic stress disorder.

When we turn from combatants to noncombatants, while civilian populations have always been the indirect victims of war—through the famine or pestilence that often accompanies war—civilians have increasingly become the direct targets of war. Total war deaths rose from ap-

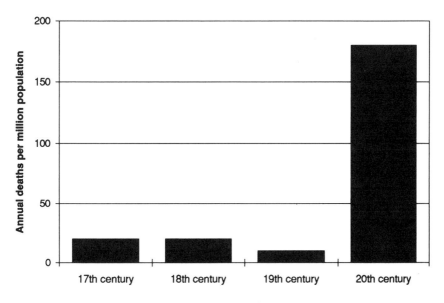

Figure 2. Military deaths in war (Garfield & Neugut, 1991).

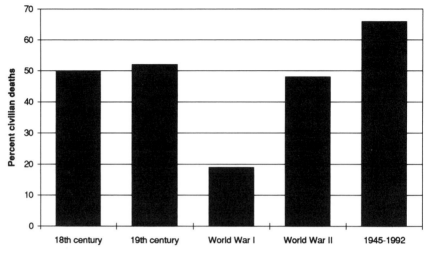

Figure 3. Civilian deaths in war (Sivard, 1991).

proximately 6 million in the 17th century to over 100 million in the first 90 years of this century. Indeed, these 100 million deaths in the 20th century are over four times as many deaths as in the preceding 400 years. Since World War I, with its emphasis on trench warfare, and World War II, in which military casualties paralleled the large number of civilian deaths, the proportion of civilians among the deaths rose to approximately 65 percent, and in the 1980s and 1990s the proportion of civilian deaths appears to have been close to 90 percent (Sivard, 1991). While these figures do not include deaths due to war-related starvation and infectious diseases, which are more difficult to document, it seems clear that direct and "collateral" attacks on civilian populations are becoming an increasingly important part of war. (See Figure 3.)

CAUSES OF VIOLENCE AND WAR

Attempts to prevent these deaths, injuries, and disabilities by outlawing specific types of weapons will clearly not be sufficient. As opponents of gun control in the United States delight in arguing, "Guns don't kill, people kill." Indeed, human beings pull the triggers, drop the bombs, push the buttons, and bury the landmines. In efforts directed toward the primary prevention of war, it is necessary not only to attempt to outlaw weaponry but also to attempt to deal with the political, economic, social, cultural, and psychological factors that lead people to use weapons to kill and maim.

On an individual level, the unprovoked use of violence has been attributed to a number of factors, including psychological disturbances that weaken the internal controls against the initiation of violent behavior, societal anomie (normlessness) that weakens the external controls, and societal models of violent behavior (such as images on television) that seem to make violence more acceptable. The latter two, being societal factors, are amenable to societal change.

The issue of the individual use of violence in response to provocation is even more complex. Freud, in "Instincts and Their Vicissitudes" (1915), distinguished two basic drives in human nature: the sexual drive as essential for reproduction and the aggressive drive as essential for survival. Both drives are developmentally related to the survival of the human species. But at the end of the 20th century, both drives can be dangerous to individual survival or even species survival. It is not irrelevant to the prevention of war that unrestrained reproduction in the presence of lower death rates can lead to dysfunctional overpopulation; 4 million years were required for the human population to reach 2 billion, 30 years to add a third billion, and now population increases by 100 million annually. Similarly, aggression, particularly with the widespread availability of powerful weapons, can lead to individual or mass destruction. These primal individual drives, in short, are often increasingly destructive to rather than protective of human survival.

Nonetheless, the desire of the individual to have control over day-to-day life is basic to satisfying human existence. When danger threatens habitual patterns of life, threatens the quality of life, or threatens health or even life itself, intense anxiety arises. The fight-or-flight response, well known from studies in physiology and biology, is dominant in animal life in response to direct physical threat. We know from traumatic stress studies that attempts by human beings to regain control in the face of overwhelming danger and disruption of life can also trigger such a fight-or-flight response (Kleber & Brom, 1992; Lifton, 1968).

We also know from traumatic stress studies that, in the face of perceived danger to individuals, there can be a sharp reduction in analytic capacity (Gersons & Carlier, 1992). It is very difficult under such circumstances to analyze a situation fully and rationally. Behavior in such cases is called *instrumental,* being aimed at the destruction of the perceived danger. Other emotions and values—such as respect for human life—and analytic thought are suppressed because concern for others and reflective thought hinder instrumental functioning.

In addition to vulnerability to physical danger and loss of control over the circumstances of their lives, human beings are extremely vulnerable to humiliation and insult, sometimes called *loss of face*. We know from the tradition of dueling in the 19th century that men often preferred to die in a duel than to live after an insult. Because humiliations are so common in current day-to-day life, at school, in the family, at work, and even between friends, many people fantasize about invulnerability. When further combined with the availability of weapons, the combination of a perceived insult and the fantasy of invulnerability may lead to behavior destructive to both oneself and others. There is considerable evidence that men—whether because of in-born characteristics such as male hormone levels or because of socialization and acculturation—are more prone to resort to violent behavior in response to perceived insults or threats, but women are also capable of such responses (Miedzian, 1991; Ruddick, 1989).

FROM THE INDIVIDUAL'S PERSPECTIVE TO THE COLLECTIVE

Moving from an analysis of the causes of individual violent behavior to an analysis of violent behavior by large groups of people—which is known as war—is even more difficult. We must start with a recognition that, in almost every society, those with power and wealth will use all the means at their disposal to maintain that power and wealth. When a perceived threat arises from outside a nation-state, as when the supply of oil or other natural resources is threatened, or inside a nation-state, as when unemployment arises, those in power may attempt to convince the population that it is in their self-interest to respond to the perceived threat. Techniques, all the more effective in these times of electronic communication, of appeal to private interests or self-preservation are used to prepare a nation for war. These techniques can also be used to provoke hatred and violence against a group that is scapegoated, for example, for "taking away the jobs" (Weerts, 1993).

Furthermore, leaders of nations sometimes fantasize themselves as invulnerable, and this seems at times to endear them to the population or at least to elements of it. Nationalism is often built around these fantasies of supremacy or of at least not being as vulnerable as others. These fantasies, perhaps less dangerous in times of less destructive weaponry, in modern times can become the starting point for massively destructive war or civil conflict. The recognition of vulnerability as part of realistic individual or national self-appraisal may serve to increase the possibility of maintaining peace in human life.

Part of the effort must be the reduction of the symbols of militarism and invulnerability that envelop us. In France, for example, Madame Mitterand and other prominent citizens support the effort, suggested by retired firefighter Armand Thuair, that the words of the French national anthem, "La Marseillaise," be changed (Riding, 1992). The current words are:

> Marchons! Marchons!
> Qu'un sang impur
> Abreuve nos sillons!
>
> March on, march on,
> And drench our fields
> With their tainted blood.

The proposed words are

> Chantons, chantons
> Que nos chansons
> Fassent taire tous les canons.
>
> Sing on, sing on,
> Until our songs
> Silence all cannons.

While efforts to change the omnipresence of violent images and of calls to violence will of course not, by themselves, bring an end to violence and war, it is not unreasonable to hope that the readiness to resort to military responses to presumed or even to actual affronts will be less.

Of course, there are other reasons, perhaps more just and more rational ones than response to personal or national affronts or the preservation of power or wealth, for the initiation of war or revolution. The world's resources are extraordinarily inequitably distributed. The population of the United States, for example, makes up only 5% of the world's population, but it consumes per capita 11 times the world's average in energy, 6 times the world's average in steel, and 4 times the world's average in grain. For much of the rest of the world, UNICEF has called the 1980s "The Decade of Despair." For the world's poorest people, average incomes have dropped by 10%–25%. Today, more than 1 billion people—1 in every 5—lives in absolute poverty. In the 37 poorest countries, spending on health has been reduced by 50% and in education by 25%. In over 50 nations, primary-school enrollment has been falling (Grant, 1991).

Within the United States, the bottom 40% of the households receive 16% of household income, and the top 40% receive 67% of household income, the greatest gap in the history of the collection of these statistics. The wealthiest 1% of the U.S. population own 37% of the nation's wealth, the highest percentage since 1929, just before the Great Depression. The concentration of hunger, homelessness, illiteracy, and hopelessness among those who live in poverty in the United States is well known (R. Sidel, 1992).

People who live under unbearable conditions of economic or social exploitation, such as those in poorly industrialized countries of the Southern Hemisphere or in poverty-ridden areas of the United States or South Africa, may recognize that these conditions are maintained by those of wealth and power through what has become known as *institutionalized violence*. Adolfo Perez Esquivel (1984) from Argentina, recipient of the 1980 Nobel Peace Prize, stated the equivalence clearly: "Usually we speak of violence only when it has reached an extreme, but it is also violence when children are dying of malnutrition, when there is no freedom of unions, when there is not enough housing, not enough health care" (p. 29).

The oppressed under these circumstances may come to believe that only armed action can lift the yoke of exploitation and oppression. A considerable amount of human experience suggests that this view is correct, since those who hold power and wealth will usually not willingly share it with the powerless and the poor. Yet, under current conditions of widespread armaments and widespread potential for destruction, leaders of this century, such as Mohandas K. Gandhi and the Reverend Doctor Martin Luther King, Jr., have eloquently argued that nonviolence is the only effective, non-self-destructive way to make lasting and positive change in the human condition.

COLLECTIVE SECURITY

Let us return to the analysis of the psychological dimensions of disputes among nations that may lead to war. It appears that what students of international law call *confidence building* (attempts to reduce suspicions of aggressive intent) and *negotiations* (communication and agreement among political leaders along with effective mediation and training in nonviolent conflict resolution) help to maintain control and to prevent military action. Psychological analysis also helps in part to explain the "arms race"—the accelerated, competitive development and production of destructive weapons—as, in part, a means to prevent loss of control. While the profit and power, and the jobs of workers, that come from arms production will remain an important stimulus to its continuation, negotiations and confidence-building measures may nonetheless contribute to reducing and decreasing arms production and also to strengthening feelings of control by sharing with others the capability of maintaining control together, what has been called *collective security* in contrast to *national security*. A number of successful peacekeeping efforts by the United Nations are examples of such strategies.

Nonetheless, the leaders of individual nations, including the United States, speak of waging "just war" in response to what they define as aggression and may call on the United Nations or regional alliances to support such a "just war." The issue of what is a "just war," debated since at least the time of St. Thomas Aquinas and Maimonides, can be touched on only briefly here. There are generally held to be two elements in a just war: *jus ad bellum* (When is it just to go to war?) and *jus in bello* (What methods may be used in a just war?). Among the elements required for *jus ad bellum* are a just grievance and the exhaustion of all means short of war to settle the grievance. Among the elements required for *jus in bello* are the protection of noncombatants and proportionality of force, including avoiding the use of weapons of mass destruction such as chemical, biological, and nuclear weapons and massive bombing of cities (Seabury & Codevilla, 1989; Walzer, 1992).

Many believe that, in the military action against Iraq called Desert Storm, the two fundamental principles of what is generally accepted as constituting a just war were violated. It is not clear that all means short of war to force the withdrawal of Iraq from Kuwait were exhausted, and it is not clear that the massive destruction of the civilian-supporting infrastructure, which has caused widespread civilian death, was necessary (Geyer & Green, 1992; V. W. Sidel, 1991). In recognition of the increasing mutual- and self-destructiveness of war and therefore its obsolescence as an "extension of foreign policy," only few effective mechanisms have emerged for the settlement of international disputes without recourse to war.

THE ROLE OF HEALTH PROFESSIONALS IN THE PREVENTION OF WAR

There are a number of ways in which health professionals, including those working on traumatic stress, can work for the prevention of war and for the acceptance of alternative methods of international and intranational conflict resolution (see Table 4).

Documentation and Presentation

One activity of many health professionals concerned with traumatic stress is the documentation and the widespread presentation of the ter-

Table 4. Roles for Health Professionals in Prevention of War

I. Documentation and presentation
   A. Health consequences of war and preparation for war
   B. Social and economic consequences of war and preparation for war
II. Advocacy
   A. Arms limitation
      1. Nuclear weapons
         a. Comprehensive nuclear test ban treaty
         b. Strengthened nuclear nonproliferation treaty
         c. Reduction in nuclear stockpiles
      2. Chemical weapons
         a. Implementation of 1993 Chemical Weapons Convention
         b. Reduction in stockpiles with effective verification
      3. Biological weapons
         a. Strengthening of 1972 Biological Weapons Convention
         b. Verification that research is truly "defensive"
   B. Collective security
      1. Confidence building
         a. Bilateral and multilateral programs
         b. Bilateral and multilateral treaties
      2. Peacekeeping
         a. International aid to countries to ease tensions
         b. International forces to maintain the peace
      3. Peacemaking
         a. Economic measures, such as sanctions carefully directed at
            military rather than civilian resources
         b. Military measures, such as UN peacemaking forces
III. Action
   A. Improving health services in underserved areas
   B. Participatinag in social change to ameliorate injustice and inequity

rible effects of war on human beings, including the late aftereffects and transgenerational effects (Danieli, 1985; Figley, 1985; Figley & Leventman, 1990; Lifton, 1968; Milgram & Hobfoll, 1986; Krystal, 1988; Laufer, 1988; Lindy, 1988; Ulman & Brothers, 1988). Just as the analysis and the dramatic presentation of data on the medical consequences of nuclear war have apparently had a profound impact and earned the presenters a Nobel Peace Prize, similar information on war as a cause of traumatic stress, dramatically presented, can be an important part of the process of convincing decision makers and the public of the folly of war as a method of solving international or intranational disputes.

Advocacy

But that is only the beginning. Health professionals also have a responsibility, we believe, to be advocates for specific measures to prevent war. This includes advocacy for the limitation of nuclear arms, such as a comprehensive nuclear test ban treaty, a stronger nuclear non-proliferation treaty, and the reduction of nuclear stockpiles. It includes advocacy for effective implementation of the 1993 Chemical Weapons Convention and for strengthening the 1972 Biological Weapons Convention at the time of the next review conference.

There must also be advocacy for measures that promote collective security. This includes advocacy of the acceptance by all nations of the jurisdiction of the International Court of Justice at The Hague and support of stronger and more widely used United Nations peacekeeping forces. It includes advocacy of global environmental protection and of sustainable development and equitable economic and social policies to lessen the gap between the haves and the have nots both internationally and intranationally.

Action

Finally, health professionals can take individual action. They can help provide health services and work personally for social change that will lessen tensions and will lessen educational, economic, and social barriers. Many health professionals concerned with traumatic stress devote considerable personal effort to these activities. Those health professionals concerned with traumatic stress who may consider doing so and those who already do might find ways of expanding their activities and recruiting others.

One aspect of the health professional's role, however, remains controversial. What, if any, should be the role of the health professional in the armed forces? While the Geneva Conventions require noncombatant status for health professionals, the line between the combatant and non-combatant roles is often blurred and subject to erosion (Liberman, 1968; V. W. Sidel, 1991).

In 1967, Dr. Howard Levy, a captain in the U.S. Army Medical Department, refused to obey an order to train the Special Forces Aidmen in medical skills. He refused specifically on the grounds that the Aidmen were being trained predominantly for a combat role and that cross-training in medical techniques eroded the distinction between combatants and noncombatants (Glasser, 1967). At Levy's court-martial, Drs. Louis Lasagna, Jean Mayer, and Benjamin Spock and one of the authors of this paper (VWS) testified for the defense. Their testimony was summarized in a report in *Science:*

> First, as a physician Levy's primary duty is to his own interpretation of the ethical codes that govern medicine; second, the historic separation of military from medical functioning had practical as well as ethical roots; and third,

they would have grave doubts about training Special Forces themselves, as long as the program implied the paramountcy of military-political judgments. . . . [They] argued that the political use of medicine by the Special Forces jeopardized the entire tradition of the noncombatant status of medicine. (Langer, 1967, p. 1349)

Although Levy was a medical officer, the court-martial panel did not include a physician. Levy was given a dishonorable discharge and sentenced to three years of hard labor at Fort Leavenworth.

The "noncombatant" role of the physician in military service, even if frank combatant activities are eschewed, remains an ambiguous one. Military physicians and military psychologists must accept different priorities from those of their civilian colleagues. The primary role of the military physician is expressed in the motto of the U.S. Army Medical Department: "To Conserve the Fighting Strength" (Rubenstein, 1988). In describing this role, a faculty member of the Academy of Health Sciences at Fort Sam Houston in an article in *Military Medicine* cited as "the clear objective of all health service support operations" the goal stated in 1866 by a veteran of the Army of the Potomac:

Strengthen the hands of the commanding general by keeping his Army in the most vigorous health, thus rendering it, in the highest degree, efficient for enduring fatigue and privitation [sic], and for fighting. (Letterman, 1866, p. 100)

Principles of triage unacceptable in civilian practice may be required, such as placing a first emphasis on patching up the lightly wounded so they can be sent back to battle. In another article in *Military Medicine*, "over-evacuation" is cited as "one of the cardinal sins of military medicine" (Bellamy, 1988, p. 185). Violation of patient confidentiality unacceptable in civilian practice may be required. Perhaps most important in this contest, military physicians like all members of the armed forces, are limited by threat of military discipline in the extent to which they can publicly protest what they believe to be an unjust war.

As wars of the 20th century kill an increasing percentage of civilians with so-called conventional weapons and escalate threats of the use of weapons of mass destruction, what form of military service is appropriate for the ethical physician and other ethical health professionals? One response was suggested a half-century ago by Dr. John A. Ryle (1939), then Regius Professor of Physics at the University of Cambridge:

It is an arresting, if at present a fantastic thought, that the medical profession which is more international than any other, could, if well coordinated, of its own initiative put a stop to war, or at least increase its uncertainties, and temper its aims considerably so as to give pause to the most bellicose of governments. . . . By withholding service from the Armed Forces before and during war . . . the doctors could so cripple the efficiency of the staff and aggravate the difficulties of campaign and so damage the morale of the troops that war would become almost unthinkable. . . . In such refusal of service . . . there would be no inhumanity which medicine at present sanctions and prolongs. (p. 7)

During the Vietnam war, more than 300 American medical students and young physicians brought Ryle's fantasy a step closer to reality by signing the following pledge:

In the name of freedom the U.S. is waging an unjustifiable war in Vietnam and is causing incalculable suffering. It is the goal of the medical profession to prevent and relieve human suffering. My effort to pursue this goal is meaningless in the context of the war. Therefore, I refuse to serve in the Armed Forces in Vietnam; and so that I may exercise my profession with conscience and dignity, I intend to seek means to service my country which are compatible with the preservation and enrichment of life. (*Newsletter,* 1968, cited by Liberman et al., 1968, p. 306)

Ryle's fantasy, of course, echoes the fantasy of Aristophanes in his comedy *Lysistrata*. The title character, an Athenian woman, ends the Second Peloponnesian War by organizing all the wives of the soldiers of both armies to refuse sexual intercourse with their husbands while the war lasts. To hasten the war's end, Lysistrata recruits a nude woman to expose herself to both armies. The Athenians and Spartans make peace quickly and go home with their wives (Aristophanes, 1979). Although women in the United States were far less supportive of the Vietnam and the Persian Gulf wars than were men (Colburn, 1991), it is extremely unlikely that either Aristophanes' or Ryle's fantasy of effective mass refusal to support a war effort will come to pass.

But individual women and men, and individual health professionals, can nonetheless make a difference by refusing to support a war. One of the most dramatic examples of refusal to go along with the military option was provided by a physician, Dr. Yolanda Huet-Vaughn, a captain in the U.S. Army Medical Service Reserve. Dr. Huet-Vaughn refused, at the risk of court-martial and possible severe punishment, to obey an order for active duty in the Persian Gulf. In her statement, she explained:

I am refusing orders to be an accomplice in what I consider an immoral, inhumane and unconstitutional act, namely an offensive military mobilization in the Middle East. My oath as a citizen-soldier to defend the Constitution, my oath as a physician to preserve human life and prevent disease, and my responsibility as a human being to the preservation of this planet, would be violated if I cooperate. (Cited by V. W. Sidel, 1991, p. 102)

It should be noted that the reasons Dr. Huet-Vaughn gave for her action were quite different from the reasons given by Dr. Levy. Dr. Levy refused to obey an order that he believed required him to perform a specific act that would violate medical ethics; Dr. Huet-Vaughn refused to obey an order she believed required her to support a particular war that she felt to be unjust and destructive to the goals of medicine and humanity. One of the questions raised by Dr. Huet-Vaughn's action is whether there is a special ethical responsibility for health professionals, in view of their obligation to protect the health and the lives of their patients and the people of their communities, to refuse to support an unjust war that they believe will cause major loss of life and destroy the health and environment of both combatants and noncombatants. The U.S. armed forces recognize the right of a health professional to be a "conscientious objector" to any service in the armed forces when that objection is based on a deeply held conviction. If a health professional considers service in support of a particular war unethical on the grounds of professional ethics, may—or, indeed, must—that professional refuse to serve? Furthermore, is there an ethical difference if the service is required by the society or if the service obligation has been entered into voluntarily to fulfill an obligation in return for military support of medical training or for other reasons? And is military service indeed a "voluntary obligation" if enlistment, as for many poor and minority people in the United States, has been prodded by lack of educational or employment opportunities or by the cost of professional education or specialty training that in other societies would be provided at public expense?

While few health professionals are willing or able to take an action such as that of Dr. Huet-Vaughn, other actions are available to oppose acts of war considered unjust, to oppose a specific war, or to oppose war in general. One is the acceptance of a service alternative consistent with an ethical obligation to care for those wounded or maimed without simultaneously supporting a war effort. Opportunities for service in an international medical corps such as Medecins du Monde or Medecins sans Frontières are unfortunately limited, but health professionals may wish to demand that their governments redirect to the United Nations or the World Health Organization a considerable portion of the resources now devoted to preparation for war to help provide funds for international rather than national medical services to treat the casualties of war.

CONCLUSION

We want to pay some extra attention to the role of the mental health professional in the prevention of war. As the quote from the correspondence between Einstein and Freud indicates, Freud was taken by surprise by Einstein's question about the prevention of war. Mental health professionals may have the same experience because they focus mainly on the individual. In this chapter, we have taken the issue of awareness to be extremely important. Collective security starts with being aware of the huge destructiveness of war that currently threatens everyone on earth, not only a threat to physical existence but to the human mind itself. Mental health professionals, and especially those working in the field of traumatic stress, are in a special position to inform humankind on the traumatic sequelae of war, not only as a "disorder" but also as a trans-generational issue which provokes new destructiveness, acting out of hatred as we see in the war in the former Yugoslavia.

In sum, the primary prevention of traumatic stress due to war requires the prevention of war. Health professionals as individuals and particularly in groups have a responsibility to help to prevent war by education and by contributing to public and professional understanding of the nature of modern war, of the health consequences of the use of weapons of mass destruction and other weapons, and of the nature and effectiveness of modern alternatives to war. But beyond education, there is, we believe, a responsibility to advocate for specific measures that will promote arms limitation and collective security and for actions that will lessen tensions and reduce the gaps between the haves and the have nots that lead to war. We suggest that the responsibility to try to prevent the wounds is at least as important as the responsibility, which many health professionals carry out so well, to bind up the wounds after they have been inflicted.

ACKNOWLEDGMENTS. Adapted in part from a keynote address at the World Conference of the International Society for Traumatic Stress Studies on Trauma and Tragedy: The Origin, Management, and Prevention of Traumatic Stress in Today's World, Amsterdam, June 23, 1992, and from Sidel (1991).

REFERENCES

Aristophanes (1979) (Trans. B. B. Rogers). *Lysistrata*. Cambridge: Harvard University Press.
Bellamy, R. F. (1988). Conserve the fighting strength. *Military Medicine, 153*, 185–186.
Colburn, D. (1991, January 29). The way of the warrior: Are men born to fight? *Washington Post*, Health Section, pp. 10–12.
Danieli, Y. (1985). The treatment and prevention of long-term effects and intergenerational transmission of victimization: A lesson from holocaust survivors and their children. In C. R. Figley (Ed.), *Trauma and its wake: The study and treatment of posttraumatic stress disorder*. New York: Brunner/Mazel.

Esquivel, A. P. (1984). Quoted in R. L. Sivard, *World military and social expenditures 1985.* Washington, DC: World Priorities, 1985, p. 7.

Figley, C. R. (1985). From victim to survivor: Social responsibility in the wake of catastrophe. In C. R. Figley (Ed.), *Trauma and its wake: The study and treatment of posttraumatic stress disorder.* New York: Brunner/Mazel.

Figley, C. R., & Leventman, S. (1990). *Strangers at home: Vietnam veterans since the war.* New York: Brunner/Mazel.

Freud, S. (1915). Instincts and their vicissitudes. In J. Strachey (Ed.), *The standard edition of the complete psychological works* (Vol. 14, pp. 117–140). London: Hogarth Press.

Freud, S., & Einstein, A. (1932). Why war? In J. Strachey (Ed.), *The standard edition of the complete psychological works* (Vol. 22, pp. 199–218). London: Hogarth Press.

Garfield, R. M., & Neugut, A. I. (1991). Epidemiologic analysis of warfare: An historical review. *Journal of the American Medical Association, 266,* 688–692.

Gersons, B. P. R., & Carlier, I. V. E. (1992). Posttraumatic stress disorder; the history of a recent concept. *British Journal of Psychiatry, 161,* 742–748.

Geyer, A., & Green, B. G. (1992). *Lines in the sand: Justice and the Gulf War.* Westminster: John Knox Press.

Glasser, I. (1967). Judgment at Fort Jackson: The court-martial of Captain Howard B. Levy. *Law in Transition Quarterly, 4,* 123–156.

Grant, J. P. (1991). *State of the world's children 1991.* Oxford: Oxford University Press.

International Physicians for the Prevention of Nuclear War. (1986). *Nobel Peace Prize (1985): Speeches and lectures.* Cambridge, MA: Author.

Kleber, R. J., & Brom, D. (1992). *Coping with trauma: Theory, prevention and treatment.* Amsterdam and Berwyn, PA: Swets & Zeitlinger International.

Krystal, H. (1988). *Integration and self-healing: Affect, trauma, alexithymia.* Hillsdale, NJ: Analytic Press.

Langer, E. (1967). The court-martial of Captain Levy: Medical ethics v. military law. *Science, 156,* 1346, 1349.

Last, J. M. (1992). Scope and methods of prevention. In J. M. Last & R. B. Wallace (Eds.), *Public health and preventive medicine* (pp. 3–11). Norwalk, CT: Appleton & Lange.

Laufer, R. S. (1988). Human response to war and war-related events in the contemporary world. In M. Lystad (Ed.), *Mental health response to mass emergencies: Theory and practice.* New York: Brunner/Mazel.

Letterman, J. (1866). *Medical recollections of the Army of the Potomac.* New York: Appleton, (p. 100). Cited by Rubenstein, 1988.

Liberman, R., Gold, W., & Sidel, V. W. (1968). Medical ethics and the military. *New Physician, 17,* 299–309.

Lifton, R. J. (1968). *Death in life: Survivors of Hiroshima.* New York: Random House. (Reprinted by Chapel Hill: University of North Carolina Press, 1991)

Lindy, J. D. (1988). *Vietnam: A casebook.* New York: Brunner/Mazel.

Lown, B. (1986). Nobel Peace Prize lecture: A prescription for hope. *New England Journal of Medicine, 314,* 985–987.

Miedzian, M. (1991). *Boys will be boys: Breaking the link between masculinity and violence.* New York: Doubleday.

Milgram, N. A., & Hobfoll, S. (1986). Generalizations from theory and practice in war-related stress. In N. A. Milgram (Ed.), *Stress and coping in time of war: Generalizations from the Israeli experience.* New York: Brunner/Mazel.

Newsletter of the Medical Student Peace Movement, Associated Students of Stanford University (1968). (Cited by R. Liberman, W. Gold, & V. W. Sidel, 1968)

Physicians for Social Responsibility. (1962). The medical consequences of thermonuclear war. *New England Journal of Medicine, 266,* 1126–1155.

Riding, A. (1992, March 5). Aux barricades! "La Marseillaise" is besieged. *New York Times.*

Rubenstein, D. A. (1988). Health service support and the principles of war. *Military Medicine, 153,* 145–146.

Ruddick, S. (1989). *Maternal thinking.* Boston: Beacon Press.

Ryle, J. A. (1939). Foreword. In H. Joule (Ed.), *The doctor's view of war* (pp. 7–10). London: Allen & Unwin.

Seabury, P., & Codevilla, A. (1989). *War: Ends and means.* New York: Basic Books.

Sidel, R. (1992). *Women and children last: The plight of poor women in affluent America* (rev. ed.). New York: Penguin.

Sidel, V. W. (1989). Weapons of mass destruction: The greatest threat to public health. *Journal of the American Medical Association, 262,* 680–682.

Sidel, V. W. (1991). Quid est amor patriae? *PSR Quarterly, 1,* 96–104.

Sidel, V. W., Onel, E., Geiger, H. J., Leaning, J., & Foege, W. H. (1992). Public health responses to natural and human disasters. In J. M. Last & R. B. Wallace (Eds.), *Public health and preventive medicine* (pp. 1173–1186). Norwalk, CT: Appleton & Lange.

Sivard, R. L. (1991). *World military and social expenditures 1991.* Washington, DC: World Priorities.

Ulman, R. B., & Brothers, D. (1988). *The shattered self: A psychoanalytic study of trauma.* Hillsdale, NJ: Analytic Press.

Walzer, M. (1992). *Just and unjust wars.* New York: Basic Books.

Weerts, J. M. P. (1993). Nationalities in Europe: The risk of war and the medical responsibility. *Medicine and War, 9,* 326–333.

16

Epilogue

ROLF J. KLEBER

The chapters in this volume differ in emphasis from the prevailing trend in the scientific study of traumatic events and their aftermaths. In the past, research on the consequences of war, combat, violence, disasters and loss has been overwhelmingly directed toward the individual victim. It has been dominated by a perspective emphasizing intrapsychic variables and processes. This is rather understandable, since professional psychologists and psychiatrists from the Western world have been involved in a capacity of caring for victimized or traumatized people. Thus, their consequent publications have been oriented toward the personal problems and suffering of those who have been affected by terror, abuse, and catastrophes.

The title of the book, *Beyond Trauma,* has to do with the conviction of the authors that trauma has a meaning that goes beyond the individual level. Trauma destroys the social system of care, protection, and meaning that surrounds an individual. The victim has been set apart from other human beings. Impaired social relationships are the result. The person feels isolated and depressed. Trust has disappeared. There is a loss of connectedness. Moreover, the process of recovery following an event or a series of events is inseparable from the social and cultural context.

Social and cultural dimensions are, therefore, relevant to the consequences of traumatic events in two ways. First, such events disrupt the

ROLF J. KLEBER • Department of Clinical and Health Psychology, Utrecht University, and Institute for Psychotherapy, 3584 CS Utrecht, The Netherlands.
Beyond Trauma: Cultural and Societal Dynamics, edited by Rolf J. Kleber, Charles R. Figley, and Berthold P. R. Gersons. New York, Plenum Press, 1995.

normally self-evident system of human ties in which the individual takes part. Suddenly, social relationships are not that certain any more; they have lost their natural character. Secondly, social processes facilitate or hinder the process of working through the experience. They shape the ways of restoring control and self-esteem.

The title *Beyond Trauma* also refers to our belief that the scientific study of traumatic experiences has to evolve beyond the present state of knowledge. Perhaps this is a cliché, but it is a significant and critical cliché. The trauma field has grown immensely in the last 15 years and major contributions from various disciplines have been made. Victims of violence, war and disaster are being recognized by society, and as such receive support. Knowledge on trauma has reached a large audience, and many ideas that were novel in the seventies and eighties have become well-known and well-accepted in the nineties. It is nonetheless evident that we have to surpass the current insights, concepts and ideas. New perspectives on adaptation to trauma and disturbances have to be developed, and new ideas on helping people have to be formulated. If this is not done, then the field could reach an impasse. The chapters in this book show that there are definite challenges for the near future. The authors, coming as they do from a variety of backgrounds, have raised many issues that demand a solution in order that the study of traumatic stress can proceed to a new stage. What are some of the common themes?

THE HIDDEN MAJORITY

One of the baffling issues of the traumatic stress field is the following question: What happens to those people who do not come to the clinics, the institutes and the private practices of therapists?

It has become clear in research as well as in clinical practice that most people confronted with war, violence and loss do not see a psychiatrist, a psychologist or other professional. Thus, the findings of most scientific publications are based on a minority: the minority of patients asking for help and people applying for some kind of compensation.

Of course, it is possible that these unseen people who have been confronted with serious life events suffer from delayed posttrauma reactions. Nevertheless, a more plausible explanation is that people are able to handle horrifying experiences on the basis on their own resilience and with the help of their own close network. Consequently, many people do not develop posttraumatic stress disorders or other disturbances. The repercussion of a model that diagnoses people in terms of disorders is that healthy and adequate coping strategies are in danger of being ignored and that we remain ignorant of non-disorder oriented ways of helping people.

POSTTRAUMATIC STRESS DISORDER AND COMPLEX TRAUMA

Posttraumatic stress disorder is a reasonably well-defined and useable concept. It is an easily understandable construct that is now part of the official psychiatric nomenclature of the *Diagnostic and Statistical Manual of Mental Disorders,* Fourth Edition (DSM-IV) (American Psychiatric Association, 1994) and the *International Classification of Diseases,* Tenth Edition (ICD-10) (World Health Organization, 1992). Nevertheless, there are serious dilemmas in the definition of the concept and in its daily use in scientific research and clinical work.

As was shown in the first chapters of the book, several of these dilemmas have to do with dividing lines, such as in the distinction between "healthy" and "disordered" forms of coping with violence, war, and disaster. Which stressors are part of the definition of an extreme stressor and which stressors are to be excluded? For instance, it is rather strange that the sudden loss of a spouse or of a child is often omitted. What is the distinction between posttraumatic stress disorder and other disorders that may be produced by extreme stressors, such as mood disorders and dissociative disturbances? Close reading of the DSM-IV shows that there are at least five to ten other disorders that may be induced by traumatic events. Is the concept of posttraumatic stress disorder adequate for defining all disturbances resulting from extreme stressors? There is an increasing tendency in research and clinical work to emphasize the differences between acute, single events and prolonged, enduring events. Studies of refugees and violations of human rights demonstrate that the concept of posttraumatic stress disorder is rather limited. The circumstances are so complicated and prolonged that individual adjustment is damaged to a far greater degree than it is after a single event in a stable society. There appears to be plural traumatization. Life has definitely changed and will probably never be the same anymore. It is highly significant in this context that many authors in the second part of the book use the concept of multiple traumatization or sequential traumatization.

Almost all discussions in trauma research are nowadays conducted in terms of posttraumatic stress disorder. There is, to some extent at least, a tyranny of PTSD. However, we should not forget that the DSM-

IV and ICD-10 are simply classification systems and nothing more. Nevertheless, people (including scientists) consider the terms to be existing entities that are applicable outside the realm of clinical work and scientific research. As such, this general concept may be a serious handicap for further development in therapy and research.

THE ILLUSION OF *POST*

By definition, the prevailing view on posttraumatic stress disorder and related disturbances is focused on "*post*traumatic." These concepts deal with psychological disturbances that arise after extreme stressors. As a result, mental health care is also focused on the posttrauma situation. But what about an ongoing exposure to shocking circumstances? As of this writing, the citizens of Sarajevo, the capital of Bosnia–Herzegovina in the former republic of Yugoslavia, are being exposed to a continuous condition of terror, siege, violence, and the constant threat of war. They are stricken by an ongoing situation of disempowerment and disruption. There seems to be no termination of the war situation. The situation is similar in many other countries. In Somalia and Chechenya, people are continuously confronted with terror and violence.

A key question is whether the reactions of citizens to the situation in their homelands can be presented in terms of the concept of posttraumatic stress disorder. To some extent, the answer is yes. First, many responses are characteristic of extreme stress and are not at variance with the symptoms of posttraumatic stress disorder: for example, avoidance reactions, reenactments, flashbacks, hyperalertness, and despair. Furthermore, people in a condition of prolonged strain and terror are already attempting to cope with events that have happened in the recent period, since the siege of a war-stricken city is not one massive event, but a sequence of many distinguishable, stressful experiences that have to be integrated one by one: the loss of a loved one, the bombing of one's own neighborhood, the loss of a house, and the terrifying confrontation with a sniper. But to some extent the answer is also no. The characteristic reactions, usually classified as stress reactions, are also signs of survival and adaptive coping. For instance, hypervigilance and denial are ways to endure the events. Hypervigilance keeps people alert for possible dangers in a besieged city. Emotional numbing keeps the realization of the hopelessness of the situation at a distance. One has not begun to recover from the situation, but is coping with an ongoing traumatization instead.

The example of Sarajevo shows how much the treatment of posttraumatic stress disorder, as portrayed in the scientific literature, is rooted in the belief systems and customs of Western Europe and the USA. Counseling and psychotherapy are to be implemented only after conditions of safety and certainty have been established. Many influential authors on treatment state that the first task of recovery is the establishment of a safe environment. Therapeutic work cannot succeed unless safety has been adequately secured. To take this assumption literally would mean that helping people exposed to trauma is not possible in the case of Sarajevo. This is a rather cynical viewpoint, if one realizes that 300,000 to 400,000 people are living in a situation of ongoing terror. Some safety may in fact occur: within a small community, within a family, within a group of connected people. Structuring support, safety and recognition is no doubt essential, but such a situation needs more flexible methods of help.

The example of Sarajevo makes another current notion of the Western perspective on posttraumatic stress clear: namely that helpers can only provide help when they have integrated their own traumatic experiences. This is in itself a rather noble thought, but it is unrealistic in situations where a population is still under constant stress. Everybody, including the helpers, belongs to the same group. There is a strong sense of communality. People feel connected to others in the same situation.

A good illustration of the kind of mental health care dedicated to these problems is a trauma counseling project currently conducted in Sarajevo. Counseling centers have been established, involving in depth training of local professionals by psychologists and psychiatrists from abroad as well as by local experts. A professional support structure has been created. Recovery from trauma is being encouraged in many ways: psychological education, house calls, short-term psychotherapy, group sessions for family members, and information programs about traumatic stress on the local radio station. Of course, one has to realize that the inhabitants of Sarajevo are still in a relatively advantageous position. They are a European population used to a public health care system. The implementation of trauma care becomes more complicated in countries where basic health care is lacking or where people are not used to mental health care institutions.

COPING AS A COLLECTIVE PROCESS

A person victimized by a traumatic experience does not live in a vacuum. He or she is surrounded by others, not only the people in the close environment, but also the members of the society as a whole and the legacies of earlier generations. All these people shape the processes of coping with trauma and its consequences.

Society provides people with "tools" in relation to the aftermath of traumatic experiences. Norms and values as well as symbols and rituals channel thoughts and emotions and consequently create opportunities for individual ways of adjustment. Fifty years after World War II, people all over Europe are surrounded in both literal and figurative senses by signs referring to the past in all kinds of forms and presentations: statues and monuments in parks and squares, memorials, films and documentaries on television, national myths, history lessons at school, resistance fighters educating young school children about their struggles, arguments in political discussions and debates, ruins of vanished city centers, and museums such as the Anne Frank House in Amsterdam. These are all public manifestations of the collective memory of the war. They provide public acknowledgment of the suffering of individuals and form a tribute to the victims and the survivors. These buildings, statues, songs and other memorials are called *lieux de mémoire* in French.

Such collective recollection is not confined to war. After a recent plane crash in Amsterdam, a statue was unveiled dedicated to the victims of the disaster. One year after a large explosion in a chemical plant in a small town, a commemorative service was held, which included speeches, songs and moments of silence. Ceremonies, monuments and memorials are points of reference for a continued identity and for specific meanings that members of a society can attach to the horrors. The significance and the cost of the experiences are consequently—and often tacitly—recognized. In this way, cultural images and rituals help the person in his or her attempts to master the horrendous recollections. They create order and enable the construction of a narrative in which the events find a place.

Cultural belief systems, along with cultural objects and social role expectations, greatly affect psychosocial adjustment in individuals attempting to master severe trauma. This is why any assessment or treatment of traumatic stress or stress disorders must consider the social and cultural context as well. Yet both the psychotraumatology literature and the psychotherapy literature generally focus almost exclusively on the functioning of the individual victim or survivor. This book has attempted to make the reader sensitive to the collective factors within which social support is provided to traumatized persons. These dimensions should be taken into account in counseling and treatment.

Finally, we should not forget that there is the essential conception of *beyond trauma* as overcoming the traumatic experience. A victim or a survivor has to transcend the traumatic event and its implications. The individual's sense of continuity has been dramatically disrupted by an event or a series of events. He or she has to derive meaning from the traumatic experience and to discover significance in the confrontation with violence and loss. The individual has to find a new formula to go on living in peace. The final outcome of the process of coping with trauma should be that recollections do not intrude involuntarily anymore and that the person is no longer involved in the continuous struggle to integrate the experience in his or her own life. Only scars such as unpleasant memories or a sad feeling should ultimately remain.

REFERENCES

American Psychiatric Association (1994). *Diagnostic and statistical manual of mental disorders,* (4th ed.). Washington, DC: Author.

World Health Organization (1992). *International classification of diseases and related health problems* (10th ed.). Geneva: Author.

About the Editors

Rolf J. Kleber is Associate Professor of Psychology at Utrecht University, and Head of Research at the Institute for Psychotrauma in Utrecht, The Netherlands. He has been a lecturer at the University of California, Irvine, and has held positions at several Dutch universities. He has conducted research projects on psychotherapy of posttraumatic stress disorder, work-related trauma and intervention programs, transgenerational aspects of war stress, late sequelae of World War II, health issues of refugees, and cross-cultural aspects of mental health. He is chief editor of the Dutch scientific journal *Gedrag and Gezondheid (Behavior and Health)*. As cofounder of the Institute for Psychotrauma, he is a consultant in the field of health care and occupational trauma. Recently, he has been an invited lecturer in Sarajevo, Bosnia-Herzegovina. Dr. Kleber has published many scientific and professional articles and books on stress, trauma, and coping. Together with Daniel Brom, he published *Coping with Trauma: Theory, Prevention and Treatment* (1992).

Charles R. Figley is Director of the Florida State University Psychosocial Stress Research Program and Marriage and Family Therapy Center, Tallahassee, Florida. He has edited many books on psychosocial stress, posttraumatic stress disorder, and marriage and family counseling. His most recent compilation is *Compassion Fatigue: Coping with Traumatic Stress Disorder in Those Who Treat the Traumatized* (1995). Dr. Figley is the founding president of the International Society of Traumatic Stress Studies and founding editor of the *Journal for Traumatic Stress*. He is also consultant to numerous mental health and treatment agencies and associations. He is the recipient of the 1994 Pioneer Award in Traumatology.

Berthold P. R. Gersons is Chair of the Department of Psychiatry of the Academic Medical Center, University of Amsterdam, Amsterdam, The

Netherlands. He was Chair of the First World Conference, "Trauma and Tragedy" of the International Society for Traumatic Stress, held in Amsterdam in 1992. He has written about crisis intervention, bereavement, mental health consultation, the history of the trauma concept, and preventive psychiatry. In 1980, Dr. Gersons initiated the first self-help team for police officers confronted with shooting incidents. He also started the Dutch longitudinal study on critical incidents in police work and psychotherapy for posttraumatic stress disorder. Currently, he is involved in studies on disaster sequelae and debriefing. He is also active in the fields of community psychiatry and the transformation and innovation of mental health services. He is a regular consultant to the World Health Organization.

Index

Amnesty International, definition of torture, 184
Aquino, Corazon, 134–135

Bettelheim, Bruno, 105
Breuer, Josef, 11
Buffalo Creek disaster, 5–6
Burnout, and secondary traumatization, 93–95

Camus, Albert, 200
Chernobyl disaster, 213–232
    characteristic reactions of inhabitants, 222–227
    health problems attributed to radiation, 224–227
    psychological significance of radiation, 229, 231
    psychosocial stressors as consequence, 219–222, 228, 229
    psychotraumatic consequences, 223–224
    stress-related illness behaviors and health problems, 228–230
    traumatic and chronic stress reactions, 227–228
Children
    and secondary traumatic stress, 84–87
    and transgenerational traumatization, 85–87
Chile, human rights violations in, 115–130
    effect on Chilean society, 117–118
    during political transition period, 128–130

Chile, human rights violations in (cont.)
    psychotherapeutic treatment approach, 122–125
    and retraumatization, 123–124
    "social imaginary" concept of human rights issues, 118–120
    testimony as catharsis, 122, 129
    therapists' professional challenges, 126–128
    therapy under dictatorship, 120–122
Cognitive appraisal and coping theory, 135
Cognitive processing model of posttrauma reactions, 57–63
    and cognitive theory, 14, 52, 55–57
    empirical validation of, 67–69
    methodoloy and measurement strategies, 64–69
Coping
    affective-focused, 144, 146
    as collective process, 303–305
    and diagnostic errors, 161
    dissociation as, 124–125
    escape and avoidance as, 39, 60–62, 65, 66
    and existential belief system, 139–140
    of "hidden majority," 300–301
    need for survivor-focused inquiry, 23
    optimism as cultural factor in, 141, 146–147
    problem-focused, 135, 140
    and religious behavior, 146
    stress reactions as, 302
Countertransference
    and moral conflicts, 240, 246
    and secondary traumatic stress, 92
Cumulative traumatization, 122

Dagan, Gabriel, 102–103
Depression, and coping style, 135
Desert Storm, 289
DESNOS (disorders of extreme stress not
    otherwise specified), 192
*Diagnostic and Statistical Manual of Mental
    Disorders (DSM)*, PTSD concept, 2,
    12, 18, 34, 99
  as adequate diagnostic system, 192–193,
    301–302
  concerns about causal sequence, 198–199
  constitution of traumatic experience, 77
  as major milestone, 76
  misleading interpretations of defining
    criteria, 196
  problems with diagnostic criteria, 193–
    194
Dissociation response, 40, 124–125

Einstein, Albert, 277
El Salvador, psychosocial trauma in, 26
Esquivel, Adolfo Perez, 288
Extreme traumatization, 105, 107, 109, 122

Family stress. *See* Secondary traumatic
    stress
First World Conference on Traumatic
    Stress, 4–5
Freud, Anna, 123
Freud, Sigmund, 11, 33, 52, 78, 105, 185,
    277, 285

Health professionals
  and language problems, 161, 162–165
  in military service, 291–294
  moral and ethical issues, 233–235, 237–
    247
  role in facilitating torture, 27, 200–
    209
  role in prevention of health problems,
    279–280
  role in prevention of war, 280–284, 289–
    295
  stress reactions of, 79, 91–92
Holocaust, the
  German youth study, 249–274
    aggressive-defense postures, 254–258
    defense structures, 256, 258, 261–262,
      271–272
    failure to learn from history, 271
    identity conflicts, 256–257, 259, 260–
      261, 263–264

Holocaust (*cont.*)
  German youth study (*cont.*)
    intergenerational communication,
      265–270
    knowledge and comprehension qual-
      ity, 252, 257–258, 259, 264
    and narcissistic trauma versus existen-
      tial trauma, 260–261
    partial-relevance approach in, 252
    and phenomenon of narcissistic defen-
      siveness, 260–262, 271–272
    recognition of historical guilt, 262–264
    rejection and rationalization reac-
      tions, 258–259
    resigned acceptance of guilt and suf-
      fering, 259–262
    role of schools, 271–272
  long-term and transgenerational effects,
    23–24, 85–87
  sequential traumatization of victims, 3
Huet-Vaughn, Yolanda, 293–294
Human rights violations
  deficiency of PTSD diagnosis, 99–109
  role of health professionals in, 200–209

Incestuous abuse, defined, 173
Incestuous abuse of females, 171–186
  and exposure to mass media and pornog-
    raphy, 182–183
  and ineffectiveness of social control,
    183–184
  prevalence of, 173–176
  and society's conception of masculinity,
    179–181, 185
  as torture and political offense, 184–186
  trauma of, 176–178
Institutionalized violence, 288
International Classification of Disease (ICD-
    10), 34, 193, 198, 302
International Physicians for the Prevention
    of Nuclear War (IPPNW), 281
Israeli war veterans, 238, 240–242
  conflictual situation for therapists, 245–
    246
  secondary stress of families, 80–82

Janet, Pierre, 11

Lasagna, Louis, 291
Latin American Institute for Mental
    Health and Human Rights
    (ILAS), 100

Levi, Primo, 26
Levy, Howard, 281–292
Lysistrata, 293

Madisha, Donald, 187
Marcos, Ferdinand, 134
Mayer, Jean, 291
Medical Association for the Prevention of
    War (MAPW), 281
Memory network
    activation and modification of, 59–60,
        65, 66, 70–71
    formation of, 58–59, 64–65, 70
    voluntary activation of, 60–61

National Commission of Truth and Recon-
    ciliation (Chile), 115
Nederlandse Vereniging voor Medische
    Polemologie (NVMP), 281
Neuroticism, 46, 47

Oppenheim, Hermann, 11

Philippines, effect of political instability
        on women's mental health, 137–
        147
    cultural interpretation of findings, 137–
        144
    culture as buffer, 139–144, 146
    research questions and instruments, 135–
        137
Physicians for Social Responsibility (PSR),
    281
Political instability, culture as buffer to,
    139–147
Political trauma, as context-bound, 108–
    109
Posttorture syndrome, lack of evidence for,
    192
Posttraumatic stress disorder
    and complex trauma, 192, 301–302
    as conflict of values, 234
    and countertransference, 240, 246
    cultural and societal dimensions of, 2–
        5
    as diagnostic tool, 99–109, 192–200
    dilemmas in definition and use of term,
        301
    as expression of conflict, 234, 238–239
    and refugees, 161–162
    role of political beliefs and validation in,
        21

Posttraumatic stress disorder (*cont.*)
    stressor, 31–52
        measurement of severity of, 38–44
        and passage of time, 49–50
        and threshold effects, 44–46
        triggers and vulnerability factors, 46–49
        and technological disasters, 223–224
        theoretical conceptions of, 100, 238–242
        and torture victims, 192–200
        treatment and prevention issues, 35
        use of term "disorder," 103–104, 242–
            245
        use of term "post," 100–103, 302–303
        in Western psychiatry, 17–19, 303
Primary prevention
    defined, 278
    as therapists' responsibility, 235–236,
        280–284, 289–95
Psychosocial trauma, concept of, 117–118

Rape, and definitive injury, 20
Recall
    impact of social and cultural issues on,
        40
    and issue of test–retest reliability, 39
Recovery
    escape and avoidance responses, 60–62,
        65, 66
    formation of traumatic memory net-
        work, 58–59, 64–65, 70
    intrusion process, 59–60, 65, 66, 70–71
    and trauma severity, 57–58
    voluntary activation of memory net-
        work, 60–61
Refugees, 18
    cumulative traumatization of, 152–154
    psychotherapeutic work with, 151–168
        cultural bias and differences in, 155–
            162
        language problems, 161
        therapist's attitude in, 165–168
        use of interpreters, 162–165
    stress of, 22–23
    uprooting and adjustment problems,
        154
Rushdie, Salman, 31
Ryle, John A., 292–293

Secondary prevention, defined, 278
Secondary traumatic stress, 75–95
    of colleagues in high-risk occupations,
        87–89

Secondary traumatic stress (*cont.*)
  compassion fatigue of support system,
    93–95
  of crisis workers, 89–91
  defined, 77–79
  of family and significant others, 80–87
  versus primary traumatic stress, 80
  psychotherapists' vulnerability to, 91–92
Selling of DSM: The Rhetoric of Science in Psychiatry, The, 194
Social Psychiatric Service for Refugees,
    Amsterdam, Netherlands, 151
South Africa, torture and repression in,
    187–210
  and forensic application of PTSD criteria, 194–196
  perversion of social and behavioral sciences in, 201–202
  political abuses of mental health services in, 208–209
  role of health professionals in, 206–207
  role of ideologies and belief systems in,
    189–192
  traumas of apartheid system, 188–190
South African Nationalist Party, 201
Soviet Union, political abuses of psychiatry
    in, 208
Spock, Benjamin, 291
Symptom recruitment, 46

Tertiary prevention, 278
Therapy
  cultural bias and cultural differences in,
    155–162
  emphasis on capacity to function, 25
  human rights framework in, 25–27
  victimological focus in, 23–24
  Western individual-based model, 17–19,
    303
Three Mile Island nuclear plant, Harrisburg, Pennsylvania, 227–228
Torture
  avoidance and denial reactions, 39, 60–
    62, 65, 66
  and cultural framework, 156–157
  defined, 123, 184
  dissociation as coping mechanism, 124–
    125
  distinctions between traumatic and
    pathogenic elements, 123
  hospitable environment for, 204–205
  incestuous abuse as, 184–186

Torture (*cont.*)
  and PTSD diagnosis, 192–193
    forensic application of PTSD criteria,
      194–196
    problems with stressor criterion, 196–
      198
    role of health professionals in, 200–209
  social and familial rupture as definitive
    injury, 20
Trauma and traumatization
  and anticipation and acceptance of risks,
    42–43
  as collective experience, 19–22
  constant reinterpretation of, 43–44
  as continuous experience, 102–103
  cumulative and sequential, 105–106,
    122, 152–154, 301
  elements of traumatic event, 78
  extreme situation and extreme traumatization, 105–107
  as individual-centered event, 17–19
  influences on threshold effects of, 44–
    46
  long-term and transgenerational effects,
    23–24, 85–87
  narcissistic versus existential, 260–261
  political and historical context of, 32–
    34
  and posttrauma phase, 21
  and religion, 146, 156–157
  scientific study of, 11–12
  and social/cultural context, 19–22, 141,
    146–147, 299–300, 304
  stressor role, 31–38
    in retrospective assessment, 39
    significance of, 35
  temporal duration of traumatic event,
    43
  vicarious, 91
  in Western biomedicine and psychoanalysis, 18
Trauma measurement, 38–44, 64–69
  development of exposure scales, 40–42
  Global Severity Index (GSI), 65
  Impact of Events Scale (IES), 65
  impact of social and cultural issues on recall, 40
  and representations of trauma, 42–44
  Symptom Check List 90 Revised (SCL-90-
    R), 65
  use of additive scales, 39
Traumatic neurosis, 11

Verwoerd, Hendrik, 201
Vietnam war veterans
  PTSD lifetime rate, 19
  secondary traumatic stress of spouses,
    82–84
  societal estrangement of, 3, 20

War, 17–28
  battle trauma
    conceptualization of effects, 32–33
    genetic and environmental factors in,
      48–49
  causes of, 286–288
  civilian trauma care during, 303
  and collective recollection, 304
  and collective security versus national se-
    curity, 288–289

War (*cont.*)
  health consequences of, 280–284
  health professionals' role in prevention
    of, 280–281, 289–295
  and individual violence, 284–286
  just war concept, 289
  low-intensity, 200
  social and cultural damage from, 21–
    22
  and transgenerational traumatization,
    85–87
  traumatic stress on family, 80–87
  use of terror as social control, 17
Western psychotherapeutic techniques,
  limitations of, 17–19
World Health Organization (WHO),
  25